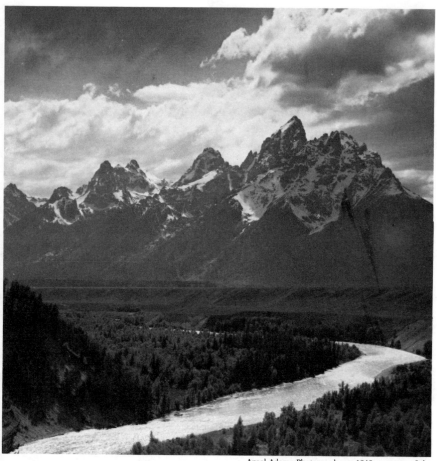

Ansel Adams Photograph, ca. 1940, courtesy of the
National Archives

Teton Mountains and Snake River.

NATIONAL PARKS

The American Experience

Third Edition

Alfred Runte

UNIVERSITY OF NEBRASKA PRESS
LINCOLN AND LONDON

♾ The paper in this book meets the minimum requirements of
American National Standard for Information Sciences—
Permanence of Paper for Printed Library Materials,
ANSI Z39.48-1984.

First Bison Books printing: 1997
Most recent printing indicated by the last digit below:
10 9 8 7 6 5 4 3 2 1

Library of Congress Cataloging-in-Publication Data
Runte, Alfred, 1947–
National parks.
Bibliography: p.
Includes index.
1. National parks and reserves—
United States—
History. I. Title.
E160.R78   1987   973   86-11368
ISBN 0-8032-8963-4 (alk. paper)

In Memory of My Mother and Father

Contents

Illustrations

Preface to the Third Edition

Yellowstone at 125:
Anniversary Remarks on the Recent History of National Parks

Now a century and a quarter old, Yellowstone maintains its popularity as the landscape closest to every ideal of what comprises a national park. Nor should the story of its exploration and founding as a scenic refuge ever grow tiresome. It is just that the story may never again seem as inspirational as when the country itself was young. Mounting pressures on the environment now betray the erosion of cultural attachments to both regional and national landscapes. Initially, in 1972, my research itself dampened the celebration of the Yellowstone Centennial. A hundred years earlier, I noted, the opponents of Yellowstone Park had insisted that it include nothing of proven commercial value.[1] My cause for despair was my own preference for the utopian version of the evolution of national parks, in the words of the historian Wallace Stegner still "the best idea we ever had."[2]

The lost innocence of the national parks may indeed be the dominant theme of preservation in the twenty-first century. When this book originally went to press, the United States was preoccupied with the protection of national parks and wilderness. Now the future of Yellowstone, its fame aside, is but one of many concerns competing for the attention of the public and the media. Historians themselves remain divided between sentiment and objectivity. Like Wallace Stegner, many are tempted to celebrate national parks as the ideal expression of landscape democracy, despite evidence reaffirming that many parks have also been compromised or mismanaged.[3]

One inescapable cause of management problems is the extraordinary growth in traffic and visitation. The country that invented national parks held just thirty million people. As late as World War I, Yellowstone's annual visitation rarely exceeded 50,000. Moreover, the large majority came by train and stagecoach, part of a community of travelers bound to responsibility by limited access, poorer roads, and rustic accommodations.

The nation about to carry Yellowstone into another millennium has ten times the population of 1872. Park visitation, both domestic and foreign, now exceeds three million every year. The park's sense of timelessness and benediction, of summer renewal and winter sleep, is lost amid a million cars and the drone of a hundred thousand snowmobiles. No different from any urban landscape, Yellowstone is constantly importuned, providing digression, but hardly sanctuary, from the complexities of the modern world.[4]

Meanwhile, economic forces dictate that extractive industries are still of greater value to the West than either wilderness or tourism. Thus, Noranda Minerals Inc., a Canadian conglomerate, opened the 1990s by pressuring federal officials to authorize a large gold and silver mine near Cooke City, Montana, barely two miles outside Yellowstone's northeastern boundary. For obvious reasons, any prior conviction that the region should be added to Yellowstone National Park had never been taken seriously, even though mining, first advanced more than a century ago, suggested only a modest strike. Over the years, existing mines were occasionally reworked and other mountainsides freshly scarred, little of which, it was argued, had spilled over into the park. Finally, technology overtook preservation with the invention of new extractive options. One technique, using cyanide as a leaching agent, coaxed as little as an ounce of gold from several tons of low-yield ore. Suddenly, what had once been only a marginal deposit was being hailed as the West's newest bonanza. Unfortunately, this time the mounds of tailings and a reservoir of toxic wastes might loom over a watershed feeding directly into Yellowstone.[5]

The so-called New World Mine brought home in the twilight of the twentieth century what had been true of the park ever since its establishment. Even as Congress in 1872 pledged its commitment to scenic preservation, it qualified repeatedly that Yellowstone's future indeed hinged on reassurances that only scenery was at stake. The mine was just the latest example of that historical precondition. In the end, the ambitions of American materialism still favored development over the ideals of conservation.

To be sure, Congress had established many additional categories of national parks and their equivalent, including recreation areas, historic sites, wild rivers, and scenic trails. However, most tended to be corridors or islands on the American landscape, the majority significantly altered by prior development. Urban parks especially portended enormous costs for cleanup and maintenance, expenses generally not associated with areas traditionally reserved from the western public lands. Accordingly, if federal budgets persistently dwindled, as a mounting deficit seemed logically to predict, there was reason to fear that protection in the original natural units would also erode as one result.

As if to sharpen that debate, in the summer and fall of 1988 Yellowstone was swept by a series of unprecedented wildfires. Virtually all of the park was affected by drifting smoke and ash, and approximately half of its forests burned, although intensities and tree loss widely varied. Dramatically, in late August and early September flames literally raced across the park, forcing firefighters into "last stands" around Yellowstone's endangered historic buildings. Other contingents battled to protect adjacent forests framing its primary scenic wonders. Weeks later, costs had surpassed a hundred million dollars to maintain an assault force still numbering several thousand people, including rangers, military personnel, and members of the National Guard.[6]

Finally, as the first snows of autumn snuffed out the still stubborn flames and hard-to-reach embers, the country began taking stock of its legendary landscape. The obvious reaction was despair, to pronounce Yellowstone hopelessly burned beyond historical recognition. And yet, the biological value of fire had many defenders, most insisting that any talk of tragedy had been grossly overstated. Granted, the fires had been serious and their intensity unforeseen. Too late, the Park Service had moved to suppress back-country burns worsened by lengthening weeks of heat and drought. Even so, Yellowstone in time would surely recover. In retrospect, fire seemed less an enemy of preservation than did a century of human abuse and manipulation.[7]

As another pivotal event in the history of the national parks, the Yellowstone fires refocused every debate regarding when to intervene in the management of natural environments. For a majority of Americans, Yellowstone's obvious appeal was still as the nation's distant, fabled "wonderland." Much relieved, everyone applauded that its geyser basins, canyon, and waterfalls had survived the flames intact. For others, however, wilderness was indeed the new criterion for maintaining the integrity of every natural area. In Yellowstone, the wolf had been exterminated and the grizzly bear long threatened with extinction. By implication, Yellowstone itself was hardly perfect. The term *wilderness* implied sanctuary, a landscape reserved for every native plant and animal as well as scenic wonders.

Literature buttressed such convictions, including environmental history, which by now had also left the romanticism of the nineteenth century far behind. Notable books included *Yellowstone: A Wilderness Besieged* (1985), by the historian Richard A. Bartlett, and *Playing God in Yellowstone: The Destruction of America's First National Park* (1986), by a journalist, Alston Chase. Using different styles and approaches, both authors challenged the historical and contemporary priorities of the National Park Service. Development, they argued, often took precedence over the protection of key natural features.[8] In another critical review, the historian Stephen J. Pyne noted the agency's tendency to ignore obvious distinctions between good and bad fires. Yellowstone, he concluded, had survived only because the park was truly big enough to absorb a million-acre holocaust, defined either as a natural occurrence or a management mistake.[9]

Regardless, within months of the fires, efforts to assess their long-term damage evinced a dwindling air of certainty. Through winter and into spring precipitation returned to normal. A minuscule percentage of the park, that portion where soils had been sterilized by the flames, showed no signs of imminent recovery. Elsewhere, in 1989 Yellowstone came alive in a sea of grass and wildflowers. It was, even skeptics admitted, one of the most glorious springs on record. Off through the blackened trees, long-forgotten vistas had reopened while, underfoot, millions of new seedlings were already taking root. Granted, many areas would take decades, even a century or more to recover fully. Then again, fires historically had reduced forest litter and undergrowth in cycles measured in years instead of centuries. What had appeared "natural" before the fires might be deceptive in its own right, self-generating, perhaps, but a landscape no less artificial than any of Yellowstone's most popular, developed areas.[10]

In that respect, the question of natural fire was part of the larger

issue of Yellowstone's long-term survival. In the 1990s a new definition, Greater Yellowstone, addressed the park in further relation to the
health of its neighboring lands. The thrust of its argument obvious,
Greater Yellowstone included all potential wilderness surrounding the
national park, another eight to ten million acres in addition to Yellowstone's original two. In short, Greater Yellowstone departed dramatically from cultural biases limiting preservation only to "worthless" lands.
Inside the park, that criterion still prevailed; adjacent, however, lay
many areas now designated for all forms of commercial development,
including ranches, mining claims, logging operations, resorts, and summer homes.[11]

True, Greater Yellowstone referred primarily to lands still held in
trust by the federal government. The vast majority, in national forests,
further embraced several million acres already protected under the Wilderness Act of 1964. Even so, the national forests themselves were often pockmarked with commercial claims and private property. More
critically, the U.S. Forest Service fundamentally disagreed that so much
territory deserved set-asides as wilderness. On paper, the idea of buffer-
ing Yellowstone with everything outside the park might seem comforting and attainable. The hurdle, so easily discounted, was that it was no
longer 1872.

The reintroduction of the wolf in 1995 further aroused complaints
of government indifference to the needs of local residents. Like the grizzly bear, wolves were prone to wander beyond the boundaries of the
park itself. Among critics, the reintroduction cemented arguments that
Greater Yellowstone presaged a government "taking," allegedly, a subtle
but overt attempt to limit the rights of property holders without just
compensation.[12] Once again, the matter illustrated the futility of visual-
izing wilderness as something behind a fence. Wilderness was hardly
real estate; it was a landscape immune to zoning or other forms of sub-
division. Short of some sentiment for wilderness on private lands bordering any national park, wildlife as mobile as the wolf and grizzly
bear was certain to face continuing persecution.

Once again, any expansion of the national park system to round
out the integrity of natural environments was restricted to topographic
provinces where such additions would not impinge on civilization. Thus,
the battle for Alaska behind them, preservationists renewed their interest in the deserts of California, Nevada, and Arizona. Yellowstone, as
one result, ironically lost its preeminence as the largest national park in

the continental United States. Under terms of the Desert Protection Act of 1994, Death Valley National Monument, expanded and redesignated as Death Valley National Park, now surpassed Yellowstone by more than a million acres.[13]

The successful outcome of the Desert Protection Act had indeed hinged on the matter of expansion without sacrifice. Greater Yellowstone conflicted with productive forests, growing communities, and several important watersheds. In contrast, the word *desert* seemed self-explanatory. The barren outcroppings of Joshua Tree National Monument, simultaneously expanded and renamed a national park, suggested, like Death Valley, the absence of traditional commercial values. Weeks earlier, Saguaro in southern Arizona made the same transition from a monument into a park. However, where mining, hunting, and grazing were still deemed significant, principally in California's East Mojave Desert, even a landscape so inextricably linked with visions of waste and hopelessness guaranteed no priorities for wilderness preservation. Designated only a national preserve, the East Mojave Desert served further notice of that enduring contradiction, the one bent on appeasement rather than closure of commercial claims to the nation's public lands.[14]

Although a century and a quarter old, the national park idea still awaited true consensus, a confirmation of cultural significance unaffected by expedience or remoteness. Indeed, earlier visionaries had considered parks but a necessary stage in the evolution of a more enduring ethic, one transcending political and social boundaries to see all land as sacred space.[15] The proper evolution from Yellowstone into Greater Yellowstone was ultimately America the Beautiful. National parks should be more than reservations separating wilderness from the grasp of civilization. Rather, they should inspire Americans to care for every landscape, especially those enveloping their daily lives. Ideally, the future of the parks was projection, awareness rippling outward as well as people flowing in. A new philosophy, as it were, first demanded a new maturity. Behavior inappropriate to a national park was likely to be inappropriate anywhere.

In that respect, the events preceding another major Yellowstone anniversary foretold an uncertain future for national parks and wilderness. For every achievement there was still ambivalence; for every success an element of national doubt. At least on the eve of the anniversary the news was mostly positive. In August 1996, President William Clinton announced an agreement with the Noranda company liberating

Yellowstone from the proximity of the New World Mine. On payment of $65 million, and in exchange for other federal properties yet to be determined, Noranda pledged to relinquish all of its historical claims to the controversial New World site.[16]

Apparently, both Yellowstone and Greater Yellowstone had dodged a crippling blow to their respective identities as national park and wilderness. History alone raised the discomforting question: How long would any such agreement last? The euphoria of the moment conveniently masked that larger reality. For every victory came only the certainty of a different renewal of the threat.

In that respect, Yellowstone at one hundred and twenty-five was really no more secure than Yellowstone at any anniversary in between. Earlier preservationists simply had the luxury of a smaller, less demanding population. No longer could Yellowstone, or any national park, survive all that civilization now portended. Contemporary celebrants could only hope the twenty-first century would bring no threat so serious it might undo every past success. If so, the original conviction of American nationalism would obviously have to hold. The glory of the United States lay in landscapes still pristine and undeveloped. Only then might wilderness survive the social and cultural changes spilling over into the next millennium. Only then might restraint possibly sustain the limitations of tradition, ensuring the timelessness of the national parks as the best idea America ever had.

NOTES

1. Alfred Runte, "Yellowstone: It's Useless, So Why Not a Park?" *National Parks and Conservation Magazine: The Environmental Journal* 46 (March 1972): 4–7.

2. Wallace Stegner, "The Best Idea We Ever Had," *Wilderness* 46 (Spring 1983): 4.

3. The interpretive "edge" in management histories of the national parks is visibly underscored by the combative symbolism of several recent titles. See, for example, Carsten Lien, *Olympic Battleground: The Power Politics of Timber Preservation* (San Francisco: Sierra Club Books, 1991); and Alfred Runte, *Yosemite: The Embattled Wilderness* (Lincoln: University of Nebraska Press, 1990). Other important works include Richard J. Orsi, Alfred Runte, and Marlene Smith-Baranzini, eds., *Yosemite and Sequoia: A Century of California National Parks* (Berkeley: University of California Press, 1993); and

George M. Lubick, *Petrified Forest National Park: A Wilderness Bound in Time* (Tucson: University of Arizona Press, 1996). A comprehensive history of the national monuments is Hal K. Rothman, *Preserving Different Pasts: The American National Monuments* (Urbana: University of Illinois Press, 1989). See also Mark W. T. Harvey, *A Symbol of Wilderness: Echo Park and the American Conservation Movement* (Albuquerque: University of New Mexico Press, 1994).

4. On the issue of population and development pressures now affecting the national parks, see Michael Frome, *Regreening the National Parks* (Tucson: University of Arizona Press, 1992).

5. Timothy Egan, "New Gold Rush Stirs Fears of Exploitation," *New York Times*, August 14, 1994, pp. 1, 11; Todd Wilkinson, "Fool's Gold," *National Parks* 68 (July–August 1994): 31–35; Greater Yellowstone Coalition, *"Mine From Hell" Threatens Yellowstone*, undated brochure, ca. 1994; James Brooke, "Montana Mining Town Fights Gold Rush Plan," *New York Times*, January 7, 1996, p. 8.

6. The literature generated by the Yellowstone fires was exceptionally large, if highly repetitive. For a critical listing of the first major titles, see Alfred Runte, "Man Bites Dog in Yellowstone: The Fire Books of 1989," *Montana: The Magazine of Western History* 39 (Autumn 1989): 86–87.

7. See, for example, Richard A. Bartlett, "Nature is the Least of Yellowstone's Adversaries," *Los Angeles Times*, September 26, 1988, pt. 2, p. 5.

8. Richard A. Bartlett, *Yellowstone: A Wilderness Besieged* (Tucson: University of Arizona Press, 1985); Alston Chase, *Playing God in Yellowstone: The Destruction of America's First National Park* (Boston: Atlantic Monthly Press, 1986).

9. Stephen J. Pyne, "The Summer We Let Wild Fire Loose," *Natural History* (August 1989): 45–49. See also idem, "Letting Wild Fire Loose: The Fires of '88," *Montana: The Magazine of Western History* 39 (Summer 1989): 76–79. Another critical analysis is Alston Chase, "Greater Yellowstone and the Death and Rebirth of the National Parks Ideal," *Orion Nature Quarterly* 8 (Summer 1989): 44–55.

10. For an early analysis of Yellowstone's recovery, see George Wuerthner, "The Flames of '88," *Wilderness* 52 (Summer 1989): 41–54.

11. U.S. Department of the Interior, National Park Service, and U.S. Department of Agriculture, U.S. Forest Service, *The Greater Yellowstone Area: A Briefing Guide* (Washington, D.C.: Government Printing Office, 1987).

12. Jim Robbins, "Return of Wolves to West Brings Back Fear and Anger," *New York Times*, December 29, 1995, p. 7. U.S. Department of the Interior, National Park Service, Yellowstone National Park, *Yellowstone Today* (Autumn 1995), p. 6. Recent books tracing the evolution of American attitudes toward wildlife and wilderness include Thomas R. Dunlap, *Saving America's*

Wildlife (Princeton: Princeton University Press, 1988); and Lisa Mighetto, *Wild Animals and American Environmental Ethics* (Tucson: University of Arizona Press, 1991).

13. Marc Reisner, "A Decision for the Desert," *Wilderness* 50 (Winter 1986): 33–53; California Desert Protection League, *The California Desert: A Time to Protect Our Western Heritage*, May 1993; Katharine Q. Seelye, "House Approves Desert Preserve in a Vast Expanse of California," *New York Times*, July 28, 1994, pp. 1, 10.

14. Timothy Egan, "New Parks Mix Public and Private, Uneasily," *New York Times*, December 26, 1994, pp. 1, 9.

15. The classic statement of this conviction remains Aldo Leopold, *A Sand County Almanac* (New York: Oxford University Press, 1949). For another twist on the argument, see William Cronon, "The Trouble with Wilderness; or, Getting Back to the Wrong Nature," *Environmental History* 1 (January 1996): 7–28. A seminal defense of the national parks as natural environments is Robin Winks, "Dispelling the Myth," *National Parks* 70 (July–August 1996): 52–53.

16. John M. Broder, "Clinton Unveils Deal to Stop Yellowstone Mine," *Los Angeles Times*, August 13, 1996, p. 1.

Preface

No institution is more symbolic of the conservation movement in the United States than the national parks. Although other approaches to conservation, such as the national forests, each have their own following, only the national parks have had both the individuality and uniqueness to fix an indelible image on the American mind. The components of that image are the subject of this volume. What follows, then, is an interpretative history; people, events, and legislation are treated only as they pertain to the *idea* of national parks. For this reason I have not found it necessary to cover every park in detail; similarly, it would be impossible in the scope of one book to consider the multitude of recreation areas, military parks, historic sites, and urban preserves now often ranked with the national parks proper. Most of the themes relevant to the prime natural areas still have direct application throughout the national park system, particularly with respect to the problems of maintaining the character and integrity of the parks once they have been established. The indifference of Congress to the infringement of commercialization on Gettysburg National Military Park, for example, is traceable to the same pressures for development which have led to the resort atmosphere in portions of Yosemite, Yellowstone, Grand Canyon, and other parks.

The reluctance of most historians and writers to dwell on the negative themes of national park history is understandable. National parks stand for the unselfish side of conservation. Take away the national park idea and the conservation movement loses its spirit of idealism and altruism. National parks justify the conviction that the United States has been as committed to do what is "right" for the environment as what is mandatory to ensure the productivity of the nation's natural resources. Without the national parks the history of conservation becomes predictable and therefore ordinary. Taking precautions to ward off the possibility of running out of natural resources was only common sense.

The history of the national park idea is indeed filled with examples of statesmanship and philanthropy. Still, there has been a tendency among historians to put the national parks on a pedestal, to interpret the park idea as evidence of an unqualified revulsion against disruption of the environment. It would be comforting to believe that the national park idea originated in a deep and uncompromising love of the land for its own sake. Such a circumstance—much like the common assertion that Indians were the first "ecologists"—would reassure modern environmentalists they need only recapture the spirit of the past to acquire ecological wisdom and respect. But in fact, the national park idea evolved to fulfill cultural rather than environmental needs. The search for a distinct national identity, more than what have come to be called "the rights of rocks," was the initial impetus behind scenic preservation. Nor did the United States overrule economic considerations in the selection of the areas to be included in the national parks. Even today the reserves are not allowed to interfere with the material progress of the nation.

It has been as hard to develop in the American public a concern for the environment in and of itself within the national parks as it has outside of them. For example, despite the public's growing sensitivity to environmental issues, the large majority of park visitors still shun the trails for the comfort and convenience of automobiles. Most of these enthusiasts, like their predecessors, continue to see the national parks as a parade of natural "wonders," as a string of phenomena to be photographed and deserted in haste. Thus while the nation professes an awareness of the interrelationships of all living things, outmoded perceptions remain a hindrance to the realization of sound ecological management throughout the national park system.

Previous editions of this book have gratefully acknowledged the many friends, relatives, and colleagues who contributed to its research and completion. All, accordingly, will understand if I now refrain from simply listing them yet again. Instead, I would like to give brief acknowledgment to the debt I owe an era, that time when history was about achievement more than about who had done what to whom.

Perhaps, in everyone's insistence to be inclusive, historians have forgotten what true achievement means. I came from that side of the tracks where history now spends most of its time. No one need tell me how hard it was for immigrants, minorities, and working class families to get ahead. I know, because my parents were part of that struggle, wondering like everybody else how to get through another day.

The point is that struggle also meant advancement, not only heartache but opportunity. History as I discovered it lifted the story of America to a higher plane, and me as well. I thank that age for its inspiration if not for its perfectibility, leaving perfection to those who really believe only remorse is now the answer.

Prologue

The Heritage of Achievement and Indifference

Happily the United States Government (warned by the results of having allowed the Falls of Niagara to become private property) determined that certain districts, discovered in various parts of the States, and noted for their exceeding beauty, should, by Act of Congress, be appropriated for evermore "for public use, resort, and recreation, and be inalienable for all time."

Lady C. F. Gordon-Cumming,
British traveler, 1878

More than a century ago, a small group of Americans pioneered a unique idea—the national park idea. It was the contention of this group that the natural "wonders" of the United States should not be handed out to a few profiteers, but rather held in trust for all people for all time. Gradually, as perceptions of the environment changed, national parks also became important for wilderness preservation, wildlife protection, and purposes closer to the concerns of ecologists. To be sure, the national park idea as we know it today did not emerge in finished form. More accurately, it evolved. Still, the values of the nineteenth century have remained influential, a fact which does much to explain why many national parks are still torn between the struggle for preservation and for use. Especially because most Americans still seek out spectacular scenery and natural phenomena, environmentalists caution that

1

the public has little understanding of the restraints on visitation needed to protect the diversity of the parks as a whole.[1]

Who first conceived the idea of preservation is not known. Ancient civilizations of the Near East fostered landscape design and management long before the birth of Christ. By 700 B.C., for example, Assyrian noblemen sharpened their hunting, riding, and combat techniques in designated training reserves. These were copied by the great royal hunting enclosures of the Persian Empire, which flourished throughout Asia Minor between 550 and 350 B.C. It remained for the Greeks to democratize landscape esthetics; their larger towns and cities, including Athens, provided citizens with the *agora*, a plaza for *public* assembly, relaxation, and refreshment. Known for its fountains and tree-shaded walkways, the agora has been compared to the modern city park.[2]

Although urbanization throughout the Roman Empire led to similar experiments, Medieval Europe, like Asia Minor, reverted to the maintenance of open spaces exclusively for the ruling classes. Hunting once more became a primary use of these lands; in fact, the word "park" stems from this usage. Originally "parc" in Old French and Middle English, the term designated "an enclosed piece of ground stocked with beasts of the chase, held by prescription or by the king's grant."[3] Trespassers were punished severely, especially poachers who often were put to death.

With the possible exception of the Greeks and Romans, therefore, the park idea as now defined is modern in origin; only recently has it come to mean both protection and public access. Not until the eighteenth and nineteenth centuries did the appreciation of landscapes and democratic ideals rise to prominence throughout the Western world. In Europe, and later the United States, with the rapid spread of cities, factories, and their attendant social dislocations, people came to question whether the Industrial Revolution really represented progress. Locked into the drudgery and grime of manufacturing communities, more and more people followed poets and philosophers in embracing nature as the avenue of escape. The Romantic Movement, for example, in its praise for the strange and mysterious in nature, by definition preferred landscapes only suggestive of human occupation. Thus ruined castles or crumbling fortresses were valued because of what they implied; a concern for detail would have destroyed the enjoyment of trying to recall their former grandeur through one's own imagination. Others held that the ultimate state of nature might be the absence of civilization altogether. So argued deists and primitivists, at least, the former because man's works supposedly obscured God's truths, the latter in the conviction that man seemed happiest in direct proportion to the absence of his own creations.[4]

The egalitarian ideals of the American and French revolutions further joined urbanization and industrialization in undermining traditional beliefs. As a result, throughout Europe royalty finally lost the power to dictate solely when and how parklands were to be opened to the public at large. In 1852, for example, the city of Paris took over the popular Bois de Boulogne from the crown, with the agreement that its woods and promenades would be cared for and improved. London's royal parks, initially opened to the populace during the eighteenth century at the discretion of the monarch, similarly were enlarged and maintained for public benefit. Another important milestone on the road to landscape democracy in Great Britain was Victoria Park, carved from London's crowded East End. Authorized in 1842, it was the first reserve not only managed, but expressly purchased, for public instead of private use. Its counterpart in Liverpool, Birkenhead Park, likewise was to remain, in the words of one American admirer, Frederick Law Olmsted, "entirely, unreservedly, and for ever, the people's own. The poorest British peasant is as free to enjoy it in all its parts as the British queen. . . . Is it not," he concluded, "a grand, good thing?"[5]

Olmsted, the son of a prosperous Connecticut family, returned home from his first visit to the Continent in 1850. He was then twenty-eight years old, and his career as America's foremost designer and proponent of urban parks lay some years in the future.[6] Yet even as he praised Great Britain's commitment to provide urban refuges for the common man, the climate of opinion in the United States was already swinging decidedly in favor of the city park idea. As early as 1831 the Massachusetts legislature approved a "rural cemetery" on the outskirts of Boston, to be known as Mount Auburn. Shortly after its completion urban residents favored the site for picnicking, strolling, and solitude. Rural cemeteries caught on throughout the Northeast. By 1836 Brooklyn and Philadelphia, among other cities, were equally renowned for this popular, if unconventional, means of providing open space.[7]

If the nation could provide parklands for the dead, parklands for the living might also be realized. Two of the earliest proponents of the city park idea were Andrew Jackson Downing, a horticulturist, and the poet William Cullen Bryant. During the 1840s they called for the establishment of a large reserve within easy reach of New York City. Finally, in 1853 the New York legislature agreed to the plan by purchasing a rectangular site (the equivalent of approximately one square mile) on the outskirts of the metropolis. To be known as Central Park once the city had built up around it, the project launched Frederick Law Olmsted and his partner, Calvert Vaux, on their distinguished careers.[8]

Central Park set a precedent for preservation in the common interest more than a decade before realization of the national park idea. Still, while its debt to the city park is obvious, the national park evolved in response to environmental perceptions of a dramatically different kind. City parks were an eastern phenomenon, a refuge from the noise and pace of urban living. City dwellers wanted facilities for recreation, not scenic protection per se. Convenient access was of primary concern; a city park could be located anywhere, however distasteful the site. Portions of Central Park itself replaced run-down farms, pig sties, and garbage dumps. Once a site had been obtained, the landscape architect readily made it pleasing to the eye by adding lakes, walkways, gardens, or playing fields as public demand warranted.

Later, of course, the placement of roads, trails, and overnight lodgings in the national parks called upon similar artistry and sensitivity to existing natural features. Yet beyond these concessions to access and convenience, from the outset Americans understood intuitively that the national parks were different.

The striking dissimilarity was topographical. Unlike those who sought relief from the crowdedness and monotony of city streets, proponents of the national parks unveiled their idea against the backdrop of the American West. Grand, monumental scenery was the physical catalyst. The pioneers and explorers who emerged from the more subdued environments of the East found the Rocky Mountains, Cascades, and Sierra Nevada overpowering in every respect. Cliffs and waterfalls thousands of feet high, canyons a mile deep, and soaring mountains covered with great conifers were awesome to people born and bred within reach of the Atlantic seaboard. It is therefore understandable why many national parks, as distinct from urban parks, were established long before their potential for recreation could be realized. In the West the protection of scenery by itself was justification enough for modifying the park idea.

As a visual experience, national parks went beyond the need for physical fitness or outdoor recreation. Indeed, the parks did not emerge merely as the end product of landscape appreciation for its own sake. Simply admiring the natural world was nothing unique to the people of the United States; the transcendentalists, including Ralph Waldo Emerson and Henry David Thoreau, themselves followed the example of the likes of Shelley, Byron, Wordsworth, and Keats. The intellectual subtleties of transcendentalism, in any case, could hardly sustain the national park idea in a country as firmly committed to material progress as the United States.

The decision not only to admire nature but to preserve it required stronger incentives. Specifically, the impulse to bridge the gap between appreciation and protection needed catalysts of unquestionable drama and visibility. In the fate of Niagara Falls Americans found a compelling reason to give preservation more than a passing thought. Although then recognized both at home and abroad as the nation's most magnificent natural spectacle, as early as 1830 the falls suffered the insults of so-called sharpers and hucksters of every kind. While some located adjacent to the cataract to tap its endless stream of power, still more came to fleece the growing number of tourists attracted by completion of the Erie Canal, and, close behind, the railroads. The mixed blessings of Niagara's popularity were soon apparent. Private developers quickly acquired the best overlooks, then forced travelers to pay handsomely for the privilege of using them. By 1860 gatehouses and fences rimmed the falls from every angle. No less offensive were hackmen, curio hawkers, and tour guides, who matched their dishonesty with annoying persistence.[9]

A continuous parade of European visitors and commentators embarrassed the nation by condemning the commercialization of Niagara.[10] To be sure, although half the falls belonged to Canada, few mentioned this fact in defense of the United States; if Americans had no pride in their portion of the falls, they deserved no excuse. Among the earliest critics to write in this vein was Alexis de Tocqueville. In 1831, during the extended visit to the United States that led to his classic work, *Democracy in America*, he urged a friend to "hasten" to Niagara if he wished "to see this place in its grandeur. If you delay," he warned, "your Niagara will have been spoiled for you. Already the forest round about is being cleared. . . . I don't give the Americans ten years to establish a saw or flour mill at the base of the cataract."[11]

By 1834 Tocqueville's worst fears had been confirmed, most memorably in the observations of a pair of English Congregational ministers, Andrew Reed and James Matheson. They noted that the American side now boasted the "shabby town" of Manchester. "Manchester and the falls of Niagara!" They made no effort to veil their disgust. "One has hardly the patience to record these things." Surely some "universal voice ought to interfere and prevent the money-seekers." The divines followed with nothing less than an appeal for international protection of the cataract. "Niagara does not belong to [individuals]; Niagara does not belong to Canada or America," they asserted. Rather "such spots should be deemed the property of civilized mankind." Their destruction, after all, compromised "the tastes, the morals, and the enjoyments of all men."[12]

If Reed and Matheson could have inspired their own countrymen to take action, perhaps England, and not the United States, would now be credited as the inventor of the national park idea. England certainly had a comparable opportunity, until Canada won its independence in 1867; the provinces boasted a variety of natural wonders, many on a par with those of the western United States. European countries simply lacked an equal provocation to originate the national park idea. If not for Great Britain, whose cultural identity was secure, for the United States each disparagement about its indifference to the fate of its natural wonders hit home. Although only verbal barbs, they unmistakably accused Americans of having no pride in themselves or in their past. "By George, you would think so indeed, if you had the chance of seeing the Falls of Niagara twice in ten years," said another English traveler, Sir Richard Henry Bonnycastle, repeating the popular charge in 1849. Granted, by now the fate of the falls was "a well-worn tale." Yet "so old a friend as the Falls of Niagara; for you must have read about those before you read Robinson Crusoe," surely deserved better than injury "by the Utilitarian mania." But "the Yankees [have] put an ugly shot tower on the brink of the Horseshoe," he lamented, "and they are about to consummate the barbarism by throwing a wire bridge . . . over the river just below the American Fall. . . . What they will not do next in their freaks it is difficult to surmise," he concluded, then echoed Reed's and Matheson's disgust: "but it requires very little more to show that patriotism, taste, and self-esteem, are not the leading features in the character of the inhabitants of this part of the world."[13]

Later in United States history, when intellectuals had greater confidence in their nation's achievements, such derision would be more easily discounted. But now the United States agonized in the shadow of European standards. Unlike the Old World, the new nation lacked an established past, particularly as expressed in art, architecture, and literature. In the Romantic tradition nationalists looked to scenery as one form of compensation. Yet even the landscapes of the United States, knowledge of which was then confined to those in the eastern half of the continent, were nothing extraordinary. Confronted with the obvious, Americans had little choice but to admit that the landmarks of Europe, especially the Alps, were no less magnificent. Prior to 1850 America's best claim to scenic superiority was Niagara Falls, which, most Europeans themselves conceded, surpassed comparable examples in the Old World. But the onslaught of commercialism robbed the cataract of credibility as a cultural legacy. A monument, whether human or natural in origin, implies some semblance of public control over its fate. But the private ownership of the land adjoining Niagara Falls compromised that ideal, as noted by Tocqueville, Reed, Matheson, Bonnycastle, and their contemporaries.

Redemption for the United States lay in westward expansion. As if reprieved, between 1846 and 1848 the nation acquired the most spectacular portions of the continent, including the Rocky Mountains and Pacific slope. Distance magnified their appeal, the more so as easterners endured urban drudgery, crowdedness, and monotony. This dichotomy between the settled East and frontier West further explains the timing of the national park idea. In effect the East was the audience to frontier events. For the West was a stage, a setting for the adventure stories, travel accounts, and dramatic paintings that characterized so much of the period. Indeed, Americans conquered the region precisely as popular literature, art, and professional journalism came of age. While the last frontier passed into history, the nation watched intently, if not in the field then through its dime novelists, newspaper correspondents, engravers, artists, and explorers.[14]

As each of these groups glorified the West, Americans became aware that here the nation could redeem itself of the shame of Niagara Falls and prove its citizens worthy of great landmarks. Much as Europe retained custody of the artifacts of Western Civilization, so in the West the United States had one final opportunity to protect a truly convincing semblance of historical continuity through landscape. Niagara Falls, as the lesson of past indifference, warned Americans about the need to guard against similar encroachments on their new-found wonderland. For although the grandeur of the Far West inspired the national park idea, eastern men invented and shaped it. Thus as the nation moved west, the specter of Niagara remained fresh in the minds of those many people who had witnessed its disfigurement firsthand. These included Frederick Law Olmsted, whose familiarity with the cataract dated as far back as boyhood visits in 1828 and 1834.[15] Between 1879 and 1885 he and a few close associates aroused the nation in support of efforts by the state of New York to restore the cataract and its environs to their natural condition.[16] (Ontario followed suit with dedication of its provincial park in 1888.) Still, having opened the West, Americans finally could admit that the East as a whole was too commonplace to surpass the scenic landmarks of Europe. The likes of Yosemite Valley and Yellowstone, by way of contrast, needed no apologies. But only if they were faithfully preserved from abuse (the fate of Niagara still aroused the nation's conscience) would they be truly convincing proof of the New World's cultural promise. Here at last—in the blending of the eastern mind and the western experience—was the enduring spark for the American inspiration of national parks.

1

Catalysts: Nationalism, Art, and the American West

The eastern half of America offers no suggestion of its western half.

Samuel Bowles, 1869

Why should we go to Switzerland to see mountains or to Iceland for geysers? Thirty years ago the attraction of America to the foreign mind was Niagara Falls. Now we have attractions which diminish Niagara into an ordinary exhibition.

New York Herald, 1872

When national parks were first established, protection of the "environment" as now defined was the least of preservationists' aims. Rather America's incentive for the national park idea lay in the persistence of a painfully felt desire for time-honored traditions in the United States. For decades the nation had suffered the embarrassment of a dearth of recognized cultural achievements. Unlike established, European countries, which traced their origins far back into antiquity, the United States lacked a long artistic and literary heritage. The absence of reminders of the human past, including castles, ancient ruins, and cathedrals on the landscape, further alienated American intellectuals from a cultural identity.[1] In response to constant barbs about these deficiencies from Old World critics and New World apologists, by the 1860s many thoughtful Americans had embraced the wonderlands of the

11

West as replacements for man-made marks of achievement. The agelessness of monumental scenery instead of the past accomplishments of Western Civilization was to become the visible symbol of continuity and stability in the new nation.

Of course the great majority of Americans took pride in the inventiveness and material progress of the nation; the search for a "traditional" culture was not among the public's chief concerns. Yet in order to claim that the general populace did not at least sympathize with the doubts of artists and intellectuals, first it would be necessary to discount the observance of their ideals in the popular as well as professional literature of the period. Indeed, much as Henry David Thoreau, Ralph Waldo Emerson, and others fostered an appreciation of landscapes on an intellectual plane, so publicists of a more common bent aroused support for preservation while introducing their readers to the scenery of the Far West. Among the more articulate spokesmen of this genre was Samuel Bowles, editor and publisher of the *Springfield* (Mass.) *Republican*. Learned, socially respected, and well-to-do, Bowles typified the class of gentlemen adventurers, artists, and explorers who conceived and advanced the national park idea during the second half of the nineteenth century.[2] With the conclusion of the Civil War in 1865, Bowles realized a long-held dream to see the West firsthand. The trip was made all the more enjoyable by the companionship of two prominent friends, Schuyler Colfax, Speaker of the U.S. House of Representatives, and Albert D. Richardson, recently distinguished for his coverage of the war as a correspondent for the *New York Tribune*.

The overnight success of Bowles and Richardson confirms how important the popular press was in laying the foundations of the national park idea. In contrast to the writings of Thoreau, which had a very limited following during his own lifetime, the *Springfield Republican* as early as 1860 enjoyed a strong circulation as far afield as the Mississippi Valley. The *New York Tribune*'s circulation of 290,000 nationwide similarly reflected the growing popularity of general publications. Although much of this readership can be linked to interest in the Civil War, articles about the West remained in great demand throughout the conflict. And with the close of hostilities both

Bowles and Richardson became best-selling authors. Bowles' essays for the *Republican* alone sold 38,000 copies when collected and republished as *Across the Continent* and *Our New West*, released in 1865 and 1869 respectively.[3]

Richardson's *Beyond the Mississippi*, published in 1867, was equally popular. Like Bowles, Richardson therefore excited the East's fascination with the West. Curiosity about the great physical disparity between the landscapes of the two regions was especially great. "The two sides of the Continent," Bowles observed, "are sharp in contrasts of climate, of soil, of mountains, of resources, of production, of everything." Indeed, only in the "New West" had nature wearied "of repetitions" and created so "originally, freshly, uniquely, majestically." Throughout the Rocky Mountains and along the Pacific slope lay scenery "to pique the curiosity and challenge the admiration of the world." Surely none could doubt, he therefore concluded, that the West would contribute to the lasting fame and glory of the entire United States.[4]

Although Bowles addressed the issue of preservation only briefly, the evolution of his thinking demonstrates how cultural anxiety turned appreciation of the West into bona fide efforts to protect it. He arrived in Yosemite Valley in 1865 to find the gorge already set aside by Congress the previous year. The "wise cession," as he immediately praised the grant, should be looked to as "an admirable example for other objects of natural curiosity and popular interest all over the Union." New York State, for example, "should preserve for popular use both Niagara Falls and its neighborhood"; similarly, the state would be well advised to set apart "a generous section of her famous Adirondacks, and Maine one of her lakes and surrounding woods." By 1869, when Bowles revised the statement, he had grown even more outspoken. He now considered it nothing less than "a pity" that the nation had failed to duplicate the Yosemite grant during the past four years. Moreover, the rewritten paragraph concluded with an appeal to national pride. Consider "what a blessing it would be to all visitors" for these areas to be "preserved for public use," he asked, "what an honor to the Nation!"[5]

Widespread indifference was still a major hurdle. Especially during the nineteenth century, distance and income prohibited most Americans from ever knowing the wonders of the West firsthand. Nor could literature alone bring its wonderlands within reach. As a result, landscape painters and photographers were equally important in furthering the spirit of concern that led to the national park idea. Foremost among artists to portray the region were Albert Bierstadt and Thomas Moran, whose works gave impetus to the establishment of Yosemite and Yellowstone parks respectively.[6] Indeed, the success of scenic protection depended on visual proof of the uniqueness of western landmarks. Once their beauty had been confirmed by artists as well as nationalists, Congress responded favorably to pleas that the most renowned wonderlands should be set aside, first as symbols of national pride and, in time, as areas for public recreation.

The reliance on nature as proof of national greatness began in earnest immediately following American independence from Great Britain. A clearly undesirable side effect of political freedom was the rending of former ties with European culture. No longer could the United States lay claim to the achievements of Western civilization merely by recalling its membership in the British Empire. In recognition of this disquieting fact, patriots tried to reassure themselves that the United States was destined for a grand and glorious future in its own right. Yet doubts were bound to persist, especially when American intellectuals dared to consider whether or not their culture really could survive apart from Europe. Since the achievements of their own artists and writers were negligible, nationalists turned to nature as the only viable alternative. As early as 1784, for example, Thomas Jefferson singled out portions of the American landscape to support his conviction that the environment was ideal for future national attainments. He was especially proud of two wonders native to Virginia, the Natural Bridge, south of Lexington, and the Potomac River Gorge, which pierces the Blue Ridge Mountains at Harpers

Ferry. High above the river, on a large rock later named in his honor, he declared the panorama of rapids and cliffs "worth a voyage across the Atlantic."[7] Other essayists were far less restrained. Philip Freneau, for example, focused his defense of national pride farther westward, where he crowned the Mississippi the "prince of rivers, in comparison of whom the *Nile* is but a small rivulet, and the *Danube* a ditch."[8]

Even the most spirited nationalists, however, could not be blind to the obvious distortions of such claims. That the Danube was not a ditch went without saying. And why should Europeans risk the long and dangerous Atlantic crossing just to see the Potomac River, especially when the Old World possessed its equivalent—or better—in the scenery of the Rhine? Clearly Americans had to do more than stretch reality if Europeans were to concede any validity to the New World point of view.

Unfortunately for America's nationalists, their subsequent attempts to distinguish the United States from Europe through the medium of nature proved no more convincing. Landscapes in the New World were simply too lacking in history for those many intellectuals who longed for stronger emotional attachments to their culture than great rocks, waterfalls, or rivers. Few voiced their doubts more poignantly than Washington Irving. In 1819 he confided to his *Sketch Book* that he preferred "to wander over the scenes of renowned achievement—to tread, as it were, in the footsteps of antiquity—to loiter about the ruined castle—to meditate on the falling tower—to escape, in short, from the commonplace reality of the present, and lose myself among the shadowy grandeurs of the past." Thus Irving was among those who satisfied his fantasies abroad, although he conceded that no American need "look beyond his own country for the sublime and beautiful of natural scenery."[9]

Irving's qualification, however, was little more reassuring than nationalists' prior distortions. At best it allowed the United States to claim equality with European landscapes only in the category of visual impact. This did nothing to ease the discomfort of those who still struggled to link American scenery with deeply emotional and spiritual values as well. In this vein James Fenimore Cooper revealed the inner misgivings of everyone concerned when he admitted their dilemma was beyond resolution until civilization in the New World had also advanced to "the highest state." Meanwhile Americans must "concede to Europe much the noblest scenery . . . in all those effects which depend on time and association."[10] Shortly before his death, in September 1851, Cooper still maintained that "the great distinction between American and European scenery, as a whole," lay "in the greater want of finish in the former than in the latter, and to the greater superfluity of works of art in the old world than in the new." Specifically, European landscapes included castles, fortified towns, villages accented by towering cathedrals, and similar "picturesque and striking collections of human habitations." Although nature had "certainly made some differences" between the two continents, still no one could deny Europe's superiority over the United States in the possession of landscapes blessed with "the impress of the past."[11]

First published in *The Nation*, Cooper's assessment later appeared in *The Home Book of the Picturesque*. Among the volume's other contributors were William Cullen Bryant, Washington Irving, and Nathaniel Parker Willis, all of whom had achieved prominence in writings about the American scene. Indeed no book contains a more comprehensive overview of the anxieties aroused by America's search for distinction through landscape. Cooper's daughter, Susan, for example, who also contributed to the collection of articles, likewise revealed the depth of misgivings about the sense of impermanence and instability in a typical northeastern landscape. One "soft hazy morning, early in October," she began, "we were sitting upon the trunk of a fallen pine, near a projecting cliff which overlooked the country for some fifteen miles or more; the lake, the rural town, and the farms and valleys beyond, lying at our feet like a beautiful map." Yet when she compared the scene below to similar examples in Europe, her cheerfulness faded. Suddenly the taverns and shops of the village only reminded her of the "comparatively slight and furtive charac-

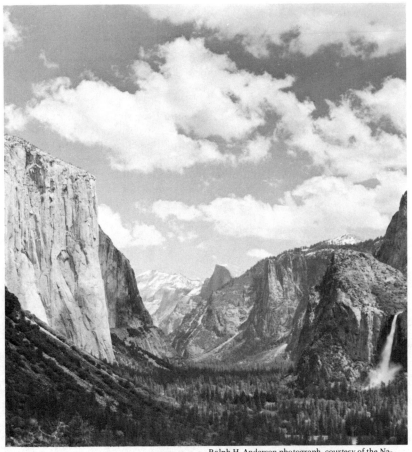

Ralph H. Anderson photograph, courtesy of the National Park Service

The sheer cliffs and waterfalls of Yosemite Valley epitomize the notion of monumentalism that lay behind the national park movement in the United States. Yosemite Valley was ceded to California for protection as a state park in 1864; a national park surrounding the gorge was established by Congress in 1890.

Courtesy of the National Collection of Fine Arts,
Smithsonian Institution

George Catlin (1796–1872), best known for his paintings of American Indians, painted Niagara Falls in 1827. Perhaps he was thinking of the commercial disfigurement of Niagara that has already begun when, in 1832, he proposed "A *nation's Park*"; Frederick Law Olmsted, Ferdinand V. Hayden, and other later leaders of the national park movement held Niagara up as an argument for the protection of scenic wonders.

Courtesy of the National Park Service

"The passage of the Patowmac through the Blue ridge" at Harpers Ferry, wrote Thomas Jefferson, "is perhaps one of the most stupendous scenes in nature. . . . This scene is worth a voyage across the Atlantic." Even so, most European travelers, as well as American nationalists, considered such landscapes commonplace, especially when compared with the Rhine Valley and similar Old World landmarks with a long human history.

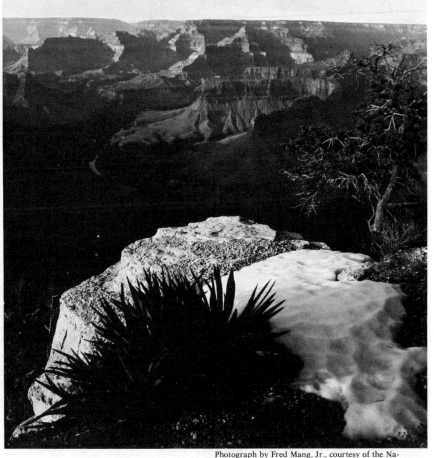

Photograph by Fred Mang, Jr., courtesy of the National Park Service

In a 1974 survey by the United States Travel Service, Americans ranked the Grand Canyon as the nation's supreme natural spectacle. President Theodore Roosevelt proclaimed the Grand Canyon a national monument in 1908; Congress made it a national park in 1919.

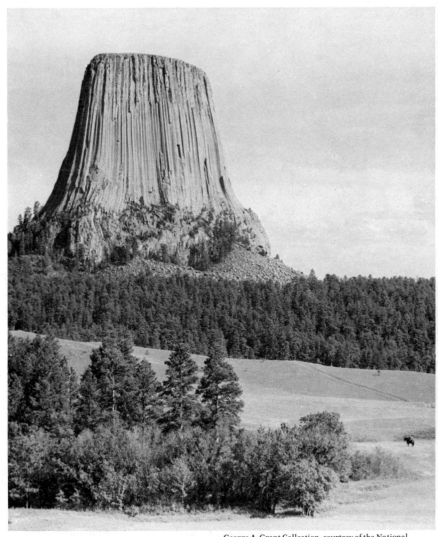

George A. Grant Collection, courtesy of the National
Park Service

Devils Tower, Wyoming, was proclaimed the first national monument in 1906.

William S. Keller, courtesy of the National Park Service

The ruggedness and harsh environment of Mount McKinley, Alaska, discouraged profitable exploitation, but mining and mineral exploration were allowed to continue in the foothills and lowlands following the establishment of Mount McKinley National Park in 1917.

Glacier National Park, Montana, was introduced to the Congress in
1910 as "1,400 square miles of mountains piled on top of each other."

The Lower Falls and the Canyon of the Yellowstone River have been a
favorite subject for painters and photographers since the first expeditions of scientific exploration entered the Yellowstone country.

The ruggedness of Mount Rainier (which is here reflected in the waters of Eunice Lake) makes for breathtaking scenery and, like other national park landscapes, offers little else to exploit—only marginal amounts of timber and arable land.

Preservationists working for the establishment of Olympic National Park, Washington, during the 1930s encountered stiff opposition from lumbermen who were determined to draw the park boundaries closer to the timberline.

All the elements of monumentalism, especially rugged terrain and falling water, are missing from the proposed Prairie National Park in Pottawatomie County, Kansas. Yet it was just such a "monotonous" landscape that George Catlin had in mind when he proposed a nation's park in 1832. That his dream was realized in quite different form attests to the limitations of the national park idea in the United States.

ter of American architecture." Indeed, she said, echoing her father's lament, "there is no blending of the old and new in this country; there is nothing old among us." Even if Americans were "endowed with ruins"—her bitterness grew—"we should not preserve them"; rather "they would be pulled down to make way for some novelty." She could only imagine that the village had been miraculously transformed into an Old World hamlet, but this fantasy, too, failed in the least to comfort her. Forced to abandon her daydream, her visionary bridge "of massive stone, narrow, and highly arched," the "ancient watch-tower" rising above the trees, and the old country houses and thatched-roof cottages all vanished into nothingness. Her spell broken, "the country resumed its every-day aspect."[12]

As the writings of the Coopers further demonstrate, attempts to use nature as a basis for cultural superiority had clearly been less than successful. All rhetoric aside, American intellectuals themselves were far from convinced that landscapes in the United States were worthy of special recognition. Against the claim stood the realities of geography. Prior to 1848 the United States was limited to the eastern two-thirds of the continent. Except for portions of the Appalachian Mountains and a scattering of natural wonders such as Niagara Falls, the remainder of the American scene was, in truth, nothing extraordinary. Time and time again European and American writers alike used words such as "common" or "monotonous" to describe a majority of the East.[13] Its failure to measure up to scenery of the magnitude of the Swiss Alps, for example, prompted James Fenimore Cooper to add: "As a whole, it must be admitted that Europe offers to the senses sublimer views and certainly grander, than are to be found within our own borders, unless we resort to the Rocky Mountains, and the ranges in California and New Mexico."[14]

In fact, westward expansion would resolve the dilemma of America's cultural nationalists. Only a few years earlier Cooper's suggestion that they take refuge in the landforms of the West would have been pointless, inasmuch as both Mexico

and Great Britain contested with the United States for possession of the wonderlands he identified. But meanwhile events
had moved swiftly to make his alternative a credible one. As
the 1840s drew to a close, the tide of American expansion
finally reached the shores of the Pacific Ocean. It was, supporters justified, the "manifest destiny" of the nation to possess all
of the territory in between. The Louisiana Purchase of 1803
was the first major step toward this goal; from France the
United States acquired the heartland of the continent between
the west bank of the Mississippi River and the eastern slope of
the Rocky Mountains. Texas, annexed in 1845, secured the
territory from the south. The following year Great Britain
reluctantly, but peaceably, relinquished her claim to the
Pacific Northwest, which included all of present-day
Washington, Oregon, Idaho, and western Montana. In 1846 the
United States also declared war on Mexico, whose defeat two
years later brought California and most of the Southwest
under American control.[15] These acquisitions, in addition to
settlement of the boundaries in the Pacific Northwest, assured
the United States dominion over some of the most varied
scenery on the continent.

As James Fenimore Cooper had implied, this heritage
might relieve the frustration of trying to uncover landscapes
truly unique to the United States. Of course the search for
material well-being was the overriding motivation behind
conquest of the West itself. Still, exploration of the region soon
revealed distinct opportunities for the nation's cultural advancement as well. Above all, the West assured nationalists
that the growth and development of the United States were not
to close, environmentally speaking, on an anticlimactic note.
Rather, as Americans embarked on their final era of expansion,
the boldest and most magnificent setting in their experience
opened before them. It followed that the West's lack of art and
architecture would not disturb cultural nationalists nearly as
much as had been true in the East. After all, crudeness was
easily overlooked in an environment whose natural endowments were unparalleled worldwide.

Accompanied by the force of appeals for cultural identity

through nature, the opening of the Far West further explains the timing of the national park idea. In the region there remained not only the opportunity to appreciate nature unspoiled, but to preserve it intact as well. As distinct from the misfortune of eastern wonders such as Niagara Falls, which long since had fallen victim to private abuse, those in the West still belonged to the federal government as part of the public domain. The West, in either case, was the last chance for cultural nationalists to prove their sincerity.

The modern discovery of Yosemite Valley and the Sierra redwoods, in 1851 and 1852, respectively, provided the first believable evidence since Niagara Falls that the United States had a valid claim to cultural recognition through natural wonders.[16] Suddenly, as if to show their relief, nationalists belittled the geography of even their most magnificent trans-Atlantic rivals. Switzerland, long renowned as the gem of mountain landscapes, was an obvious first target. In this vein the sentiments of Lieutenant Colonel A. V. Kautz, a decorated veteran of the Civil War, were typical. Recalling his nearly successful ascent of Mount Rainier, Washington, in 1857, he declared the surrounding Cascade Range in possession of "mountain scenery in quantity and quality sufficient to make half a dozen Switzerlands." With good reason, of course, a majority of writers favored Yosemite Valley for drawing such comparisons. "When we come to the Yosemite Falls proper," noted one admirer, "we behold an object which has no parallel anywhere in the Alps." Nor could any valley in Switzerland, he maintained, match the symmetry and magnificence of Yosemite. William H. Brewer, a graduate of Yale University and member of the California Geological Survey, was among the majority of transplanted easterners who shared an identical view. In 1863 he described Yosemite Falls as the "crowning glory" of the entire gorge. "It comes over the wall on the far side of the valley," he began, "and drops 1,542 feet the first leap, then falls 1,100 more in two or three more cascades, the entire height being over 2,600 feet! I question if the world furnishes a parallel," he continued, "certainly there is none known." Even Bridal Veil Falls—only a fraction as high as the greater cataract—itself seemed "vastly finer than any water-fall in Switzerland," he concluded, "in fact finer than any in Europe."[17]

The common practice of not merely describing each wonder, but in the same breath depreciating its counterparts abroad, confirms how pervasive cultural anxiety was in the United States during this period. Nor were these correspondents an intellectual elite whose writings may be discounted because they were limited to a professional clientele. As early as 1859 Horace Greeley, owner and editor of the *New York Tribune*, wrote for a circulation approaching 300,000 when he visited Yosemite Valley and dubbed it "the most unique and majestic of nature's marvels." Indeed, he maintained, "no single wonder of nature on earth" could surpass it. Six years later Samuel Bowles further revealed the popularity of scenic nationalism in his series of articles for the *Springfield Republican*. "THE YOSEMITE!" he exclaimed. "As well interpret God in thirty-nine articles as portray it to you by word of mouth or pen." Again it seemed more effective to rely upon culturally-inspired descriptions. Specifically, everyone should agree that "only the whole of Switzerland" eclipsed the valley; in fact, he concluded, "no one scene in all the Alps" could match its "majestic and impressive beauty."[18]

The temptation to view Yosemite Valley as a nationalistic resource was also encouraged by the Reverend Thomas Starr King. His impressions of the gorge in 1860 soon appeared as a series of articles in the *Boston Evening Transcript*. Undoubtedly he excited New Englanders by noting that only twenty minutes after entering Yosemite Valley, his party came to "the foot of a fall as high and more beautiful than the celebrated Staubach,[19] the highest in Europe." And the cataract was only a sample of what California's fabled wonderland had to offer. Indeed, as he and his companions moved farther up the valley, King pondered whether "such a ride" would be "possible in any other part of the planet?" Like his contemporaries he answered himself predictably: "nowhere among the Alps, in no pass of the Andes, and in no Canyon of the mighty Oregon range," he stated, "is there such stupendous rock scenery."

Only "the awful gorges of the Himalaya" might challenge the summits and defiles of the Sierra Nevada.[20]

Comparisons between the natural wonders of the United States also had advantages. After all, most Americans of the period would never get to see Yosemite Valley, let alone the mountains of Asia. Thus travel accounts had more meaning when commentators measured Niagara Falls, Natural Bridge, or some other eastern landmark against its counterpart in the West. Readers of the *Springfield Republican*, for example, shared the enthusiasm of Samuel Bowles upon his discovery that Yosemite Falls was in fact "fifteen times as high as Niagara Falls!" Albert D. Richardson of the *New York Tribune* nudged the figure slightly upward, to "sixteen times higher than Niagara," but the purpose of both descriptions was unchanged. "Think of a cataract of half a mile with only a single break!" Richardson challenged his followers. And as if that statistic were not enough to boggle their minds and soothe their provincial doubts, "Niagara itself," he noted, "would dwarf beside the rocks in this valley."[21]

With this self-examination of America's own wonders came added assurance that only in the United States did a gorge like Yosemite Valley exist. The Sierra redwoods[22] were still further consolation for the absence of a long American past, one redeemed, at least mentally, through creative fantasizing in the midst of ancient ruins and other objects of human achievement. The explorer and surveyor Clarence King also considered this approach to "the perspective of centuries" much too "conventional." Although a native of Connecticut and graduate of Yale University, beneath the Sierra redwoods, in 1864, he rejected the common assertion that culture derived solely from man-made artifacts. Instead he found stability and continuity in the "vast bulk and grand, pillar-like stateliness" of the great trees. Indeed, he insisted, no "fragment of human work, broken pillar or sand-worn image half lifted over pathetic desert,—none of these link the past and to-day with anything like the power of these monuments of living antiquity...." The argument recalled the doubts of nationalists such as Washington Irving and the Coopers, who felt that American society had nothing suggesting age and permanence. In rebuttal King noted that the Sierra redwoods "began to grow before the Christian era," let alone the flowering of European civilization. The antiquity of the United States, in other words, predated that of Europe. In this vein Horace Greeley himself anticipated the explorer's argument; similarly moved in 1859 by a visit to the Sierra redwoods, he assured readers of the *Tribune* that the trees "were of very substantial size when David danced before the ark, when Solomon laid the foundations of the Temple, when Theseus ruled in Athens, when Aeneas fled from the burning wreck of vanquished Troy," and "when Sesostris led his victorious Egyptians into the heart of Asia." It followed that the United States had its own claim to antiquity; America's past simply must be measured in "green old age," King said. In either case, as living monuments the redwoods were superior ties to the past, since, unlike still-life artifacts, they would be growing "broad and high for centuries to come."[23]

These claims, however trivial from today's perspective, then filled an important intellectual need. For the first time in almost a century Americans argued with confidence that the United States had something of value in its own right to contribute to world culture. Although Europe's castles, ruins, and abbeys would never be eclipsed, the United States had "earth monuments"[24] and giant redwoods that had stood long before the birth of Christ. Thus the natural marvels of the West compensated for America's lack of old cities, aristocratic traditions, and similar reminders of Old World accomplishments. As Albert D. Richardson summed up the standard perception of the region: "In grand natural curiosities and wonders, all other countries combined fall far below it."[25] Such statements, so often repeated throughout the 1850s and 1860s, yet so implausible beforehand, might now comfort people still living under the shadow of Milton, Shakespeare, and the Sistine Chapel.

The search for a unique national identity inevitably influenced the arts in the United States as well as personal correspondence and popular literature. With the rise of the Hudson River School of landscape painting, cultural nationalists found their first vindication. Prior to evolution of the genre during the 1820s and 1830s, its predecessors usually did little more than imitate European styles and subject matter. In contrast the Hudson River School broke the bonds of tradition and looked directly to nature for guidance and inspiration. For the first time American artists disdained merely reinterpreting Old World buildings and ruins for the hundredth or thousandth time. Instead the Hudson River School searched for truth and realism in the natural world, confident that only the unchanging laws of the universe contained real wisdom and meaning for mankind. Artists were advised to depict mountains, forests, river valleys, and seacoasts, where, despite random human interruptions, the hidden but ever-consistent laws of nature could still be deciphered.[26]

It followed that the Hudson River School had no reason to look beyond the Northeast for subject matter; nature in all its moods could be located or imagined throughout the region. Moreover, the quest for realism common to the Hudson River School led to a concern for detail that discouraged the interpretation of landforms on a scale such as that found in the West. The popularization of its natural wonders awaited what has been labeled as the Rocky Mountain School of landscape painting, which emerged during the late 1850s and 1860s. Indeed, much as the relatively subdued landscapes of the Northeast affected the subtleties of the Hudson River School, so, inevitably, the horizons and grandeur of the West defined the Rocky Mountain School as well. One distinction was the compulsion of artists in the West to cut their canvas by the yard instead of by the foot. Others sacrificed realism, as if to suggest that the mountains of the region were even higher, its canyons far deeper, and its colors more vivid than in real life.[27] Still, while exaggeration was out of place in the Hudson River School, its practice in the West was in keeping with pronouncements that the region was in fact America's repository of cultural identity through landscape.

The popularity of the Rocky Mountain School thus further

prepared the United States to turn from simply appreciating its natural wonders to preserving them. To be sure, although artists such as George Catlin, Karl Bodmer, and George Caleb Bingham preceded the Rocky Mountain School into the West, as pioneers none was privileged to visit those wonderlands whose uniqueness later evoked cultural as well as artistic acclaim. The popularization of Yosemite Valley and the Yellowstone, in particular, respectively awaited the co-founders of the Rocky Mountain School, Albert Bierstadt and Thomas Moran.[28] Bierstadt, drawn west by the Rocky Mountains in 1859, painted the region more than a decade prior to Moran, which explains his earlier fame and importance. After sketching the Wind River Mountains and other large peaks in what is now the state of Wyoming, Bierstadt returned east and moved his studio from New Bedford, Massachusetts, to New York City, where, shortly afterward, the first of his paintings went on display at the National Academy of Design. Among them was *The Base of the Rocky Mountains, Laramie Peak*, shown in April 1860. Measuring a full 4½ by 9 feet, it not only established his reputation but alerted the public to expect similar interpretations of the West in subsequent years.[29]

Bierstadt's second trip west in 1863 led him to California, where he became intimate with perhaps his most familiar trademark—Yosemite Valley. For seven weeks during August and September he rambled through the gorge, retracing the footsteps of Horace Greeley, the Reverend Thomas Starr King, and other early visitors. From his sketches evolved a lengthy series of paintings, including *Valley of the Yosemite* (1864), which sold the following year for $1,600. An even more dramatic success awaited *The Rocky Mountains* (1863). In 1865 the 6-by-10-foot canvas commanded $25,000, then the highest sum ever awarded an American artist. Two years later Bierstadt repeated the triumph with *Domes of the Yosemite*. A whopping 9½ by 15 feet, it too was commissioned for $25,000.[30]

While Bierstadt's accomplishments affirmed the popularity of the American West, still others turned to the rising profession of photography to substantiate nationalists' claims. Carleton E. Watkins, for example, photographed Yosemite

Valley and the Sierra redwoods as early as 1861, two years prior to Bierstadt's arrival. With fanfare no less than that accorded the painter, his pictures also made the rounds of major galleries in the East.[31] Bierstadt's advantage as a painter was his freedom to break with reality. *Domes of the Yosemite*, for instance, imparts a starkness and rigidity to the valley which imply that it is even more dramatic and magnificent than in real life. Similarly, the Indian encampment in the foreground of *The Rocky Mountains* draws the viewer's attention back to the peaks, whose outline, although subtle, again suggests an abruptness and boldness uncommon to most of the region. The style was in keeping with the preferences of those who needed reassurance that the mountains of the West were in fact rivals of the Alps. Bierstadt revealed his own uneasiness about the validity of such claims in a series of paintings oddly suggestive of alpine rather than western scenery.[32] In either case, his followers readily forgave his tendency to exaggerate the summits of the region; only as Americans became more self-confident about their cultural identity did their acceptance of the genre lapse into criticism. Meanwhile, if Bierstadt embellished his landscapes for dramatic emphasis, he merely copied what European masters themselves had encouraged for years regarding interpretations of their own famous ruins and buildings.

Translated into engravings and woodcuts for popular distribution in newspapers and magazines, the works of Albert Bierstadt, C. E. Watkins, and other artists provided the visual component of cultural nationalism. Their achievement alone, of course, did not inspire the national park idea. Still, by dramatizing what the nation stood to lose by its indifference, artists contributed immeasurably to the evolution of concern. Scenic monuments, no less than man-made ones, would never become credible symbols of American culture if the nation simply allowed them to slip from public ownership into private control. As early as the 1830s European critics all but charged the United States with hypocrisy over the defacement of Niagara Falls; further examples of such callousness, it followed, would only lead to equally harsh condemnation.

Perhaps George Catlin, since recognized as one of the foremost artists of the American Indian, overheard similar reprimands while painting Niagara Falls during the late 1820s.[33] In any event, his is perhaps the most quoted response to the problem of preservation in general. A native of Pennsylvania, in the year 1832 he was at Fort Pierre, in present South Dakota, where, like Alexis de Tocqueville beside Niagara Falls, he urged his countrymen to consider the price of sweeping aside the native animals and inhabitants of the prairies for all time. The alternative, he concluded, was "A *nation's Park*, containing man and beast, in all the wild and freshness of their nature's beauty!" The cultural possibilities of such a legacy also did not escape his attention; what "a beautiful and thrilling specimen" the park would be "for America to preserve and hold up to the view of her refined citizens and the world, in future ages!"[34]

Of course Catlin was far ahead of his time. Indeed, not until the twentieth century was well advanced—as exemplified in 1934 with authorization of Everglades National Park in Florida—did national park enthusiasts recognize wild animals as fully worthy of protection alongside spectacular scenery. Similarly, "practical" considerations actually motivated the first legislation to protect natural areas. In 1832 Congress set aside the Arkansas Hot Springs, but in recognition of its medicinal value, not with the intent of protecting scenery. As scenery the Hot Springs reservation hardly compared with wonders such as Niagara Falls or Virginia's Natural Bridge, which, although more deserving of protection, received none despite annual visitation approaching the tens of thousands.[35]

A spirited exchange between English and American botanists over the proper classification for the Sierra redwoods was more indicative of the type of catalyst needed to effect scenic preservation in the United States. Once the British realized that the trees were not a hoax, their search for a scientific name appropriate to the giants led to the adoption of *Wellingtonia gigantea*, after England's revered statesman and war hero, the Duke of Wellington. To say that American nationalists opposed the commemoration of an Englishman with a New World wonder would be an understatement. *Washingtonia gigantea* was their alternative; whether George Washington's defeat of the British during the Revolutionary War sweetened the substitution has not been spelled out.[36] Regardless, the debate is further evidence of the degree of cultural importance the United States ascribed to the wonders of the West during the nineteenth century. Well after 1900 American botanists still chided British correspondents for occasionally lapsing into use of *Wellingtonia gigantea* to identify the big trees. In what might be considered a compromise, the Sierra redwoods are now generally called *Sequoia gigantea*, after the Indian chief Sequoyah, inventor of the Cherokee alphabet.

Given America's defense of its right to name the Sierra redwoods, it followed their impending destruction would precipitate a cry of protest. The fate of the "Mother of the Forest," among the largest specimens in the Calaveras Grove, was a dramatic case in point. In 1854 promoters stripped the tree of its bark to a height of 116 feet, then cut the shell into sections and shipped it to New York for exhibit. Later it made its way to England where, until 1866, the mammoth bedazzled thousands at the Crystal Palace.[37]

Yet there were critics of this and even earlier exhibits of Sierra redwoods. In 1853 *Gleason's Pictorial*, a widely read British journal, published a letter from an irate Californian who protested disfigurement of the "Discovery Tree" for public display as "a cruel idea, a perfect desecration." If native to Europe, he charged, "such a natural production would have been cherished and protected, if necessary, by law; but in this money-making, go-ahead community, thirty or forty thousand dollars are paid for it and the purchaser chops it down and ships it off for a shilling show."[38] A similar accusation in 1857 by James Russell Lowell was no less pointed, especially in the wake of America's long and often frustrating search for cultural recognition apart from Europe. If the United States hoped to compensate for its lack of human works by substituting the wonders of nature, Americans would have to do better than allow the redwoods, Niagara Falls, or any other landmark to be auctioned off to the highest bidder.

Further incentive to turn from the appreciation of land-scapes to their preservation appeared as Yosemite Valley itself seemed destined to fall victim to the whims of private indi-viduals. Some entrepreneurs already claimed portions of the gorge in anticipation of the thousands of visitors sure to follow in their footsteps. The situation posed a dilemma. If the exploiters were allowed to confiscate Yosemite Valley as well as the Sierra redwoods, whatever cultural symbolism they lent the nation might soon become meaningless. Niagara Falls already demonstrated the absurdity of taking cultural refuge in wonders whose uniqueness had been sacrificed to indi-vidual gain; again the United States risked the charge that its claim to an identity through landscape was totally ridiculous.

The crystallization of cultural anxiety into realization of the national park idea may be traced to the winter of 1864. Moved by concern for the Sierra redwoods and Yosemite Val-ley, a small group of Californians persuaded their junior Unit-ed States senator, John Conness, to propose legislation pro-tecting both marvels from further private abuse. Precisely who conceived the campaign itself remains largely a mystery. The known advocate is Israel Ward Raymond, the state representa-tive of the Central American Steamship Transit Company of New York. On February 20, 1864, he addressed a letter to Senator Conness, urging preservation of Yosemite and a grove of the big trees "for public use, resort and recreation." Raymond was equally insistent that the wonders be "inalien-able forever." Perhaps this wording was suggested to him by Frederick Law Olmsted, then managing the nearby Mariposa Estate, although there is no evidence the landscape architect played a direct role in the park movement. In any event, Con-ness was more than cooperative. He forwarded Raymond's letter to the commissioner of the General Land Office with the request that a bill be prepared, and, significantly, he repeated Raymond's words: "Let the grant be inalienable."[39]

Raymond's insistence on the terminology suggests that he

and his associates had considered how the park would reflect on the credibility of the United States from the outset. Especially from a cultural perspective, preservation without permanence would be no real test of the nation's sincerity. As if in accord with that interpretation, in the Senate John Conness justified the clause as a patriotic duty that already was long overdue. The heart of his speech recalled that the British once had derided the Sierra redwoods in particular as nothing but "a Yankee invention," a fabrication "made from beginning to end; that it was an utter untruth that such trees grew in this country; that it could not be."[40] Whether or not Conness himself seriously endorsed his statement, or whether he merely considered his appeal to national pride and patriotism as good strategy, his reliance on the argument substantiates its popularity and importance. The Congress was also receptive, and on June 30, 1864, President Abraham Lincoln signed the bill into law.

The purpose of the park, as indicated by the placement of its boundaries, was strictly scenic. Only Yosemite Valley and its encircling peaks, an area of approximately forty square miles, comprised the northern unit. A similar restriction applied to the southern section of the park, the Mariposa Grove of Sierra redwoods, where a maximum of four square miles of the public domain might be protected.[41] Obviously such limitations ignored the ecological framework of the region, especially its watersheds; indeed, the term *ecology* was not even known. Monumentalism, not environmentalism, was the driving impetus behind the 1864 Yosemite Act.

Senator Conness's drawn-out reminder that Great Britain initially debunked the existence of the Sierra redwoods substantiates the cultural overtones to his legislation. Indeed, its provisions prove that Congress intended the park to be in the national interest all along. Although Yosemite Valley and the Mariposa Grove were to be turned over to California for administration, the federal government clearly spelled out beforehand what management by the state must embody. These conditions of acceptance included the retention of the park for "public use, resort and recreation"; similarly, both the valley and big trees must be held "inalienable for all time."[42] Nor did this rhetoric merely mask a state-inspired project divorced of nationalistic overtones; two years elapsed before California even agreed to take over the park.

In fact, therefore, if not in name, Yosemite was the first national park. Although Congress never enforced the restrictions imposed on California's acceptance of the grant (at least not until 1905, when the state ceded the valley and big trees back to the federal government), their presence indicates that Congress had acted with the national interest in mind. The consensus that national parks had to be permanent was also recognized as early as 1864. The concept itself had cultural significance; in landscape, no less than in art and architecture, the certainty of permanence was essential for preserving any sense of continuity between the present and past. Indeed, if Congress had simply intended to satisfy the public's urge for outdoor recreation, it should hardly have looked as far afield as California for an appropriate site. By any stretch of the imagination, the realization of Yosemite's potential as a tourist retreat was still many years distant in 1864.

Until recreation in the valley became a serious possibility, Yosemite and the Sierra redwoods filled a cultural role. To be sure, that this was the park's immediate purpose was soon confirmed by those who looked beyond its monumental attributes to the enhancement of its other natural values. As early as 1865, for example, Frederick Law Olmsted warned the Yosemite Park Commission that most Americans considered the grant a mere "wonder or curiosity." It followed they did not appreciate the preserve's "tender" esthetic resources, namely the "foliage of noble and lovely trees and bushes, tranquil meadows, playful streams," and the other varieties "of soft and peaceful pastoral beauty." A quarter of a century later he repeated the charge; the traditional perception of Yosemite as a spectacle, he maintained, was still "a vulgar blunder." To the contrary, the valley's charm did not depend "on the greatness of its walls," the "length of its little early summer cascades; the height of certain of its trees, the reflections in its pools, and other such matters as can be entered in statistical tables" or "pointed out by guides and represented within picture frames." Rather the attraction of the gorge lay "in the rare association" achieved by combining its spectacular features with the "very beautifully dispersed great bodies, groups and clusters of trees." These, too, contributed to the Yosemite experience, not just those landforms that excited public acclaim because they were so awesome.[43]

John Muir, who first entered Yosemite Valley in 1868, soon shared much the same opinion. A self-styled "poetico-trampo-geologist-bot. and ornith-natural, etc!-!-!," like Olmsted he had also trained himself to look beyond the spectacular in nature.[44] Writing in 1875, however, he declared the rest of the world still "not ready for the fine banks and braes [hills] of the lower Sierra." His choice of words did more than reflect his early boyhood in Scotland. Nearer the point, Muir recognized that the public ranked scenery according to its size and ruggedness. "Tourists make their way through the foot-hill landscapes as if blind to all their best beauty," he observed, "and like children seek the emphasized mountains—the big alpine capitals whitened with glaciers and adorned with conspicuous spires." Although he optimistically concluded that "the world moves onward," and one day "lowlands will be loved more than alps, and lakes and level rivers more than water-falls,"[45] he would, like Olmsted, close an illustrious career still far from having convinced the public at large that the commonplace in nature was as worthy of protection as the spectacular.

Such understanding awaited an age receptive to the life-giving properties and esthetic beauty of all ecosystems. Well into the twentieth century, Americans valued the natural wonders of the West almost exclusively for their scenic impact. The perception was in keeping with the origins of the national park idea as a response to cultural anxiety. To reemphasize, most Americans expressed their nationalism by drawing attention to the material advancement of the nation. But again, to admit that a distinct minority inspired the national park idea does not discount that minority's social and political influence. The opening of the Far West, coupled with nationalists' long search for an American identity, gave form and meaning to the myriad emotions historians have defined as "nature appreciation." Conceivably, the United States might have originated the national park idea in the absence of cultural nationalism; with it, however, the nation had clear and immediate justification to go beyond simply appreciating its natural wonders to preserving them.

Cultural insecurity, as the catalyst for concern, speeded the nation's response to the threatened confiscation of its natural heritage. Indeed, to suggest that the national park idea evolved from the search for national pride alone, rather than out of anxiety about America's failure to live up to the achievements of Europe, is to ignore that pride and anxiety had one and the same source. Precisely because American intellectuals lacked confidence in their record, their quest for national pride became so all-consuming. Even those writers and artists who provided the United States with its strongest basis for cultural recognition, including James Fenimore Cooper and Washington Irving, were still the most easily discouraged by comparisons of their nation's attainments to the record of Europe. As anxious provincials they found it impossible to ignore statements such as that popularized by the English clergyman, Sydney Smith, who asked derisively in 1820: "In the four quarters of the globe, who reads an American book? or goes to an American play? or looks at an American picture or statue?"[46] America's landscapes, shorn of all links with the past, only dramatized the nation's cultural deficiencies. Not until the discovery of landmarks of unquestionable uniqueness did nationalists feel confident in urging Europeans to heed Thomas Jefferson's advice and cross the Atlantic to visit the wonders of the New World. Such were the reassuring magnets of the American West, the cornerstones of a nationalistic park idea.

2

Monumentalism Reaffirmed: The Yellowstone

As an agricultural country, I was not favorably impressed with the great Yellowstone basin, but its brimstone resources are ample for all the matchmakers in the world. . . . When, . . . by means of the Northern Pacific Railroad, the falls of the Yellowstone and the geyser basin are rendered easy of access, probably no portion of America will be more popular as a watering-place or summer resort. . . .

Walter Trumbull, 1871

We pass with rapid transition from one remarkable vision to another, each unique of its kind and surpassing all others in the known world. The intelligent American will one day point on the map to this remarkable district with the conscious pride that it has not its parallel on the face of the globe.

Ferdinand Vandiveer Hayden, 1872

In 1872 the national park idea, shaped beneath the monumental grandeur of Yosemite Valley and the Sierra redwoods, was realized in name as well as in fact with the establishment of Yellowstone National Park, Wyoming. In subsequent years, however, what appeared to be differences between Yosemite and Yellowstone overshadowed the origins of the national park idea during the 1860s. In marked contrast to the Yosemite grant, Yellowstone Park was huge, more than 3,300 square miles in area. In addition, it was truly a national park, since the federal government retained exclusive jurisdiction over the area. Still, in no way was Yellowstone intended to break with the visions of 1864. Its spaciousness resulted from concern for the safety of yet undiscovered wonders, not because park advocates in 1872 were any more aware of the advantages of protecting an integral ecosystem. Nor was Yellowstone so large because it was meant to protect wilderness; Americans were still ambivalent about wild country.[1] Like Yosemite Park, Yellowstone owed its existence to more immediate concerns. Similar to the natural phenomena of the High Sierra, Wyoming's fabled wonderland of geysers, waterfalls, canyons, and other "curiosities" appealed to the nation as a cultural repository. Although it was much larger than its predecessor, therefore, and was first to be *called* a national park, Yellowstone merely reaffirmed the ideals and anxieties of 1864.

Thus if more had been known about Yellowstone[2] at the same time, perhaps the two parks would have been established simultaneously. Well into the 1860s, however, its steep mountains, deep canyons, and remoteness discouraged most explorers, let alone tourists whose cultural biases might have carried the sentiment for protection from California to Wyoming. Precisely who first explored the region still is not known. Sometime between 1806 and 1810 the mountain man John Colter may have traversed it, although his exact route—if in fact he ever crossed the heart of what is now Yellowstone National Park at all—has never been verified. Evidence that James Bridger saw the territory is far more reliable; his stories, at least, suggest that he had a substantial knowledge about the Yellowstone by the 1830s.[3] There are other accounts, but only a few; the trappers, after all, were not in the West to arouse publicity about its natural wonders. The enjoyment and description of the wilderness awaited adventurers of a far different persuasion.

The discovery of gold in neighboring Montana Territory during the 1860s foretold the opening of Yellowstone to permanent disclosure. The period of revelation began as the goldseekers made inroads into the region via the Yellowstone River. And, occasionally, some deposits were unearthed. Yet more often "strikes" consisted of spectacular scenery and natural phenomena. In 1866 Jim Bridger added excitement to these reports with new renditions of his already fabled (though still widely disbelieved) adventures in the so-called mythical Yellowstone. Still, such publicity stirred several Montanans to entertain thoughts about an expedition of their own. During the summer of 1869 one was organized. As the date of departure drew near, however, most of the men dropped out, ostensibly because of unforeseen business engagements, but more likely because they now feared Indian reprisals. Their apprehension only grew on word from Fort Ellis that no military escort could be provided that year. With the season drawing to a close, only three of the men, Charles W. Cook, David E. Folsom, and William Peterson, dared risk the consequences and go it alone. On September 6 they left the settlements behind and headed south for the Yellowstone wilderness.[4]

No less than their counterparts in Yosemite Valley and beneath the Sierra redwoods, the adventurers returned with descriptions whose cultural overtones proved decisive in molding America's first impression of the region. When Cook, Folsom, and Peterson[5] reemerged from Yellowstone early in October, their list of discoveries included the Grand Canyon of the Yellowstone River, Yellowstone Lake, and the thermal wonders of what has come to be known as the Lower Geyser Basin. For a second time exploration of the West had revealed a made-to-order wonderland where the handiwork of nature grandly compensated for the Old World associations and sense of the past so painfully absent in the United States. As Charles W. Cook was comforted to note, a limestone formation on the outskirts of the wilderness "bore a strong resemblance to an old castle," whose "rampart and bulwark were slowly yielding to the ravages of time." Still, "the stout old turret stood out in bold relief against the sky, with every embrasure as perfect in outline as though but a day ago it had been built by the hand of man." Indeed the explorers "could almost imagine," he concluded, "that it was the stronghold of some baron of feudal times, and that we were his retainers returning laden with the spoils of a successful foray."[6]

Charles Cook's attempt to ascribe human intervention to the formation was no less sincere than prior efforts by Samuel Bowles, Horace Greeley, Clarence King, and their contemporaries in the High Sierra. Nor were Cook, Folsom, and Peterson to be disappointed. Continuing on to the Grand Canyon of the Yellowstone River, they further discovered that here, too, "it required no stretch of the imagination to picture," deep within the recesses of the chasm, "fortresses, castles, watchtowers, and other ancient structures, of every conceivable shape." Similarly, near Yellowstone Lake the men later sighted other "objects of interest and wonder," including "stone monuments," formed "by the slow process of precipitation, through the countless lapse of ages."[7] Wherever appropriate, such descriptions reaffirmed that the United States could salvage a past from the timelessness of natural forces, which, if suitably directed, themselves could be imagined to have resulted from human initiative.

The success of Charles W. Cook and his associates helped inspire an even more elaborate expedition the following summer. Meanwhile, back in Montana, Cook collaborated with David Folsom on a special diary of their descriptions, which eventually appeared in the July 1870 issue of *Western Monthly Magazine*.[8] By then the second expedition was making its final plans and preparations. To be composed of nineteen men in all, its leader would be Henry Dana Washburn. Following two terms as an Indiana representative to the United States Congress, Washburn in 1869 was appointed surveyor-general of Montana, where he soon joined in the discussions that led to the expedition. Its other participants included Nathaniel Pitt Langford, a native of New York State turned territorial politician, and Cornelius Hedges, a young lawyer with a degree from Yale University. Both men, as amateur correspondents, were authenticated by Walter Trumbull, formerly a reporter for the *New York Sun*; his father, Lyman, was the senior United States senator from Illinois. Lieutenant Gustavus C. Doane, another native of New York State, commanded the military escort of six men.[9] Again these brief biographies are instructive of the cultural baggage the men, as Eastern-bred professionals, carried with them into the Yellowstone wilderness. Here, no less than in Yosemite Valley, the combination of eastern perceptions and the wonders of the West fostered the earliest glimmerings of the national park idea.

With the Washburn-Langford-Doane Expedition,[10] the popularization of Yellowstone's cultural possibilities was assured. Indeed, the outpouring of publicity that followed completion of the venture soon overshadowed the prior exploits of Cook, Folsom, and Peterson. On August 22, 1870, Washburn and his associates left Fort Ellis, Montana Territory, and, four days later, approached what is now Yellowstone National Park. Their adventures over the next month aroused the imaginations of people nationwide. Like their predecessors, Washburn and his companions marveled at the Grand Canyon of the Yellowstone River and its spectacular upper and lower falls, over 100 and 300 feet high respectively. "A grander scene than the lower cataract of the Yellowstone was never witnessed by mortal eyes," Langford stated. "It is a sheer, compact, solid, perpendicular sheet, faultless in all the elements of grandeur and picturesque beauties."[11] On September 1 the men resumed their march south toward Yellowstone Lake, but delayed enroute to examine the Mud Volcano. Following their sighting of the lake on the third, they exhausted themselves for several days in a trek around its southern shore through mile after mile of tumbled pines. The maze soon claimed a member of the party, Truman C. Everts, who became hopelessly separated from his companions. No one could be confident that he had survived; in fact he made his way out of Yellowstone several weeks later, although much weakened and emaciated. Still, if inadvertently, Evert's brush with death invited considerable comment and soon contributed as much publicity to the expedition as the popularization of Yellowstone's wonders.[12]

With the abandonment of their search for Everts, the explorers, understandably subdued, continued westward to the headwaters of the Firehole River. Here their spirits lifted with the sighting of the Upper Geyser Basin, which Cook and his party had missed the previous year. To the Washburn Expedition went the honor of locating and naming the basin's thermal attractions, including Old Faithful geyser, destined to become the enduring symbol of the national park idea. Yet whatever emotions the Upper Geyser Basin arouses among modern visitors, its first publicists welcomed the opportunity to draw comparisons between its wonders and the attractions of Europe. "To do justice to the subject would require a volume," Lieutenant Doane assured Congress. "The geysers of Iceland sink to insignificance beside them; they are above the reach of comparison." Similarly, Nathaniel P. Langford proclaimed the geyser the "new and, perhaps, most remarkable feature in our scenery and physical history." Again the wonder was touted all the more because its counterpart was not even present in Europe. "It is found in no other countries but Iceland and Tibet," Langford stated. "Taken as an aggregate," the officer added, "the Firehole Basin surpasses all other great wonders of the continent."[13] It followed that the scenery of the Old World, especially the Alps, had found its equal in the Rocky Mountains as well as the Sierra Nevada. For the geyser was America's alone—at least with respect to Europe—to the delight of every nationalist concerned.

Yellowstone, to be sure, was soon the talk of the popular press. No sooner did the Washburn Expedition return to Montana than several of its participants, including Washburn, Langford, and Hedges, composed a series of descriptive articles for the *Helena Daily Herald*.[14] Within days the accounts also spread to the East. On October 14, for example, the *New York Times* carried a lengthy editorial praising Washburn's skill in reporting the discoveries. "Accounts of travel are often rather uninteresting," the editorial began, "partly because of the lack of interest in the places visited and partly through the defective way in which they are described." But Yellowstone as portrayed by the surveyor-general of Montana struck the reader "like the realization of a child's fairy tale." Everywhere the expedition had encountered formations "that constantly suggested some mighty effort at human architecture." For instance, one stream coursed "between a procession of sharp pinnacles, looking like some noble old castle, dismantled and shivered with years, but still erect and defiant."[15] And "beauti-

ful" hardly seemed "the word for the Lower Falls of the Yellowstone. Here the height more than doubles Niagara." The
revelation of this magnificent wonder, the *Times* concluded, in
addition to "geysers of mud and steam that must exceed the
size and power of those of Iceland," clearly explained why
Washburn's writings were "so gilded with true romance."[16]

Such publicity soon provided additional opportunities for
the explorers to market their achievement. During the winter
of 1870–71, for example, Nathaniel P. Langford contracted
with the Northern Pacific Railroad to deliver a series of lec-
tures in Washington, D.C., New York, and Philadelphia. In
Washington his audience included Dr. Ferdinand Vandiveer
Hayden, a professor of geology at the University of Pennsylvania, and, of significance for Yellowstone's future, the director of the United States Geological and Geographical Survey of
the Territories. Langford's speech—added to the growing list
of reports and articles by Cornelius Hedges, Lieutenant Doane,
General Washburn,[17] and others—convinced Hayden to drop
his plans for operating in Dakota and Nebraska that summer.
Instead he would take the survey into Yellowstone.[18]

Congress appropriated $40,000, a sum that enabled the
men to accomplish far more than another description of Yellowstone's natural phenomena. In marked contrast to the Cook
and Washburn forays, Hayden's team included entomologists,
topographers, a zoologist, mineralogist, meteorologist, and
physician.[19] Thomas Moran, the artist, and William Henry
Jackson, a frontier photographer, were also invited to provide
the all-important visual record of the expedition's discoveries.[20] Moran, today regarded with Albert Bierstadt as
co-founder of the Rocky Mountain School of landscape painting, complemented Jackson's surprisingly detailed pictures
with a series of sketches and watercolors. Of those translated
onto canvas, the most famous and impressive is *The Grand
Canyon of the Yellowstone*. In June 1872 Congress purchased
the work for $10,000 and later hung it in the Senate lobby. A
full 7 by 12 feet, the painting firmly established Thomas Moran
as Bierstadt's rival.[21]

The Hayden Survey, which departed Fort Ellis on July 15,

constituted the third major investigation of Yellowstone in as many years. Yet a fourth expedition, a military reconnaissance commanded by one Colonel John W. Barlow and Captain David P. Heap, accompanied the Hayden party off and on during its travels, but, for obvious reasons, never achieved the distinction of the latter. Hayden and his men were among the first to see Mammoth Hot Springs,[22] a phenomenon of limestone terraces and streaming fountains on the northern outskirts of the Yellowstone wilderness. In prior seasons Cook, Washburn, and their associates had missed the wonder because they chose a slightly different route. The Hayden party spent two days exploring the area, then resumed its march southward toward the Grand Canyon of the Yellowstone River. Here the great falls and richly colored cliffs inspired Thomas Moran's great painting, which still is recognized as the most famous of his career. Its style, after all, was in keeping with the grandiose imagery of the West so popular during the period. In the middle of the picture, off in the distance, the Lower Fall leaps into the canyon, half-shrouded in mist. In the foreground and to the sides of the painting, the rocks, walls, and trees of the chasm grow progressively bolder and more angular in appearance, as if to suggest that the formations may in fact be thought of as castles, fortresses, or ruins. Indeed in real life, Ferdinand V. Hayden maintained, the pinnacles stood out like "Gothic columns . . . with greater variety and more striking colors than ever adorned a work of human art."[23] Only William Henry Jackson's photographs restricted the expedition to recording the scene without embellishment; still, nothing about the canyon's appearance deterred its publicists from declaring the formations superior to man-made art and architecture.

On the evening of July 28 the men arrived at Yellowstone Lake. While some members of the party stayed behind to map the shoreline, on the thirty-first Hayden and four others, including W. H. Jackson, struck off for the Firehole River. Three days later they sighted the Lower Geyser Basin; on August 6 and 7 they further investigated the Upper Geyser Basin and its hourly sentinel, Old Faithful. Soon afterward Hayden and his contingent returned to their comrades at Yellowstone Lake. Following yet another week of separate forays to the west and south, Hayden regrouped the men for the march northward and home. Back in Montana, on August 27, the geologist officially closed all operations in the field.[24]

Like the discovery of Yosemite Valley and the Sierra redwoods, the revelation of Yellowstone to the world offered the United States still another opportunity to acquire a semblance of antiquity through landscape. The protection of Yellowstone as a further outgrowth of America's cultural nationalism has simply been overshadowed by the debate concerning *when* the national park idea evolved rather than *why* it evolved. Those who place greater emphasis on terminology rather than ideology, for example, contend that Yellowstone marks the true origins of both the idea and the institution. Yellowstone, after all, and not Yosemite, was first to be *called* a national park.[25] This line of reasoning begins with the diary of Nathaniel Pitt Langford, whose entry for September 20, 1870, opened as follows: "Last night, and also this morning in camp, the entire party had a rather unusual discussion. The proposition was made by some member that we utilize the result of our exploration by taking up quarter sections of land at the most prominent points of interest," specifically, those that "would eventually become a source of great profit to the owners." Following this suggestion, however, and others of a similar bent, Cornelius Hedges declared "that he did not approve of any of these plans—that there ought to be no private ownership of any portion of that region, but that the whole of it ought to be set aside as a great National Park, and that each one of us ought to make an effort to have this accomplished."

According to Langford, the proposal then "met with an instantaneous and favorable response from all—except one—of the members of our party, and each hour since the matter was first broached, our enthusiasm has increased." Indeed, Langford concluded, "I lay awake half of last night thinking about it;—and if my wakefulness deprived my bedfellow (Hedges) of any sleep, he has only himself and his disturbing National Park proposition to answer for it."[26]

A monument on the site of the discussion, at the junction of the Firehole and Gibbon rivers, testifies to the widespread acceptance of Langford's account. But that the explorers used the term *national* park at this time is more than open to question. Doubts have been cast on Langford's diary itself, which he edited and revised for publication in 1905, thirty-five years after the event. There is also no mention of the term "national park" in any of the numerous publications prepared by the members of the Washburn Expedition following their exploits; the omission is very surprising in light of the plan's supposed adoption by all but one of the explorers. Thus it seems reasonable to conclude that while Langford did not intentionally distort his recollections, they magnified over time in response to the growing popularity of the national park idea. In all probability, what the Washburn Expedition discussed the night of September 19, 1870, if in fact the men had resolved to campaign for a park at this early date, was something on the order of the Yosemite grant, which preserved the gorge and Mariposa Redwood Grove in two distinct sections. Similar small parcels might easily have been established to preserve only Yellowstone's major points of interest, including the canyon, falls, and geyser basins. In either case, only later, as the men clarified their own thoughts and determined to really push for protection of the region, did the term "national park" evolve.[27]

Even then it appeared nowhere in the enabling act itself; the title *public* park was consistently used.[28] The omission lends credence to the argument that Yellowstone was in fact modeled after the Yosemite grant and retained by the federal government only because Wyoming, unlike California, was a territory rather than a state. Nor should the comparative insignificance of Yosemite in terms of size hide the striking similarity between the intent of its advocates and those who supported a Yellowstone park. While Yellowstone's explorers admitted that the region as a whole was "picturesque," they, too, invariably sought out those wonders whose uniqueness suggested the human intervention found so wanting in the American scene. It followed that wilderness preservation was the least of their aims. Nathaniel P. Langford's visions for Yellowstone Lake, for example, might well have been inspired by Lake Como or the French Riviera. "How can I sum up its wonderful attraction!" he exclaimed. "It is dotted with islands of great beauty, as yet unvisited by man, but which at no remote period will be adorned with villas and the ornaments of civilized life." Even at the moment, he confided to his diary, Yellowstone Lake "possesses adaptabilities for the highest display of artificial culture, amid the greatest wonders of Nature that the world affords. . . ." Not many years would elapse, he predicted, "before the march of civil improvements will reclaim this delightful solitude, and garnish it with all the attractions of cultivated taste and refinement."[29]

Eventually his dream would be realized, at least partially, with construction of the grand hotels beside the lake, the canyon, and the geyser basins. Granted, today Yellowstone is highly valued because it also has wilderness. The park's first publicists, however, did not embrace its wild country with the same enthusiasm, at least not in 1870. Rather the charge of crudeness often leveled at the United States aroused precisely the opposite reaction. As with Langford, the Upper Falls of the Yellowstone River furnished Cornelius Hedges with a vision more appropriate for the future. "I fancied I could see in the dim distance of a few seasons an iron swing bridge," he declared in the pages of the *Helena Daily Herald*, "with bright, happy eyes gazing wondrously upon this beauty of nature in water colors." In the meantime a "convenient ledge, with a surface accommodation for 20 persons," provided access for those who preferred to view the cataract in a more genteel fashion.[30]

With that statement Hedges joined Langford in revealing his innermost yearnings about the possibility of refining the region. While the United States lived in the shadow of European art and architecture, the absence of villas, iron bridges, and other ornaments was as unsettling in Yellowstone as anywhere else. The appreciation of nature for its own sake was not yet widely accepted. Indeed, as late as 1905 Langford might have stricken his conviction that Yellowstone should be "civilized" from his diary; that he instead published the passage intact bears out the depth of his original commitment to popularize the region as a tourist resort rather than a wilderness preserve.

The decision was in keeping with the explorers' urge to lend their exploits cultural as well as historical significance. As vindicated provincials, they freely joined Langford in further dismissing European culture with their newly discovered "spires of protruding rocks," "pillars of basalt," and other forms of the "majestic display of natural architecture." Nor did Langford seem in the least embarrassed when he claimed to have located a geyser whose crater resembled "a miniature model of the Coliseum."[31] As long as the United States lacked comparable examples of the real thing, the New World masterpieces of the Yellowstone would also help ease the period of transition.

As in the case of Yosemite Valley and the Sierra redwoods, therefore, to ignore the threatened confiscation of Yellowstone's wonders by private interests would again be the equivalent of admitting that the United States had no pride in its culture. No sooner had the explorers confirmed the existence of the natural phenomena than attempts to exploit them arose. Even as the Hayden Survey entered Yellowstone in the summer of 1871, two claimants were cutting poles in anticipation of fencing off the geyser basins along the Firehole River.[32] Supposedly the Washburn Expedition had discussed and rejected a similar scheme the previous year; whether or not the surveyor-general and his companions further considered the park idea at this time, however, did nothing to diminish the influence of cultural anxiety as a spur for its advancement.

The events of the park campaign itself, as distinct from the perceptions that inspired it, are still unclear. Langford's diary aside, the financier Jay Cooke and officials of the Northern Pacific Railroad may actually have suggested the park bill and motivated the interested parties. The interpretation does have considerable support. As early as January 1871 Nathaniel P.

Langford lectured in the East under sponsorship of the line. Similarly, that summer Cooke extended financial aid to Thomas Moran so that the artist might accompany the Hayden Survey into Yellowstone. Finally, on October 27, 1871, Professor Hayden himself received an official request from an agent of the Northern Pacific project to lobby on behalf of the park proposal. "Let Congress pass a bill reserving the Great Geyser Basin as a public park forever," the letter suggested, "just as it has reserved that far inferior wonder the Yosemite Valley and big trees. If you approve this, would such a recommendation be appropriate in your official report?"[33] Cooke and his associates realized, of course, that if Yellowstone became a park, their railroad would be the sole beneficiary of the tourist traffic.

With the introduction of the park bill in Congress, however, officials of the Northern Pacific apparently stayed out of the limelight. At least in public, the House and Senate placed their trust in the writings of the explorers themselves. The arguments of Dr. Hayden were especially influential. At the request of the House Committee on the Public Lands, he prepared a detailed summary of Yellowstone's qualifications for park status. When the geologist presented the statement, the committee released it verbatim as its own report in favor of the bill.[34] No document does more to reveal the explorers' reliance on promoting the region as another cultural oasis. After decrying the callousness of those laying claim to Yellowstone's wonders, Hayden objected that they intended "to fence in these rare wonders so as to charge visitors a fee, as is now done at Niagara Falls, for the sight of that which ought to be as free as the air or water." The failure of Congress to intervene decisively, he concluded, would doom "decorations more beautiful than human art ever conceived" to be, "in a single season," despoiled "beyond recovery."[35]

Hayden's outspoken reminder about the nation's failure to prevent the disfigurement of Niagara Falls was highly effective, especially in providing park backers a fitting analogy for their case. Similarly, his exposure of the superiority of Yellowstone's "decorations" over "human art" challenged Congress either to approve the park or risk further national embarrassment. Although the formations of the West invited obvious comparisons to castles, ruins, and other storybook structures, nationalists were not so nebulous in their analogies, but rather debunked specific examples of Old World art and architecture. The geologist, by again specifying where the nation had failed to match its rhetoric with a commitment to action, thus helped revive the formula for protection found successful in 1864.

Congress further asked Professor Hayden to suggest suitable boundaries for the park, although again, they were drawn large to insure the preservation of Yellowstone's wonders, not its wilderness per se.[36] Meanwhile, he, Langford, Walter Trumbull, and others worked long and hard to effect a favorable vote. For example, they placed 400 copies of Langford's article in the May and June, 1871, issues of *Scribner's Monthly* on the desk of each senator and representative prior to the debates in both houses. Similarly, William H. Jackson's photographs and Thomas Moran's watercolors and sketches were displayed prominently in the halls of the Capitol. News that Moran was nearing completion of his great canvas of the Grand Canyon of the Yellowstone River also evoked widespread publicity. Finally, Hayden and his associates tried to meet personally with as many members of the Congress as possible. In retrospect, it was a very thorough campaign, one that paid off on March 1, 1872, when President Ulysses S. Grant signed the Yellowstone Park Act into law.[37]

Precisely who authored the bill still is not known. The leading candidate for the honor, however, would be Representative Henry L. Dawes of Massachusetts. Not only did he support the Hayden Survey with great enthusiasm, but also his list of acquaintances, including Frederick Law Olmsted and Samuel Bowles, indicates that he must have been favorably disposed to the idea of preservation from an early date.[38] In either case, similar to Yosemite and the Mariposa Redwood Grove, Yellowstone was "dedicated and set apart as a public park or pleasuring ground for the benefit and enjoyment of the people." Like Yosemite, of course, it would be decades before Yellowstone enjoyed any appreciable visitation; the Northern Pacific Railroad itself was not completed, nor would it link up with the park until 1883. An immediate justification for the reserve was its symbolic importance. As soon as possible, the secretary of the interior was to prepare regulations providing "for the preservation from injury or spoliation, of all timber, mineral deposits, natural curiosities, or wonders within said park," which must be retained "in their natural condition."[39] The striking similarity between the intent of these stipulations, and those of the Yosemite Park bill, lends credence to the claim that the national park *idea* was first realized in 1864. To be sure, only because Yosemite was not called a national park has its identical role as a wonderland set aside in the national interest occasionally been discounted.

Comparisons between the area of the two parks undoubtedly contributed to any confusion about their parallel intent. In 1864 Yosemite was a very small affair, barely forty square miles surrounding the valley and redwoods. As a result, not only was Yellowstone the first national park, but, by virtue of its size, it was the first to anticipate the "ideal" national park as the idea came to evolve. But again, whatever resemblance Yellowstone bore in 1872 to the modern standard was purely unintentional. Had more been known about the region, namely, that the best of its natural phenomena had in fact been located, in all probability Yellowstone, like Yosemite, would have been established as a fragmented series of parcels encompassing little more than its major attractions.

Rarely would national parks of the future be as large or inclusive. Indeed, this was to become the great paradox of the national park idea. Granted, the United States sought out and protected the "earth monuments" of the West as replacements for the landmarks of human achievement still absent in the New World. Yet in few instances did the credibility of preservation for cultural ends require more than protection of a wonder by itself. In the meantime the nation had another reputation to encourage and protect, one more in keeping with its pioneer origins and expansionist ideals. Fortunately for preservation, the time when the United States would have to decide between parks and profits was not yet quite at hand.

3

Worthless Lands

Nothing dollarable is safe, however guarded.
John Muir, 1910

Yosemite and Yellowstone would be models for the national park idea for all time. But later endorsements of the philosophy were not unqualified, nor did the establishment of either of the two parks themselves set an unconditional precedent for strict preservation. Instead there evolved in Congress a firm (if unwritten) policy that only "worthless" lands might be set aside as national parks. From the very beginning Congress bowed to arguments that commercial resources should either be excluded from the parks at the outset, or be opened to exploitation regardless of their location. John Conness himself opened the Yosemite debates of 1864 with this assurance: "I will state to the Senate," he began, "that this bill proposes to make a grant of certain premises located in the Sierra Nevada mountains, in the State of California, that are for all public purposes worthless, but which constitute, perhaps, some of the greatest wonders of the world." In closing he returned to the question of their utility rather than beauty for emphasis. "It is a matter involving no appropriation whatever," he stated. "The property is of no value to the Government. I make this explanation that the Senate may understand what the purpose is."[1]

Precisely because the landscapes of the national parks are so impressive, the economic limitations imposed on scenic preservation in the United States have long been minimized. Simply, the grandeur of the national parks has distracted attention from the major precondition behind their establishment. How indeed could anyone refer to such inspiring landscapes as "worthless"? But although Americans as a whole admit to the "beauty" of the national parks, rarely have perceptions based on emotion overcome the urge to acquire wealth. The development of the United States in the midst of abundance could not help but strengthen materialism and the nation's commitment to the sanctity of private property. As a result, while more Americans came to believe that no individual had the right to own a national monument, such as Yosemite Valley, only rarely was the same standard enforced when the scenery in question was both esthetically and economically significant. A surplus of rugged, marginal land enabled the country to "afford" scenic protection; national parks, however spectacular from the standpoint of their topography, actually encompassed only those features considered valueless for lumbering, mining, grazing, or agriculture. Indeed, throughout the history of the national park idea, the concept of useless scenery has virtually determined which landmarks the nation would protect as well as how it would protect them.[2]

In 1864 Congress authorized only Yosemite Valley and four square miles of Sierra redwoods for park status; this was hardly an area large enough to jeopardize the nation's economy. Besides, the park was so high and so rugged it already appeared to be valueless.[3] In short, the Yosemite grant was a clear instance where scenic preservation could be allowed to take precedence over economic goals because the land in question seemed worthless. Efforts to establish parks in the future were not always to be so noncontroversial.

With consideration of the Yellowstone park bill, Congress restated its reluctance to protect the area if it contained anything of appreciable value. Whatever spirit of altruism the debates evoked quickly evaporated in the determination of both the House and Senate to establish the worthlessness of the territory beforehand. The bill came up for final discussion in the Senate on January 30, 1872, and, on February 27, the House debated the measure. Still, while the sessions confirmed that a majority of the Congress sympathized with the intent of the legislation, clearly its approval hinged on whether or not the park would interfere with the future of the West as a storehouse of natural resources.

In the absence of firsthand knowledge about the area proposed for park status, the House and Senate turned to the reports and articles submitted by participants of the Washburn and Hayden expeditions. Of these gentlemen, none was more crucial to the decision of Congress than Hayden himself. While his associates might afford some embellishment of their accounts, as head of the U.S. Geological and Geographical Survey of the Territories, the geologist staked his own reputation on the accuracy of his assessment. His belief that priority should be given to the exploitation of natural resources was also well known on Capitol Hill.[4] Thus confident of his position, those who would have to decide the issue could speak with conviction, ever secure in both the source and accuracy of their information.

Indeed the striking similarity between Hayden's report to the House Committee on the Public Lands and the tone of the congressional debates documents the depth of his influence. Not only did the committee publish Hayden's comments verbatim as its personal endorsement of the park bill, but Senate records also bear testimony to the pervasiveness of his ideas. For example, his observation that Yellowstone was practically worthless for anything but tourism in the first place was constantly paraphrased. "The entire area comprised within the limits of the reservation contemplated in this bill is not suscep-tible of cultivation with any degree of certainty," he began, "and the winters would be too severe for stock-raising." Yel-lowstone averaged well above 6,000 feet in altitude; under these conditions settlement would be "problematical unless there are valuable mines to attract the people." Yet even this seemed a remote possibility in light of the region's "volcanic origins"; indeed it was "not probable that any mines or miner-als of value will ever be found there." Nor was there much credibility behind the assertion that Yellowstone would prove profitable for agricultural interests. To the contrary, the re-gion suffered "frost every month of the year."[5]

The description would have been convincing regardless of its author. Because Hayden backed it with his own reputation, however, his statement assured supporters of the Yellowstone park bill that most objections might readily, if not completely, be overcome. Taking instruction from Professor Hayden, those who favored the proposal immediately sought to establish the park's uselessness for all but scenic enjoyment. In the Senate, for example, George Edmunds of Vermont opened the brief but spirited debates with a declaration that Yellowstone was "so far elevated above the sea" that it could not "be used for private occupation at all." He therefore assured his colleagues they did "no harm to the material interests of the people in endeavoring to preserve" the region.[6]

The only rebuttal of significance came from Senator Cor-nelius Cole of California. "I have grave doubts about the pro-priety of passing this bill," he responded. Although he was convinced of there being "very little timber on this tract of land," surely it was not, as claimed, off limits to grazing and agriculture. The fate awaiting Yellowstone's wonders also seemed to have been overstated. No harm would come to the geysers and other natural curiosities if their environs reverted to private control, he maintained; besides, there was an "abundance of public park ground in the Rocky Mountains" that never would be occupied at all. Perhaps Yellowstone, however, was a place "where persons can and would go and settle and improve and cultivate the grounds, if there be

ground fit for cultivation." Further guarantees by Senator
Edmunds that Yellowstone was "north of latitude forty" and
"over seven thousand feet above the level of the sea" failed in
the least to quiet Cole's objections. "Ground of a greater height
than that has been cultivated and occupied," he retorted; then
he asked: "But if it cannot be occupied and cultivated, why
should we make a public park of it? If it cannot be occupied by
man, why protect it from occupation? I see no reason in that."[7]

Passage of the bill, of course, confirms that a majority of
the Senate felt differently. Still, Cole's intensity alerted supporters of the park to redouble their assurances of its worthlessness, especially in light of the importance of the industries
he defended to the emerging economy of the West. Appropriately, the assignment fell to Senator Lyman Trumbull of Illinois. His son, Walter, it will be recalled, had participated in
the Washburn Expedition of 1870. Added to Professor Hayden's personal observations of the area in question, Walter's
firsthand knowledge convinced his father that Yellowstone's
value was negligible. "Here is a region of country away up in
the Rocky Mountains," Senator Trumbull said, stressing its
isolation as proof of the claim. Clearly Yellowstone was "not
likely ever to be inhabited for the purposes of agriculture."
Rather it was more probable "that some person may go there
and plant himself right across the only path that leads to [its]
wonders, and charge every man that passes along between the
gorges of these mountains a fee of a dollar or five dollars."[8]
Surprisingly, his scenario made no mention of Niagara Falls as
the classic example of such avarice. Still, by 1872 the foundation of his analogy was common knowledge. Professor Hayden,
in his own report to the House Committee on the Public Lands,
left no doubt that the explorers' determination to avoid another Niagara was indeed a primary incentive for the Yellowstone park campaign.

With consideration of the park bill by the House, however,
once again concern about the region's potential value took
precedence. To be sure, remarks supposedly in support of the
reserve still seemed distinctly noncommittal. For example, the
Yellowstone "is a region of country seven thousand feet above

the level of the sea," the bill's sponsor, Henry L. Dawes of Massachusetts, said; "there is frost every month of the year, and nobody can dwell upon it for the purpose of agriculture." His response to potential opposition was equally familiar. Not only was the entire area "rocky, mountainous, and full of gorges," but even "the Indians," he added for emphasis, "can no more live there than they can upon the precipitous sides of the Yosemite Valley."[9]

Such conviction, however exaggerated, was more than a tactic to persuade Congress to enact the legislation. While Senators Trumbull and Edmunds and Representative Dawes undoubtedly weighed the advantages of their reliance on the worthless-lands argument, even they had already committed themselves to abolishment of the park in light of new evidence. From the outset the enabling act bore no "inalienable" clause, nor was its omission an oversight. In sharp contrast to the Yosemite Act, which contained the commitment to perpetual protection, the generosity of the Yellowstone bill suggested the wisdom of a more conservative approach. Senator Trumbull, for example, assured his colleagues that "at some future time, if we desire to do so, we can repeal this law if it is in anybody's way, but now I think it a very appropriate bill to pass."[10] His qualification, of course, did nothing to dilute the meaning of his preceding statement. Simply, if development of Yellowstone became a real possibility, Congress would have legitimate reason to rescind the park act. The only condition, to paraphrase Trumbull, was that the exploiters then be people who would make a solid contribution to the economy of the West, not just "anybody" out to make a fast buck at the expense of potential tourists.

The distinction made between legitimate and nonlegitimate developers marks the origins of the national park idea's enduring double standard. The sin of exploitation was not the pursuit of personal gain, but personal gain that could not be defended as being in the national interest. The integrity of the national parks might in fact be compromised; restitution to the United States through industrial and technological advances simply had to be insured. That wealth of resources, not wealth of scenery, had become the nation's ultimate measure of achievement was made even more explicit by Representative Henry L. Dawes. "This bill reserves the control over [Yellowstone]," he told the House, "and preserves the control over it to the United States, so that at any time when it shall appear that it will be better to devote it to any other purpose it will be perfectly within the control of the United States to do it." And as if his meaning still were not clear, he reworded the statement time and time again. "If upon a more minute survey," he elaborated, "it shall be found that [Yellowstone] can be made useful for settlers, and not depredators, it will be perfectly proper this bill should [be repealed]." And still his qualifications continued. "We part with no control," he finally concluded, "we put no obstacle in the way of any other disposition of it; we but interfere with what is represented as the exposure of that country to those who are attracted by the wonderful descriptions of it . . . and who are going there to plunder this wonderful manifestation of nature."[11]

Few speeches do more to confirm that the park's great size stemmed from uncertainty rather than from a deliberate attempt to protect the totality of Yellowstone's wilderness and ecological resources. Had more data about the region been available to Congress, especially that its best "wonders," "freaks," and "curiosities" had in fact been located, undoubtedly both the House and Senate would have taken a dim view of the boundaries submitted by Professor Hayden for their approval. Then, too, in keeping with his own perception of the region as a parade of beautiful "decorations," in all probability his own proposal would have been far more conservative if drawn up with the confidence that his information about the territory was complete.

In either case, proof of Yellowstone's vulnerability to development soon appeared. Congress itself literally ignored the park for the next five years. When funding finally was approved in 1877, the amount was still woefully inadequate to manage and protect the reserve.[12] A proposal advanced in 1884 for construction of an access railroad across the northeast corner of the park spelled more problems. For the remainder of the decade promoters defended the line as the only practical method of transporting gold-bearing ores from Cooke City, just east of the park, to the recently completed branch line of the Northern Pacific Railway at Gardiner Gateway, Yellowstone's northern entrance. But although Congress turned down the plan each time it was broached, the project was denied more because of what the mines lacked rather than what the tracks would have threatened. Despite the glowing predictions of their boosters, the Cooke City mines never lived up to expectations; had they done so, Congress would have had stronger reason to side with the miners.[13] In truth, Dr. Ferdinand V. Hayden had been vindicated; his assessment in 1871 that few of Yellowstone's volcanic formations contained precious metals was correct. But that Congress even considered the so-called Cinnabar and Clark's Fork Railway—and on more than one occasion—confirmed that Yellowstone's integrity still hinged on its worthlessness. Promoters who later eyed the national parks would not always come up empty-handed, nor drop their schemes merely on the threat of bitter controversy.

Denial of the railroad, to be sure, did not mark a turning point in congressional attitudes toward scenic preservation. When the federal government once more considered the establishment of national parks, in all but name and location the precedents of 1864 and 1872 were little changed. Well into the twentieth century national parks emphasized only the high, rugged, spectacular landforms of the West; invariably park boundaries conformed to economic rather than ecological dictates. Even later awareness about a growing need for wilderness, wildlife, and biological conservation did not change the primary criterion of preservation—national parks must begin worthless and remain worthless to survive.

As if the cultural nationalism of the nation had been assuaged, Congress established no national parks for nearly two decades following Yellowstone.[14] In 1875 a small reserve was set aside on Mackinac Island, in Michigan, yet it hardly qualified as a scenic wonderland and eventually was turned over to the state.[15] When the national park idea enjoyed a true resurgence, the areas set aside were unmistakably in the image of Yellowstone and Yosemite. No less than during the 1850s and 1860s, when concern about the permanence and stability of American culture provided an incentive for scenic preservation, anxiety about the future of the United States played a key role in revival of the park idea. The added catalyst was a disturbing report released in 1890 by the United States Bureau of the Census. For the first time in nearly three hundred years, the document noted, the nation no longer possessed a distinct boundary between the settled and unsettled portions of the West. While large islands of uninhabited land remained, most were in mountainous or desert provinces of marginal economic potential. Knowledgeable Americans found the news upsetting to say the least. Since the first English settlements along the Atlantic coast and the dawn of westward expansion, the frontier had symbolized the essence of personal and economic freedom. It followed that the passing of the frontier had deprived the United States of something truly unique. Like Europe, suddenly the New World itself faced the prospect of growing older and more complacent. And few Americans relished the thought of confinement.[16]

The prospect seemed all the more objectionable when viewed against the rise of urban America. Just when the citizenry at large had begun to seek out open spaces, it realized that cities had even less than before. By 1890 the largest metropolitan areas of the Eastern seaboard were either near or past a million inhabitants; just thirty years later one of every two Americans would live in an urban community of 2,500 or above.[17]

Anxiety among intellectuals about the nation's future was now to be dominated by doubts about the strength, patriotism, and stamina of urban-based Americans. Charles Eliot Norton, for example, the Harvard scholar and former editor of the *North American Review*, was among those who drew pessimistic conclusions. "Men in cities and towns feel much less relation with their neighbors than of old," he lamented to a close friend in 1882. Urban life threatened instead to sap the nation of its "civic patriotism" and "sense of spiritual and moral community."[18] Thus for those of Norton's persuasion the Census Bureau only confirmed what most of them already feared—the twentieth century would find the United States a very different nation indeed.

Convinced that cities discouraged cultural greatness, Norton reasserted his support of nature as the antithesis of urban stagnation. Similar rejections of urban growth breathed new life into the park idea throughout the United States. In 1885 New York State achieved two breakthroughs with dedication of the Niagara Falls Reservation and establishment of the Adirondack Forest Preserve. At long last the signboards, fences, shops, gatehouses, stables, and hotels which so long had rimmed Niagara Falls were to give way to a free public park. Largely the realization of efforts by Frederick Law Olmsted and Charles Eliot Norton, the Niagara Falls Reservation ranks with Central Park, Yosemite, and Yellowstone as a preservation triumph of the nineteenth century.[19] Other park advocates embraced the Adirondack state forest as a milestone, despite their admission that its potential for recreation ranked second behind efforts to protect its watersheds.[20]

Neither park, to be sure, could be called an unqualified victory for preservation. The Adirondack Forest Preserve was best described as a patchwork quilt instead of an integral unit. Rather than purchase the land outright, the state obtained most of the forest's original 715,000 acres piecemeal, as penalties for unpaid taxes. As a result, few of the properties supported prime woodlands; the common practice was to strip one's holdings and abandon them before the tax collector arrived. The Niagara Falls Reservation likewise came into existence hamstrung by prior development and unsettled claims. Indeed, the cataract remained a classic example of the futility of trying to reverse exploitation once the process was well underway. From the beginning the park was a mere 400 acres, and fully three-fourths of these were below water. Hydroelectric interests, moreover, now denied access to the brink of the cataract proper, simply retaliated with proposals to divert the flow of the Niagara River around the falls to other suitable drops. It followed that long-range improvements to the falls would be mainly cosmetic. After 1885 visitors could expect, at the very least, to view the cataract without enduring the visual pollution, and without paying exorbitant charges for access to the prime observation points.[21]

Niagara Falls, as part of the settled, industrialized Northeast, graphically portrayed the impracticality of campaigning for larger parks in areas already lost to development. Most national parks especially would have to be won from lands west of the Mississippi River, where broad, unclaimed, marginal tracts of the public domain still survived. Yet even in the West protection would not come easily. Here, too, what preservationists wanted to save still had to conform to what the economic biases of the nation allowed them to save. As Congress began to renege on some of the more spectacular portions of existing national parks, preservationists themselves realized how much their movement rested on what scenery lacked as opposed to what it contained.

By 1900 the first glimmerings of a national park *system* had begun to emerge; still unresolved was how long and how well the nation would be committed to maintaining it. Yosemite Valley and its environs were among the first to provide unsettling clues. The Census Report of 1890 found John Muir himself ready to admit the vulnerability of his beloved High Sierra to defacement. Immediately following his entry into Yosemite Valley in 1868, he showed little anxiety about the future of the region as a whole. Throughout the 1870s the naturalist believed that remoteness would protect the California high country indefinitely. As late as 1875, for example, he described the Sierra Nevada as a "vast wilderness of mountains" remaining "almost wholly unexplored," save for "a few nervous raids . . . from random points adjacent to trails." By 1890, however, reality had sapped his confidence. He now conceded that the Sierra had been transformed from flowered slopes into "rough taluses" totally devoid of flora and fauna. Sheep were primarily responsible for the destruction; in the animals' wake wildflowers had been forced to become "wallflowers," Muir lamented, "not only in Yosemite Valley, but to a great extent throughout the length and breadth of the Sierra."[22]

Yosemite, supposedly protected from defacement as a state park, had also become the victim of its own popularity. Indeed, much as Frederick Law Olmsted had predicted in 1865, tourists in the valley welcomed the proliferation of eyesores which catered to their wants. Over the years the park commissioners, many of whom were political appointees, also ignored the intrusions. The narrowness of the valley, of course, quickly exposed such indifferent management; any development was readily noticeable. Sheds, stables, and fences, for instance, necessitated the clearance of woodlands and underbrush. Similarly, although livestock provided transportation and produce in the valley, their presence sacrificed its wildflowers and other vegetation. Inevitably, preservationists once again compared Yosemite's predicament to that of Niagara Falls. As early as 1868, for instance, Josiah Dwight Whitney, director of the California Geological Survey, warned that Yosemite Valley, rather than being "a joy forever," instead also faced the sadder prospect of turning into a great swindle "like Niagara Falls, a gigantic institution for fleecing the public. The screws will be put on," he predicted, "just as fast as the public can be educated into bearing the pressure." By 1890 Whitney had been more than proven correct. One hotel keeper, for example, actually cut a swath through the trees to provide his barroom with an unobstructed view of Yosemite Falls.[23]

Among those outraged by such callousness was Robert Underwood Johnson, associate editor of *Century Magazine*. A resident of New York City, he reflected the continuing fascination in the West and its preservation initially fostered among eastern writers and newspapermen such as Samuel Bowles and Horace Greeley. In 1889 he visited San Francisco and met John Muir, who persuaded him to tour the High Sierra in and about Yosemite Valley. Inevitably their evenings around the campfire and rambles through the back country sparked discussions about the calamity that had befallen the gorge and its environs. At least Yosemite Valley, as a park, had a chance for better protection, but the high country was still totally at the mercy of exploitation. Sheepmen remained among the worst offenders; Muir himself immortalized their flocks by labeling the animals "hoofed locusts." The insinuation was more than justified, especially since it was common practice to allow overgrazing of the grasses, young trees, and underbrush so critical to the stability of the area's watersheds.[24] Thus evolved Muir's lament about the survival of nothing but "wall-flowers" in the High Sierra; indeed only the steepest peaks were off limits to the flocks.

As a solution, Muir and Johnson proposed a national park surrounding Yosemite Valley. Although the idea was not new, the men added great vitality and prestige to the effort. Muir agreed to write two articles describing the region for *Century Magazine*; Johnson, upon returning east, promised to lobby for the park both through his journal and in the nation's capital.[25]

That each man sought to protect more than the "wonders" of the High Sierra is unquestionable. Muir especially appreciated the complexity and interdependence of nature. It followed that the future of Yosemite Valley hinged especially on the preservation of its environs. "For the branching canyons and valleys of the basins of the streams that pour into Yosemite are as closely related to it as are the fingers to the palm of the hand," Muir wrote, "as the branches, foliage, and flowers of a tree to the trunk." As a result, he firmly believed "all the fountain region above Yosemite, with its peaks, canyons, snow fields, glaciers, forests and streams, should be included in the park to make it a harmonious unit instead of a fragment, great though the fragment may be."[26] Not only were generous boundaries vital to protect Yosemite's watersheds, but also "the fineness of its wildness." This, too, was a worthy objective, he insisted, especially to the "lover of wilderness pure and simple."[27]

But although more Americans now sympathized with Muir's endorsement of wild country, not until the 1930s would wilderness preservation be recognized as a primary justification for establishing national parks, at least in the eyes of Congress. At the moment a more traditional perspective aided Muir's efforts to arouse public concern about the Sierra

Nevada as a whole. The fate of the Sierra redwoods, specifically, was an issue more in keeping with the popular origins of the national park idea. By the 1880s a number of major groves had been discovered along the western face of the mountains. However, it appeared that all but the most inaccessible stands would fall victim to lumbermen and curiosity seekers. Preservationists still considered any logging totally unjustified, since the Sierra redwoods, as distinct from their distant cousins along the California coast, were so brittle they shattered when toppled to the ground. Even trees that withstood the crash were impractical for little more than grape stakes or shingles. In fact, in mixed stands loggers often considered the Sierra redwoods a nuisance because they hindered felling of other conifers, especially sugar pine. To economize, the lumberjacks simply felled both species.[28]

In 1878 several prominent Californians, including George W. Stewart, editor of the *Visalia Delta*, organized a movement to supplement the holdings of the Mariposa Grove, set aside by the Yosemite Act of 1864. In time both the American Association for the Advancement of Science and the California Academy of Sciences also lent their support. By 1885 Stewart and his group were campaigning to protect groves surrounding what is now the Giant Forest in Sequoia National Park. Among the standouts of the unit was the General Sherman Tree, the largest of all living things.[29]

Several practical considerations also aided Muir, Johnson, Stewart, and their associates in furthering their respective campaigns. California irrigators, for example, recognized the need for setting aside those watersheds vital to the agricultural regions of the state. In addition, the Southern Pacific Railroad—perhaps taking instruction from the Northern Pacific Railway's promotion of Yellowstone National Park—seems to have lent support to the preservationists' cause.[30] Period advertisements, at least, confirm that the Southern Pacific was very committed to boosting tourism throughout the Sierra Nevada.

None of these considerations, of course, overrode the criterion that no material interests should suffer because of park development. For example, the brittleness and inaccessibility of the Sierra redwoods were preconditions for their preservation. Similarly, John Muir himself stressed the importance of deflecting potential challenges to Yosemite Park by assuring opponents of its worthlessness. "As I have urged over and over again," he began in a letter to Robert Underwood Johnson in May 1890, "the Yosemite Reservation ought to include all the Yosemite fountains." For although they "are glorious scenery," none "are valuable for any other use than the use of beauty." Only the summits of the mountains "are possibly gold bearing," he continued—in language highly reminiscent of F. V. Hayden's Yellowstone report of 1872—"and not a single valuable mine has yet been discovered in them." Rather the watershed was best described as "a mass of solid granite that will never be valuable for agriculture," although "its forests ought to be preserved."[31] Irrigators and farmers downslope strongly agreed with this point; perhaps their support offset what must have been strong opposition from grazing interests intent on maintaining their hold in the high country.

Such details of the campaign have been lost because of incomplete records. As a result, clues to explain why preservationists were successful must be sought from the legislation itself. During late August and September of 1890, bills providing for what were to become Yosemite, Sequoia, and General Grant national parks slipped through Congress with little fanfare.[32] The apparent lack of opposition can be laid to the language of each bill. Yosemite, for example, was not introduced as a national park, but as "reserved forest lands." This wording, while not in conflict with preservationists' immediate goals, was still far closer to the utilitarian aims of California's agricultural interests. Perhaps the emphasis placed on protecting the watersheds of the Yosemite high country, rather than its scenery, also explains why Congress allowed the reserve to encompass more than 1,500 square miles. Sequoia, by comparison, authorized as "a public park," was much smaller, only 250 square miles in area. And its neighbor to the north, General Grant, barely included four square miles of government land surrounding the great redwood bearing its name.[33]

The restriction of Sequoia and General Grant to the territory in and about their focal "wonders" was in keeping with their introduction as "parks" rather than "forest" reservations. The decision that Yosemite should also be managed as a park was made by Secretary of the Interior John W. Noble, to whom was entrusted the care of all three areas.[34] Following the turn of the century, when "national forests" became synonymous with the controlled exploitation of natural resources (as opposed to strict preservation), the significance of his interpretation stood out.

Even as authorized, Yosemite, Sequoia, and General Grant national parks were not immune from assault. Not only did sheepmen continually invade the reserves, but portions of all three were pockmarked with numerous private inholdings. Yosemite, in addition, suffered from the absence of centralized, unified management; not until 1905 did California cede the valley proper, and the Mariposa Grove of Sierra redwoods, back to the federal government. The perennial efforts of congressmen in the region to abolish large portions of Yosemite Park and return them to the public domain were equally threatening. Although the park today is nearly circular, when it was originally surveyed, in 1890, it was almost square but for extensions along its eastern side. The vulnerability of these protrusions lay in their real or imagined wealth. On the western flank timber and grasslands had been taken into the park; to the south and southeast timber and mineral claims had been included. Finally, in 1904, a special government commission recommended that these portions be deleted from the reserve. The following year, in accordance with that endorsement, Congress removed the sections and reopened them to exploitation. All told the area deleted comprised 542 square miles, fully one-third of the original reservation. In a gesture of compensation, Congress extended the boundary northward to encompass an additional 113 square miles of territory. Prior surveys of the addition, however, coupled with knowledge of its ruggedness and high altitudes, had already established its worthlessness beyond any reasonable doubt.[35]

The reduction of Yosemite National Park confirmed that Congress was in fact willing to reverse its prior endorsements of scenic preservation where expedient. Granted, at the time few but John Muir strongly opposed the realignment of Yosemite National Park.[36] After all, little had been done to interfere with the standard perception of national parks as a unique visual experience. Much of the territory deleted consisted of foothills and similar topography; although such features had scenic merit in their own right, they were not yet prized for inclusion in *national* parks. Only later would esthetic conservationists themselves fully subscribe to John Muir's appreciation of wildness and scenic beauty exclusive of the grandiose in nature. His was a perception for a later age, one that grasped the appeal of ordinary as well as extraordinary ecosystems. Molded in the worship of the great or near-great in landscapes, the national park idea moved into the twentieth century little changed from the standards and limitations of 1864 and 1872. The issue of worthless lands, it followed, must also be dealt with again.

4

New Parks,
Enduring Perspectives

*Be it enacted by the Senate and House of Representatives of
the United States of America in Congress assembled*, That
any person who shall appropriate, excavate, injure, or
destroy any historic or prehistoric ruin or monument, or
any object of antiquity, situated on lands owned or controlled by the Government of the United States, . . . shall,
upon conviction, be fined . . . or be imprisoned . . . or
shall suffer both fine and imprisonment, in the discretion
of the court.

Antiquities Act, 1906

Much as for Yosemite Valley and Yellowstone, monumentalism and economic worthlessness were predetermining factors leading to the establishment of Yosemite, Sequoia, and
General Grant national parks. And even if it was an unwritten
policy, no qualification outweighed the precedent of "useless"
scenery; only where scenic nationalism did not conflict with
materialism could the national park idea further expand. First
to exemplify the interplay of both forces after 1890 was
Washington State's Mount Rainier. Rising majestically above
its encircling forests, the extinct volcano invited the cultural
fantasies so prevalent during the opening decades of the national park idea. "I could have summoned back the whole
antique world of mythology and domiciled it upon this greater
and grander Olympus," declared one preservationist. Before
Mount Rainier "the mild glories of the Alps and Apennines

grow anemic and dull," while from its summit "the tower of Babel would have been hardly more visible than one of the church spires of a Puget Sound city." Yet only as a national park, he cautioned in conclusion, would "its fame widen with the years," and "our great army of tourists gain a new pleasure, a larger artistic sense, and a higher inspiration from the contemplation of the grandeur and beauty of this St. Peter's of the skies."[1]

Again it remained for John Muir to sound a note of caution and thereby reveal the second and more important criterion of scenic preservation. Specifically, he feared the proposed park would in fact include only the high country and ignore the foothills where protection was required most. "The icy dome needs none of man's care," he maintained, "but unless the reserve is guarded the flower bloom will soon be killed, and nothing of the forests will be left but black stump monuments."[2]

Monumentalism, of course, was precisely what Congress had in mind. As Muir agonized, Congress' generosity in the Cascade Mountains, no less than in the Rockies or Sierra Nevada, was still bound by the compulsion to keep parks to the minimum area necessary for highlighting their focal "wonders." As written in 1899, the Mount Rainier Park Act failed to preserve many of the lowland environments Muir initially singled out as equally worthy of protection. Moreover, even above timberline Congress did not relax its caution. Just in case first impressions of the peak's worthlessness proved erroneous, Congress allowed both mining and exploring for minerals in the park to continue. A still more obvious concession to economic interests was perpetrated in the form of a land exchange between the government and the Northern Pacific Railroad. In return for the company's claim to portions of the mountain, the government allowed the line to select compensation from federal property in any other state served by its tracks. Naturally the trade worked to the advantage of the Northern Pacific, which divested itself of rugged, marginally-productive land at the expense of the nation at large.[3] Thus Mount Rainier National Park itself can be interpreted as an example of scenic preservation designed to the specifications of big business and frontier individualism, not the needs of the environment.

The prerequisite that national parks be worthless was also mandatory in the discussions leading to the protection of Crater Lake in Oregon. Originally the site formed the crest of ancient Mount Mazama, which, like Rainier, was once among the active volcanoes of the Cascade Range. Several thousand years ago a violent eruption capsized the summit and left the huge cavity in its stead. Over the centuries rain and melting snows filled the crater to a depth of nearly 2,000 feet.[4] It was therefore evident natural resources in the area would be limited; again the value of the wonderland was recognized to be strictly monumental. Among the earliest visitors to publicize Crater Lake in this vein was William Gladstone Steel, the Portland judge whose dedication and persistence led to park status in 1902. "To those living in New York City"—he said, offering the standard form of description—"I would say, Crater Lake is large enough to have Manhattan, Randall's, Wards and Blackwell's Island dropped into it, side by side without touching the walls, or, Chicago and Washington City might do the same." At Crater Lake "all ingenuity of nature seems to have been exerted to the fullest capacity to build one grand, awe-inspiring temple" the likes of which the world had never seen.[5]

Approval of the park by Congress, however, still hinged on proof of its worthlessness for all but the most marginal economic returns. In this vein Thomas H. Tongue of Oregon introduced Crater Lake to the House of Representatives as "a very small affair—only eighteen by twenty-two miles," containing "no agricultural land of any kind." Instead the proposed park was simply "a mountain, a little more than 9,000 feet in altitude, whose summit [had] been destroyed by volcanic action," and was "now occupied by a gigantic caldron nearly 6 miles in diameter and 4,000 feet in depth." In addition, he reassured his colleagues, he had insisted at the outset that the boundaries be laid out "so as to include no valuable land." The object of the bill was "simply to withdraw this land from public settlement [to protect] its great beauty and great scientific value."[6]

Few members of the House opposed the preservation of Crater Lake; they merely wished to make certain that a park would in fact protect no more than the wonder itself. John H. Stephens of Texas, for example, quizzed Representative Tongue about the potential for mineral deposits within the reserve proper. Tongue answered by repeating his assurance that "nothing of any value" was to be set aside. Yet the bill as introduced actually prohibited exploring for minerals. He clarified that the restriction was meant only to keep people from entering the reserve "under the name of prospecting" when their real intent was to destroy "the natural conditions of the park and the natural objects of beauty and interest." The House grew more skeptical, however; indeed, no one supported Tongue's confidence that the nearest mineral deposits of consequence were "in the other range of mountains opposite from" Crater Lake. Not until he had agreed to amend the bill to allow mining in the preserve did the House reconsider the motion and call for a vote. The compromise in effect negated wording that the national park was to be "forever." This phrase was the first recognition of the concept of "inalienable" preservation since the Yosemite Act of 1864. Thus amended, the Crater Lake park bill cleared the House, passed the Senate without debate, and received President Theodore Roosevelt's signature on May 23, 1902.[7]

As exemplified by the restriction of Mount Rainier and Crater Lake national parks to their focal wonders, the national park idea at the beginning of the twentieth century was little changed from its original purpose of protecting a unique visual experience. Those who challenged the inadequacy of the parks in terms of their size, moreover, still did so against growing pressures for systematic reductions of the reserves instead. The frustration of compromise was further compounded by the rising popularity of what has come to be called the "utilitarian" conservation movement. Professional foresters, for example, argued that trees should not be preserved indefinitely, but rather should be grown much like crops, albeit ones "harvested" at 50-, 75-, or 100-year intervals. Similarly, hydrologists and civil engineers maintained that rivers should be dammed and their waters distributed for irrigation, desert reclamation, and other "practical" ends; to allow natural drainage was considered "wasteful." Americans must work to stabilize their environment by manipulating natural cycles to achieve greater industrial and agricultural efficiency. Only then would mankind's historical dependence on the whims of nature be overcome.[8]

The persuasiveness of utilitarian conservation, as opposed to absolute preservation, lay in its obvious link with the pioneer ethic. After all, to use resources wisely was still to *use* them. It followed that advocates of the national parks remained at a great disadvantage. Not only did each park suffer from the reluctance of Congress to abolish outright any claims to existing resources, but also until park visitation itself measurably increased, preservationists had no recognized "use" of their own to counter the objections of those who considered scenic preservation an extravagance. In this regard the geography of preservation worked against the permanence of the national park idea. Although nine-tenths of the population lived in the eastern half of the country, prior to 1919 every major preserve was in the West.[9] On a positive note, each year the number of rail passengers to the national parks showed decided increases. Still, not until the 1920s, when mass production of the automobile democratized long-distance travel, were the reserves truly within reach of middle-class as well as upper-class visitors.

Meanwhile, a threatened shortage of natural resources only enhanced the prestige of the park idea's competing philosophy, utilitarian conservation. The Census Report of 1890 added a special note of immediacy to such fears by calling attention to dwindling supplies of timber and arable lands on the public domain. Congress responded in May 1891 with passage of the Forest Reserve Act, which slipped past opponents from the West in the confusion surrounding the close of the lame-duck session. But although the legislation was largely unpublicized, it was far-reaching. Under the act Congress gave the president unilateral authority to proclaim appropriate areas of the public domain forest reservations. President Benjamin Harrison acted promptly by designating 13,000,000 acres of the mountain West in this category by 1893. Subsequent additions by presidents Grover Cleveland and William McKinley swelled the system to approximately 46,000,000 acres.[10] Here the figure stood in September 1901, when Theodore Roosevelt entered the White House in the wake of McKinley's assassination.

With the accession of Roosevelt, the prominence of utilitarian conservation over scenic preservation was virtually guaranteed. By the end of his administration he had tripled the national forest system in the West to its present size of nearly 150,000,000 acres. In addition, he strongly endorsed most of the tenets of utilitarian conservation still practiced today, including land reclamation, forestry, and leasing of the public domain.[11] These were policies preservationists also supported; what dismayed them was the tendency of utilitarian conservationists to deny categorically the legitimacy of scenic protection. Utilitarianists argued instead that the failure to seek out natural resources, wherever located, was every bit as wasteful as traditional abuses of the environment. "The first duty of the human race is to control the earth it lives upon," stated Roosevelt's chief advisor, Gifford Pinchot.[12] Strict preservation, in short, benefited no one. In 1905 Congress vindicated Pinchot by authorizing the U.S. Forest Service. Not only was he appointed chief forester, but also in keeping with his firm conviction that trees should not be protected for their beauty alone but rather managed as crops, Congress placed the new bureau under the U.S. Department of Agriculture.[13]

That establishment of the Forest Service coincided with the reduction of Yosemite National Park was symbolic of the emerging power structure within the conservation movement as a whole. While esthetic advocates still struggled to consolidate their gains, resource managers enjoyed growing popularity and prestige. After all, only in means, not ends, did utilitarian conservationists break with the pioneer spirit of the nation.

As scientists they merely promised America a new frontier of technological innovation and expansion. The conservation of natural resources, as opposed to the establishment of national parks, meant to regulate use rather than totally restrict it. Indeed, at every opportunity Gifford Pinchot and his counterparts assured cattlemen, lumbermen, and miners that the government had no intention of "locking up" the bounty of the public domain, but merely wished to insure its long-term productivity through "efficient" and "proper" management.[14] From an economic standpoint scenic preservationists had nothing comparable to support their ideology; by its very nature scenic protection hinged on the exclusion of logging, mining, or grazing. One approach to the problem, of course, was to demonstrate how tourism might generate more revenue than that achieved by exploiting the limited resources of the parks. The argument, however, simply lacked credibility until greater numbers of people did in fact visit the reserves.

Expansion of the national park system still relied on scenic nationalism. The one overriding criterion was proof that the territory set aside was, as claimed, worthless for all ends but preservation. With settlement of the American Southwest in particular, Indian ruins and artifacts were jeopardized by souvenir hunters and other vandals. Among those aroused by the impending loss of these treasures was John F. Lacey, an Iowa congressman. A staunch preservationist in his own right, in 1906 he pushed a bill through Congress to preserve all "objects of historic or scientific interest that are situated upon the lands owned or controlled by the Government of the United States." The bill's obvious departure from national parks' legislation was Lacey's emphasis on artifacts as distinct from scenic wonders. Still, his identical motivation was much in evidence with the provision that the new sites be called *national monuments.*[15]

The continuing influence of cultural nationalism also stood out in the title of the bill: "An Act for the Preservation of American Antiquities." Never before had the nation so openly admitted that doubts about its past were in fact a primary catalyst for scenic preservation. As established by precedent with the Forest Reserve Act of 1891, Congress left the choice of sites to be set aside solely to the president. As a result, although the Antiquities Act did not provide for the protection of landscapes per se, the discretion accorded the president likewise afforded him the opportunity to broaden the impact of the legislation considerably. To be sure, it was by means of the Antiquities Act that Theodore Roosevelt broke with the utilitarian leanings of his administration and won himself the lasting respect of preservationists as well. Almost immediately he interpreted the word "scientific" to include areas noted for their geologic (hence scenic) as well as man-made significance. Thus Devils Tower, an imposing monolith of volcanic basalt rising 865 feet above the plains of northeastern Wyoming, became the first national monument on September 24, 1906. Three additional sites followed in December—Petrified Forest and Montezuma Castle, both in Arizona, and El Morro, New Mexico, also known as Inscription Rock. The rock, with its carvings by ancient tribes, early Spanish explorers, and American adventurers, qualified for protection with the castle—a magnificent five-story cliff dwelling—as an historic structure. Similarly, Petrified Forest met the spirit of the Antiquities Act as a scientific phenomenon. Unfortunately, its prehistoric giants, which had solidified into colorful mineral formations, already had been vandalized extensively by rock hunters and other collectors.[16]

Any lack of objection to these monuments, nonetheless, still could not be laid to widespread public support for Roosevelt's initiative. More to the point, none of the areas set aside to date had been large enough to interfere with the material progress of the West. The same assurance could not be offered as readily in the case of two of his later contributions to the national monument system. Following another year distinguished only by the protection of Indian cliff dwellings and obviously "worthless" wonders on the order of Lassen Peak, California—a volcano—early in 1908 President Roosevelt declared a national monument of more than 800,000 acres surrounding the Grand Canyon of Arizona, famed as the outstanding "textbook" of erosion and rock stratification in the world. Yet despite the chasm's unmistakable value for scientific research, clearly the president had stretched the intent of the Antiquities Act beyond the limit. Indeed, as if to invite a serious challenge to his authority, just before leaving office, on March 3, 1909, he provided equivalent protection for 600,000 acres of land encircling Washington state's Mount Olympus.[17]

In neither case had President Roosevelt adhered to the guidelines of the Antiquities Act to preserve only man-made wonders or scientific curiosities. In "all instances," the act stated, each monument must be "confined to the smallest area compatible with the proper care and management of the objects to be protected." Whatever their scientific worth, the Grand Canyon and Mount Olympus were far from mere "objects." Still, for the moment Congress had no reason to restrain the president's initiative. Much as in the case of the national parks proper, neither the Grand Canyon nor Mount Olympus seemed to be of immediate economic value. Small deposits of minerals had been unearthed in the Grand Canyon, but the chasm was so rugged and inaccessible that no prospector had seriously attempted to bring them out. Similarly, Mount Olympus National Monument, although partially forested, lay walled in behind the peaks of the Olympic Peninsula. When lumbermen did in fact penetrate the region a few years afterward, President Woodrow Wilson, in accordance with the nation's traditional precondition for scenic preservation, in 1915 reduced the monument by its most valuable half.[18]

The lasting significance of the Antiquities Act lay in its title and decree that the new reserves be called "national monuments." Rarely had the nation so openly revealed that its efforts to protect the uniqueness of the West had been strongly motivated by the search for cultural identity. Americans now made the dwellings of prehistoric Indians suffice for the absence of Greek and Roman ruins in the New World. It followed that the more impressive monuments eventually would be considered for national park status. Prior to winning the honor, they, too, simply had to be proven worthless.

The establishment of government agencies determined to practice utilitarian ethics only sharpened the conflict between those who wished to preserve the national parks intact and those who considered full protection unjustified. Originally, legislation establishing the parks had been worded to anticipate any change in their value. Now the bills included specific references to the rights of competing government bureaus as well. The Reclamation Service, created by Congress in 1902 to construct and regulate dams and irrigation works throughout the West, complemented the Forest Service as the most prominent agency to win these concessions. Reclamation was the one major form of development in its infancy when Yosemite and Yellowstone parks were created. To be sure, if more had been known then about the potential of their rivers and canyons for hydroelectric power and water storage, in all likelihood the national park idea as thought of today, with wild streams and broad expanses of wilderness as well as scenic wonders, would have stood even less chance of coming to fruition.

The knowledge of past oversight made Congress even more determined to restrict the national parks to the minimum area necessary for public access to their prominent features. The establishment of Mesa Verde National Park in 1906, for instance, was facilitated by limiting its area to a series of Indian cliff dwellings and adjacent rugged terrain in southwestern Colorado.[19] By way of contrast, the Glacier and Rocky Mountain national park projects, whose territories were to be substantially larger, aroused suspicions among the standard variety of local, regional, and national economic interests. None were more influential than the Forest Service and Reclamation Service. Both now strongly opposed expansion of the national park system as being contrary to the proper management of the public domain. Although preservationists argued that even existing national parks had been proven barren of most natural resources, the rebuttal was still ineffective. Never before had technology so forcefully demonstrated that lands once considered worthless might become otherwise. Thus only if park legislation guaranteed the utilitarian agencies the option to enter and use the reserves wherever feasible could preservationists hope for their antagonists' even qualified endorsement of the national park idea.

The terms of the Glacier park bill impressed preservationists with the growing power and prestige of the Forest Service and Reclamation Service. Among the project's champions were George Bird Grinnell, author, sportsman, and explorer,[20] and Louis W. Hill, president of the Great Northern Railway. Grinnell, a New York City gentleman of means, provided the initial impetus for the park following his exploration of northwestern Montana in 1885. His commitment to scenic protection was already a matter of record. Angered by vandalism and poaching within Yellowstone National Park, he was among those whose drive for better management of the reserve brought the U.S. Cavalry to its rescue in 1886.[21] Like John Muir he now turned to the popular press to arouse support for his beliefs. One of his more insightful vignettes of western Montana appeared in the September 1901 issue of *Century Magazine*, the same publication so skillfully used a decade previously by Muir and Robert Underwood Johnson in calling attention to the fate of Yosemite Valley and its environs.[22]

Grinnell's explanation of the need to protect what is now Glacier National Park soon won the endorsement of Louis W. Hill. The son of James J. Hill, founder of the Great Northern Railway, Louis shared his father's instinct for a profitable investment. Following his succession to the presidency of the line in 1907, therefore, he promoted the Glacier wilderness as the rival of Yellowstone and Yosemite Valley. Of course his incentive was the knowledge that the Great Northern, which closely paralleled the southern boundary of the proposed park, would enjoy a virtual monopoly over passenger traffic.[23]

Still, Congress remained skeptical about the project until the region had been scrutinized to the satisfaction of everyone concerned, including, and especially, those with potential claims to its wealth. Thus although the park bill was introduced in 1908, it was not approved until two years later, and then only after many second thoughts. Senator Boies Penrose of Pennsylvania set the tone of the deliberations. Speaking in support of the bill's sponsors, senators Thomas H. Carter and Joseph M. Dixon of Montana, in January 1910 he opened debate on a personal, although familiar note. "I have hunted and traveled over almost every inch of the [Glacier] country," he began. It "is one of the grandest scenic sections in the United States, absolutely unfit for cultivation or habitation, and as far as I know not possessing any mineral resources." Only after this disclaimer did he then proclaim the region "admirably adapted for a park." But still his colleagues were in no hurry to reach a decision; therefore when debate resumed in February, it remained for Senator Dixon to remind them of Glacier's worthlessness for all but scenic enjoyment. "This is an area," he said, "of about 1,400 square miles of mountains piled on top of each other." Such territory was much too rugged to be exploited; "there is no agricultural land whatever," he confirmed. "Nothing is taken from anyone. The rights of the few settlers and entrymen are protected in the bill."[24] At last won over by constant repetition of the worthless-lands argument, the Senate voted in favor of the national park.

Although the discussion in the House was brief, an amendment tacked onto the legislation required conferees from both branches to iron out their differences. Once more Senator Dixon defended his assessment that Glacier was useless for all but park status. Of course skeptics, among them Senator Joseph W. Bailey of Texas, still remained. "It will involve a considerable expenditure of public money to make much of a park out of mountains piled on top of each other," he maintained. But finally, he, too, conceded that preservation was "as good a use as can be made of that land." In the unlikely event resources were discovered, however, the act provided for mining, settlement, reclamation, and sustained-yield forestry in the park. Section 1, for example, empowered the Reclamation Service to "enter upon and utilize for flowage or other purposes any area within said park which may be necessary for the development and maintenance of a government reclamation project." Similarly, as a concession to the Forest Service, the secretary of the interior was authorized to "sell and permit the removal of such matured, or dead or down timbers as he may deem necessary or advisable for the protection or improvement of the park." The contradiction was obvious; precisely how logging might "protect" or "improve" Glacier was not spelled out. In reality the provision was another blank check for development in case there were possible changes in knowledge about the region and its "worth." Thus amended, the Glacier National Park bill was approved on May 11, 1910.[25]

Sixty miles northwest of Denver, Colorado, lay the high country proposed for inclusion in Rocky Mountain national park. Again, a similar set of restrictions confirmed the preeminence of utilitarian conservation over scenic preservation. Even before a park bill was introduced on Capitol Hill in 1915, sponsors of the project had been forced to reduce its intended area by two-thirds to quiet protests from mining and grazing interests.[26] The Senate, apparently satisfied, did not debate the measure, but discussion in the House was quite spirited. Predictably, the bill's sponsor, Representative Edward T. Taylor of Colorado, espoused the beauty yet uselessness of the area under review. The park would be "marvelously beautiful," he began; then he injected a dose of nationalism, stating that the region surpassed "Switzerland in the varied glory of its magnificence." It followed that such rugged topography supported "comparatively little timber of merchantable value" and the altitude was much "too great for practical farming." The territory simply had "no value for anything but scenery." This was not merely his opinion, he added, but the consensus of "thousands [of people] from all over the world." But although the House now passed the bill, both branches of Congress made certain that it provided for railroaders, prospectors, and the Reclamation Service to enter and use Rocky Mountain National Park, just in case Congressman Taylor and the other supporters of the park were mistaken.[27]

If preservationists once hoped that Congress did not seriously intend to open the national parks to development where feasible, the return of the best timber, mineral, and grasslands of Yosemite National Park to the public domain in 1905 was unavoidable evidence to the contrary. And already the park had become the setting for a still greater and more dramatic controversy. As early as 1882 the city of San Francisco looked to the canyons of the High Sierra for a permanent fresh-water supply. Eight years later, however, the site considered most ideal for a dam and reservoir, Hetch Hetchy Valley, was included in Yosemite National Park. The potential for conflict sharpened as preservationists came to appreciate that Hetch Hetchy was the rival of Yosemite Valley itself. Indeed, the prominent cliffs and waterfalls of the two gorges were strikingly identical. The Tuolumne River completed the resemblance by splitting the floor of Hetch Hetchy, much as the Merced River divides Yosemite. The former's claim to distinction was wildness. The absence of roads retained for Hetch Hetchy the wilderness charms long ago sacrificed to tourism in Yosemite, including meadows, open woodlands, and an abundance of wildflowers. In either case, preservationists considered the nation extremely fortunate to have a single wonderland of its type; the fact there were two was cause for celebration indeed.[28]

San Francisco, however, was adamant against looking elsewhere for its source of fresh water. The very ruggedness which included Hetch Hetchy among the nation's great natural wonders fated it to remain the favorite site for the dam. From a technical standpoint nothing stood in the way of the project; the one and only major obstacle was Hetch Hetchy's location within a national park.

Time, moreover, was on the side of San Francisco. In 1901, following completion of the city's engineering report, Mayor James D. Phelan petitioned the secretary of the interior, Ethan Allen Hitchcock, for permission to dam the gorge. Hitchcock, however, whose sympathies lay with preservationists, denied the request in 1903 as "not in keeping with the public interest."[29] San Francisco simply waited for a more opportune moment to resubmit its proposal; city fathers, after all, needed no reminder that Hitchcock's term of office would not last forever.

Following his resignation four years later, San Francisco

filed a new request. As had been expected, Hitchcock's successor, James A. Garfield, was far more receptive to the idea of damming Hetch Hetchy. An early barometer of his position was his close association with Chief Forester Gifford Pinchot, whom Garfield greatly admired. As a result, his decision the following year to grant San Francisco's second petition came as no surprise.[30]

Approval of the permit set the stage for the greatest cause célèbre in the early history of the national park movement in the United States.[31] For preservationists the stakes were especially high. Prior schemes to exclude lands and resources from the national parks, particularly Yosemite, for the most part had been limited to the edges of the reserves. Generally speaking, foothills predominated in these areas; preservationists themselves often shared honest differences of opinion about the suitability of giving national park status to commonplace topography. The Hetch Hetchy issue invited no such spirit of compromise. Developers and preservationists no longer battled for the fringes of a national park, but for the very heart of one. Conceivably, the outcome would determine whether or not the national park idea itself could survive. If even the inner sanctum of Yosemite could not be protected in perpetuity, no national park, then or in the future, could be considered safe from exploitation.

The Hetch Hetchy controversy was indeed a struggle over precedent. Both before Congress and in the popular press, esthetic conservationists justified their crusade as an effort to prevent what they considered to be the inevitable ruination of the national park idea. Thus when Congress made its decision, in the closing months of 1913, preservationists believed they had suffered a major setback. By wide majorities both houses upheld the Garfield permit of 1908 and allowed San Francisco to begin construction of its reservoir.[32]

From the start preservationists had been at a disadvantage. First, it was still too early to demonstrate widespread public interest in the Hetch Hetchy Valley. The argument that two or three thousand enthusiasts camped on its floor every season could not prevail against the rejoinder that 500,000 San

Franciscans needed fresh water. Similarly, to contend that Hetch Hetchy was a second Yosemite was, in effect, to admit that the valley was the opposite of unique. Opponents were quick to ask that if the nation already had one Yosemite, why did it need two?[33] "The question [is] whether the preservation of a scenic gem is of more consequence than the needs of a great and growing community," wrote John P. Young, managing editor of the *San Francisco Chronicle*. Although he agreed "the meadows and trees of the valley would be submerged," preservationists had failed to consider that "the immense reservoir created would substitute in their place a vastly more attractive feature" and "a far more powerful attraction to persons in search of inspiring scenery than the eliminated beauties of the past." The lake would "still be enclosed by towering peaks and massive walls, and the falls of the Hetch Hetchy [would] still tumble"; in addition, all of these features would be mirrored "in the waters of the new creation." Granted, some of the "present adornments will disappear," Young admitted, but "in their place will be substituted that which will make Hetch-Hetchy incomparable and cause it to rank as one of the world's great scenic wonders."[34]

San Francisco engineers illustrated the claim by retouching a photograph to suggest how the valley would look once the reservoir had filled. Few scenes promised a more idyllic result. Not a ripple stirred the lake; rather its surface reflected the cliffs and waterfalls with mirror-like precision.[35] But preservationists challenged the conception, asserting that in reality the reservoir would be ringed by ugly mudflats and bleached rocks, especially when the water level fell during periods of peak demand. "Under conditions of nature lakes occur," stated J. Horace McFarland, one of the project's leading opponents, while "under conditions brought about by men ponds are created. Flooding the Hetch Hetchy will make a valley of unmatched beauty simply a pond, a reservoir, and nothing else."[36]

The photograph, although contrived, was symbolic of the dilemma preservationists faced in updating their own traditions. Except for an occasional prophet such as John Muir or

The Sunday finery of these tourists, visiting a thermal basin in
Yellowstone at the turn of the century, confirms the view of Yellowstone's first explorers, who saw the region as a future "resort"
rather than a wilderness preserve.

Stephen T. Mather, first director of the National Park Service, was instrumental in furthering a "pragmatic alliance" between the western railroads and the Park Service. The North Coast Limited was the premier passenger train of the Northern Pacific Railroad, which was one of five major lines serving Yellowstone National Park.

Mark R. Daniels, while superintendent of national parks in 1915, said that Americans who spent from fifty to one hundred million dollars annually to visit the Alps "are taking this money out of the United States to spend it in foreign lands upon a commodity that is inferior to the home product." As part of the "See America First" campaign, these waitresses at Glacier National Park in 1933 recreated Switzerland in the American wilderness.

Cars meet Yellowstone-bound passengers beside the train at Gardiner, Montana, in June 1930. Only fifteen years earlier, trains and stagecoaches had enjoyed a monopoly of national park patronage.

The western railroads played up the romantic side of tourism in advertisements like this one from the December 1910 issue of *McClure's*.

The National Park Service interpretative program, inaugurated in the 1920s, led tourists off the road to such places as Mount Stanton, Glacier National Park.

Union Pacific Railroad
Photograph by Wayne B. Alcorn, courtesy of the
National Park Service, Bryce Canyon National Park

An advertising artist's conception of Bryce Canyon from the May 1927 issue of *National Geographic Magazine*, above, contrasts fancifully with a photograph of two actual formations, Thor's Hammer and the Temple of Osiris, below. The advertisement also attempts to link Bryce Canyon with the architecture of Europe and the Orient.

Glacier Park Lodge, opened by the Great Northern Railway in 1913, at first was welcomed by preservationists who thought that the tourists it attracted would support the national park idea. The great timbers in the lobby are Douglas fir, with the bark on. It is the only national park hotel, except for Mount McKinley Hotel in Alaska, that is directly accessible by long-line passenger trains.

Hileman Photograph, courtesy of the National
Archives

The Great Northern Railway purchased the site of Glacier Park Lodge
from the Piegan Indians and retained a group of Indians to meet the
trains. The lodge, now owned by Glacier Park, Inc., is still outside the
national park proper.

Unlike the railroads, automobiles won admittance to the parks themselves and, once inside, could go almost anywhere. Oliver Lippincott, a Los Angeles photographer, posed on Glacier Point, Yosemite, with a horseless carriage, a flag, and a lady who may represent motherhood.

Frederick Law Olmsted, for almost half a century preservationists, like San Francisco's "ghost" photographer, had sought to win converts by highlighting the extraordinary. By and large national parks were considered a visual experience; their purpose was not to preserve nature as an integral whole, but to seek out the most impressive waterfalls, canyons, and mountain peaks of the West. With the Hetch Hetchy controversy the pitfalls of this perspective came sharply into focus. Before preservationists learned to verbalize the valley's other redeeming values, especially its wildness, time ran out. On December 19, 1913, President Woodrow Wilson signed the legislation granting San Francisco all rights to the gorge.[37]

The city's trump was proof that Hetch Hetchy could be used for something more than recreation. Thus, even as the national park idea matured, the belief that its units must remain worthless exacted built-in limitations on ecological needs long before these needs came to be realized. Utilitarian agencies compounded the dilemma by reserving to themselves the right of future access to national park resources, especially water-power sites. It followed that preservationists must identify and publicize those methods by which the parks could pay dividends to the national purse without being destroyed in the process. The need for haste was evident; if history, at least, were any indication, the likes of the Hetch Hetchy controversy could be expected again.

5

See America First

See Europe if You Will, but See America First
Soo Railroad Brochure, ca. 1910

War with Switzerland!
Mark Daniels, 1915

The influence of [the national parks] is far beyond what is usually esteemed or usually considered. It has a relation to efficiency—the working efficiency of the people, to their health, and particularly to their patriotism—which would make the parks worth while, if there were not a cent of revenue in it, and if every visitor to the parks meant that the Government would have to pay a tax of $1 simply to get him there.
J. Horace McFarland, 1916

Coming so soon after the reduction of Yosemite National Park, the loss of Hetch Hetchy in December 1913 was a double blow to the defenders of scenic preservation. Then, the following year, John Muir died. His friends sincerely believed that his death had been hastened by his own remorse. Yet Hetch Hetchy was a beginning as well as an end. Indeed, no defeat so forced the issue of how best to guard the national parks in an urban, industrial age. For inspiration, preservationists might still turn to the writings of John Muir. "Thousands of tired, nerve-shaken, over-civilized people," he had written, "are beginning to find out that going to the mountains is going home, that wildness is a necessity, and that mountain parks and reservations are useful not only as fountains of timber and irrigating rivers, but as fountains of life." If most preservationists still did not fully subscribe to the need for wilderness protection, a majority was agreed that the national parks no longer could be defended on scenic merit alone. As a result, by further pirating the slogans of utilitarian conservation, preservationists followed Muir in defending the national parks as a means of preventing "waste" in their own right. As distinct from proper management of the national forests, the stakes were merely in terms of human "efficiency." But if "we must consider [the national parks] from the commercial standpoint," Allen Chamberlain, a New England advocate said, "let it not be forgotten that Switzerland regards its scenery as a money-producing asset to the extent of some two hundred million dollars annually."[1]

When further tied to scenic nationalism, nothing did more for the preservationists' cause. Just when Americans had largely overcome their cultural doubts, the reminder of the amount Americans spent in Europe for scenic travel recalled those doubts to good advantage. Unfortunately for Hetch Hetchy, the money lost to tourism abroad was not popularized until well into the eleventh hour of the battle for the valley; even then its remoteness, and proximity to the better-known Yosemite, were insurmountable factors against Hetch Hetchy's protection. But if ever the cloud over the valley did have a silver lining, it was in teaching preservationists to rely as much on economic rationales for protection as on the standard emotional ones. As far back as the creation of Yellowstone National Park in 1872, the railroads of the West promoted scenic protection, not out of altruism, of course, but in appreciation that the attraction of more tourists into the region meant greater revenues. Increasingly cognizant of the significance of this fact, preservationists turned to the railroads for political and financial aid during the Hetch Hetchy campaign. The rewards of this "pragmatic alliance"[2] were soon confirmed by growing public support for a bureau of national parks, an agency fully committed to the principles of esthetic as opposed to utilitarian conservation. Such were the foundations of the National Park Service, approved by Congress in August 1916.

The "Hetch Hetchy Steal," as it would always be known,

aroused preservationists to the need for strengthening the position of the national parks in terms of the country's economy. Much as the national park idea evolved in response to concern about the wonders of the West, so now growing confidence in reclamation, forest regeneration, and other utilitarian sciences signaled that the years of peaceful coexistence between the two branches of conservation were fast drawing to a close.[3] Prior to the turn of the century, presupposed similarities between national parks and forest reservations worked against a permanent split between the two philosophies. The confusion of preservationists in particular stemmed from legislation such as the Yosemite Act, which referred to the park as "reserved forest lands."[4] It followed that resource professionals seemed no less in agreement that strict protection of the public domain took precedence over exploitation of any kind. Only as foresters, reclamationists, and civil engineers boldly advocated sustained-yield management for all lands in the West, including the national parks, did preservationists realize their assumptions had been mistaken.

Never before was the necessity of finding ways to exploit the reserves without destroying their basic integrity more apparent. Clearly, protection precluded in-park developments of the scope advocated by resource managers, most notably large dams and reservoirs. Still, without some concessions to the comfort and convenience of tourists, public support for the parks might not be forthcoming at all. Accordingly, preservationists conceded the Hetch Hetchy campaign must be waged on two fronts. Above all, they hoped to win a political victory in Washington. Should their direct approach fail, however, they also worked simultaneously to influence Congress by arousing the public to greater awareness about the national parks through the mass media, the railroads, and promotional literature. Inevitably the need to communicate their philosophy caused preservationists themselves to reevaluate the traditions and reasoning behind their movement. The national park idea, it followed, would never be quite the same again.

To its advantage, scenic preservation was now in fact a

movement. Initially only a scattering of individuals and interest groups supported the national parks, most notably the Appalachian Mountain Club (1876), Boone and Crockett Club (1888), and Sierra Club (1892). By 1910, however, nearly twenty distinct organizations directly advocated scenic protection.[5] To these could be added a host of garden clubs, women's clubs, horticultural societies, and other sympathetic coalitions. The accelerating transformation of the United States from a rural to an urban-based nation foretold that the increasing appreciation of nature would continue. For most people, few factors more quickly erased the memories of rural hardships than the confinement of city streets. Those recollections which survived were happy thoughts of changing seasons, holiday gatherings, close friendships, and childhood dreams. Literature further encouraged this method of escape; indeed, during this period writings about nature soared in popularity. Still another means of retreat available to people of modest wealth was a home in the suburbs, or, better yet, farther out in the country, where stables, spacious lawns, and other accessories of rural living could be re-created. Of course what evolved on the urban fringe was a romanticized version of rural America. Still, to those caught between the undeniable economic advantages of city life and its obnoxious side effects, reality was beside the point. Even at the price of one or two hours of commuting, many thought the opportunity to escape the grime, noise, and overcrowding of city life a bargain by comparison.[6]

Among them was still to be found the large majority of national park supporters. Much as Eastern men of urban backgrounds conceived and advanced the national park idea, so modern urbanites and suburbanites now supplemented the thinning ranks of the original enthusiasts. Frederick Law Olmsted, Jr., for example, a co-author of the National Park Service Act of 1916, thus followed in the footsteps of his illustrious father, who died in 1903. The younger Olmsted was further encouraged by an even more outspoken preservationist, J. Horace McFarland, a successful printer, publisher, and horticulturist from Harrisburg, Pennsylvania. McFarland was long the chief proponent of the need to establish a bureau of national parks. Indeed, no lobbyist did more to both strengthen and broaden the national parks platform during the trying years of the Hetch Hetchy debate. Ironically, it was a second campaign to save Niagara Falls that launched his career. In 1904, when the American League for Civic Improvement merged with the American Park and Outdoor Society, McFarland was elected first president of the new organization, the American Civic Association. Immediately he marshalled its forces against the latest scheme to harness the Niagara River for the production of hydroelectric power. The developers, thwarted by protection of the falls proper as a state park in 1885, had since retaliated with plans to construct huge conduits to capture the river and divert its flow around the cataract to powerhouses set elsewhere in the Niagara Gorge. If, as a result, the flow of the falls were substantially reduced, McFarland noted that the prior campaign to save the cataract and its environs from structural blight would be rendered meaningless.[7]

Due largely to McFarland, the diversion controversy attracted notoriety nationwide. From his Harrisburg office, he alerted scores of government, civic, and business leaders to the pending tragedy of a waterless Niagara. Simultaneously, his dedication to horticulture (his specialty was roses) and urban beautification won him the editorship of the "Beautiful America" column in the *Ladies' Home Journal*, already a leading women's magazine. In October 1906 the column provided a platform for one of the most ringing essays of his career, "Shall We Make a Coal-Pile of Niagara?" "Every American—nay, every world citizen," he wrote, "should see Niagara many times, for the welfare of his soul and the perpetual memory of a great work of God. . . ." Yet "the engineers calmly agree that Niagara Falls will, in a very few years, be but a memory. A memory of what? Of grandeur, beauty and natural majesty unexcelled anywhere on earth, sacrificed unnecessarily for the gain of a few!" Before and after illustrations suggested the result: "The words might well be emblazoned," McFarland concluded, "in letters of fire across the shamelessly-uncovered bluff of the American Fall: 'The Monument of America's Shame and Greed.' "[8]

As a businessman himself, McFarland did not oppose appealing to America's pocketbook as well as to its conscience. Based on tourism alone, the destruction of Niagara was truly "folly unbounded. To the railroads of the country and to the town of Niagara Falls visitors from all the world pay upward of twenty million dollars each year—a sure annual dividend upon Nature's freely-bestowed capital of wonders. . . ." Extended to the nation at large the figure "would thus stand at over three hundred million dollars," he estimated. But at Niagara "all this will be wiped out, for who will care to see a bare cliff and a mass of factories, a maze of wires and tunnels and wheels and generators?"[9]

With that question J. Horace McFarland voiced the argument that rallied the entire preservation movement. On the West Coast his denouncement of water-power interests caught the eye of William E. Colby, secretary of the Sierra Club. Faced with a similar struggle to protect the Hetch Hetchy Valley from defacement, the Sierra Club was searching anxiously for allies of its own. Letters from Colby to McFarland confirmed that the American Civic Association would close ranks on the Hetch Hetchy issue in exchange for whatever support the Sierra Club could muster for Niagara. Colby's negotiations with the Appalachian Mountain Club in Boston, then pushing for legislation to protect the forests of the East, likewise guaranteed its aid against the Hetch Hetchy dam permit. From this East-West alliance he formed the Society for the Preservation of National Parks. Its masthead included the slogan: "To preserve from destructive invasion our National Parks—Nature's Wonderlands." John Muir accepted the nomination as president; Allen Chamberlain, director of exploration for the Appalachian Mountain Club, Robert Underwood Johnson of *Century Magazine*, and J. Horace McFarland, among others, agreed to serve on the Advisory Council.[10]

Noticeably absent from the roster were the names of respected resource conservationists. Gifford Pinchot's skepticism in particular concerned William Colby and his associates; few government employees, after all, enjoyed greater influence with the president and Congress. Indeed, if past experience were any indication, where Pinchot stood in the Hetch Hetchy controversy might in large part determine its outcome. Accordingly, preservationists considered the lessening of his antagonism to the national parks to be of first priority. "We had counted on you for support in this fight," wrote Colby in reference to Hetch Hetchy. "Does it not give you pause when you stop to consider that such men as John Muir . . . and the leaders of the Appalachian [Club] and the American Civic Association, and other kindred organizations—all of them men who have stood in the fore front of your fight for the preservation of our forests and who helped create public sentiment for you in your noble work, . . . should now be standing shoulder to shoulder in most earnest opposition to this attempt to enter and desecrate one of our most magnificent National Parks? We need you as a friend in this cause," he pleaded in conclusion, "and call upon you to assist us."[11]

Pinchot's refusal came as no real surprise; still, his polite evasion of specifics in the Hetch Hetchy controversy struck Colby and McFarland as condescending and thus unprofessional. Other than remaining persistent, of course, they had few options to force his hand. Yet while their disappointment and irritation grew, the dialogue forced the men to grapple head-on with examples of the rhetoric so convincingly used against them. Soon, for example, they sensed the effectiveness of diluting utilitarian arguments by ascribing human "waste" and "inefficiency" to the lack of scenic rather than material conservation. "I feel that the conservation movement is now weak," J. Horace McFarland wrote Gifford Pinchot in November 1909, for example, "because it has failed to join hands with the preservation of scenery, with the provision of agreeable working conditions, and with that suggestion which is the first thing to produce patriotism." Although he was still groping for the proper formula, McFarland continued. "I want to say that somehow we must get you to see that the man whose efforts we want to conserve produces the best effort and more effort in agreeable surroundings; that the preservation of forests, water powers, minerals and other items of national prosperity in a sane way must be associated with the pleasure to the eye and the mind and the regeneration of the spirit of man."[12] If lacking the eloquence of John Muir's prior rationales for wilderness and parks, this statement went far beyond the position that scenery was merely to be seen. McFarland's equation of preservation with greater productivity, a relationship first implied in his articles about Niagara Falls, especially held untapped possibilities. Until Americans at large accepted preservation for its own sake, economic persuasion was better insurance for the movement than unilateral appeals for a spiritual and emotional understanding of landscapes.

Before the argument could be fully credible, of course, park visitation must be dramatically increased. Nor could wilderness be singled out as a separate inducement for preservation until more people experienced the rewards of solitude firsthand. As late as 1908 barely 13,000 tourists enjoyed Yosemite National Park as a scenic wonderland, let alone as one of Muir's "fountains of life." Of these visitors, only a few hundred shunned the localized points of interest and hiked into the Tuolumne River watershed and Hetch Hetchy Valley. Such figures typified the preservationists' dilemma. While San Francisco officials could demonstrate a current need for fresh water among 500,000 constituents—a demand soon to grow by thousands more—the Sierra Club and its supporters were easily portrayed as selfish "nature cranks" and traveling elitists.[13] Some preservationists, among them John Muir, refuted the charge by agreeing to construction of a road into the valley. Others maintained that a large hotel should also be built.[14] The weakness of each compromise stemmed from preservationists' lack of evidence to justify an immediate need for the projects. Until park visitation actually increased, San Francisco held the upper hand in the numbers argument.

Still, in the long run the association of scenic protection with economic growth was the most innovative approach for defending the national park idea. Taking up where he left off during the Niagara debate, for example, J. Horace McFarland returned to the popular press as a springboard for sparking discussion. "Are we to so proceed with the conservation of all our God-given resources but the beauty which has created our love of country," he questioned in *Outlook* during March 1909, "that the generation to come will increasingly spend, in beauty travel to wiser Europe, the millions they have accumulated here, being driven away from what was once a very Eden of loveliness by our careless disregard for appearance?" Allen Chamberlain of the Appalachian Mountain Club was first to reply: "Your article on 'Ugly Conservation' in a recent *Outlook* is the right sort," he wrote. He also underscored the importance of equating preservation with patriotism and economic well-being. "Our friends the conservationists, that is the professionals, are exceedingly loath to recognize this point of view." Chamberlain suggested that the argument be made more specific, however, especially in light of the evolving Hetch Hetchy debate. "It seems to me that we should try in this connection to stimulate public interest in the National Parks by talking more about their possibilities as vacation resorts," he offered as one example. Indeed, only "if the public could be induced to visit these scenic treasurehouses," he concluded, "would they soon come to appreciate their value and stand firmly in their defense."[15]

McFarland's encouragement speeded an article of Chamberlain's own. Appropriately titled "Scenery as a National Asset," it, too, was published in *Outlook*, on May 28, 1910. In keeping with his title and suggestions to McFarland, Chamberlain focused on the problems of the national parks and national monuments. "Here are some of the world's sublimest scenes," he noted, not to mention "many wonderful records of past ages" and "relics of the prehistoric occupants of portions of our land." Unfortunately, many of the parks were "so remote from railways" the public was "only just beginning to realize" they existed. Within the reserves proper, the lack of visitor facilities hampered greater awareness. "Take the Yosemite Park as an example," Chamberlain observed. "Everyone is herded into the great valley, and little is done to encourage people to go into the magnificent country farther back in the mountains."

As a result, two equally beautiful attractions, the Hetch Hetchy Valley and Tuolumne Meadows, were effectively off-limits to park visitors. "The extension of the present road for nine miles will open the former," he said, alluding to the compromise suggested by preservationists to thwart the dam, "and the latter can be reached by repairing the old Tioga road." Following the improvements, "hotels, or boarding camps at the very least, would undoubtedly be established at both of these points."[16]

The widespread belief that some development must be allowed in the parks may explain why most preservationists, including Chamberlain, did not make direct reference to Hetch Hetchy's wilderness attributes.[17] To save the valley, indeed the entire park system, seemed to hinge on the encouragement of much greater visitation, not less. By definition today, the policy is inconsistent with wilderness preservation. Yet, given a choice in 1910, preservationists clearly preferred roads, trails, hotels, and crowds to dams, reservoirs, powerlines, and conduits. "In short," Chamberlain concluded, "the nation has in these parks a natural resource of enormous value to its people, but it is not being developed and utilized as it might be." Instead, as dramatized by the Hetch Hetchy affair, "selfish interests" likely would "steal an important part of our birthright."[18]

The argument that one day national parks, if properly managed, would stimulate the economy in their own right certainly enhanced their defenders' position. The problem for the moment was the need to rely on the future tense; immediate gains from promoting the reserves must be realized as well. Fortunately, the railroads of the West, beginning with the Northern Pacific, had endorsed scenic protection as far back as agitation for the Yellowstone Park Act of 1872. Granted, the railroads did not back the national park idea out of altruism or environmental concern; rather the lines promoted tourism in their quest for greater profits. Still, preservationists recognized the value of forming an alliance with a powerful corporate group committed to similar goals, if not from similar motivation. Tourism, however encouraged, was the prerequisite for providing the national parks with a solid economic justification for their existence. Equally important, boosting travel in no way endangered the basic integrity of the scenic reserves, as was true of most utilitarian projects.[19]

No one better voiced these arguments than Richard B. Watrous, secretary of the American Civic Association. Taking up where J. Horace McFarland and Allen Chamberlain left off, during the summer of 1911 he defined travel promotion as the only "dignified exploitation of our national parks." He therefore urged preservationists nationwide to join the association in publicizing "the direct material returns that will accrue to the railroads, to the concessionaires, and to the various sections of the country that will benefit by increased travel." Specifically, the cooperation of the railroads, as feeders to the parks, was especially "essential" as "one of those practical phases of making the aesthetic possible."[20]

It remained for Secretary of the Interior Walter L. Fisher (1911–13) to give these views the sanction of the government. In September 1911, at Yellowstone, he convened the first national parks conference, largely to air problems common to the reserves. Yet it soon became apparent that the gathering also marked a turnabout in support of the park idea by both government and industry. The large delegation of officials from the railroads was one indication of coming changes; Fisher's opening remarks before the conferees were equally revealing. The "enlightened selfishness" of the railroads, he declared, entitled them to the "grateful recognition" of all park advocates.[21] Immediately company executives returned the compliment with promises to assist the government in upgrading park hotels, roads, and trails.[22] Without doubt, preservationists rejoiced, the railroads were firmly committed to national park improvements and publicity efforts.

Over the next several years the railroads affirmed their dedication in a flurry of national park promotion. As a group the lines spent hundreds of thousands of dollars on advertising brochures, complimentary park guidebooks, and full-page magazine spreads, some in luxurious color. Their unspoken purpose to swell the coffers of the lines did nothing to discredit their effectiveness in also heightening public awareness about the parks. Congress as well, it followed, could no longer be indifferent to the parks' rising popularity.

The first debates to dwell at length on the need to market American scenery were those leading to the establishment of Glacier National Park in 1910. "Two hundred million dollars of the good money of the people of the United States are paid out annually by Americans who visit the mountains of Switzerland and other parts of Europe," asserted Senator Thomas H. Carter in defense of the bill. "I would say that our own people might direct their course to our own grand mountains, where scenery equal to that to be found anywhere on this globe may be seen and enjoyed." Just five years later, with consideration of the Rocky Mountain national park bill, the amount Americans spent overseas on scenic travel supposedly had soared to an estimated $500 million yearly, a "considerable portion" of which, agreed Representative Edward T. Taylor of Colorado, "goes to see scenery that in no way compares with our own." Indeed, he continued, "the American people have never yet capitalized our scenery and climate, as we should. It is one of our most valuable assets, and these great assets should be realized upon to the fullest extent."[23]

Here was cultural nationalism with a new twist. Now the United States would not be satisfied until its landmarks measured up to Europe's monetarily as well as symbolically. "We receive comparatively nothing for [our scenery]," Congressman Taylor elaborated, "while Switzerland derives from $10,000 to $40,000 per square mile per year from scenery that is not equal to ours. But Switzerland knows that the public is ready and willing to pay for scenery, and they have developed it for selling purposes." Not to profit from the prudence of the Swiss, he concluded, especially since World War I was "closing European resorts to American travel this year," would cost the United States a golden opportunity to teach its "citizens to visit and appreciate our own parks."[24]

Although tinged with the self-doubts about the quality of native scenery that still lingered in the American mind, Carter's and Taylor's sentiments reassured preservationists that they were making progress toward new rationales for scenic protection. Still, just as for Washington Irving, James Fenimore Cooper, and earlier nationalists, there remained the problem of how to turn American eyes from foreign to native scenery. One prerequisite, park advocates and rail executives agreed, was the construction of "proper" tourist accommodations. Grand, rustic lodges were of particular importance, since the wealthy, after all, still comprised the majority of travelers. Luxury hotels also proved that civilization had in fact edged into the American wilderness and softened its discomforting rawness.[25] With these ends in mind, in 1904 the Santa Fe Railroad, for example, completed the majestic El Tovar Hotel on the South Rim of the Grand Canyon. (This was just three years after the Santa Fe extended a branch line to the chasm; four more years elapsed, however, before the canyon became a national monument.) Similarly, in Yellowstone the Northern Pacific underwrote a string of hostelries as early as 1886. Yet no structures were more elegant or varied than those provided visitors to Glacier National Park by Louis W. Hill and the Great Northern Railway. Between 1911 and 1915 Hill personally supervised the construction of two sprawling lodges and a series of Swiss-style chalets within and immediately adjacent to the reserve. Mary Roberts Rinehart, the novelist, was among those so impressed by the buildings that she concluded in 1916: "Were it not for the Great Northern Railway, travel through Glacier Park would be practically impossible."[26]

Yet despite the cooperation of the railroads, preservationists still could not escape the certainty of head-on confrontations with the advocates of utilitarian conservation. The promise of immediate returns to the national economy, as opposed to what the national parks *might* contribute to the gross national product, demanded constant rebuttal. Nor were preservationists unaware that Congress, despite an occasional burst of eloquence in defense of the national park idea, was no less committed to the standards of the past. However impressive were the Rocky Mountains, the Cascades, and Sierra Nevada, the remnants of their beauty that Congress saw fit to protect were still the easiest to protect. In describing Glacier National Park as "the wildest part of America," for example, Mary Roberts Rinehart was nonetheless moved to admit: "If the Government had not preserved it, it would have preserved itself. No homesteader would ever have invaded its rugged magnificence and dared its winter snows. But you and I would not have seen it," she added, although "so far most niggardly provision has been made" for park management.[27]

The admission that the national parks were still the step-children of federal conservation policy, coupled with the controversy over Hetch Hetchy and its eventual loss, spurred preservationists' efforts to create a separate government agency committed solely to park management and protection. This campaign would lead to the National Park Service, approved by Congress in 1916. In the interim, preservationists redoubled their search for new ways to justify the national park idea. The combination of mounting world tensions and urban expansion, for example, provided another creative, if somewhat improbable platform—military preparedness. One of the more outspoken testimonials to link scenery with defense was that of Robert Bradford Marshall, chief topographer of the U.S. Geological Survey. "I come now to a hobby of mine—our national parks," he said in a March 1911 speech before the Canadian Campers Club in New York City. "Now, you may think I am a national park crank, but I am going to prove to you that a fine, generous national park system is absolutely essential to the proper handling of an American war Fleet in case of a great war, or to the establishment and maintenance of an army which, in the event of such a catastrophe shall be invincible against the armed hosts of the world." The rapid development of cities and the increasing proportion of urban inhabitants had been unforeseen, he continued. Thus while "city soldiers in the past have made good," as urban areas became "more and more congested" the "physical status" of boys and men "deteriorated" and would "continue to deteriorate." Hanging "from the straps of crowded [street] cars" working men "forget they have legs." What was the prescription for restoring their physical vitality? "Give them national parks," places "where they can go every year or so and forget something of the rush and jam and scramble of the modern life . . . and build up their bodies by being next to nature. Then, should there be a call to arms, the dwellers of the city canyons will be able to meet the physical needs of a strenuous field service."[28]

George Otis Smith, director of the U.S. Geological Survey, had already endorsed Marshall's appraisal. "The nation that leads the world in feverish business activity requires playgrounds as well as workshops," he agreed in 1909. For the maintenance of "industrial supremacy" presupposed "conserving not only minerals but men." Thus "arguments for scenic preservation need not be limited to aesthetic or sentimental postulates"; to the contrary, the "playgrounds of the nation are essential to its very life." The statement was not original; indeed, perhaps John Muir had said it best, Smith admitted, when he defined mountain parks as "fountains of life," for only there "can be had the recreation that makes for increased and maintained efficiency." Still, "the materialist" as well must not "turn aside from this demand of the times," Smith added, "for no greater value can be won from mountain slopes and rushing rivers than through the utilization of natural scenery in the development of [our] citizens." R. B. Marshall's speech also lent itself to a reminder about the economic advantages of scenic protection: "Manage the national parks on a business basis and work for good transportation facilities to and from them," Marshall directed, "so that the multitude may visit them."[29] Like Smith, he hoped to thwart the rigid interpretation of resource conservationists that the national parks must, above all, be exploited for their material wealth to benefit the American people.

A respected landscape engineer, Mark R. Daniels of the Interior Department, was another who challenged the viewpoint as "due principally to the popular misconception of the value of idealism as a factor in our economic development. The capitalist has been prone to call the idealist an impractical crank," he stated in an address before the American Civic Association on December 3, 1914. Similarly, "idealists

Voyageurs NP

Isle Royale NP

Apostle Islands NL

Pictured Rocks NL

Acadia NP

St. Croix National
Scenic Riverway

Cape Cod NS

Sleeping Bear
Dunes NL

Delaware NSR

Fire Island NS

Indiana Dunes NL

Shenandoah NP

Assateague Island NS

New River
Gorge NR

Ozark National
Scenic Riverway

Mammoth Cave NP

Cape Hatteras NS

Big South Fork NR

Obed NSR

Great Smoky
Mountains NP

Cape Lookout NS

Buffalo NR

Congaree
Swamp NM

KEY TO ABBREVIATIONS

NL—National Lakeshore
NM—National Monument
NP—National Park
NS—National Seashore
NR—National River
NSR–National Scenic River
Pres–National Preserve

Cumberland
Island NS

Thicket
National Preserve

Canaveral NS

Gulf Islands NS

PRIMARY NATURAL UNITS
OF THE
NATIONAL PARK SYSTEM

Big
Cypress
National
Preserve

Biscayne NP

Everglades NP

Virgin Islands NP
(not shown)

SCALE

| 0 | 200 | 400 | MILES |

| 0 | 200 | 400 | 600 | KILOMETERS |

SOURCE: Forest Service, United States Department of Agriculture, Rare II Map A, 1978, and U.S., Department of the Interior, National Park Service, Map and Guide: National Parks of the United States, 1983

... have called the capitalists, or accused them, rather, of being utterly devoid of any sense of the ideal." The only solution was for both to appreciate that what "is fundamentally idealistic cannot fail to be eventually economic," that "idealism and economics are inalienably related" by virtue of the former's "tremendous commercial value." Seen in this light national park advocates and planners did not compromise their beliefs by considering "the economic phase" of their calling; instead they added "a new dignity to it." Indeed, he concluded, "the problem which confronts us is a systematic and organized effort to administer these national parks." Thus "any plan" which was "to be successful" must also "be functional."[30]

Daniels' conclusion alluded to what preservationists now perceived as the major threat to the future of the national parks—the absence of a separate government bureau committed solely to their welfare and management. Without permanent administrative safeguards for the reserves, all efforts to broaden the role of the parks to include fostering patriotism, worker efficiency, and commercial success seemed pointless. Past legislation offered little reassurance. Although each national park was the responsibility of the secretary of the interior, the Hetch Hetchy affair underscored the lack of continuity in decision-making. In 1903, for example, Secretary Ethan Allen Hitchcock disallowed the dam permit, but his decision was overturned five years later by his successor, James A. Garfield. Another serious discrepancy was the absence of uniformity among the park acts themselves. As a primary illustration, J. Horace McFarland contrasted "the Yellowstone—having a satisfactory, definite, enabling act," with "the Yosemite—being no park at all but actually a forest reserve." The nonexistence of "national legislation referring to the federal parks in general terms" also dismayed preservationists, as did what McFarland called "confused and indefinite" management procedures.[31]

Passage of the Antiquities Act of 1906 further complicated the problem of controlling the parks systematically. Rather than entrust the national monuments to a single, centralized agency, Congress left each under the care of the bureau holding original administration of the land. As a result, "of the twenty-eight national monuments created by executive action," McFarland noted in 1911, "thirteen are under the Forest Service and fifteen under the Interior Department." Inevitably "none were being adequately controlled or logically handled."[32] Preservationists found special cause for alarm at the Grand Canyon and Mount Olympus, the two largest monuments. Since both were carved from property managed by the U.S. Forest Service, and thus had remained with that agency, it seemed reasonable to conclude that utilitarian biases would prevail in the parks. In 1915 President Woodrow Wilson confirmed preservationists' worst fears when, partly in response to pressure from the Forest Service, he reduced the size of Mount Olympus National Monument by more than half to allow lumbering operations.[33]

The War Department made up the final but no less significant layer of confusion in park management. In 1883 Congress finally authorized protection for Yellowstone under the direction of the United States Army. Three years later the cavalry entered the park, and, after 1890, provided similar enforcement against vandalism, illegal grazing, and poaching at Yosemite, Sequoia, and General Grant national parks. But although the troopers did a superb job (one historian contends they actually "saved" the reserves), they, too, testified to the absence of unified management.[34] The same might be said of the U.S. Army Corps of Engineers, which primarily planned and built roads in the parks, most notably in Yellowstone.[35]

The first serious attempt to redress the problem came in 1900, when Representative John F. Lacey of Iowa, later chief proponent of the Antiquities Act, introduced legislation "to establish and administer national parks."[36] The proposal got no further, however, until 1910, when Secretary of the Interior Richard A. Ballinger bowed to pressure from J. Horace McFarland to draft a bill providing for a "Bureau of National Parks." Following suggestions and rewrites by other members of the American Civic Association, most notably Frederick Law Olmsted, Jr., in 1911 the document was presented on Capitol Hill by its sponsor, Senator Reed Smoot of Utah.[37]

Opposition to the measure was strong. The Forest Service—now among the federal government's principal landholding agencies—was especially aroused because it suspected that any new parks would be carved primarily from its tracts in the West.[38] Gifford Pinchot also remained strongly opposed to increasing the prestige of the national parks, despite his removal as chief forester in 1910 following a rupture between him and Theodore Roosevelt's successor, President William Howard Taft.[39] Finally, some members of Congress were antagonistic to the formation of still another full-fledged bureaucracy. Accordingly, in January 1912 preservationists renamed their proposed organization the National Park *Service*. As distinct from the word "bureau," "service" implied that the new agency would not have as much political power. Others noted the significance of changing the title to suggest that the National Park Service, rather than starting off as superior to its existing rivals—especially the Forest Service—in reality must compete with them directly for its own federal funding and support.[40]

Even with these compromises, however, the campaign to pass the Park Service bill remained difficult. For example, the Forest Service fought to retain not only its existing national monuments, but all future national parks carved from its holdings. Congress's concession to the former request temporarily undermined any hope of managing the national parks and monuments as an integral system. The views of Gifford Pinchot were no less divisive; throughout the contest he spoke out against any attempt to coordinate scenic protection unless the program were handled "efficiently, economically, and satisfactorily by the Forest Service."[41]

Preservationists' ability to thwart an unworkable compromise stemmed in large part from their evolving alliance with the western railroads. Encouraged by J. Horace McFarland, Richard B. Watrous, and others close to the American Civic Association, advocates of the Park Service bill carefully nurtured the spirit of cooperation aroused during the Yellowstone conference of 1911. Over the next five years their homework paid off handsomely as the campaign to establish the Park Service moved through the maze of congressional hearings and similar legislative roadblocks. On occasion, the railroads themselves sent prominent officials to testify on behalf of the agency and to elaborate on what the lines were doing to promote travel in the meantime.[42] Again there was little altruism involved; rather "these men have reached that degree of enlightenment in their selfishness," Secretary of the Interior Walter L. Fisher reasserted in 1912, "that they have come to the conclusion that it is for their own best interest to have a national park bureau established."[43]

It followed that as preservationists played their hand before Congress, the monetary appeal of scenic protection was still trump. "For instance," Secretary Fisher said in leading off testimony on the Park Service bill before the House Public Lands Committee, "we should try to make our people spend their money in this country instead of abroad, and certainly as far as spending it abroad for the scenic effect." With respect to landscape the United States did "not have to ask any odds of any other country on earth."[44] Examples of the value of national parks to worker productivity strengthened the argument. In this vein J. Horace McFarland seconded the pronouncements of George Otis Smith and Robert Bradford Marshall, then added a variation uniquely his own. "I think sometimes we fall into a misapprehension," he stated at the congressional hearings in 1916, "because the word 'park' in the minds of most of us suggests a place where there are flower beds . . . and things of that kind." Congress should be aware "that the park has passed out of this category in the United States." Beyond esthetics the parks met a very practical need. The "park is the direct competitor . . . of the courts, of the jail, of the cemetery, and a very efficient competitor with all of them," McFarland elaborated. By providing rest and relaxation, parks alone kept "at work men who otherwise would be away from work. That is the park idea in America," he concluded—with a final challenge to the utilitarian persuasion—"as it has come to be the idea of service and efficiency, and not an idea of pleasure and ornamentation at all."[45]

McFarland's dismissal of scenic protection for its own sake was a sincere attempt to link the national park idea to the tenets of utilitarian conservation. Indeed, while the statement seems out of character at first glance, more accurately it reflected the quiet desperation among preservationists that followed in the wake of their losing Hetch Hetchy. Privately, preservationists took comfort from the support of the railroads, whose promotion of the national parks confirmed that the park idea was in fact coming into its own. The efforts of Senator Reed Smoot on Capitol Hill to win passage of the Park Service bill added to the growing prestige of esthetic conservation.[46] Thus heartened, interested members of the American Civic Association used their office in Washington, D.C., to rally their own campaign on behalf of the National Park Service.

By 1915 campaign headquarters had also been established at the Interior Department. Two men in particular, Stephen T. Mather and Horace M. Albright, worked to enlist the backing of political and industrial leaders. Mather, a skilled promoter, member of the Sierra Club, and self-made millionaire in the mining and distribution of borax, had been attracted to Washington the previous December by Secretary of the Interior Franklin K. Lane, who, like Mather, was an alumnus of the University of California. Following his graduation in 1887, Mather became a reporter for the *New York Sun*, stayed five years, then turned his energies to the borax industry, in which he eventually made his fortune. By 1914 he was restless and ready for a different challenge. Quite by accident, an opportunity presented itself following a summer sojourn into the High Sierra. Angered by the poor management of Yosemite and Sequoia national parks, Mather penned a letter to Secretary Lane in protest. Coincidentally, someone of Mather's wealth, dedication, and business experience was precisely the man Lane was looking for to put the national parks in order. Thus his reply: "Dear Steve, If you don't like the way the national parks are being run, come on down to Washington and run them yourself." Mather wavered, then accepted the challenge, provided that Secretary Lane found someone to shield him from the inevitable red tape and legal hassles. Lane gladly complied by introducing Mather to a young, energetic lawyer in the Interior Department, Horace M. Albright, who agreed to become Mather's assistant.[47]

Mather stayed fourteen years, the first two as assistant to Secretary Lane, the remainder as director of the National Park Service. Several months before his death (in January 1930), Horace Albright took over as director and preserved the Mather tradition until 1933, when he, too, resigned to become president of the American Potash Company. With good reason no names are more closely linked with the success of the National Park Service than those of Mather and Albright. The business acumen of both men was of inestimable value in the day-to-day meetings, speech-making, and promotional campaigns that characterized the Park Service in its opening decades. At times the railroads themselves needed a little arm-twisting, as in 1915, when Mather asked them to provide excursion tickets which would be honored on any line serving the major parks.[48] In other instances the problem might be a balky politician opposed to increased appropriations, or a reporter whose ignorance of the parks jeopardized what the Park Service was trying to accomplish. Against such hurdles Mather and Albright were at their best. Whether as writers, public speakers, or out-and-out lobbyists, none better understood the fickleness of human nature and the art of overcoming it.

Indeed the effectiveness of their promotion was not due to new ideas per se; John Muir, J. Horace McFarland, R. B. Marshall, Mark Daniels, and others had long since laid the rhetorical basis for justifying the national parks in an urban, industrial society. Mather's and Albright's original contribution was the institutionalization of the national park idea within the political and legal framework of the federal government. Henceforth an attack on a reserve would not be an affront to it alone, but to the very fabric of American society.

It followed that the struggle to associate scenic preservation with long-ingrained American values had been a success. As early as 1915 Stephen Mather confirmed the potential of the relationship by joining preservationists in equating the national parks with the country's economic health. "Secretary Lane has asked me for a business administration," he wrote just four months after taking office. "This I understand to mean an administration which shall develop to the highest possible degree of efficiency the resources of the national parks both for the pleasure and the profit of their owners, the people." With that statement Mather gave credence to the theme developed by J. Horace McFarland and his contemporaries during more than a decade. "A hundred thousand people used the national parks last year," Mather continued. "A million Americans should play in them every summer." To emphasize his reasoning, he again invoked the profit motive: "Our national parks are practically lying fallow, and only await proper development to bring them into their own."[49]

The National Park Service bill had long been seen as the best hope of guarding the parks against the changing whims and uncertainties of the political climate. Success finally was achieved on August 25, 1916, when President Woodrow Wilson affixed his signature to the National Park Service Act. Here at last, preservationists congratulated themselves, was a clear-cut blueprint of what the national parks stood for and how they should be administered. Section 1, for example, provided for a director, assistant director, chief clerk, draftsman, and messenger, in addition to "such other employees as the Secretary of the Interior may deem necessary." Title to all existing and future national parks passed to the new agency; similarly, the Park Service took over each of the national monuments directly controlled by the Interior Department. Not until 1933 were the Forest Service and War Department also forced to give up the monuments under their jurisdiction. For this reason management of the parks and monuments as a whole was still temporarily frustrated.[50]

The setback, nonetheless, was incidental to the integration of park goals under a single statement of purpose, the clause originally drafted by Frederick Law Olmsted, Jr. From these words preservationists gained confidence for an end to any uncertainty about the "fundamental purpose" of the national parks. That "purpose," the clause clarified, "is to conserve the scenery and the natural and historic objects and the wild life therein and to provide for the enjoyment of the same in such manner and by such means as will leave them unimpaired for the enjoyment of future generations."[51] In time preservationists discovered that the paragraph itself was subject to broad differences of opinion. Precisely what, for example, was meant by "unimpaired"? Did the word make allowances for roads, trails, hotels, and parking lots? One day the potential for such debates would seem endless. Still, at the very least the clause provided a basis for consensus; indeed, given the circumstances behind its passage, especially the recent loss of Hetch Hetchy, it was more than preservationists reasonably could have expected.

The defense of the parks, in any event, had been elevated from the throes of indifferent management to the full responsibility of the federal government. At last esthetic conservationists had an agency of their own to counter the ambitions of those who considered Hetch Hetchy merely the opening wedge in gaining access to all of the public domain, including the national parks and monuments. Nor did Stephen T. Mather and Horace Albright have any intention of waiting for the inevitable confrontations. Instead they worked to dilute utilitarian rhetoric by playing upon the value of the national parks as an economic resource. The first national parks conference called by Mather as director of the Park Service underscored the timelessness of this approach. In January 1917 delegates from Congress, the parks, the railroads, and many civic groups gathered at the National Museum in Washington, D.C., to discuss the future of the Park Service and its charges. The list of opening speakers was impressive. It included, for example, Senator Reed Smoot of Utah, who related to the audience his role in introducing the Park Service bill. Preservationists found additional cause for optimism in the speech of Scott Ferris of Oklahoma, chairman of the House Committee on the Public Lands. "The amount of money that goes abroad every year by tourists is no less than alarming," he said, endorsing the "See America First" campaign. "The best estimate available is that more than $500,000,000 is expended by our American people every year abroad vainly hunting for wonders and beauties only half as grand as nature has generously provided for them at home." Surely, he concluded, such overseas spending demanded "that we of the Congress and you members of the conference" find some way "to keep at least a part of that money at home where it belongs."[52]

Especially from someone as powerful as Congressman Ferris, the statement bore testimony to the persuasiveness of the "See America First" ideology. By channeling cultural nationalism into both an esthetic and economic defense of the national parks, preservationists considerably strengthened the park idea in the United States. Similarly, their association of human "efficiency" and productivity with outdoor recreation turned the rhetoric of resource conservationists into an asset for preservation rather than a total liability. The National Park Service provided the foundation on which to build the popularity of these themes within the government. Confronted with evidence that the national parks were capable of paying economic as well as emotional dividends, for the first time Congress had good reason to add to the system rather than dismantle it.

6

Complete Conservation

Our national parks system is a national museum. Its purpose is to preserve forever . . . certain areas of extraordinary scenic magnificence in a condition of primitive nature. Its recreational value is also very great, but recreation is not distinctive of the system. The function which alone distinguishes the national parks . . . is the museum function made possible only by the parks' complete conservation.

Robert Sterling Yard, 1923

It is now recognized that [national] Parks contain more than scenery.

Harold C. Bryant, co-founder,
Yosemite Free Nature Guide Service,
1929

The success of the "See America First" campaign reassured preservationists that the national parks would survive in some form. Still open to question was whether they would survive as *originally* established. Hetch Hetchy was only the most recent example of the resistance of Congress to larger parks on the order of Yellowstone, whose expanse protected (if unintentionally) other natural values besides scenic wonders. The growing belief that total preservation should in fact be the role of national parks in the twentieth century only heightened the tension regarding their integrity. Increasingly Americans recalled the pronouncement of the Census Bureau in 1890 that the frontier was no more. Indeed "it has girdled the globe," Mary Roberts Rinehart confirmed in May 1921 for readers of the *Ladies' Home Journal.* "And, unless we are very careful," she cautioned, "soon there will be no reminders of the old

West," including "the last national resource the American people have withheld from commercial exploitation, their parks." That others had said as much did nothing to lessen the urgency of her own statement. Outside the parks it seemed the transformation of the West would be total. Plans to dam the Columbia River, for example, already threatened the perspective of those who would imagine Lewis and Clark reaching out "on their adventurous journey into the unknown." Soon the river would "be harnessed, like Niagara, and turning a million wheels. Our wild life gone with our Indians, our waterfalls harnessed and our rivers laboring, our mountains groaning that they might bring forth power, soon all that will be left of our great past," she restated emphatically, "will be our national parks."[1]

As a catalyst of the national park idea, the search for an American past through landscape was nothing new. The difference in articles such as Mrs. Rinehart's lay in their insistence that the national park idea would not be fully realized until all components of the American scene were represented. The preservation of a sense of history itself, for example, as recalled through broad expanses of native, living landscapes, was coming to be considered as crucial to establishing the identity of the United States as the protection of specific natural wonders. It followed that preservationists might, for the first time, draw a clear distinction between all parks and *national* parks. Formality of any kind, Mrs. Rinehart herself believed, smacked too much of the city park experience. In the West one came to appreciate "that a park could be more than a neat and civilized place, with green benches and public tennis courts." The word "park" itself was "misleading." "It is too small a name," she maintained, "too definitely associated with signs and asphalt and tameness."[2] Indeed, one of the more noticeable outcomes of the Hetch Hetchy controversy was preservationists' determination to defend the parks as a vestige of primitive America. "In this respect a national and a city park are wholly different," two vertebrate zoologists, Joseph Grinnell and Tracy Storer, agreed in 1916. "A city park is of necessity artificial . . .; but a national park is at its inception entirely natural and is generally thereafter kept fairly immune from human interference."[3]

Notable exceptions in the parks included the lodges and grand hotels, which, however rustic, still could not seriously be considered "entirely natural." If most preservationists did not insist that the parks be kept absolutely free of development, it was in appreciation of the need to attract more visitors, or—as in the case of Hetch Hetchy—risk far more damaging forms of commercial enterprise. Yet "the great hotels are dwarfed by the mountains around them, lost in the trees," Mrs. Rinehart assured her readers. "The wilderness is there, all around them, so close that the timid wild life creeps to their very doors."[4]

Such concessions were necessary until patronage in the parks reached a level sufficient to justify the protection of both animate and inanimate scenery. To be sure, hardly had Stephen T. Mather taken office as director of the National Park Service than ranchers and farmers in the state of Idaho launched a concerted effort to tap Yellowstone Lake and the falls of the Bechler River—in the southwestern corner of Yellowstone Park—for irrigation.[5] Preservationists quickly perceived the scheme as a threat to their own proposal to extend the boundaries of the park southward to include portions of the Thorofare Basin, Jackson Hole, and the Teton Mountains. The addition, they maintained, was necessary if Yellowstone were now to be managed along natural rather than political boundaries. Out of the plan emerged Grand Teton National Park, established in 1929 as a "roadless" preserve. Any pretext that the park was a serious break with tradition, however, was dispelled by failure to include the lowlands and wildlife habitat of Jackson Hole.

It remained instead for Everglades National Park, Florida, authorized in 1934, to mark the first unmistakable pledge to total preservation. The commitment seemed all the more convincing in light of the kind of topography represented in the Everglades. For the first time a major national park would lack great mountains, deep canyons, and tumbling waterfalls; preservationists accepted the protection of its native plants

A California camper, facing the perils of the roadside to shoot a bison in Wind Cave National Park, illustrates the impact of the automobile upon the way modern American tourists see the national parks.

Before being toppled by heavy snowfall in the winter of 1969, the Wawona Tunnel Tree, in the Mariposa Redwood Grove of Yosemite National Park, was the scene of countless snapshots, publicity stunts, and gags, usually involving cars. Above, a carriage carrying President Theodore Roosevelt (standing tallest in the carriage) and John Muir (partly hidden, second from left) visits the landmark in May 1903.

Hileman photograph, courtesy of the National Archives

These touring cars of the 1920s, east of St. Mary Lake in Glacier National Park, were the precursors of the modern air-conditioned tour buses operated by park concessionaires.

Courtesy of the National Park Service

These women at Old Faithful Inn, Yellowstone, in 1922, were given a tour in a Park Service car.

George A. Grant Collection, courtesy of the National Park Service

The elaborate masonry, turnouts, and tunnels of National Park Service roads helped to make the parks a unique visual experience for motorists. Above, an automobile negotiates the east slope of the Logan Pass (Going-to-the-Sun) Highway in Glacier National Park. Below, the dedication of the Going-to-the-Sun Highway, July 15, 1933, brought dignitaries, Indians, and a brass band to their feet for the singing of "America."

The rapid growth of automobile traffic encouraged the development of areas on the fringes of the national parks like West Yellowstone, Montana, shown here in August 1939.

The automobile has been accused of contributing to the degradation of wildlife in the national parks, particularly by causing changes in habits and feeding patterns; here, a buck deer begs at a car in Yellowstone, 1926.

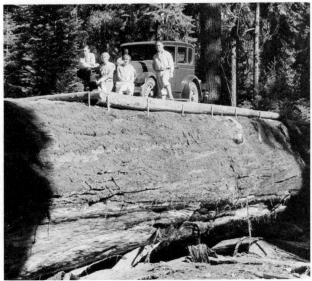

George A. Grant Collection, courtesy of the National
Park Service

Tourists pose on the Auto Log in Sequoia National Park during the
summer of 1929.

Cecil W. Stoughton photograph, courtesy of the National Park Service

Modern snowmobilists watch an eruption of Old Faithful. By opening the parks to new recreational machines, critics say, the National
Park Service is paying more heed to the whims of visitors than to the
complex needs of park environments.

Visitors regularly speak of the national parks as Nature's cathedrals; Easter sunrise services were first offered at Mirror Lake in Yosemite Valley in 1932.

Bert Taylor, United States skating champion, performs at the Yosemite Winterclub in February 1937. Preservationists protest that an ice rink, let alone such theatrics, is an amusement more appropriate to big cities and resorts than to a park set aside to preserve a natural environment.

William S. Keller photograph, courtesy of the National Park Service

A workman removes debris from Blue Star Spring while Old Faithful erupts in the background, March 1968. Too many callous visitors bring too many pop bottles.

Courtesy of the National Park Service, Yellowstone National Park

Grizzlies and gulls hold visitors' fascination at the bear feeding grounds near the Grand Canyon of the Yellowstone sometime during the 1930s. The twilight "shows" were last held in the fall of 1945, but the question of bears and garbage in Yellowstone is still controversial.

and animals alone as justification for Everglades National Park. Later fears that its pristine character might also be sacrificed to development stemmed from mounting pressure to restrict the park to an area considerably under the ceiling approved by Congress. In the quest for total preservation, no less than the retention of significant natural wonders, the worthlessness of the area in question was still the only guarantee of effecting a successful outcome.

The conviction that national parks were fast becoming the last vestiges of primitive America was an important catalyst for management of their resources as a whole. Since the creation of Yosemite and Yellowstone, in 1864 and 1872 respectively, the overriding criterion for the selection of national parks was the presence of natural wonders. Occasionally Congress seemed aware that the parks might fill other roles; the Yellowstone Act, for example, provided against "the wanton destruction of the fish and game found within said park, and against their capture or destruction for the purposes of merchandise or profit."[6] But precisely what was meant by "wanton destruction" was open to broad interpretation. Nor can it be argued seriously that game conservation inspired Yellowstone National Park. It remained for sportsmen and explorers such as George Bird Grinnell, co-founder of the Boone and Crockett Club, to impress upon the secretary of the interior and the Congress the need for better wildlife protection in Yellowstone.[7] Of course, simply to provide shelter for the animals could hardly be called game management; both the science and public appreciation of its importance did not mature until the twentieth century.[8]

The federal government still weighed new parks primarily on the basis of their physical endowments; only then might other factors bearing on the decision to establish a reserve be openly advanced. "So with the Yellowstone," Stephen T. Mather asserted in the *National Parks Portfolio*, in 1916; "all have heard of its geysers, but few indeed of its thirty-three-hundred square miles of wilderness beauty." The inclusion of wilderness in the park in 1872 had been purely unintentional.

The park "is associated in the public mind with geysers only," Robert Sterling Yard, author of the *Portfolio*, agreed. "There never was a greater mistake. Were there no geysers, the Yellowstone watershed alone, with its glowing canyon, would be worth the national park." Of course the chasm was a scenic wonder in its own right. But "were there also no canyon," Yard continued, "the scenic wilderness and its incomparable wealth of wild-animal life would be worth the national park."[9]

Seen in light of his capacity as Mather's director of public relations, Yard's assessment could be interpreted as a sign of new directions in park management. Free distribution of the *National Parks Portfolio* to 275,000 leading Americans underscored the significance of his and Mather's reappraisal of the role of national parks. What they initially envisioned as a publicity volume was in fact an invitation to join in rethinking the national park idea. "That these parks excelled in grandeur and variety the combined scenic exhibits of other principal nations moved the national pride," Yard recalled. Now Americans were awakening to the realization that the national parks "embodied in actual reality . . . a mighty system of national museums of the primitive American wilderness." Indeed "the national parks are much more than a playground," Mary Roberts Rinehart agreed. "They are a refuge. They bring rest to their human visitors, but they give life to uncounted numbers of wild creatures." Certainly the animals "are of no less consequence than the scenery," Joseph Grinnell and Tracy Storer concurred. "To the natural charm of the landscape they add the witchery of movement." Management of the national parks ultimately must consider the sum total of these phenomena. "Herein lies the feature of supreme value in national parks," the naturalists concluded in defending their assessment; "they furnish examples of the earth as it was before the advent of the white man."[10]

Like the analogy that natural wonders served as cultural mileposts, the claim that primitive America might be suspended in the national parks promised to secure the national park idea for the future. Destruction of the reserves, for example, might be decried as dismembering the bond between history and prehistory. In this vein public education stood to become a beneficiary of complete conservation; indeed the national park system, Robert Sterling Yard lamented, "may be compared to a school equipped with every educational device, filled with eager pupils [but] with no teachers." Both individually and collectively, the reserves provided a superb illustration of "the geological sequence of America's making," of "the tremendous processes of the upbuilding of gigantic mountain systems, their destruction by erosion, and their rebuilding." Similarly, Yard added: "In all of them wild life conditions remain untouched."[11]

The latter, unfortunately, was not yet the case. Actually the National Park Service pursued a vigorous program against predators well into the 1930s. As early as October 1920, for example, Stephen T. Mather reported a "very gratifying increase in deer and other species that always suffer through the depredations of mountain lion, wolves, and other 'killers.'" In truth the application of "complete conservation" to both wildlife and landscapes was still largely compromised by human values and emotions. Until the evolution of that degree of detachment based on ecological understanding, allowances would continue to be made for "desirable" as opposed to "undesirable" features of the natural world. This major lapse in objectivity aside, however, the defense of total preservation as a vehicle for education still had considerable appeal. After all, the promotion of national parks as America's "outdoor classrooms" was a practical rationale for preserving "living" landscapes as well as natural wonders. "It seems to have been demonstrated that Uncle Sam's famous playgrounds have a much greater value than merely that of attracting tourists to see geysers and glaciers and waterfalls," summed up one supporter. The reserves, agreed Stephen Mather, "in addition to being ideal recreation areas, serve also as field laboratories for the study of nature."[12]

The first park museums and interpretive programs, which appeared in the 1920s, formally recognized the educational role of scenic preservation. Instructing visitors in complete conservation, however, was to prove far easier than actually applying the theory. Congress still resisted additions to the parks which would compensate for their existing limitations. Moreover, in the face of opposition from vested economic interests, efforts to expand the park system had little chance of success unless the new areas themselves were restricted in size. Invariably they, too, stressed physical phenomena. Because the parks were meant to take in only scenic wonders, such as a mountain or canyon, they failed to include enough habitat to give sanctuary to all resident species of plants and animals.

No one, of course, opposed additions to the park system of a traditional nature; by no means had the United States protected representative examples of every major kind of landscape. Those close to the issue of total conservation might also overlook their setbacks amid the excitement of rediscovering the wonders of the continent. John Burroughs, for example, was one of several contemporary naturalists who still reached the height of popularity with a style of description more suggestive of nineteenth-century explorers. "In the East, the earth's wounds are virtually all healed," he noted in 1911, "but in the West they are yet raw and gaping, if not bleeding." The Grand Canyon in particular did "indeed suggest a far-off, half-sacred antiquity, some greater Jerusalem, Egypt, Babylon, or India," he wrote. "We speak of it as a scene; it is more like a vision, so foreign is it to all other terrestrial spectacles, and so surpassingly beautiful."[13]

As Burroughs reminded his readers, the stark landforms of the Southwest provided Americans yet another opportunity to achieve a semblance of historical continuity through landscape. The protection of the region's outstanding natural wonders was therefore a strong possibility. Grand Canyon National Monument, set aside by President Theodore Roosevelt in January 1908, was preceded only by Petrified Forest National Monument, proclaimed two years earlier to protect the remnants of an ancient woodland in eastern Arizona. Later, in 1919, Congress elevated the Grand Canyon to full national park status. The same year marked the creation of Zion National Park, Utah, located approximately 100 air miles to the north. Justly renowned as "the Yosemite of the Desert" by virtue of its steep, brilliantly colored sandstone cliffs, Zion itself had nearby rivals, most notably Bryce Canyon, dedicated as a national park in 1928, and Cedar Breaks National Monument, established five years later.[14]

The inclusion of these unique areas in the park system rounded out what another popular writer, Rufus Steele, dubbed "the Celestial Circuit." (The route has since been broadened with the creation of several parklands of the same genre, including Canyonlands [1964], Arches [1971], and Capitol Reef [1971].) "It leads to canyons set about with majestic peaks," he depicted, "and to other canyons that are filled with cathedrals and colonnades, ramparts and rooms, terraces and temples, turrets and towers, obelisks and organs," and similar "incredible products of erosion." In testimony to the excitement aroused by his descriptions, during the late 1920s the Union Pacific Railroad resurrected the "See America First" campaign as part of a massive publicity effort to attract rail travelers to the region. "The Grand Canyon?" one of the railroad's posters asked. "Nowhere on the face of the globe is there anything like it." But even Bryce Canyon, although far smaller, was no less worthy of a rail pilgrimage west. Its "great side walls are fluted like giant cathedral organs," the Union Pacific insisted. "Other architectural rockforms tower upward in vast spires and minarets—marbly white and flaming pink." Royalty itself seemed present, "high on painted pedestals" and "startlingly real. Figures of Titans, of kings and queens!" Finally came Zion, with "tremendous temples and towers" rising "sheer four-fifths of a mile into the blue Utah sky." Surely, therefore, "every true American" would want to see the wonders of his own country first, especially those covered throughout the Southwest "on an exclusive Union Pacific tour."[15]

New mountain-based national parks likewise affirmed that monumentalism was still a preeminent force behind the advancement of scenic preservation. Included among the reserves established in 1916 were Mount Lassen Volcanic National Park, California, and Hawaii Volcanoes National Park, on the islands of Hawaii and Maui. The following year Congress added Mount McKinley in Alaska to the park system, ostensibly as a game preserve. Yet, ecologically speaking, all of the new parks were disappointments. Much like their predecessors, they, too, were rugged, restricted in size, or, regardless of their area, compromised to accommodate economic claims to the detriment of preservation objectives. Congress still allowed mining in Mount McKinley National Park, for instance; moreover, the prospectors might kill "game or birds as they may be needed for their actual necessities when short of food." To say nothing of the mining, the discretion accorded the hunters seriously undercut any pretensions of wildlife conservation in the reserve.[16] In either case, preservation had not been achieved without rugged scenery as its focus, in this instance Mount McKinley.

Proof that the United States was indeed committed to wildlife protection in the national parks could not seriously be demonstrated until Congress recognized the parks because of their wildlife instead of their imposing topography. For example, the establishment of reserves in the East, whose landforms were relatively modest, would confirm the nation's sincerity to protect other natural values besides scenery. As early as 1894 the North Carolina Press Association petitioned Congress for a national park in the state; five years later the Appalachian National Park Association, organized at Asheville, seconded the proposal. Other preservation groups rapidly followed suit, including the Appalachian Mountain Club, the American Civic Association, and the American Association for the Advancement of Science. It still remained for Mount Desert Island, a rugged fragment of Maine seacoast, to form the nucleus of the first eastern park. This was Acadia, established in 1919. Several New England gentlemen of means inspired the project, including Charles W. Eliot, president of Harvard University, and George B. Dorr, a wealthy Bostonian. As early as 1901 they financed a program to secure portions of the island threatened by development; large contributions from other philanthropists, most notably John D. Rockefeller, Jr., furthered the cause. In 1916 the group persuaded President Woodrow Wilson to proclaim the 6,000 acres acquired to date a national monument. In 1918 Congress provided $10,000 for its management; then the following year—largely at the insistence of Mr. Dorr and Park Service director Stephen T. Mather—authorized that the reserve be made into a national park.[17]

Meanwhile the drive for reserves in the highlands of Virginia, Tennessee, or North Carolina also continued. Out of these efforts came the Southern Appalachian National Park Committee. In 1924 Secretary of the Interior Hubert Work asked the five-man commission to assess the region's suitability for representation in the national park system. "It has not been generally known that eastern parks of *National* size might still be acquired by our Government," the delegation advised in its report. But surprisingly, not one but "several areas were found that contained topographic features of great scenic value" which compared "favorably with any of the existing parks of the West." In order of ruggedness two were preeminent—the Great Smoky Mountains, forming the border between North Carolina and Tennessee, and the Blue Ridge Mountains of Virginia. Yet the need to guard against overconfidence about the chances of actually preserving each highland remained. "All that has saved these nearby regions from spoliation for so long a time," the commissioners warned, "has been their inaccessibility and the difficulty of profitably exploiting the timber wealth that mantles the steep mountain slopes." Now these woodlands, too, were jeopardized by the "rapidly increasing shortages and mounting values of forest products." Thus it seemed probable "that the last remnants of [the] primeval forests will be destroyed," the men concluded, "however remote on steep mountain side or hidden away in deep lonely cove they may be."[18]

Predictably, the commissioners stressed ruggedness as the primary criterion for awarding the Appalachians one or more national parks. Still, their reference to the "primeval" character of the highlands was evidence they had considered broader roles for the reserves. The emerging importance of total preservation was further reflected in the appearance of articles calling attention to the value of the Great Smoky Mountains as a botanical refuge. "There are 152 varieties of trees alone," observed Isabelle F. Story, editor-in-chief of the National Park Service. Indeed "it is impossible to describe the Great Smoky forest," agreed Robert Sterling Yard, "so rich is it in variety and beauty."[19] Yet no one denied that spectacular topography was still the major criterion for selecting a national park. Ruggedness first attracted the Appalachian National Park Committee to the Blue Ridge and Great Smokies. Other features unique to the Appalachians, especially their forests, initially were singled out largely to overcome doubts that neither region had enough topographical distinction to warrant park status. "It may be admitted that they are second to the West in rugged grandeur," Commissioner William C. Gregg conceded, "but they are first in beauty of woods, in thrilling fairyland glens, and in the warmth of Mother Nature's welcome." Stephen T. Mather added to Gregg's assessment: "The greater portion of the lands involved in these two park projects are wilderness areas." Still, even he felt compelled to add immediately, "and in the Smoky Mountains are found the greatest outstanding peaks east of the Rocky Mountains."[20]

In the East, of course, the public domain had long since passed into private control. The establishment of a national park here was not simply a matter of transferring land from one federal bureaucracy to another. As with Acadia, the land must be repurchased. From the outset Congress made it clear that either the states or private donors would have to assume the financial and legal costs of acquiring any reserves east of the Rockies. To coordinate such efforts, preservationists organized the Shenandoah National Park Association of Virginia, the Great Smoky Mountain Conservation Commission, and Great Smoky Mountains, Inc. Swayed by this outburst of citizen support, in May 1926 Congress authorized the secretary of the interior to accept, on behalf of the federal government, a maximum of 521,000 acres and 704,000 acres for Shenandoah and Great Smoky Mountains national parks respectively.[21] Still, in the absence of any immediate assistance from Washington, both projects were sorely compromised from the start. Estimates for acquiring sufficient property in the

Smokies alone approached $10 million. Residents of North Carolina, Tennessee, and other private citizens raised half the amount; long plagued by substandard economies, however, neither state seemed capable of attaining its goal. Again the cause of preservation had a rescuer in John D. Rockefeller, Jr., who made up the difference between the $5 million subscribed to date and the amount needed for a national park worthy of the name. A substantially smaller, but no less welcome Rockefeller contribution aided the Shenandoah project in Virginia as well. Thereby spared the certainty of truly crippling delays, in 1934 and 1935 respectively Great Smoky Mountain and Shenandoah national parks joined the system as full-fledged members.[22]

Shenandoah and the Great Smokies are best seen as transition parks. While both anticipated the ecological standards of the later twentieth century, Congress first required each region to approximate the visual standards of the national park idea as originally conceived. The persistence of monumentalism dictated that landscapes represented in the East also be of some topographic significance. Whatever the merits of the Great Smokies and the Blue Ridge Mountains as wilderness, wildlife, and botanical preserves, none of these features had as yet been recognized apart from its scenic base. Mountains were the framework of protection; what lived or moved on their surfaces might buttress preservationists' arguments for the parks, yet not guarantee them a full and complete victory. Still unresolved was whether or not large areas devoid of geological wonders might win permanent admittance to the national park system. Confidence that the United States was moving closer to concern for the environment for its own sake awaited the outcome of more heated controversies. With the addition, specifically, of the Florida Everglades to the national park family, preservationists could point with greater assurance to evidence of a more enlightened environmental perspective.

The cornerstone of that perspective was total preservation. Its meaning was not yet fully defined; still, gradually more Americans were coming to realize that, essentially, the difference between all parks and *national* parks lay in the one feature that the latter had had from the beginning—primitive conditions. State and city parks could be said to be scenic; few but the national parks offered scenery unmodified. "Except to make way for roads, trails, hotels and camps sufficient to permit the people to live there awhile and contemplate the unaltered works of nature," Robert Sterling Yard described the distinction, "no tree, shrub or wild flower is cut, no stream or lake shore is disturbed, no bird or animal is destroyed." The national parks, in short, were unique by virtue of "complete conservation."[23] It followed that they were best where modified the least.

It was symbolic that Yellowstone National Park would be central to the first major test of that new resolve. Approval of the park in 1872 realized the campaign to protect the region's unique "freaks" and "curiosities" of nature. Yet its boundaries had been drawn in some haste and in the absence of complete knowledge about the territory. Only gradually did a later generation of preservationists fully appreciate that many features worthy of protection had been left outside the park. Of these none were considered more inspiring than the mountains of the Teton Range. Sheer and glacier-carved, the summits guard the southern approach to Yellowstone on a north-south axis approximately forty miles in length. The highest peak, Grand Teton, rises well above 13,700 feet. To the east the mountains fall off abruptly into Jackson Hole, which, at roughly 6,000 feet in elevation, often is referred to as the Tetons' "frame." The valley supports a variety of native vegetation as a foreground, including woodlands, grasslands, and sagebrush flats. Several lakes and streams also mirror the peaks, among them Jackson Lake, lying astride the northern flank of the range, and the Snake River, which roughly divides the remainder of Jackson Hole into an eastern and a western half.[24]

Like its neighbor to the north, Yellowstone National Park, prior to 1880 Jackson Hole was wild and relatively unnoticed.[25] This was the ideal time to protect the region as a whole, before anyone seriously claimed it. Yet with the nation's attention fixed on the wonders of Yellowstone, the opportunity vanished before it was realized. By the late 1880s ranchers and settlers began filtering into Jackson Hole from the south and east; hard evidence of civilization inevitably followed, including roads, cabins, barns, and fences.[26]

With settlement came permanent disruptions to the wildlife as well as the natural vegetation. For centuries Yellowstone's southern elk herd had migrated through Jackson Hole to winter in the Green River basin, west of the Wind River Mountains. Other large mammals, including moose and antelope, were also dependent on a far larger range than the national park originally included. With settlement of the Green River basin, then Jackson Hole, the elk found themselves squeezed off their wintering grounds by barbed-wire fencing and roads. In addition, domestic livestock consumed much of the forage previously reserved for the elk. They could not stay in Yellowstone; the snow was too deep and the cold too bitter. As a result, thousands of the animals starved, weakened, and died. To worsen matters, each fall the herd also fell victim to poaching. The professional hunters simply lined up just outside Yellowstone Park to await the animals' forced exit. Sport hunting, although legal, also took its toll. The sportsmen, after all, no less than the market hunters, sought out those elk whose strength and vitality were essential to maintaining the herd's reproductive capacity.[27]

Because scenic phenomena, not wildlife, inspired Yellowstone National Park, no one at the time seriously considered laying out its boundaries to protect both resources. Still, even if the fate of the elk had been foreseen, it is doubtful Congress would have added Jackson Hole to the national park in 1872. The valley floor is an average of 2,000 feet below Yellowstone; at this elevation grazing and agriculture are still practical, and certainly would have preempted any claim that a wildlife preserve was Jackson Hole's legitimate role. Indeed, as late as 1898 Congress shelved a report by Charles D. Walcott, director of the U.S. Geological Survey, and Dr. T. S. Brandegee, a San Diego botanist, which called for the extension of Yellowstone Park southward to include the upper portion of the valley and most of the neighboring Thorofare Basin. The men noted that by restricting the addition to the northern segment of Jackson Hole, few vested interests should feel threatened, inasmuch as most of the settlers and ranchers had been drawn to the southern end of the valley because of its superior fertility. Besides, the territory to be included was primarily government land as part of the Teton Forest Preserve.[28]

It soon became evident, nevertheless, that preserving access to the forest reserve was reason enough for valley residents to oppose the plan. As a concession to local needs, settlers and ranchers were allowed to graze their livestock, hunt, gather fenceposts, and cut firewood in the forest. For obvious reasons few of the tenants wanted to forego these privileges for the sake of Yellowstone Park. Accordingly, in 1902 approximately sixty residents of Jackson Hole petitioned against the extension as another infringement on their right of entry to the public domain. It remained for the state of Wyoming, in 1905, to declare a large portion of the region a game preserve and curtail the poaching of the elk.[29] However, in the absence of a comprehensive approach to the issue of development in Jackson Hole itself, the effectiveness of the measure was compromised from the start.

The lines were now drawn for one of the longest and most emotional battles in the history of the national park idea. Over the next several years the tragedy of the elk occasionally focused attention on the fate of Jackson Hole. Then, in July 1916, Stephen T. Mather and Horace Albright briefly visited the valley with a party of government officials. It was this trip, Albright later recalled, that convinced him, Mather, and their associates that "this region must become a park" to protect forever its "beauty and wilderness charm."[30] The following winter he and Mather "looked up the status of Jackson Hole lands and tried to formulate some feasible park plans." Predictably, their own proposal strayed little from the earlier recommendation of Walcott and Brandegee to extend Yellowstone National Park southward into Jackson Hole. After all, Mather himself noted, the northern half of the valley "can never be put to any commercial use," while "every foot naturally belongs to Yellowstone Park."[31]

Opponents, however, were still not convinced by the worthless-lands argument. The Park Service agreed to preserve grazing privileges in the addition, and, true to Mather's word, pursued only the inclusion of Jackson Hole's least desirable portion. Yet on February 18, 1919, the extension bill died in the Senate under objections raised by John F. Nugent of Idaho. Speaking on behalf of state sheepmen and cattlemen, Nugent claimed that certain grasslands to be included in the park would not, as promised, in fact be open to grazing.[32] Once again the mere possibility that a national park would jeopardize commercial ventures had been enough to kill the Yellowstone extension.[33]

The controversy now took a new twist. Although the skepticism of the ranchers had been foreseen, an unexpected source of opposition suddenly appeared. Its target—a road-building program endorsed by the National Park Service—also came as quite a surprise. In part to counter objections raised against the economic impact of the Yellowstone extension, the Park Service had gone on record in support of an enlarged and improved system of roads for Jackson Hole, including a direct link with the Cody Road (Yellowstone's east entrance) via Thorofare Basin. "In Washington we were constantly impressed by visiting callers from the West with the demand for more and better roads," Horace Albright explained later in justifying the decision. It followed that the people of Jackson Hole would be thinking along much the same lines. "We even put this tentative idea on a map, believing that it was what Wyoming wanted. How many times later," he confessed, "we wished that map had never seen the light of day."[34]

But although the proposal was tentative, as Albright noted, publication of the map in the Park Service's *Annual Report* strongly implied that the roads would go through.[35] In August 1919, Albright, now superintendent of Yellowstone, returned to Jackson Hole to attend a public meeting called to discuss the Yellowstone extension. His hope of reenlisting support for the project evaporated in a storm of opposition.

Behind the hostility of those present at the gathering, he determined, were the dude ranchers. As opposed to traditional ranching interests, who by and large welcomed the opportunities opened by public-works projects, the dude ranchers favored precisely the opposite flavor of the West. Like their clients, most were not native Westerners, but well-to-do Easterners who escaped to Jackson Hole to run their businesses during the tourist season. It was they, Albright reported, "who felt that park status meant modern roads, overflowing of the country with tourists, and other encroachments of civilization that would rob it of its romance and charm."[36] They even "refused to abide by the daylight-saving law," he complained to Director Mather in October. "They do not want automobiles . . . they will not have a telephone; and they insist that their mail should not be delivered more than three times a week." His veiled disgust was understandable; the National Park Service was charged with the task of making it easier to see the West rather than more difficult. Providing access to the national parks still had its serious side as well. Without greater public support for the reserves brought about by increased visitation, none might continue to exist. "One must, of course, feel a certain sympathy for these people who are trying to get away from the noise and worries of city life and go as far into the wilds as possible," Albright conceded, "but they can not expect to keep such extraordinary mountain regions as the Tetons and their gem lakes . . . all for themselves."[37]

In view of the determined opposition of the dude ranchers to more development in the Jackson Hole country, however, the Park Service reassessed its priorities. "Should the extension of the park be approved," Stephen T. Mather stressed hardly a year after Albright's run-in with valley residents, "it would be the policy of this service to abstain from the construction or improvement of any more roads than now exist in the region. . . ." Mather further stated it to be his "firm conviction that a part of the Yellowstone country" likewise "should be maintained *as a wilderness* [italics added] for the ever-increasing numbers of people who prefer to walk and ride over trails in a region abounding in wild life." Moreover, as if to deny that the Park Service had, at the very least, encouraged a false impression about its commitment to the highway program, he would now go so far as to claim that any roads around Yellowstone Lake and across the Thorofare Basin "would mean the extinction of the moose." His overcompensation had a twofold purpose; first, it was obvious the Park Service had lost the trust of the dude ranchers in Jackson Hole. In addition to regaining their confidence, Mather also had to restore the credibility of the National Park Service as the agency of complete conservation. "I am so sure that this view is correct," he concluded, "that I would be glad to see an actual inhibition on new road building placed in the proposed extension bill, this proviso to declare that without the prior authority of Congress no new road project in this region should be undertaken."[38]

As testimony to his sincerity, he immediately extended the restriction against roads to other large parks, particularly Yosemite. The ban was not total; rather new roads must not be considered until old ones proved inadequate. Still, Mather insisted: "In the Yosemite National Park, as in all of the other parks, the policy which contemplates leaving large areas of high mountain country wholly undeveloped should be forever maintained."[39]

In 1926 there appeared another opportunity to follow through on his promise. After several years of delay and litigation, Congress was finally prepared to enlarge Sequoia National Park by taking in a substantial portion of the Sierra Nevada east of the Giant Forest, including Mount Whitney. Debate in the House of Representatives inevitably led to the question of developing the new section. The bill's sponsor, however, Henry E. Barbour of California, would hear none of it. "It is proposed to make this a trail park and keep it a trail park," he stressed. "It is now a trail park . . . ; there are no roads contemplated into this new area at this time." The bill itself underscored the point by providing "for the preservation of said park *in a state of nature* [italics added] so far as is consistent with the purposes of this Act."[40] Although the clause left substantial leeway for development, with the enlargement of Sequoia National Park came proof that complete conservation was winning converts, especially with regard to the placement of roads.

It was one thing, of course, to prohibit roads in the rugged back country of the national parks, where their construction was nearly impossible in the first place, and quite another to discourage highways where topography posed no obstacles. In this regard Horace Albright conceded that the Sierra Nevada and Jackson Hole were worlds apart. "Good roads for the hurrying motorist, on the one hand," he noted in discussing the complexity of the issue facing the valley, "and protection of the dude ranchers from invasion by automobiles, on the other, were foreseen as difficult problems soon to be faced." Valley residents traced the day of reckoning to 1923. By then "it seemed that road development might get entirely out of hand," Albright recalled. Struthers Burt, a partner of the famous Bar BC dude ranch, agreed. Each year "the increasing hordes of automobile tourists" swept Jackson Hole "like locusts." Few motorists had "the slightest perception . . . that there existed other and equally important philosophies and vital, fundamental human desires." The charge foreshadowed Burt's own change of heart toward the National Park Service. "In the beginning I was bitterly opposed to park extension, and remained so for some time," he admitted. "The advent of the automobile alone would have changed my mind. . . ."[41]

Finally convinced of at least Horace Albright's sincerity, in July 1923 the dude ranchers invited him back to Jackson Hole to discuss the feasibility of protecting it as a living outdoor museum or recreation area. The threat of public-works projects sponsored by the U.S. Forest Service and the Bureau of Reclamation added to the sense of urgency in the valley over auto-related commercialism. By 1916, for example, the bureau had increased the surface area of Jackson Lake approximately 50 percent through damming of its outlet. As the water level rose, piles of dead trees and other debris littered the shoreline for miles. Despite the destruction, irrigationists backed the bureau's search for other reservoir sites, including the wilderness lakes surrounding Jackson Hole. Whether such schemes could be thwarted by an outdoor museum or its equivalent was highly questionable; who, for example, would invest in such a proposal? Still, Albright went along with the dude ranchers with the hope of eventually substituting a project more likely to succeed.[42]

Three years later, in July 1926, an opportunity presented itself in the form of Mr. and Mrs. John D. Rockefeller, Jr. While they and their sons vacationed in Yellowstone, Albright suggested the family round out its stay with a visit to Jackson Hole. He further offered to escort them in person. Naturally he anticipated their reaction to the assortment of gas stations, billboards, dancehalls, and other tourist traps now dotting that remarkable valley. On the spot Rockefeller requested that Albright forward him a list of the affected properties and estimates for the cost of restoring them to their former condition. Late that fall, however, when Albright hand-delivered the data requested by the philanthropist to his New York City office, Rockefeller surprised him by outlining an even more ambitious plan. While Albright's proposal called for spending approximately $250,000 to acquire only the land nearest the mountains, Rockefeller wished to invest four times that amount to purchase and restore private property on both sides of the Snake River. Understandably jubilant, Albright quickly compiled the necessary additions.[43]

To expedite the program, in 1927 Rockefeller and his staff, on advice from Albright, incorporated the Snake River Land Company out of Salt Lake City, Utah. The objective was to conceal Rockefeller's identity to ward off speculation in Jackson Hole once the purchasing began. Although the philanthropist intended to pay a fair price for the land, he agreed that knowledge of his interest in the valley would make completion of his program extremely difficult, if not impossible. Not until 1930, after most of the key real estate had been acquired, did Rockefeller's sponsorship of the Snake River Land Company, and his intention to deed its holdings to the National Park Service, become public information.[44]

All told, Rockefeller purchased approximately 35,000 acres, nearly 22 per cent of that portion of Jackson Hole eventually accorded park status. By February 1929 his subordinates had also persuaded President Calvin Coolidge to withdraw most of the adjoining tracts of public domain from entry. This, too, was a crucial victory, since, without the withdrawals, nothing legally prevented speculators, or those farmers and ranchers just bought out, from filing new homesteads as fast as Rockefeller acquired their existing holdings in the valley.[45]

But while he intended his gift to be free of cost to the nation, he could hardly have realized that Congress would not accept it for another twenty years. Once more the roadblock to preservation was the issue of "uselessness." Congress chose sides in 1929, when it set apart only the Teton Mountains as a national park. The protection of such rugged terrain, of course, could not seriously be considered a threat to any established economic interest. The park also gave preservationists the appearance of a victory, when in fact only those who still looked for monuments were satisfied. Fritiof M. Fryxell, for example, a geologist, could not have been more pleased with the result. "The peaks—these are the climax and, after all, the *raison de'etre* of this park," he maintained. "For the Grand Teton National Park is preeminently the national park of mountain peaks—*the Park of Matterhorns*."[46] Congress itself saw no reason to make the reserve contiguous with Yellowstone; similarly, Jackson Hole was excluded. Indeed, Jenny, Leigh, and String lakes, which hug the mountains' eastern flank, were just about the only level land in the entire 150-square-mile preserve. Its western boundary also excluded major watersheds, forests, and wildlife habitat by paralleling the tips of the peaks themselves, well above timberline. Yet even at this altitude Congress felt free to change its mind. Specifically, when the U.S. Forest Service protested that the northern third of the range contained asbestos deposits, Congress deleted the entire area prior to approving the enabling act.[47]

Granted, even without this section, no park was more magnificent. Yet only if monumentalism had been the overriding concern of preservationists could all of them have joined Fritiof M. Fryxell in praising the reserve as established. Since the inception of the movement to extend Yellowstone south-ward to include Jackson Hole and its neighboring environments, protection of the mountains themselves had been advanced as only one element of the need to preserve the region in its greater diversity. Without Jackson Hole, the park was simply a mountain retreat, too high, too cold, and too barren for all but summer recreation.

The one concession to complete conservation—a ban against any new roads, permanent camps, or hotels in the park—had also been challenged and revised accordingly. As initially worded, the clause opened with a declaration stating it to be the "intent of Congress to retain said park in its original *wilderness* character" [italics added]. The preface was a concession to the dude ranchers, whose opposition to the Park Service over the issue of roads had helped kill the Yellowstone extension in its original form. Yet some in Congress charged that the provision might now exclude trails from the park. As a result, all reference to "wilderness" was dropped. Even when an amendment exempted new trails from the ban against tourist facilities, the word "wilderness" was not reinstated in the clause.[48] The term, after all, was coming to stand for the ultimate commitment to total preservation. This might be going too far, even in the Tetons.

The ruggedness of the mountains was some guarantee total preservation must be followed, if only by default. Yet without Jackson Hole the test of the nation's commitment to complete conservation was meaningless. A park that preserved itself was, by its very nature, inadequate for protecting all forms of wildlife and plant life. Imposing landscapes were coming to be seen as but one component of the national park idea. The movement to set aside the Tetons themselves had evolved as part of the campaign to provide sanctuary for the Yellowstone elk and their winter range in Jackson Hole. As Struthers Burt put it, until the valley itself was fully protected, there remained the distinct possibility that "the tiny Grand Teton National Park, which is merely a strip along the base of the mountains, [will be] marooned like a necklace lost in a pile of garbage."[49]

Given the failure of Congress in establishing Grand Teton National Park to break with tradition by including the woodlands and sagebrush flats of Jackson Hole, it remained for approval of park status for the Florida Everglades to confirm the nation's pledge to total preservation.[50] Isle Royale National Park, in Michigan, authorized in 1931, preceded approval of the Everglades by three years; but although Isle Royale was advocated as a wilderness and wildlife preserve, nothing within its enabling act actually bound the National Park Service to manage the reserve for these values. Its supporters just as often singled out the island's "boldness" and "ruggedness"—in short, its topographic as opposed to its wilderness qualities.[51]

Jackson Hole, by virtue of its proximity to the Grand Tetons, might also be defended solely as the mountains' "frame." The Everglades had no dramatic geology to distract the American public from preservationists' sincere belief that its primitive conditions alone qualified the region for national park status. Rather then as now, the Everglades was best described as "a river of grass." As such it lacks a distinct channel with banks on either side; in reality its "streambed" averages forty miles in width. Its flow arcs southward from Lake Okeechobee—in the south-central portion of the state—to the tidal estuaries and mangrove forests of the Gulf Coast and Florida Bay, some 100 miles distant. The entire drop in elevation is but seventeen feet, barely two inches per mile. But although the current moves slowly, indeed almost imperceptibly, the lack of visible runoff is misleading as to its importance. The creep of the water, for example, allows much of it to seep underground, where it may be stored for future use by the region's large, invisible aquifers. Similarly, nearer the coast, the flow buttresses the tidelands against invasions of brackish seawater, whose salinity might jeopardize certain species of flora and fauna.[52]

The present water cycle began approximately 5,000 years ago, when glacier-fed seas last ebbed and exposed the southern Florida peninsula. The rainy season between June and October rejuvenated the flow; in wetter years Lake Okeechobee itself often spilled, providing the Everglades' "source." Storms moving in off the ocean contributed additional runoff, until, by late fall, the sawgrass filled to a depth of between one and two feet. Hurricanes and drought broke the rhythm periodically, but they were temporary conditions and did little to endanger the long-range survival of the plant and animal populations. The threat of permanent interference awaited twentieth-century profiteers, who disrupted, perhaps irreparably, the drainage pattern of which the Everglades had long been a crucial link.[53]

The birdlife was first to suffer. By the turn of the century feathers had become the rage of women's fashion, and southern Florida, with its teeming populations of American and snowy egret, was a prized source. Year after year the market hunters shot out the rookeries. To thwart the poachers, responsible sportsmen and conservationists organized the Association of Audubon Societies, after the famed nineteenth-century naturalist John James Audubon. The murder of one of its wardens by poachers in 1905, and the slaying of another three years later, aroused public opinion and helped speed legislation outlawing traffic in feathers. Yet the preservationists' victory was by no means complete. Denied a steady source for plumage, many hunters merely switched to poaching alligators, whose hides were also in growing demand for belts, shoes, luggage, and handbags. Not until 1969, despite the loss of 100,000 animals per year throughout the South as early as 1930, was the alligator fully protected by Congress as an endangered species.[54]

Farming the Everglades proved equally threatening to the longevity of its ecosystem. Because the mucklands immediately south of Lake Okeechobee were especially rich, after World War I construction began on a series of canals, locks, and dams to check its seasonal overflows and drain the excess water to the sea. Yet these early precautions against flooding were woefully inadequate. In 1926, and again in 1928, severe hurricanes spilled the lake at a cost of 2,300 lives. The toll overshadowed the widespread flooding, crop, and property damage. Conceivably, no time would have been more appropriate to conclude that the Everglades should not have been settled in the first place. Instead, in keeping with the nation's overriding utilitarian philosophy, most of the survivors looked upon the disasters as proof of the need for even greater control over Lake Okeechobee. In 1929, therefore, the Florida legislature authorized the state to cooperate with the federal government in placing a much more efficient system of holding basins and drainage canals throughout the region. During the next thirty years this network was continually expanded, largely under the auspices of the U.S. Army Corps of Engineers.[55]

And so, as with Jackson Hole, the time when the Everglades might have been set aside intact had slipped away. Once again preservationists could only hope to stem the tide of development. But that they would even make the attempt in the Everglades marked a radical about-face for the national park idea. Devoid of topographical uniqueness, no region lent more convincing testimony to the growing popularity of complete conservation. Dr. Willard Van Name, for example, associate curator of the American Museum of Natural History, spoke for a growing number of preservationists when he asked if the absence of "Yosemite Valleys or Yellowstone geysers in the eastern States" was all that prevented the enjoyment and protection of "such beauties of nature as we do have. National Parks have other important purposes besides preserving especially remarkable natural scenery," he stated, "notably that of preserving our rapidly vanishing wild life." In this regard no portion of the East loomed as a more logical candidate for national park status than the Everglades. "The movement to establish an Everglades National Park in Florida appeals strongly to me," Gilbert Grosvenor, president of the National Geographic Society, also testified. "Mount Desert [Acadia], Shenandoah, Great Smoky, and Everglades—what a magnificent string of Eastern Seaboard parks that would make!"[56]

The formation of the Tropic Everglades National Park Association in 1928 officially launched the campaign. Over the next six years the association's founder and chairman, Ernest F. Coe, a Miami activist, worked tirelessly to introduce the

Everglades to influential congressmen, newspaper editors, journalists, scholars, and other park devotees. To both aid the effort and lend it credibility in scientific circles, Coe invited Dr. David Fairchild, an internationally recognized botanist with the U.S. Department of Agriculture, to head the association as president.[57]

Establishment of the citizen's group provided a sounding board for the inevitable debate regarding the suitability of the Everglades for national park status. Indeed, as Ernest Coe and Dr. Fairchild soon discovered, not all preservationists were in fact agreed that a national park in the region would be desirable. Some suggested that if the area warranted protection, a state park would be more than adequate. Still others advocated a botanical reserve of some sort, perhaps, but not necessarily under federal jurisdiction. Few rumblings of dissent, however, were more disconcerting than the opposition of William T. Hornaday, long hailed as one of America's leading spokesmen for wildlife conservation. In the Everglades "I found mighty little that was of special interest, and absolutely nothing that was picturesque or beautiful," he asserted, recalling visits dating back to 1875; "both then and now, . . . a swamp is a swamp." On a more charitable note, he conceded that "the saw-grass Everglades Swamp is not as ugly and repulsive as some other swamps that I have seen"; still he concluded: "it is yet a *long ways* from being fit to elevate into a national park, to put alongside the magnificent array of scenic wonderlands that the American people have elevated into that glorious class."[58]

Especially in light of his own lifelong commitment to wildlife conservation, Hornaday's rejection of an Everglades national park on the basis of its physical shortcomings underscored how fixed the image of parks as a visual experience had become in the American mind. It followed that Ernest Coe, Dr. Fairchild, and their supporters had to break down the barriers of that perception before they could educate the nation to understand the Everglades' own brand of uniqueness. The process of determining its suitability for national park status took the form of several so-called "special" investigations. The first, conducted by the National Park Service in February 1930, observed the requirements of a bill passed by Congress under the auspices of Senator Duncan U. Fletcher of Florida. Director Horace M. Albright led the inspection; the first day out the party circled above the proposed park in a blimp provided by the Goodyear Dirigible Corporation. "I believe," Albright reported, "that the old idea of an Everglades with dense swamps and lagoons festooned with lianas, and miasmatic swamps full of alligators and crocodiles and venomous snakes was entirely shattered." In their stead the group found forests, rivers, and plains supporting "many thousands of herons and other wild waterfowl." Each member of the investigation could well imagine, he concluded, "what an exceedingly interesting educational exhibit this entire area would be if by absolute protection these birds would multiply and the now rare species come back into the picture for the enjoyment of future generations."[59]

Toward this end the Albright committee reached accord that the Everglades would best be protected as a national park. "Before leaving I sounded out the opinion of the individual members," he assured the secretary of the interior, "and all were agreed that all standards set for national park creation would be fully justified in the establishment of this new park."[60] Skeptics might still be found elsewhere, however. Those in Congress, for example, succeeded in stalling the park bill another four years. The suspicion of the National Parks Association, chaired by Stephen Mather's former assistant, Robert Sterling Yard, also frustrated Albright, Ernest F. Coe, and their associates. In 1919 Mather had sponsored the formation of the National Parks Association in an effort to secure a private, nonpartisan watchdog for national park standards. Yard, whom Mather endorsed as first president, still took his job seriously—perhaps, Albright now believed, too seriously. For example, the National Parks Association would not, under any circumstances, accept pre-existing man-made structures, especially dams and reservoirs, in new national parks. Yard's reasoning was well-intentioned; like most preservationists he feared setting a precedent which would lead to another Hetch

Hetchy. Might not their acceptance of extant dams, for example, be interpreted by Congress as an admission of its right to dam Hetch Hetchy in the first place? Yard's insistence on absolute purity, of course, left little room for compromise. Indeed, not only was he skeptical of the qualifications of the Everglades for national park status,[61] he also unequivocally opposed the enlargement of Grand Teton National Park for fear the inclusion of Jackson Lake—dammed as early as 1906—would be misconstrued as proof of the legitimacy of such projects in any reserve.[62]

The preponderance of private land throughout the Everglades gave rise to similar doubts. Some opponents even argued that the national park project was simply a scheme advanced by real-estate promoters to exaggerate the value of their holdings. Such skepticism in part led to a second major investigation of the Everglades under the auspices of the National Parks Association. Other sponsoring agencies included the American Civic Association, the American Society of Landscape Architects, and the National Association of Audubon Societies. It was therefore fitting that the principal investigator for the survey would be Frederick Law Olmsted, Jr., whose authorship of key portions of the National Park Service Act of 1916 had won the respect of each of these groups. William P. Wharton, a naturalist, accompanied Olmsted; on January 18, 1932, following two weeks of personal exploration in the Everglades, they presented their findings to the trustees of the National Parks Association.

Both the thoroughness of the report and the reputation of its senior author finally convinced the National Parks Association of the worthiness of the Everglades for national park status. Without question, Olmsted and Wharton agreed, the region was unique. "What we were chiefly concerned to study in the Florida Everglades," they wrote, "was the validity or invalidity of doubts . . . as to whether the area is really characterized by qualities properly typical of our National Parks from the standpoint of scenery. . . ." The major preconception to be overcome was the belief that scenery must in all cases be defined as landscape. And "in a good deal of the region," the men stated, revealing the difficulty of breaking down their own prejudice, "the quality of the scenery is to the casual observer somewhat confused and monotonous." Visitors might compare the region to "other great plains," for example, whose scenic qualities were "perhaps rather subtle for the average observer in search of the spectacular." Yet even the topography of plains might be "simpler and bolder" in appearance. The scenery of the Everglades was better described as an emotional rather than a visual experience. Apart from landscape, it consisted "of beauty linked with a sense of power and vastness in nature." Granted, this indeed was scenery of the type "so different from the great scenes in our existing National Parks"; still, the "sheer beauty" of "the great flocks of birds, . . . the thousands upon thousands of ibis and herons flocking in at sunset," could be a sight "no less arresting, no less memorable than the impressions derived from the great mountain and canyon parks of the West."[63]

To further compensate for its lack of rugged terrain, the Everglades literally enthralled the visitor with its "sense of remoteness!" and "pristine wilderness." Foremost among the elements of the region to evoke this emotion was the mangrove forest bordering the coast. "It is a monotonous forest, in the sense that the coniferous forests of the north are monotonous." Yet "it is a forest not only uninhabited and unmodified by man," they noted, "but literally trackless and uninhabitable." Ten thousand people might boat through the region every day and "leave no track upon the forest floor. . . ." Again the average visitor might not yet grasp the essence of wilderness; still, even for him, the men repeated, the Everglades should "rank high among the natural spectacles of America" by virtue of its great wildlife populations alone.[64]

Admittedly, where it called attention to the quantity of animals involved, the Olmsted-Wharton report was a throwback to the past. Much as those who felt compelled to compare the wonders of the West and Europe to the inch, their own sense of the need to speak in superlatives about the Everglades suggests some degree of self-doubt that the region could in fact stand on its own merits. Still, to now justify a national park exclusively on the basis of wildlife, indeed, to defend wildlife itself as scenery regardless of its physical backdrop, revealed how dramatically the national park idea might depart from the standards held by the great majority of early park supporters.

As testimony to the depth of that transformation, the Everglades National Park Act specifically called for total preservation of the region. While the Olmsted-Wharton report addressed the policy in principle, setbacks such as the Jackson Hole controversy convinced defenders of the Everglades that the concept would not necessarily be practiced in the field. Accordingly, they were insistent that an appropriate clause be drafted and included in the park's enabling act. "Such opposition as has been evidenced among organizations to the Everglades Bill," Horace Albright's successor, Arno B. Cammerer, explained, in April 1934, "has been directed to the form of the bill and not to the project, and solely to the alleged insufficiency that the future wilderness character of the area was not fully provided for." On the basis of the Olmsted-Wharton report, the National Parks Association spearheaded the drive for enactment of the Everglades as a wilderness preserve. "I would not object to a restatement of this principle in an amendment to the bill," Secretary of the Interior Harold Ickes agreed, "if . . . such an amendment would not endanger its passage."[65]

Congressional approval of the bill as amended, on May 30, 1934, was seen by all concerned as a major victory for complete conservation. Indeed, how else could the park be interpreted, asked Ernest F. Coe—"it has no mountains, its highest elevation being less than eight feet above sea level?" Rather the "spirit" of Everglades National Park, in fact its very inspiration, he maintained, "is primarily the preservation of the primitive."[66] For the first time the language of park legislation had been unmistakably clear in committing the federal government to such management. Section 4 of the enabling act began: "The said area or areas shall be permanently reserved *as a wilderness*" [italics added]. Similarly, no development of the park to provide access to visitors must "interfere with the preservation intact of the unique flora and fauna and the essential primitive conditions." This clause alone, Coe noted, marked a momentous "evolution" in the character and standards of the national parks. In the provision was clear evidence of the growing respect for "natural ecological relations," of "that interlocking balanced relation between the animate and the inanimate world." The national parks "have much of interest in bold topography and other uniqueness," Dr. John K. Small of the New York Botanical Garden agreed. "Why not also have a unique area exhilarating by its lack of topography and charming by its matchless vegetation and animal life?"[67]

With the authorization of Everglades National Park, Congress answered on a positive note. Of course there were the usual preconditions. Most notably, as with Shenandoah, Great Smoky, Isle Royale, and similar projects, again it remained for the state of Florida and its friends to actually purchase the land for the park. Similarly, before Congress would make the reserve official, the property must be deeded over to the federal government with no strings attached. As a result, formal dedication of Everglades National Park did not come until 1947. Still, nothing during the interval affected its guiding purpose as a wilderness and wildlife preserve. To the contrary, as early as 1937 the federal government reaffirmed the precedent set forth in the Everglades with authorization of Cape Hatteras National Seashore, in North Carolina, "as a primitive wilderness." Except for certain areas best devoted to outdoor recreation, no portion of the park was to be administered in a manner "incompatible with the preservation of the unique flora and fauna" or the original "physiographic conditions."[68] Again nothing in the salt marshes and sand dunes of Cape Hatteras could be linked with monumentalism; like the Everglades, the first national seashore in the United States was the direct beneficiary of the distinctions advanced under the heading of "complete conservation." At Cape Hatteras the nation once more paid formal recognition to the virtues of protecting an ecosystem for its own sake. And, in time, the genre of parks begun astride the breakers of North Carolina blossomed into an impressive string of preserves along all of the nation's coasts.[69] None, to be sure, were national parks in the traditional sense; simply, if the national park idea was now to be truly representative of the American scene, tradition must make way for ecological reality.[70]

Everglades National Park was the all-important precedent. The sincerity of attempts to apply total preservation to existing national parks might still be discredited by their imposing topography. Totally devoid of the mileposts of cultural nationalism, the Everglades confirmed the depth of commitments to protect more than the physical environment. Granted, preservationists initially had trouble convincing themselves of the need to break with tradition. Gradually, however, as they closed ranks, for the first time new avenues of scenic protection became a real possibility. If any single doubt remained, it was the most enduring one of all. However the United States defined "conservation" or applied it to the national parks, could their friends make it stick?

7

Ecology Denied

A park is an artificial unit, not an independent biological unit with natural boundaries (unless it happens to be an island).

George M. Wright et al., 1933

The biotic associations in many of our parks are artifacts, pure and simple. They represent a complex ecologic history but they do not necessarily represent primitive America.

Leopold Committee, 1963

That total preservation was an afterthought of the twentieth century was nowhere more apparent than in the national parks. Although "complete conservation" assumed the protection of living landscapes as well as scenic wonders, each attempt to round out the parks as effective biological units proved far from successful. Traditional opponents of scenic preservation, led by resource interests and utilitarian-minded government agencies, still maintained that protection should be on a minimum scale only. To be sure, the reluctance of Congress to provide the parks an ecological as well as a scenic framework no longer could be laid to ignorance of the principles of plant and wildlife conservation. As early as 1933 the National Park Service publicized the need for broader management considerations in its precedent-breaking report, *Fauna of the National Parks of the United States.* Its authors,

George M. Wright, Ben H. Thompson, and Joseph S. Dixon, were experts on wildlife management, natural history, and economic mammalogy, respectively.[1] "Unfortunately," they said, setting the theme of their study, "most of our national parks are mountain-top parks," comprising but "a fringe around a mountain peak," a "patch on one slope of a mountain extending to its crest," or "but portions of one slope." Each reflected the placement of "arbitrary boundaries laid out to protect some scenic feature." Park boundaries, of course, were anything but arbitrary. It was not by accident, but by design that Congress refused to accept or retain parklands with known minerals, timber, and other natural resources. Still, regardless of the reasoning behind the exclusion of such areas, the disruption of living environments which resulted was no less complete. For example, the men concluded emphatically: "It is utterly impossible to protect animals in an area so small that they are within it only a portion of the year."[2]

Yellowstone, despite its great size, already served as a dramatic case in point. While the park appeared to be a wildlife refuge by virtue of its spacious boundaries, these in fact failed to compensate for the region's high altitude, on the average of 8,000 feet. Winter cold and snow still drove most of the large mammals, including the southern elk herd, to the shelter of valleys such as Jackson Hole. Yet not until 1950, following another prolonged and emotion-charged battle, was Grand Teton National Park enlarged along its eastern flank to take in a substantial remnant of the valley and its wildlife habitat.

Although far less spectacular than the Tetons themselves, the addition was crucial to the maintenance of a living landscape. *Fauna of the National Parks* addressed this growing tendency to distinguish between animate and inanimate scenery. "The realization is coming that perhaps our greatest natural heritage," rather "than just scenic features . . . is nature itself, with all its complexity and its abundance of life." For the first time Americans could admit that "awesome scenery" might in fact be sterile without "the intimate details of living things, the plants, the animals that live on them, and the animals that live on those animals." The enduring obstacle to sound ecological management in the national parks was the prior emphasis on setting aside purely scenic wonders. "The preponderance of unfavorable wildlife conditions," the authors continued, "is traceable to the insufficiency of park areas as self-contained biological units." In "creating the national parks a little square has been chalked across the drift of the game, and the game doesn't stay within the square." Indeed "not one park," the report concluded, "is large enough to provide year-round sanctuary for adequate populations of all resident species."[3]

To the example of Yellowstone could be added the Florida Everglades. As we have seen, in 1934 Congress authorized the southern extremity of the region as the first national park expressly designated for wilderness and wildlife protection. But because the reserve failed to include the entire ecosystem, it was vulnerable to outside development from the start. Over the years an ever-greater proportion of the natural flow of fresh water southward to the Everglades was disrupted and diverted to factories, farms, and subdivisions. Similarly, the failure of Congress to protect a complete watershed within Redwood National Park—established in 1968—soon loomed as the major threat to its integrity as well. Often loggers clear-cut the adjacent forests right up to the park boundaries, thus subjecting hundreds of great trees which supposedly had been "saved" to the threat of being undermined by flash floods and mudslides from the logging sites. No longer could Congress claim ignorance about the ecological needs of the region; the redwoods, like Jackson Hole and the Everglades, were simply the latest victims of political and economic reality.

Each new controversy mirrored its predecessors. Throughout the twentieth century, parks that came easily into the fold were still, to the best of knowledge at the time, economically valueless from the standpoint of their natural wealth, if not their potential for outdoor recreation. The Big Bend country of southwest Texas, for example, authorized as a national park in 1935, drew little objection. After all, the region was predominantly rugged, arid, inaccessible, and well removed from the centers of commercial activity in the state.[4]

The exceptions to the rule could still be expected to arouse far greater opposition. The proposed Olympic national park in Washington, with its prized stands of Douglas fir, red cedar, Western hemlock, and Sitka spruce, was a noted example. Preservationists had never been pleased with the reduction of the national monument by President Woodrow Wilson in 1915; accordingly, during the 1930s they mounted a campaign to restore the lost acreage to the monument and designate the whole a national park.

The heated exchange touched off by the plan is still recalled among the protagonists. From the outset preservationists insisted that Olympic National Park protect the unique rain forests of the Olympic peninsula, not merely, in the words of one supporter, "an Alpine area [of] little or no commercial value."[5] The vociferous opposition of the lumber industry and U.S. Forest Service made it inevitable that the bulk of the reserve would be so structured; still, in 1938 preservationists won a partial victory with the inclusion of several broad expanses of rain forest in the new Olympic National Park.[6]

The presence of the tracts, of course, provided a basis for opponents of the park to request reductions. During World War II, for example, the secretary of the interior was asked to open the reserve to logging to bolster the nation's war effort. When Germany and Japan surrendered, the lumber companies merely switched back to decrying the park as a hindrance to the region's economy. Throughout the 1950s they stepped up their campaign against the reserve; occasional challenges during the 1960s served further notice that preservation remained vulnerable to attack whenever and wherever resources in quantity could be found.[7]

The establishment of Kings Canyon National Park, California, lying immediately north of Sequoia National Park, was somewhat less controversial, but no less difficult to effect. As early as 1891 John Muir called for protection of the gorge in *Century Magazine*. The forty-nine-year delay in creating the reserve was a direct reflection of strong opposition by water-power interests. Only when it became evident that dams suffi-cient to meet the need for water storage and electricity could be located elsewhere did the protests against the park subside. Congress then agreed access into Kings Canyon should be limited and the region managed to insure the protection of its "wilderness character."[8] As a result, preservationists hailed Kings Canyon National Park as another milestone on the road to total preservation.

The status of Kings Canyon as part of the public domain, nonetheless, aided its protection. The same was true of Olym-pic National Park. To create each reserve the federal govern-ment merely transferred title to the land from the U.S. Forest Service to the National Park Service.[9] Areas such as Jackson Hole, where substantial inholdings of private land made the creation of parks considerably more complex, provided a more accurate assessment of the degree of commitment to preserva-tion on the part of Congress. By 1940 still another decade of controversy lay ahead before Jackson Hole would be linked with Grand Teton National Park. The mere mention of the valley now aroused development-conscious groups through-out the West to a fever pitch. Collectively they viewed John D. Rockefeller, Jr.'s philanthropy as the epitome of outside inter-ference and the threat of government by legislative decree. The issue was not merely his purchase of the land in secret, but that he fully intended to take all of it out of production by donating it to the National Park Service.

In 1943 the Jackson Hole controversy came to a head. Acting with the assurance that Rockefeller intended to divest his holdings in the valley within a year, on March 13 President Franklin D. Roosevelt proclaimed the entire north end of Jackson Hole a national monument. The bulk of the reserve had been carved from the Teton National Forest, which, when combined with the property of the Snake River Land Com-pany, brought the addition to approximately 221,000 acres.[10]

The storm of protest unleashed by Roosevelt's decree echoed throughout the Rocky Mountain West. "It is unthink-able that this hunters' paradise should be molested in any way," Congressman Frank A. Barrett of Wyoming said, leading the attack for dissolution of Jackson Hole National Monument. There followed the standard argument that the only "real" scenery in the region was the mountains themselves. "The addition of farm and ranch lands and sagebrush flats is not going to enhance the beauty of the Tetons." That, of course, was not the point, as Newton B. Drury, director of the Park Service, testified in rebuttal. The national park idea now rested on the preservation of animate scenery as well as natural wonders. "Visitors to national parks and monuments take great pleasure and obtain valuable education in viewing many species of strange animals living under natural conditions," Drury explained. Given the proximity of Jackson Hole to Grand Teton National Park, its proper role was not, as Representative Barrett argued, simply to provide that sense of freedom sought by hunters "to pursue and kill the big game that for so many years roamed our western plains." Rather Congress must insure the protection and restoration of all parts "of the wildlife picture" in the valley, including "the largest herd of elk in America."[11]

And yet, as had happened so often in the past, the identification of commercial uses for Jackson Hole, in this instance hunting, ranching, and farming, swayed Congress to the side of development. In December 1944 a bill introduced by Representative Barrett for dissolution of Jackson Hole National Monument easily passed both the House and Senate; only President Roosevelt's veto staved off abolishment of the reserve.[12]

Such a narrow defeat, however, foreshadowed the certainty of Barrett's attempt to revive the proposal. That the bill also failed its second time around could be laid to the length and intensity of the controversy. As both sides tired of the struggle, the prospects for a compromise measurably improved. With the assurance that an agreement would be reached, on December 16, 1949, John D. Rockefeller, Jr., deeded his property in Jackson Hole (its total cost of acquisition was roughly $1.5 million) over to the federal government. It remained for Congress to work out the details of the com-

promise legislation. With its approval by President Harry S
Truman on September 14, 1950, Jackson Hole National
Monument was abolished and rededicated as a portion of
Grand Teton National Park.[13]

Cosmetically the addition was a great success. What may
rightfully be called the "frame" of the Tetons, the sweeping
vistas across Jackson Hole, Jackson Lake, and the Snake River,
no longer could be marred by billboards, tourist traps, and
other forms of visual blight. Those preservationists who still
considered the park inadequate listed its failures in terms of
total conservation. As one illustration, Congress did not accept
the recommendation that Jackson Hole and the Tetons be
made contiguous with Yellowstone, their geographic partner.
In between lay a wide corridor managed by the U.S. Forest
Service, whose philosophy of management usually clashed
with the idea of preservation for its own sake. In effect, two
agencies were responsible for what was in fact a single ecosystem. Even more revealing, however, was a provision in the
park act that provided for sport shooting. To quiet the objections of sportsmen who opposed the addition of Jackson Hole
to Grand Teton National Park as an infringement on traditional recreation, periodically a specified number might enter
the preserve as "deputized rangers," ostensibly to assist the
Park Service in maintaining the elk herd at optimum size. Of
course the "deputies" were simply hunters under a less offensive title. Even to claim they would fill the void left by the
extinction of natural predators, and cull only the weaker and
diseased elk from the herd, was naive at best.[14]

Thanks to the efforts of wildlife conservationists, the
southern elk herd no longer was threatened with extinction,
but Grand Teton National Park was still not a self-contained
biological unit. In this regard the situation in the Florida
Everglades was also very frustrating. As set forth with authorization of the park in 1934, the Everglades could not in fact be
dedicated as a national park until the state had purchased the
land and deeded it to the federal government. Furthermore,
congressional opponents of the enabling act, who in 1934
heralded the project as a "snake swamp park," had won an

amendment to the legislation prohibiting any financial support from Congress for management of the Everglades until 1939.[15]

There were also setbacks in acquiring the land. To insure the biological integrity of the Everglades, the region had to be purchased promptly and completely. The act of 1934 called for the preservation "of approximately two thousand square miles . . . of Dade, Monroe, and Collier Counties." But not until 1957, fully ten years after dedication of the park, was the process of acquisition anywhere near complete. Even then protection of the region was not assured. Fully 93 percent of the Everglades proper was outside the preserve and earmarked for additional farms, water-storage basins, and flood-control projects. Similarly, the Big Cypress Swamp, another critical aquifer to the northwest, was beyond the park boundaries and thus still subject to intensive development.[16]

Few parks, as a result, were more fitting testimony to the cliché "too little, too late." Many had held from the start that the project should be closer to 2 million acres instead of its current 1.4 million. The title "Everglades" National Park was somewhat misleading. In reality the preserve included only a representative portion of the sawgrass province, and that with the least potential for development. Nearly as much of the park consisted of the mangrove forests, sloughs, and tidelands along the coast. Still, even this far south recharges of fresh water are essential for maintaining the life-cycle of the region. Wood ibis, for example, breed successfully only when high water facilitates the reproduction of large populations of fish close to the nesting sites. In addition, the physical substrata must be replenished periodically to hold back salt-laden intrusions from the sea.[17]

It followed that the placement of new dikes and drainage canals across the watershed north of the park jeopardized the entire preserve. In 1961 that possibility became a reality as a prolonged drought occurred throughout southern Florida. Peter Farb, a naturalist and writer, described his return to the Everglades at the height of the tragedy. "I found no Eden but rather a waterless hell under a blazing sun. Everywhere I saw

Everglades drying up, the last drops of water evaporating from water holes, creeks and sloughs."[18]

Drought by itself was not unusual to the region; what turned this particular dry spell into a crisis was the policy of withholding water from the Everglades for agricultural uses, or shunting it seaward to check the mere possibility of floods. In 1962 engineers completed yet another major link in the system of levees south of Lake Okeechobee. For the first time drainage into the park could be shut off completely. Three years later, for example, engineers lowered Lake Okeechobee in anticipation of a normal wet season by flushing more than 280,000 acre feet of water directly into the sea. Yet although the Everglades was starved for water, supplying the region still would have been impossible. A hydrologist, William J. Schneider, summed up the problem: "under the existing canal system" the excess water could not be moved from Lake Okeechobee to the national park "without also pouring it across the farmlands in-between."[19]

Although the farms prospered at the expense of the park, it was pointless to suggest they be destroyed to save it in return. Instead the Park Service took advantage of near-record precipitation in 1966 to work out an interim agreement with the Florida Board of Conservation and the U.S. Army Corps of Engineers for scheduled releases of water into the park from bordering conservation districts. The extent of damage to the region nevertheless continued to haunt preservationists: Would the water be enough, they asked, and in time? And what of the future? Only Congress might seal the agreement and guarantee water to the park, the historian, Wallace Stegner, concluded the following year. "Nobody else can. The most that anyone else can do is slow down the inevitable."[20]

Guaranteed protection of the Everglades depended on unified management of the entire ecosystem south of Lake Okeechobee. Long before realization of the national park, however, any hope of acquiring such a vast area—on the order of three to four times the size of Yellowstone—had vanished. Congress might have condemned the private land, of course;

indeed, for a nation now reaching toward outer space, the cost of such a park seemed infinitesimal by comparison. Yet it required little understanding of American culture to perceive that support for technological advancement was on a level all its own. Not until 1961, with authorization of Cape Cod National Seashore, Massachusetts, did the federal government relax its own requirement that national parks outside the public domain be purchased by the states or private philanthropists. Before Congress might agree to extend the power of eminent domain to regions of the magnitude of the Everglades, however, the traditions and values of the United States would have to undergo a truly revolutionary reappraisal.

So far Isle Royale National Park, in Lake Superior, had come closest to the ideal ecological preserve by virtue of its island status, isolation, and nearly complete ownership by the federal government. But Isle Royale was to remain the classic exception. For a time during the 1960s, it seemed the retention of an entire, integral ecosystem within a single national park in the West might be accomplished in the California coast redwoods. The trees sweep down to the sea in a narrow band from the Oregon border south to Monterey Bay. Prior to white settlement, pure and mixed stands of coast redwood covered approximately two million acres, roughly the equivalent of Yellowstone National Park. In river valleys facing the coast, a combination of rich alluvial soil, ocean rains, and blanketing fog often propels many specimens to heights well above 300 feet (the present record is 367 feet). With age many of the trees also broaden at the base, commonly attaining diameters of between 10 and 15 feet. Inland the giants give way to relatives of moderate size and species of lower moisture-dependence. Yet even here, what a redwood lacks in girth and height is more than compensated for by its color and grace.[21]

During the closing third of the nineteenth century, a similar assessment had been enough to win national park status for its distant counterpart, the Sierra redwood. Loggers knew beforehand, of course, that Sierra redwood was so brittle the trees often shattered when toppled to the ground. Coast redwood, in marked contrast, turned out to be lightweight, pest-resistant, and highly durable. In short, its quality as lumber was superior. To forestall the inevitable assault against the species, as early as 1852 a California assemblyman, H. A. Crabb, called for the withdrawal of "all public lands upon which the Redwood is growing." Not surprisingly, the plan went nowhere. In 1879 Secretary of the Interior Carl Schurz resurrected a much reduced version of Crabb's proposal, one calling for the protection of a mere 46,000 acres of the trees. But again the effort was to no avail. Not until 1901, with the establishment of Big Basin Redwoods State Park, near Santa Cruz, were several major groves of the great trees spared from the logger's axe.[22]

Meanwhile, aided by weak land laws and the almost total absence of their enforcement, private claimants had defrauded the federal government of nearly 100 percent of the entire redwood region. Now properties once parkland for the taking would have to be repurchased at considerable expense. The state took the first initiative with the creation of Big Basin, in Santa Cruz County. In 1908 a California Congressman, William Kent, and his wife donated another major grove to the federal government. This was a 295-acre expanse beneath Mt. Tamalpais, just north of San Francisco. The Kents' only preconditions were that the land be managed as a park and named in honor of their friend, John Muir. President Theodore Roosevelt gladly complied with both terms and proclaimed the tract Muir Woods National Monument.[23]

Congress itself still had no intention of repossessing large portions of the redwoods, either for parks or national forests. As with Muir Woods, the initiative for protection of the trees fell largely to private groups and individuals. The Save-the-Redwoods League, organized in 1918, assumed leadership in the private sector. At first league members were committed to "a National Redwood Park." In the face of persistent congressional indifference to the proposal, however, they agreed lands purchased by the group should be donated to California for management as state parks on the order of Big Basin. By 1964 state park holdings of virgin redwood totalled 50,000 acres, thanks to the efforts of the league, John D. Rockefeller, Jr., and numerous other philanthropists large and small. In fact, of the $16 million used to establish redwood parks, better than 50 percent had been subscribed by members of the Save-the-Redwoods League.[24]

From north to south, the league gave priority to rounding out five projects—Jedediah Smith, Del Norte Coast, Prairie Creek, Humboldt, and Big Basin state parks. At first the league concentrated on purchasing the low-lying river flats and nearby benchlands, which supported the largest of the trees. As more of the giants were acquired, the focus of protection shifted to forests upslope and upstream. The league admitted to prospective members that these areas contained fewer of the "cathedral-like groves," those "stretching back into the centuries and forging a noble link with the past." But no longer was monumentalism the only perspective at stake. Logging damage adjacent to the monumental groves underscored to the league the futility of trying to save the redwoods without acquiring complete watersheds wherever possible. For example, severe flooding along Bull Creek in Humboldt State Park during the winter of 1955–56 toppled 300 of its largest redwoods and undermined an additional 225. Although preservationists conceded that record rainfall was a major contributing factor, as much of the damage, they maintained, could be laid to the effects of clear-cutting the forest adjacent to the park. With no trees or groundcover to check the rush of water down the slopes, the torrent swept on, gathering force from suspended mud and debris. When the crest finally subsided, better than 15 percent of Humboldt Park's primeval, bottomland growth lay heaped and tangled along the banks of Bull Creek.[25]

Awareness of the need to provide the redwoods an ecological framework based on the security of major watersheds reawakened serious discussion about a redwood national park. Left to private philanthropy alone the costs of such a project were far too great. Newton B. Drury, former Park Service director, and now secretary of the Save-the-Redwoods League, took stock of the enormity of the task. "It is recognized that even when all the spectacular cathedral-like stands of Redwoods along the river bottoms and the flats have been acquired, the lands surrounding them must be preserved for administrative and protective reasons." Preservationists now faced the challenge of "rounding out complete areas, involving basins and watersheds in their entirety."[26] As justification for this approach, the league recalled the flooding of Bull Creek. "The big lesson from the tragedy," another environmentalist, Russell D. Butcher, stated in pleading for Congress to intervene, "is the importance of protecting not only the particular scenic-scientific park features, in this case the unsurpassed stands of coast redwoods, but of bringing under some degree of control the surrounding, ecologically-related lands—the upper slopes of the same watershed."[27]

Mill Creek, within and adjacent to Jedediah Smith and Del Norte Coast state parks, had a financial edge. A national park here required $56 million as opposed to a minimum of nearly three times that amount along Redwood Creek, adjoining Prairie Creek Redwoods State Park.[28] In deference to these figures, the Save-the-Redwoods League endorsed the Mill Creek watershed as the best site for national park status. In 1964, however, the Sierra Club, dismayed by the league's conservatism, quoted a study by the National Park Service which concluded that Redwood Creek was indeed the superior location. Despite the report, President Lyndon B. Johnson, Secretary of the Interior Stewart L. Udall, and the National Park Service opted early for Mill Creek as the alternative most likely to receive congressional approval in time to forestall the threat of additional logging damage.[29] Disheartened, the Sierra Club took its case to the public in a series of controversial advertisements. "Mr. President," an example published in 1967 began: "There is one great forest of redwoods left on earth; but the one you are trying to save isn't it. . . . Meanwhile they are cutting down both of them."[30]

The irony of the crisis was the degree to which the preservationists' once popular imagery of the redwoods as "monuments" could now be turned against the advancement of ecological conservation. By far the most common rebuttal to either project took the form of statements to the effect that the best *individual* trees already had been set aside by the state; protection of the groves as a whole was therefore pointless. In this vein Governor Ronald Reagan of California himself reportedly remarked: "If you've seen one redwood tree, you've seen them all." Such statements implied that Americans in truth looked upon the redwoods much as the Grand Canyon, Old Faithful, or other "wonders." Setting aside the phenomenon by itself, or merely a representative sample of it, would be more than adequate. Lumber companies and their workers similarly attacked the park proposal by arguing that the area's cool, damp climate discouraged tourism in the first place. As for protection of the redwoods and their watersheds, that, too, was best left to industry officials. Surely, they concluded, their long-term investments in mills and other capital improvements testified to their commitment to practice sound environmental conservation.[31]

The point of contention was the breadth of that commitment. Where it failed to include the protection of old-growth redwoods, for example, or the avoidance of widespread damage to watersheds prior to the reestablishment of second-growth stands, preservationists remained unconvinced. In either case, once more they found the economic rationales against the national park impossible to overcome effectively. As approved in October 1968, the reserve contained neither the Mill Creek nor Redwood Creek watersheds in their entirety. Instead, Congress used the three existing state parks in the region as a core, then joined them together with narrow bands of land added to their peripheries. Accordingly, conformity of the national park to area watersheds was literally nonexistent. Of the 30,000 acres acquired to link the California parks, moreover, only 10,000 were previously unprotected virgin forest.[32]

The affected lumber companies received $92 million. Congress further authorized the exchange of 14,000 acres of government redwoods—the only such parcel then in federal ownership—for other corporate holdings within the projected park. Finally, Congress restricted cutting trees adjacent to the reserve only to the *possible* imposition of a ban against logging within a narrow buffer zone no more than 800 feet across.[33]

With this concession, preservationists might well conclude that the real victors in the controversy were the lumber companies. To allow logging so close to the national park defeated the very purpose that had guided the campaign since the tragedy of Bull Creek. It was argued, of course, that no national park in the twentieth century realistically could include everything its supporters might want. Still, the Sierra Club insisted, even higher estimates for the park on Redwood Creek—in the neighborhood of $200 million—were but a fraction of a single moon shot or segment of interstate highway. To the Sierra Club the issue was not whether the United States could afford the redwoods, but whether or not it wanted them preserved intact. "History will think it most strange," a club advertisement bitterly concluded, "that Americans could afford the Moon and $4 billion airplanes, while a patch of primeval redwoods—not too big for a man to walk through in a day—was considered beyond its means."[34]

The failure of the park as established to guarantee even the future of the world's tallest trees only reinforced the skepticism of the Sierra Club and its supporters. In 1963 a team of surveyors enlisted by the National Geographic Society discovered the giants on private land beside Redwood Creek. The following year news of their find inspired a lead article in *National Geographic* and aroused considerable interest.[35] But although discovery of the big trees influenced establishment of the national park, they were included only by virtue of a narrow corridor of land paralleling both sides of the streambed. Indeed, no portion of the reserve more graphically displayed the degree of gerrymandering involved in laying out the park to the specifications of the lumber industry. On both sides of the "thumb" or "worm," as the strip came to be known, the cutting of redwoods continued unabated. In 1975 park officials predicted the worst. With the advent of the rainy season, it appeared the tall trees would be toppled by runoff and mudslides from the nearby logging sites. The grove was still standing two years later, but neither the president, secretary of

thc interior, or the courts had yet intervened to stop the loggers. To the contrary, a state official confessed to reporters,
odds the trees would survive were still "very low."[36]

With its prized possessions thus jeopardized, Redwood
National Park testified to the entrenchment of those shortcomings identified in 1933 by George M. Wright, Ben H.
Thompson, and Joseph S. Dixon in their study, *Fauna of the
National Parks of the United States*. In the fate of the "worm"
was recent proof of their assessment that few national parks
provided for the broader, more intricate needs of biological
conservation. Indeed, scientific reports kept drawing the same
conclusions. In 1963, for example, a team of distinguished
scientists chaired by A. Starker Leopold, a zoologist of the
University of California at Berkeley, released its own appraisal
of the ecology picture, *Wildlife Management in the National
Parks*. "The major policy change which we would recommend
to the National Park Service," the Leopold Committee advised, "is that it recognize the enormous complexity of
ecologic communities and the diversity of management procedures required to preserve them." In 1967 yet another
statement of the problem appeared, *Man and Nature in the
National Parks*, by F. Fraser Darling and Noel D. Eichhorn.
"We start from the point of view that the national park idea is a
major and unique contribution to world culture by the United
States." Still, they could do little more than uncover new
evidence to vindicate their predecessors' findings. "We have
the uncomfortable feeling," they wrote, concurring with the
Leopold Committee, "that such members of the National Park
Service as have a high ecological awareness are not taking a
significant part in the formulation of policy." The statement
was hardly cause for optimism; still, Darling and Eichhorn
were confident park management could be steered in the
proper direction.[37]

The future of the national parks, however, was actually in
the hands of Congress more than the Park Service. For the
reserves to be managed as biological units, Congress first must
provide them with enough land. Its reluctance to do so said as
much about national priorities in the 1960s as when the park

idea was realized. From Jackson Hole to the Everglades to the redwoods, park boundaries were silent but firm testimony to the limitations long imposed on complete conservation in the United States. If studies by groups such as the Leopold Committee merely seemed repetitious of earlier findings, the fault lay elsewhere. Simply, Congress had not yet heeded past insight and rounded out at least a few of the parks to conform to the realities of the environment, not just the dictates of the economy.

8

Schemers and
Standard Bearers

> Congress (and the public which elects it) can always be
> expected to hesitate longer over an appropriation to ac-
> quire or protect a national park than over one to build a
> highway into it. Yet there is nothing which so rapidly
> turns a wilderness into a reserve and a reserve into a
> resort.
>
> *Joseph Wood Krutch, 1957*

The attempt to round out the national parks as self-sufficient
biological units was to be joined by a struggle of equal, if not
greater magnitude. Despite passage of the National Park Service Act of 1916, the lack of principles to govern proper management of the reserves had been only partially overcome.
Once challenged by the growing popularity of outdoor recreation, the definition of national parks as both pleasuring
grounds and natural reserves seemed a contradiction in
terms. Mixed emotions following completion of the Yosemite
Valley Railroad in May 1907 served as an early barometer of
the coming debate. "They have built a railroad into the Yosemite," declared Edward H. Hamilton, correspondent for *Cos-*
mopolitan magazine. And some park enthusiasts, he admitted,
had taken the news "very much as if the Black Cavalry of
Commerce has been sent out to trample down the fairy rings."

Actually the tracks ended just beyond the park, at El Portal, twelve miles west of the gorge proper. Still, Hamilton was reporting a common fear that protection in the parks would be compromised by greater visitation and tourist development. "In California and the far West," he noted, "there are people who insist that hereafter the great valley is to be a mere picnic-ground with dancing platforms, beery choruses, and couples contorting in the two-step." Personally he dismissed such critics as "nature cranks" and "the athletic rich," those "stout pilgrims with long purses and no ailments." But now "there is the railroad into Yosemite," he concluded, "and all the arguments since Adam and Eve will not put it away."[1]

Barely nine years later, however, more people entered Yosemite Park by automobile than by rail, 14,527 as opposed to 14,251. The following season (1917) the ratio was nearly three to one, and by 1918 almost seven to one, 26,669 in contrast to 4,000.[2] On a positive note, the growing availability of cars to middle-class Americans held forth the promise of greater public support for the national park idea. Although the railroads had "gradually lowered the barrier" between the East and the West, as a journalist, Charles J. Belden, admitted, "the subtle influence of the motor-car is bringing them into closer touch than would otherwise be possible." As evidence of the phenomenon, as early as 1918 there were only a "few places" in the West, "no matter how remote from the railroad, where fuel and oil may not readily be obtained." Accordingly, Hamilton's so-called "nature cranks," politely known as "purists," were outvoted by the large majority of preservationists who initially embraced the automobile, as they had earlier the railroad, as another opportunity to bolster the parks' popularity. "Our national parks are far removed from the centres of population," Enos A. Mills of Colorado observed, rejecting purism as impractical. "If visited by people," he stressed, "there must be speedy ways of reaching these places and swift means of covering their long distances, or but a few people will have either time or strength to see the wonders of these parks." In other words, without convenient transportation the public would not support scenic preservation. "The traveler wants the automobile with which to see America."[3]

When put in those terms, as a demand rather than a choice, the decision of preservationists was a foregone conclusion. At first they repeatedly emphasized the advantages of the automobile, especially its reduced cost and greater freedom of mobility. In this vein no less than Arthur Newton Pack, president of the American Nature Association, observed in 1929: "The greatest of all pleasures open to any automobile owner is travel through the wilder sections of our country . . . with comfort and economy." The motorist "will grow to regard railroads as uncomfortable necessities," another enthusiast affirmed. "He will laugh at himself for believing, before he bought his car, that a real pleasure trip could ever be accomplished by rail." Not only was the car "capable of penetrating into the wilds and bringing its owner into speedy touch with Nature," it returned him "before he has dropped any of the necessary threads of civilization."[4] Still another testimonial glorified "this freedom, this independence, this being in the largest possible degree completely master of one's self. . . . That horrible fiend, the railroad time-table, is banished to the far woods." Best of all, auto camps could be made "comfortably at a cost of two dollars a day per passenger," one third the expense of lodging in a luxury hotel, another promoter agreed. There was a similar note of prophecy in a succeeding endorsement: "Until this new travel idea developed, costs of travel precluded the average citizen including the whole family."[5]

Popularly known as "sagebrushing," auto camping swept the national parks throughout the 1920s and 1930s. "The sagebrusher," a Yellowstone enthusiast explained in defining the term, "is so called to distinguish him from a dude. A dude goes pioneering with the aid of Mr. Pullman's upholstered comforts and carries with him only the impediments ordinary to railroad travel." By contrast the sagebrusher "cuts loose from all effeteness," bringing "clothes and furniture and house and food—even the family pup—and lets his adventurous, pioneering spirit riot here in the mountain air."[6] "It was in 1915 that the first automobile, an army machine, entered the

Yellowstone National Park," two enthusiasts further reported. Just four years later the park "was invaded by more than ten thousand cars, carrying some forty thousand vacationists." The correspondents noted that the year 1919 marked the parade of "nearly ninety-eight thousand machines" through the national parks, ranking the automobile "as the greatest aid" to their "popularity and usefulness." Rocky Mountain National Park topped the list with 33,638 cars; Yosemite, permanently opened to private motorists since 1913, placed "second with something over twelve thousand." Yellowstone's 10,000 matched the figures for Mount Rainier National Park; as a result, both ran "a close race" for third in the standings.[7]

Although the surge in auto traffic was briefly interrupted by World War II, afterward it swelled with even greater intensity. By the mid 1950s only 1 to 2 percent of all park visitors entered the reserves by public transportation.[8] Even the most determined proponents of the automobile now faced the sobering realization that cars threatened the national parks as much as they insured their support. Perhaps no one had predicted the agony of the trade-off with greater foresight than the former British ambassador to the United States, James Bryce. In November 1912 he was invited to address the American Civic Association. "What Europe is now," he warned, "is that toward which you in America are tending." Specifically, the nation's population was also rapidly increasing and with it "the number of people who desire to enjoy nature, . . . both absolutely and in proportion." Unfortunately, "the opportunities for enjoying it, except as regards locomotion," were in decline. As for the rest of the "circumscribed" world, scenery in the United States no longer could be considered "inexhaustible." For a specific example Bryce chose the on-going debate "as to whether automobiles should be admitted in the Yosemite." Presently, he noted, "the steam-cars stop some twelve miles away from the entrance of the Yosemite Park." Surely development should come no closer. "There are plenty of roads for the lovers of speed and noise," he maintained, "without intruding on these few places where the wood nymphs and the water nymphs ought to be allowed to have the landscape to themselves." Like E. H. Hamilton he concluded with a Biblical analogy for emphasis: "If Adam had known what harm the serpent was going to work, he would have tried to prevent him from finding lodgement in Eden; and if you were to realize what the result of the automobile will be in that wonderful, that incomparable valley, you will keep it out."[9]

A subsequent exchange between J. Horace McFarland and George Horace Lorimer, editor of the *Saturday Evening Post*, reveals why Bryce's advice was largely ignored. Throughout the 1920s Lorimer opened the pages of his journal to park defenders of every persuasion, and often spiced their contributions with outspoken editorials of his own. Yet when he wrote to McFarland in November 1934, he admitted the loss of "some of my early enthusiasm for the National Parks." Lorimer's change of heart could be laid to the automobile. "Motor roads and other improvements are coming in them so fast," he complained, "that they are gradually beginning to lose some of their attraction for the out-of-door man and the wilderness lover." In fact, he closed, echoing the ambassador, "if this craze for improvement of the wilderness keeps up, soon there will be little or none of it left."[10]

Lorimer realized that a sense of wilderness, unlike a purely visual experience, presumed the absence of civilization and its artifacts. The preservationists' dilemma, McFarland cautioned him in reply, was that without the automobile there might not be parks containing natural wonders, let alone wilderness. "I am about the last person in this whole wide world to have the nerve to offer you any advice," he began tactfully. "Yet in this matter of the National Park development I am bound to say that we must accept compromises if assaults on the parks from the selfish citizens, of whom we have not a few, are to be repelled." However distasteful, there was no sense decrying what could not be changed. "I didn't want automobiles in the parks before any more than I do now," McFarland himself admitted. Yet what other choice did preservationists have? Specifically, "where would the parks have been without this means of getting the 'dear public' to know what the same dear public owns?" To prove his sincerity he ended on a personal note. Originally "my summer home at Eagles Mere [Pennsylvania] included a little bit of pure primeval forest." But that was "more than thirty years ago," he noted soberly. Since then "I have had to give up much of the primeval relationship in order to have anything at all."[11]

In microcosm, McFarland's sacrifice was not unlike that facing preservationists throughout the national park system. Although the prerequisite for public support of the national park idea was development, it invariably compromised many of the very values they had struggled to save in the first place. As preservationists soon discovered, moreover, park legislation itself offered little ammunition for their defense. As distinct from the detailed language governing administrative procedures in the reserves, to what *purpose* they should be managed was often couched in generalities or not even included. The closest thing to a working definition was the National Park Service Act of 1916. In each instance, the act specified, the parks were to be protected "in such manner and by such means as will leave them unimpaired for the enjoyment of future generations."[12] At the time preservationists were satisfied, indeed almost elated. Each new controversy, however, revealed the subjectiveness of the clause itself. Exactly what, for example, was meant by "unimpaired"? Who likewise determined whether or not the term made allowance for roads, hotels, parking lots, and similar forms of development? "The law has never clearly defined a national park," Robert Sterling Yard, as president of the National Parks Association, finally concluded in 1923. Neither the National Park Service Act, "nor other laws," he lamented, "specify in set terms that the conservation of these parks shall be complete conservation."[13] Each new objective, including wilderness or wildlife protection, would have to win recognition as a precedent on its own merits.

Much as the automobile speeded the passing of solitude, so it accelerated the confrontation between those who viewed the national parks as playgrounds and those, such as Lorimer and Yard, who now saw them as sanctuaries in the broadest sense. Only while visitation was scattered and sporadic could preservationists avoid deciding how the national parks should be used as well as defended. With the growing visitation brought about by popularity of the automobile, the luxury of postponing the issue of standards was gone.

"It is the will of the nation," Frederick Law Olmsted said in interpreting the Yosemite Park Act of 1864, "that this scenery shall never be private property, but that like certain defensive points upon our coast it shall be held solely for public purposes." With Olmsted's definition began the never-ending debate over what forms of enjoyment were appropriate in the national parks. At present, Olmsted conceded before the Yosemite Park commissioners in August 1865, travelers to the valley and Mariposa redwood grove totaled but several hundred annually. Yet "before many years," he predicted with amazing foresight, "these hundreds will become thousands, and in a century the whole number of visitors will be counted in the millions." Eventually laws to prevent Yosemite's defacement "must be made and rigidly enforced." Construction, for example, should be limited to "the narrowest limits consistent with the necessary accommodation of visitors." The alternative to imposing the standard would be the proliferation of buildings which "would unnecessarily obscure, distort, or detract from the dignity of the scenery."[14]

With the Yosemite Act of 1864 Congress established the precedent that basic accommodations and visitor services in the parks would be provided by private concessioners.[15] Olmsted also did not seek to forbid development outright but merely wished to channel it creatively. For instance, he supported the completion of an "approach road" which would "enable visitors to make a complete circuit of all the broader parts of the valley." Yet while he rejected a rigid, purist philosophy, he left no doubt that his priorities still lay with the environment. "The first point to be kept in mind then is the preservation and maintenance exactly as is possible of the natural scenery." No less than a great work of art, Yosemite Valley and the Mariposa redwoods belonged to future generations as well as to living Americans. In fact, he claimed, "the millions who are hereafter to benefit by the Yosemite Act have the largest interest in it, and the largest interest should be first and most strenuously guarded."[16]

In time, the posterity argument became a basic tenet of the preservation movement. Meanwhile the distinctions between recognized public needs, such as defense, and scenic preservation were not as clear-cut as Olmsted wished to imply in his opening analogy. His worst fears were soon confirmed. In November 1865 he resigned from the Yosemite Park commission and returned to New York City to resume work on Central Park. Gradually the commission lost touch with his ideals as individual members served political instead of environmental beliefs. Accordingly, much as he had forewarned, by the 1870s the valley looked more like a run-down farm instead of the well-designed public park he had envisioned only a decade before.[17]

Few better than Olmsted understood that Yosemite's condition stemmed from the common perception of the valley as a wonderland to enthrall rather than instruct the visitor. No less than at Niagara Falls, where curio salesmen, aerialists, and other stuntmen competed for a suitable backdrop, the urge to capitalize on its spectacular qualities was unquenchable. "There are falls of water elsewhere more finer," Olmsted claimed, "there are more stupendous rocks, more beetling cliffs, there are deeper and more awful chasms."[18] Still, there was no escaping that preservation was the by-product of monumentalism, not environmentalism. Thus while enthusiasts hailed the park idea as the nation's answer to the abuse of its natural wonders, the parks themselves could not escape the impulse to costume their features. In 1872, for example, a *New York Times* columnist, Grace Greenwood, entered Yosemite Valley and immediately protested that "a certain 'cute' Yankee" planned "cutting off the pretty little side cascade of the Nevada [Fall], by means of a dam, and turning all the water into the great cataract. 'Fixing the falls,' he calls this job of tinkering one of God's masterpieces." Like Ferdinand V. Hayden, Josiah Dwight Whitney, and others, she appealed to America's conscience by comparing the scheme to the commercialization of Niagara Falls. "Let it not be said by any visitor," she pleaded, "that [Yosemite Valley] is a new Niagara for extortion and impositions—a rocky pitfall for the unwary, a Slough of Despond for the timid and weak." Left unmarred, Yosemite would pay for itself "a hundred-fold"; surely that statistic, if none other, could be appreciated "even by fools."[19]

Yet even as Miss Greenwood gave credence to Frederick Law Olmsted's predictions, one James McCauley, an early Yosemite pioneer, launched carnivalism in the valley on a grand scale. During the early 1870s he constructed a trail to Glacier Point, where he later perched a rustic hotel. But although the view of the Sierra from the promontory was breathtaking, the drop—a dizzying 3,200 feet to the meadowlands below—fascinated early visitors all the more. Throughout the day it was common to find them on the ledge hefting rocks, boxes, and other objects over the side. "An ordinary stone tossed over remained in sight an incredibly long time," one observer recalled, "but finally vanished somewhere about the middle distance." Further experimentation revealed that a "handkerchief with a stone tied in the corner was visible perhaps a thousand feet deeper." But "even an empty box, watched by a fieldglass, could not be traced to its concussion with the Valley floor." And so the urge to test gravity remained unappeased. Sensing his opportunity, McCauley then "appeared on the scene, carrying an antique hen under his arm. This, in spite of the terrified ejaculations and entreaties of the ladies, he deliberately threw over the cliff's edge." Their outburst only added to the unfolding drama. "With an ear-piercing cackle that gradually grew fainter as it fell," the correspondent noted, "the poor creature shot downward; now beating the air with ineffectual wings, and now frantically clawing at the very wind, . . . thus the hapless fowl shot down, down, down, until it became a mere fluff of feathers no larger than a quail." Next "it dwindled to a wren's size," suddenly "disappeared, then again dotted the sight as a pin's point, and then—it was gone!"[20]

The finale, however, was still to come. As the shock of the

moment wore off, the women "pitched into the hen's owner with redoubled zest," only to learn, undoubtedly to their embarrassment, that McCauley's chicken went "over that cliff every day during the season. And, sure enough, on our road back we met the old hen about half up the trail, calmly picking her way home!"[21]

Compared to his invention of the firefall, however, McCauley's chicken-toss ranked as a sideshow. One Fourth of July during the early 1870s valley residents took up a collection for fireworks and approached McCauley to throw them over at Glacier Point. His enchantment with the scheme compelled him to reciprocate with one of his own. He would build a large fire, wait until it had burned down into a pile of smoldering embers, then push them over the cliff. The fire itself was not an original idea; prior to settlement of the valley adventurers reported Indian beacons along Yosemite's rim, for example. In either case, a full 1,500 feet separated McCauley's vantage on Glacier Point from the first outcrop below. "As time passed," his son later testified, "people wanted fires and were willing to pay for them." When alerted, tourists in the valley scrambled for a ringside seat "to view the performance, shrinking under the ear-splitting detonations of the dynamite that accompanied the fire at intervals."[22]

At the turn of the century McCauley left the hotel business and carried his dynamite with him. From then on the firefall survived as a silent spectacle under the auspices of David A. Curry, founder of the Yosemite Park and Curry Company. In 1899 he located his namesake, Camp Curry, in the valley directly below Glacier Point. As was customary, Curry's guests chipped in "to hire one of his porters to go up and gather the necessary fire wood and put the fire over in the evening," E. P. Leavitt, acting park superintendent, recalled in 1928. But gradually, as the event grew in popularity, Camp Curry assumed the entire expense of displaying the firefall nightly during the summer months. It was, after all, a superb drawing card, as testified by the Curry Company's brochures, which featured the firefall brilliantly aflame above the darkened campground. "As the embers fall over the cliff, the rush of air makes them glow very brightly," Leavitt explained. And "because of their light weight they fall slowly, which gives the appearance of a fall of living fire." Curry replaced McCauley's bombs with a violinist who played "softly," another observer reported, as the "fairy stars came drifting downwards, . . . floating from sight into some mighty hollow beneath the cliff that was yet fifteen hundred feet above our heads." And "so, for more than half a century," *Collier's* magazine concluded in 1952, "this man-made spectacle has rivaled the natural glories of Yosemite."[23]

Such blanket acceptance of the artificial was, in Frederick Law Olmsted's words, "fixing the mind on mere matters of wonder or curiosity." And that was precisely what he had condemned as inappropriate in 1865.[24] Still, attempts to costume the spectacular only multiplied, and as in the case of the firefall, persisted long after their inspiration, often under the auspices of the National Park Service itself. What the firefall was to Yosemite Valley, for example, tunnel trees became for the nearby groves of Sierra redwoods. In June 1878 a British visitor to the Tuolumne Big Trees reported another "novelty such as one does not come across every day. This was a tunnel through the stump of one of the largest Wellingtonia in the grove." He called upon his readers to imagine a tree "through which the road passes and the stagecoach is driven!" At first Yosemite Park did not include the Tuolumne specimen, yet it was not long before the brand of carnivalism he identified infected the reserve proper. Most notably, in 1881 the Yosemite Stage and Turnpike Company completed a road through the Mariposa Grove. Perhaps to honor the occasion, and certainly to attract publicity, the company commissioned a team of workmen to notch the sprawling base of the Wawona Tree large enough to permit the passage of its carriages. One witness recalled stopping in the center of the cut and standing up to touch the roof of the freshly-hewn opening. "Arriving on the other side, I stepped down and the foreman and each of the workers surprised me by shaking hands with me and congratulating me, saying I had the distinction of being the first one to pass through." Similar testimonials to the enjoyment of the novelty prompted tunneling of the nearby California Tree, in 1895.²⁵

By 1900 the tunnel trees received top-billing from a variety of publicists, among them the Southern Pacific Railroad, which featured the Wawona Tree regularly in its new passenger-department publication, *Sunset* magazine. Meanwhile, the campaign to reduce Yosemite National Park had spawned schemes with a synthetic bent of a decidedly more ominous nature. Chief among them was the so-called "restoration of Yosemite waterfalls," sponsored by the park's leading congressional opponent, Representative Anthony Caminetti of California. "The waterfalls of Yosemite Valley are seen at their best in June, and after that rapidly diminish," argued a state forester, Allen Kelley, in smoke-screening the congressman's real concern. Caminetti proposed to Congress that it "pay for surveys of reservoir sites in the mountains surrounding Yosemite Valley, with a view to storing water in the streams that supply the numerous falls." He failed to stress that the water was to be used for irrigation, not just so-called scenic enhancement. Still, both he and Kelley played upon the nation's pride to advance their case. Just "at the time of year when tourists from abroad find it convenient to visit the valley," Kelley noted, Yosemite Fall in reality was "no waterfall, only a discolored streak on the dry face of the cliff." He therefore proposed that the cataract "be maintained either by damming the creek or turning a portion of the waters of the Tuolumne River into its bed through a flume about twenty miles long." A similar embankment "100 yards in length . . . would store plenty of water for Nevada and Vernal Falls," while Bridal Veil, in autumn "a merely trickling film over the rocks," would best be augmented "by making a reservoir of the meadows along the creek." None other than *Harper's Weekly* published the argument, on July 16, 1892, replete with before and after woodcuts of the falls and potential dam sites.²⁶

Although this particular scheme made little headway, in 1913 Congress sided with Caminetti's philosophy by approving the no-less-objectionable Hetch Hetchy reservoir. Because its supporters also glossed over its damaging features as esthetic improvements, preservationists realized that to accept any kind of development in the national parks, no matter how innocent-looking initially, might in fact set a precedent with unforeseen consequences. So with the automobile, the naturalist, Victor H. Cahalane, justified the suspicions of its early skeptics. "As more and more visitors flood the parks," he noted in 1940, "demands for all kinds of 'improvements' arise. First and most numerous have been requests for elaborate structures and big-city amusements." Yet if secondary, schemes to redress the spectacular were advanced with equal persistence. "What good is a volcano if it erupts only once in a century or so?' inquire the 'efficiency experts.' Since it is futile to ask a mountain to take off its cap and spout lava, they request that tunnels be excavated into Lassen Peak so that they may see how the uneasy giant looks inside." Similarly, in Yosemite talk of reviving the Caminetti-Kelley proposal had literally become an annual event. Indeed "each year," Cahalane scoffed, "the administration is asked to build reservoirs above the valley rim where water could be stored and fed to the falls on the Fourth of July and Labor Day," with "special showings" for "the Elks, Kiwanis, Lions and Women's Clubs." Fortunately the National Park Service seemed determined to resist the "Nature-Aiders," he believed, with their "Turkish baths, tunneled volcanoes," and replumbed "waterfalls and hot springs."[27]

Like George Horace Lorimer, however, Cahalane was far less optimistic about the chances of ever curbing the automobile. Initially Stephen T. Mather and the Park Service openly promoted the horseless carriage as the best possible means of increasing park attendance quickly and economically. Most preservationists, still reeling from the loss of Hetch Hetchy, also discounted the warnings of Ambassador Bryce, and, like Enos Mills, welcomed cars to the national parks with the same enthusiasm previously accorded the railroads. Gradually, however, the distinctions between both forms of transportation became more pronounced. Most notably, the railroads went no farther than the fringes of the parks. Within the reserves proper visitors had to rely on public transportation, beginning with the stagecoach. In marked contrast, Victor Cahalane observed, the flood of visitors loosed by the automobile defended personal mobility as a right rather than a privilege. "Roads! Roads! Roads! We must have more roads! Bigger and better roads!" he stated, mimicking the "clamor of over-enthusiastic chambers-of-commerce, automobile associations and contractors. Faster roads! Roads into this wilderness. Roads into that wilderness." Apparently none of "these besiegers" realized, he concluded, echoing Lorimer's lament "that when processions of automobiles, clumps of filling stations, gasoline smells, restaurants and hot dog stands" invade the parks, "wilderness is gone."[28]

The Park Service itself could be accused of pandering to the public's baser instincts. Often the air of carnivalism was subtle. In Yellowstone, for example, a searchlight mounted on the roof of Old Faithful Inn beamed across the parking lot to illuminate the evening eruption of the fabled geyser. In 1939 a journalist, Martelle Trager, confessed that she and her family "rushed across the road to a place where we could get a better view of the colored lights playing upon the column of water and steam." And, as the Tragers were to discover, the Park Service was not above providing even more elaborate amusements. Indeed "the climax of the trip" was not the Upper Geyser Basin, but the Grand Canyon of the Yellowstone, where "the children heard about the Bear Feeding Show." A Park Service naturalist informed them there would be two performances that particular evening, "one at six and one at seven." They arrived fully an hour before the first, only "to find at least five hundred people already gathered" in the "big amphitheater built on the side of a hill about three miles from the hotel." Still, they found seats in the first row, and in full view of the "fenced-in pit where the garbage is dumped for the bears each evening." On schedule the "truck drove through the gate with a ranger-naturalist at the back, his gun loaded and ready to shoot if a bear attempted to attack the men who were emptying the garbage pails." But that night "the Bear Cafeteria" fed without incident at least 75 of the animals, including blacks, browns, and grizzlies.[29]

Critics charged that enjoyment alone was no measure of the suitability of such events. It followed that any relaxation of the natural for the artificial was an acceptable use of the national parks. Among those who argued against yielding to the temptation of promoting the reserves in this fashion was Henry Baldwin Ward, professor of landscape architecture at the University of Illinois. Tourists seeking pure entertainment "might be wisely diverted to areas of less unique and supreme value," he maintained. The bear feedings especially, however popular, had all "the flavor of a gladiatorial spectacle in Ancient Rome." Instead of people, the animals were reduced to "sadly degenerate representatives of the noble ancestors from which they have sprung." Albert W. Atwood, writing for the *Saturday Evening Post*, further condemned what he termed "the excessive danger of cleaning up, after the manner of city parks; of smoothing, rounding, straightening, manicuring, landscaping. . . . At Grand Canyon," he explained, "roadsides have been graded and the natural growth cut away; walks have been laid out—all with the effect of introducing an element of the artificial, of the smooth and conventional, into what is, perhaps, the supreme primeval landscape of the entire world." Yosemite Valley was the worst example, with "its dance halls, movies, bear pit shows, studios, baseball, golf, swimming pools, wienie roasts, marshmallow roasts and barbecues—all well advertised in bulletins and printed guides." It was not that such diversions were bad in themselves, he asserted, simply that none had "any relation whatever to the purpose for which the national parks were established."[30]

Each time preservationists singled out the agent primarily responsible for overdevelopment of the national parks, they inevitably debated the impact of the automobile. "The majority now come in motors," Robert Sterling Yard wrote, noting the shift from rails to roads as early as 1922. Thus "while we are fighting for the protection of the national park system from its enemies, we may also have to protect it from its friends." No statement was to prove more prophetic or enduring. With the surge in park visitation, suddenly even the grand hotels seemed tainted as "resort and amusement-type" features.

"The foreground of a picture is of very great importance," Wallace Atwood, Yard's successor as president of the National Parks Association, said in defense of his own reappraisal of the structures in 1931. Initially, of course, preservationists hailed the hotels, like the railroads and the automobile, as the prerequisites for increased patronage and public support. Yet there had been errors in judgment, including the location of the "hotels and other buildings too near the objects of interest. Other mistakes have been made in placing hotels or lodges at the choice observation stations." Perhaps visitors "should be brought within easy walking distance of the best outlook points," Atwood conceded, still, "hotels, lodges or camps should not be allowed to occupy those points." In addition, "no building should be erected in the parks solely for amusement purposes."[31] Although Atwood did not go into specifics, by implication he disapproved of hostelries such as the El Tovar, overlooking the South Rim of the Grand Canyon, and Old Faithful Inn, adjacent to Yellowstone's Upper Geyser Basin.

With the conviction that national parks ultimately must be justified in the broadest sense, and not merely as scenic wonderlands, the change of heart regarding the wisdom of encouraging greater visitation was inevitable. In this vein Arno B. Cammerer, director of the National Park Service, wrote in 1938: "Our National Parks are wilderness preserves where true natural conditions are to be found." While the statement was as much sentiment as fact, more park professionals at least were of the opinion that "complete conservation" *should* be advanced. "When Americans, in years to come," he continued, "wish to seek out extensive virgin forests, mountain solitudes, deep canyons, or sparsely vegetated deserts, they will be able to find them in the National Parks."[32] Once again contradictions could be laid to transportation policies and visitor facilities in sympathy with the automobile. In 1928 alone, 131,689 cars negotiated the narrow confines of Yosemite Valley, an eleven-fold increase in only nine years.[33] Anyone hopeful that the Great Depression of the 1930s would stem the tide must have been equally surprised. In fact just the reverse was true. Visitation to the national parks and monuments climbed steadily from approximately three million in 1929 to more than twelve million immediately prior to World War II. Although several new parks contributed to the increase, the original reserves, such as Yosemite and Yellowstone, averaged between 400,000 and 500,000 visitors annually, an all-time high.[34]

The postwar travel surge was also unprecedented. By 1955 Frederick Law Olmsted's prediction of annual visitation "by the millions" came true not only in Yosemite (1,060,000), but in Grand Teton (1,063,000), Yellowstone (1,408,000), Rocky Mountain (1,511,000), Shenandoah (1,760,000), and Great Smoky Mountains (2,678,000) national parks. To reemphasize, between 98 and 99 percent of these tourists now were private motorists. Indeed, as if to signal the beginning of the end of public transportation to the parks, in 1944 the Yosemite Valley Railroad, reportedly bankrupt, was auctioned off and torn up for scrap.[35] Quality trains still served most of the other major preserves, benefiting directly, if not proportionally, from the postwar travel revolution. Still, by the 1960s even these were giving way to the automobile and recreational vehicle, which, in contrast to the days of the "sagebrusher," often were as luxurious as the hotel accommodations of old.

"Are the parks doomed in their turn to become mere resorts? Ultimately perhaps." So wondered the respected American naturalist, Joseph Wood Krutch, detecting a growing consensus among preservationists. To their dismay the general public still did not grasp the standards of appreciation defended by Frederick Law Olmsted as early as a century before. Numbers were the key. In June 1955, for example, *U.S. News and World Report* featured the following headline: "This summer 19 million Americans will visit parks that are equipped to handle only 9 million people. Result: Parks overrun like convention cities. Scenery viewed from bumper-to-bumper traffic tie-ups. Vacationing families sleeping in their cars." Still, the figures by themselves were misleading, Krutch maintained; like Olmsted he doubted the *intent* of each tourist. In Olmsted's lifetime both the expense of traveling and the absence of internal improvements in the national parks had discouraged the casual visitor. Suddenly the barriers of privilege and discomfort had come down in a flurry of automobile and highway promotion. "It is indeed largely a matter of easy accessibility and 'modern facilities,'" Krutch noted. For the first time the survival of the national parks as natural areas lay in excluding that "considerable number" of motorists who desired nothing more on arrival than "what they can do at home or at the country club." Then—and only then—might the natural character of the reserves be even "fairly well preserved."[36]

It was ironic, of course, that a preceding generation of preservationists had often argued as forcefully against stringent protection as Krutch now argued for it. Until the level of visitation appeared adequate to defend the parks against utilitarian interests, preservationists themselves willingly compromised a sense of the primitive to encourage greater public solidarity behind the national park idea. "Even the scenery habit in its most artificial forms," John Muir wrote in 1898, "mixed with spectacles, silliness and kodaks; its devotees arrayed more gorgeously than scarlet tanagers, frightening the wild game with red umbrellas—even this is encouraging, and may well be regarded as a hopeful sign of the times." Muir's rare display of tolerance could be laid to the realization that without tourists there might well be no parks at all. "The problem is not to discourage amiable diversions," the historian, Bernard DeVoto, agreed in 1947, "but to scotch every effort, however slight, to convert the parks into summer resorts." Of course "it would hardly be practicable to examine every visitor . . . to make him prove that he has come for a legitimate purpose," Krutch added. But it would be "perfectly possible to make the test automatically" simply "by having the road ask the question: 'Are you willing to take a little trouble to get there?'"[37]

Simply to ask the question was not to resolve the preservationists' dilemma, however. To exclude people, whatever the means, risked loss of support for the national park idea; to accept more people as the price of support jeopardized the

George A. Grant Collection, courtesy of the National Park Service

Cecil W. Stoughton, courtesy of the National Park Service

When Everglades National Park was proposed, many partisans of the national park movement argued that it did not rank with such monumental wonders as Grand Canyon and Yellowstone. Monumental or not, the Everglades environment is threatened on all sides—by roads, canals, urban development, and the Everglades Jetport, shown below in December 1969.

Imposing scenery usually does not invite economic development. Exceptions like Hetch Hetchy Valley in Yosemite National Park, which was flooded by a reservoir of the city of San Francisco, have been the subjects of heated debate. Here the lower meadow of Hetch Hetchy is shown before and after being flooded.

Crater Lake National Park, Oregon, was established in 1902 only after businessmen were assured that mineral exploration could continue.

Courtesy of the National Park Service

Breyne Moskowitz, courtesy of the National Park
Service

Death Valley National Monument, proclaimed in 1933, was to be
compromised by extensive inholdings and mineral claims. Legislation passed in 1976 regulated, but did not abolish outright, such
operations as the stripmine shown below.

James E. Thompson photograph, courtesy of the
Thompson family

James E. Thompson photograph, courtesy of the
National Park Service

The ruggedness of places like Huggins Hell, pictured above, was the
main argument leading to the establishment of Great Smoky Mountains National Park in the 1920s, but within a decade visitors were
also drawn to the park for its wildlife and its virgin forests, dominated
by giant tulip-poplars like the one shown below.

Courtesy of the National Park Service
George A. Grant Collection, courtesy of the National Park Service

Horace M. Albright, as superintendent of Yellowstone National Park in the 1920s, above, led the campaign to establish Grand Teton National Park and to protect Jackson Hole. (Later, Albright became the second director of the National Park Service.) When a Reclamation Service dam at the outlet of Jackson Lake was raised in 1916, thousands of trees were killed. Purists therefore objected to including Jackson Lake in the park, saying it was no longer a natural lake but an artificial reservoir. The Civilian Conservation Corps removed much of the debris along the lakeshore in the 1930s, below.

Photograph by Dave Van de Mark, courtesy of the Save-the-Redwoods League

When Redwood National Park was established in October 1968, the slopes above the Tall Trees Grove, although outside the park, were also forested. In this photograph, taken in June 1976, only the narrow strip of parkland fronting Redwood Creek has not been cut. The fate of the "worm," as this section of the park came to be known, prompted Congress in 1978 to expand Redwood National Park by 48,000 acres. Still, only 9,000 acres is virgin forest. The remainder, much of it recently logged, will have to be replanted.

Shenandoah National Park, Virginia, benefitted from a broadening of national park standards to value distinctive flora and fauna as well as monumental scenery.

Only a few national parks, most notably Isle Royale in Lake Superior, can be considered integral biological units. Isle Royale, because it is a remote island, preserves not only a fine example of Great Lakes spruce-fir forest, but also the only known pack of timber wolves within a national park outside of Alaska.

parks themselves. This attempt to strike a balance between preservation and use had been greatly complicated by the popularity of the automobile. Finally strained to the limit by the postwar travel boom, the National Park Service received relief from Congress in the form of Mission 66. The ten-year program was to expand rather than reduce the carrying capacity of the national parks by reconstructing roads, adding visitor centers, and increasing overnight accommodations. Plans called for facilities sufficient to handle the estimated eighty million auto vacationers expected to crowd the reserves during the golden anniversary of the National Park Service, 1966. In February 1955 the American Automobile Association co-sponsored the kick-off dinner in Washington, D.C. Once the program got under way, preservationists were able to substantiate their fears that Mission 66 was indeed road- and big-development oriented. Their list of specifics included the reconstruction of Tioga Road over Tioga Pass in Yosemite National Park. While "the old road in a sense 'tiptoed' across the terrain," Devereux Butcher described, quoting the veteran nature photographer Ansel Adams, "the new one elbows and shoulders its way through the park—it blasts and gouges the landscape." On completion of the program, F. Fraser Darling and Noel D. Eichhorn reached a similar conclusion for the national parks as a whole. "Mission 66 has done comparatively little for the plants and animals," they charged in their 1967 report to the Conservation Foundation. "The enormous increase in drive-in campsites is an example of the very expensive facilities which do nothing at all for the ecological maintenance of a park."[38]

By enabling more tourists to visit the parks, they inevitably came. Between 1955 and 1974 visitation more than tripled, from approximately fourteen million to forty-six million in the national parks alone. Use of the national monuments rose proportionally, from roughly five million to more than seventeen.[39] To Edward Abbey the figures bore witness to the age of "Industrial Tourism." Wherever "trails or primitive dirt roads already exist," he remarked in his popular book *Desert Solitaire*, "the Industry expects—it hardly needs to ask—that these be developed into modern paved highways." However unpopular, there could be only one solution. "No more cars in the national parks. Let the people walk. Or ride horses, bicycles, mules, wild pigs—anything—but keep the automobiles and the motorcycles and all their motorized relatives out." In anticipation of the charge that preservationists thus defended elitism, Abbey concluded on an even more controversial note. "What about children? What about the aged and infirm?" he asked rhetorically. "Frankly, we need waste little sympathy on these two pressure groups." Children, with their entire lives ahead of them, could afford to be patient for their chance to experience nature untrammeled. The elderly merited "even less sympathy; after all they had the opportunity to see the country when it was still relatively unspoiled."[40]

Never before had preservationists voiced their opposition to the automobile so openly and defiantly. Their new militancy, however, rather than being the outgrowth of greater assurance that the national parks could now survive without pandering to development, could be traced to fear of the consequences in either case. Yet few echoed Abbey as convincingly as Garrett Hardin, professor of human ecology at the University of California, Santa Barbara. Partially crippled by polio since the age of four, "I am not fit for the wilderness I praise," he wrote, in defense of his sincerity; "I cannot pass the test I propose" or "enter the area I would restrict." Claiming, therefore, to "speak with objectivity," Hardin rejected all methods of park allocation except physical merit. Distribution "by the marketplace," for example, favored the wealthy. Similarly, a "first-come, first-served basis" multiplied waste and fatigue by sacrificing the talent and energies of the many who lined up outside the park for the sake of the few allowed in. In contrast, restricting access to the "physically vigorous" protected both wilderness and the joy of earning it. In this vein Yosemite Valley, for instance, might "be assigned a carrying capacity of about one per acre, which might mean that it could be opened to anyone who could walk ten miles." If "more and more people would be willing to walk such a distance, then the standard should be made more rigorous." Granted the valley would "be forever closed to people on crutches, to small children, to fat people, to people with heart conditions, and to old people in the usual state of physical disrepair." But "remember, I am a member of this deprived group," Hardin concluded, and also must "give up all claim of right to the wilderness experience."[41]

To effect such a radical change in policy, of course, preservationists must not only win but hold a majority of the American electorate. But that possibility still seemed very remote. "Ours is so much the age of technology and the machine," Joseph Wood Krutch noted as early as 1957, "that machines come to be loved for their own sake rather than used for other ends." For example, instead "of valuing the automobile because it may take one to a national park, the park comes to be valued because it is a place the automobile may be used to reach."[42] Beyond the entrenchment of auto culture lay the problem of rewording park legislation itself. The phraseology common to each act, "for the benefit and enjoyment of the people," clearly implied that every citizen, not just the educated, robust, or physically endowed, might freely enter the reserves. "Certainly," Arno B. Cammerer, director of the National Park Service, maintained as early as 1938, "no wilderness lover could selfishly demand that the National Parks be kept only for those who are physically able to travel them on foot or on horseback, for they were definitely set aside for the benefit and enjoyment of all." But "are not the intellectual, aesthetic and emotional rights of a minority just as sacred?" Joseph Wood Krutch asked, thereby anticipating Edward Abbey and Garrett Hardin. "Does democracy demand that they be disregarded?"[43] So the difficulty of striking a balance between minority rights and majority demands still haunted the national parks movement. "What of the too-old, the too-young, the timid, the inexperienced, the frail, the hurried, the out-of-shape or just plain lazy?" a Los Angeles lawyer, Eric Julber, wrote while appointing himself spokesman of these minorities. They, too, were perennial friends of the national parks and paid taxes for their maintenance; by what right, then, did the "purist-conservationist" seek to exclude them?

Only because "his philosophy is unfair and undemocratic," he concluded, with a taunt at Garrett Hardin and Edward Abbey. "His chief characteristic is that he is against everything."[44]

Of all the parks, Yosemite, especially the valley floor, remained a classic battleground of the debate. The narrowness and steepness of the gorge inevitably dramatized the smog, noise, congestion, and vandalism which followed in the wake of its popularity. By 1961, the number of visitors crowding the park regularly exceeded 70,000 daily.[45] Spread over Yosemite as a whole, 70,000 people would hardly have been noticed. Yet the valley, as the park's major attraction, was where practically everyone wanted to stay. Thus friends of the park, such as Devereux Butcher, continued to question the wisdom of providing "dancing, pool swimming, golfing," and, in season, "skating on a man-made lake and skiing" in the mountains. Following World War II the bear feedings, at least, had been discontinued. But "there is the firefall," he added, "which also draws crowds, and which, like the other artificial amusements, has nothing to do with the beauty and wonders of the park."[46] In 1968 the Park Service finally agreed and abolished the firefall, only to find the problems of overcrowding, crime, and congestion still on the rise. With the celebration of the Fourth of July weekend in 1970, matters came to a head. It was not a particularly happy season in the first place for park administrators and patrons. Drug use, anti-establishment sentiments, and visitor unrest were high after years of bitter controversy over the Vietnamese War. The confinement of Yosemite Valley exacerbated these tensions in addition to the crush of people. Finally, when a crowd of young people gathered in Stoneman Meadow to vent their emotions, National Park Service personnel lost their patience and drove the youths off by force.[47]

Although the ugliest incident to date, the confrontation was only the latest example of the conflicting demands imposed upon the national parks by an urban-based society. Whatever their legitimacy elsewhere, the purely recreational aims of many park visitors clashed with the preferences of those who now wished to see the parks kept as close to their original conditions as possible. In Yosemite, closure of the eastern third of the valley to vehicular traffic was among the first measures taken by the National Park Service to restore a sense of balance. During 1970 private transportation other than walking or riding bicycles was prohibited and replaced with a shuttle-bus system available free to the public. Similarly, in the wake of strong opposition to a master plan favoring greater development of Yosemite National Park, the Park Service opened the planning process to public input through a series of special hearings and the mailing of personal planning "kits" to all concerned citizens. Following tabulation of the results and final approval by the public, a revised master plan would be put into effect.[48]

Meanwhile the issue of Yosemite Valley had been joined on another front. In 1974 the Music Corporation of America, successor to the Curry Company, unveiled plans for expansion which included not only a new hotel on Glacier Point, but a tramway connecting it to the valley floor. The filming of the short-lived television series "Sierra" lent an immediate air of carnivalism to the gorge as production crews dyed rocks and other natural formations for the sake of the color cameras.[49] Once again preservationists found themselves rehashing a familiar argument. At what point did such activities compound the very problems the Park Service supposedly should be seeking to avoid? Temporarily, at least, the round went to the side of strict conservation.

Yet other park visitors just as readily endorsed the proposal of Eric Julber. "I would install an aerial tramway from the valley floor to Nevada Fall, thence up the backside to the top of Half Dome," he said in resurrecting another scheme prominent since the days of McCauley's chicken and the firefall. "The restaurant at the top would be one of the great tourist attractions of the world."[50] Julber's instant notoriety in the pages of *Reader's Digest* substantiated that such beliefs still could not be taken lightly by their opponents. As in the past, nothing guaranteed the continuity of park policies, whether the issue be standards of enjoying the parks or opening them to uses of a strictly utilitarian persuasion.

As distinct from outright threats to the parks, of course, codes of appreciation were more prone to being weighed by subjective criteria. Thus Joseph Wood Krutch observed in obvious frustration: "It is only hit or miss that these questions are being answered."[51] Granted, by and large the image of national parks as unmodified areas had become fixed in the American mind. And yet, as demonstrated by the continuing popularity of "developed" natural wonders, particularly Niagara Falls, preservationists had every reason to conclude that a majority of Americans would accept significant compromises even to the naturalness of major attractions, provided some semblance of the originals remained.

For example, in a 1974 survey conducted by the United States Travel Service, an agency of the Department of Commerce, Niagara Falls ranked third only behind the Grand Canyon and Yellowstone in public appeal.[52] Unlike its western counterparts, however, Niagara Falls represents the epitome of the "engineered" landmark. To accommodate power generation, up to one half of the flow of the Niagara River is diverted around the falls during daylight viewing hours. Between midnight and sunrise, when visitation is minimal, three-fourths of the river bypasses the cataract through conduits leading to huge turbines set in the Niagara Gorge. In effect, therefore, Niagara Falls is literally "turned on" and "turned off" to conform to both peak sightseeing and power demands. Similarly, although treaties between the United States and Canada limit the diversions, these have still necessitated stream-channel modifications, including a large jetty immediately above the cataract to preserve the falls "spectacle" by spreading the remainder of the flow evenly as it approaches the brink.[53]

Over the long term, perhaps the attempt to accommodate both industry and scenic preservation at Niagara Falls is an indication of the fate awaiting Yellowstone Falls, the Grand Canyon, and other natural wonders with hydroelectric potential. Widespread acceptance of such compromises, in either case, bears out that one man's civilization can just as easily be another's wilderness. Indeed, among the competing factions of park users consensus is still elusive. More than a century after inspiration of the national park idea the issue remains: at what point is conservation in fact sacrificed for the sake of novelty and convenient access? Conceivably, a definitive answer may never be possible.

9

Familiar Themes, Traditional Battles, and a New Seriousness

> The "romantic movement" of the early 19th century has long worked itself out as a cultural dominant, yet, for many of their keenest supporters, parks are still viewed as the living embodiment of romantic values. . . . Their delicious dream is proving increasingly hard to reconcile not only with an ever less romantic and more crowded world, but with the realistic tasks of park acquisition and park management.
>
> *E. Max Nicholson, Convener,*
> *International Biological Program,*
> *British Nature Conservancy, 1972*

> We can take only momentary pride in the achievements of the national park movement's first 100 years when we realize that in the second 100 years the fate of mankind possibly hangs in the balance.
>
> *Nathaniel P. Reed, 1972*

Despite rain and near-freezing temperatures, delegates to the Second World Conference on National Parks were enthusiastic. Even though the rain turned to sleet, few abandoned their places beside the Madison Junction in Yellowstone National Park. After all, the main event of the evening was to be of special significance. Exactly 102 years ago to the day, on September 19, 1870, the members of the celebrated Washburn Expedition had encircled their campfire on this very spot, and, according to the diary of Nathaniel Pitt Langford, immediately dedicated themselves to the protection of Yellowstone as a great national park. That professional historians had discredited Langford's account of the trip was immaterial to the moment at hand; like all popular movements the national park idea might also have its heroes and legends. Now the first lady of the United States, Mrs. Richard M. Nixon, accompanied by the secretary of the interior, Rogers C. B. Morton, was about to pay tribute to the Yellowstone Centennial by relighting, symbolically, the beacon of that renowned encampment. "Regardless of whether or not it is raining," she said, aware of the crowd's discomfort, "this has been a wondrous day for me, and I hope it has been for our delegates from abroad." She now turned and held aloft a large flame. "With the lighting of this torch," Secretary Morton remarked, interpreting her gesture, "we hereby rededicate Yellowstone National Park to a second century of service for the peoples of the world."[1]

Few celebrations during the centennial year did more to link both the past and present of the national park idea. As symbolized by the presence of Mrs. Nixon, national parks had become a revered American institution; from the White House down the United States took pride in the knowledge that it was both the inventor and exporter of the national park idea. The inconsistencies of the Washburn Expedition aside, major newspapers, magazines, television networks, and government reports told and retold its story literally in heroic terms.[2] The explorers "could not have anticipated," one said, "that their idea would flower into a new dimension of the American dream and would capture the imagination of men around the world."[3] While Americans must seek the roots of Western civilization abroad, by the same token the world must come to the United States to pay homage to the birthplace of the national park idea. Mrs. Nixon's rededication of Yellowstone to the world thus affirmed that Yellowstone was America's—and America's alone—to so dedicate.

Under the circumstances, Americans might overlook that the national park idea as originally conceived had been a response to romantic emotions rather than ecological needs. Even as the nation celebrated the Yellowstone Centennial, limitations long imposed on the national park system had already sparked more than a decade of discussion and controversy. In 1962 Rachel Carson, a respected naturalist and biologist, gave the so-called environmental decade of the 1960s powerful momentum with the publication of her best-selling book *Silent Spring*. Originally serialized in *The New Yorker* magazine, *Silent Spring* reached millions of Americans with its warning that the continued use of chemical pesticides spelled possible catastrophe for the natural world. For the first time in history, Carson noted, "every human being" was being "subjected to contact with dangerous chemicals, from the moment of conception until death." Her most chilling scenarios described the growing concentrations of persistent pesticides found in the bodies of animals higher and higher up the food chain. Already those concentrations had proven lethal to birds and fish, she argued: "Man, however much he may like to pretend to the contrary, is [also] part of nature. Can he escape a pollution that is now so thoroughly distributed throughout our world?"[4] The startling implications of her question for the national parks sank gradually into the American mind. If no environment was immune from chemical poisoning, it followed that even the most remote corners of the American wilderness had already suffered damage from toxic substances.

The publication of *Silent Spring* in 1962 coincided with the First World Conference on National Parks, convened at the Seattle World's Fair during the first week in July. Sixty-three nations sent delegates; the only countries conspicuously absent were Communist nations, with the exception of Poland.[5] In keeping with Rachel Carson's message, the theme of the conference was distinctly global and ecumenical. Indeed "the problem of conserving nature is not a local matter," the editor of the conference proceedings later wrote, "because nature does not respect political boundaries. The birds winging their way southward over Europe neither know, nor care, whether they are passing above a Common Market or a group of feudal duchies." Nature paid "no heed" to such "political or social agreements, particularly those that seek to divide the world into compartments. It has been—and always will be—all inclusive."[6]

That common perception of the 1960s carried through to the Second World Conference on National Parks, held in 1972 in observance of the Yellowstone Centennial. Among those who addressed the gathering in a somber vein was Nathaniel

P. Reed, U.S. assistant secretary of the interior in charge of fish, wildlife, and parks. "We would be deluding ourselves," he remarked, "if we did not recognize that with the joy of this occasion there is also sorrow over man's abuse of this lonely planet—and even well-founded foreboding over the future of man." Reed obviously had been influenced not only by Rachel Carson but by the equally grim warnings of Dr. Paul Ehrlich, a professor of biology at Stanford University. In his own best-selling monograph, *The Population Bomb,* Ehrlich predicted in 1968 that unchecked population growth would soon engulf the world with hordes of hungry, ignorant, and desperate people. In their urge simply to survive, he maintained, they would destroy not only the environment but practically any hope of international cooperation and world peace. By September 1971, on the eve of the Yellowstone Centennial, *The Population Bomb* was in its twenty-fifth printing. "Nothing could be more misleading to our children than our present affluent society," Ehrlich still argued in his introduction. "They will inherit a totally different world, a world in which the standards, politics, and economics of the past decade are dead."[7]

The impact of expanding human populations on forests, grasslands, and other wildlife habitat testified to the futility of trying to establish national parks with enough territory to protect all of their resident species of flora and fauna. Time and again throughout the 1970s, this consequence of over-population became the theme of scientific reports. Even the United States could no longer take refuge in "its continental vastness," wrote a panel of scholars working on behalf of the Conservation Foundation. In its own centennial study, *National Parks for the Future,* the foundation listed many of the problems working against the establishment of national parks with boundaries adequate for the protection of biological resources. Undoubtedly the greatest problem was the failure of the United States to confront the reality of its evolution into "an urban nation." The romance of its frontier origins aside, the United States was "becoming ever more urbanized." The sharpness of that familiar warning, reminiscent of the Census Report of 1890, lay in the realization that overpopulation in the 1970s was no longer a theory but a phenomenon whose pressures could finally be seen and experienced. For the first time, the foundation's panelists agreed, the United States itself had to deal squarely with the same "confinement, lack of opportunity, and environmental insult" that were characteristic of the Industrial Revolution in other countries. Pollution and overcrowding, as the end products of "a specialized, technological age," were tangible proof that the United States had also sacrificed its frontier innocence for the problems and complexities of the modern world.[8]

Seen from this perspective, the Yellowstone Conference merely reaffirmed what many people had already argued— the care and management of natural resources could no longer be successful if practiced piecemeal by individual countries. Ecological laws transcended synthetic political boundaries. There was, as a result, at least one reason for optimism; more than eighty nations, including Russia, were represented at the Second World Conference on National Parks, as opposed to only sixty-three countries listing delegates at the original meeting in 1962. It was further noted that the number of national parks and "equivalent reserves" around the globe in 1972 totaled more than 1,200 separate areas, truly an impressive figure.[9] Meanwhile, that each national park in particular could be traced back to the United States only swelled the nation's pride and sense of accomplishment as it celebrated the Yellowstone Centennial year.

Indeed, that many countries still looked to the United States for leadership in preservation was borne out by the First and Second World Conferences on National Parks. Both praised America's invention of the national park idea. Yet whether or not the United States would continue to set high standards for world conservation was a question still open to debate. For example, biologists worldwide had repeatedly stressed the importance of setting aside large tracts of territory if wildlife in particular was to survive.

Still, many members of the world community had simply followed America's nineteenth-century example by preserving only their most marginal tracts of land. Possible exceptions,

most notably the African game parks, often owed their establishment and survival to economic ends rather than deep-
seated environmental concern. In the pattern of the "See
America First" campaign, African governments had also recognized the advantages of attracting wealthy foreign tourists
into the reserves. Efforts to protect wildlife for its own sake,
especially wildlife whose dependence on remoteness from civilization meant that the animals might never be seen by tourists, was the last thing government officials endorsed. If ever
the flow of tourist dollars were to be interrupted for extended
periods, it followed that the parks themselves might just as
easily be sacrificed, either intentionally or simply through
neglect.[10]

Around the world, as in the United States, the least controversial approach to preservation was the protection of monumental scenery. The Second World Conference on National
Parks itself conceded that limitation while addressing the establishment of "world parks" to be administered under the
auspices of the United Nations. Delegates to the conference
frequently stressed the importance of protecting the most productive ecosystems on the planet, especially tropical rain forests rich in countless species of plant, insect, and wild animal
life.[11] Recommendations that seemed so obvious intellectu-
ally, however, were far more difficult to effect politically. It
was one thing to suggest that nation states such as Brazil and
the Philippines should protect their rain forests, quite another
to imply that neither had the right to dispose of its natural
resources as each saw fit.

The conference instead endorsed Antarctica as the first
international reserve. Its uniqueness as an ecosystem aside,
the overriding advantage was political. Existing international
treaties had agreed that Antarctica was to be shared by the
nations of the world in the interest of science. Moreover, many
scientists themselves shared the widespread popular belief
that most of the territory's natural wealth was locked under
thousands of feet of ice. The preservation of Antarctica was less
likely to be opposed because the lands in question appeared
worthless at the outset and, for all intents and purposes,
seemed certain to remain worthless in the future.[12]

Mounting threats to the national parks of the United States again underscored how attitudes toward even Antarctica might change if its resources proved both abundant and accessible. In the two decades preceding the Yellowstone Centennial, debate about the future of the Colorado River basin in the American Southwest especially dramatized the impermanence of national park status. In 1950 the Bureau of Reclamation unveiled a proposal to erect two high dams across the Colorado River as part of a comprehensive plan to manage water resources the length of the basin. The first dam was to be at Split Mountain, in the northeastern corner of Utah, and the second at Echo Park, just upstream in the northwestern corner of Colorado. The source of the controversy was the location of both potential reservoirs within Dinosaur National Monument, straddling the boundary between the two states.[13]

Thoroughly alarmed, preservationists joined forces in Washington, D.C., to protest the innundation of the national monument. Another highpoint of the campaign was the publication in 1955 of *This Is Dinosaur*. Noted contributors to the book of essays included its editor, the historian and novelist Wallace Stegner, and its publisher, Alfred A. Knopf. Stunning illustrations by Philip Hyde, Martin Litton, and other photographers complemented the text of what later came to be recognized as a model for the so-called battle books published throughout the 1960s by organizers of the environmental movement.[14]

In a compromise struck in 1956, Dinosaur National Monument was spared. Not until 1963 did preservationists fully appreciate the price of that agreement with the completion of the Glen Canyon dam, just upstream from Grand Canyon National Park and neighboring Marble Canyon. By the time preservationists came to recognize Glen Canyon's own remarkable qualifications for national park status, its redemption from the dam builders was out of the question. The Bureau of Reclamation merely shifted, but did not abandon, its dam building efforts. The cost of saving Dinosaur National Monument was the sacrifice of much of the rest of the Colorado River basin, including Glen Canyon. Downstream from Glen Canyon only Marble Canyon and the Grand Canyon remained untouched, and by 1963 even those monumental landscapes had been threatened with the construction of large reservoirs.[15]

Unlike Glen Canyon, the Grand Canyon was ostensibly protected, on its upstream or eastern side as a national park, and farther westward as a national monument. The establishment of the national park in 1919, however, had reserved to the federal government the prerogative of later relinquishing portions of the chasm for water-storage projects. That was the option exercised by the Bureau of Reclamation during the early 1960s in calling for the construction of two large reservoirs in the canyon. One of the high dams was planned for Bridge Canyon, downstream from the national monument. The flood pool itself still would back up through the monument and well into the park. The second dam site in Marble Canyon would not affect either the national monument or national park; nevertheless, preservationists argued that Marble Canyon itself was an integral part of the Grand Canyon ecosystem and should therefore be included within the adjoining national park.[16]

The ecological argument against the dams sought to demonstrate the interdependence of the Colorado River, its canyons, and its interlocking tributaries. Upstream, the construction of the Glen Canyon dam had already blocked the normal flow of water and suspended silt into the Grand Canyon; gradually the impact of that blockage could be detected in the erosion of sandbars along the river, as well as in the increasing density of shoreline vegetation no longer subject to removal by periodic flooding.[17] In the heat of battle, however, ecology was a difficult subject to explain to the American public. People at large responded far more emotionally and vociferously to the pending loss of the Grand Canyon as the supreme scenic spectacle of the continent.

In that respect, the defeat of the Grand Canyon dams in 1968 occurred on a note of irony. Confronted with the necessity of arousing public outcry against the dams, preservationists consistently appealed to the nation's historical prejudice for monumental scenery. To save the canyon, in other words, it seemed at times that preservation interests would have to sacrifice everything else. One popular argument, for example, suggested that coal-fired or nuclear power plants would more than compensate for the loss of hydroelectricity from each of the proposed dams.[18] Only when the exploitation of the coal fields in the region began in earnest did the cost of such trade-offs become apparent. Saved from the dam builders below, the Grand Canyon was now threatened by the emissions of the new power plants from above.[19] As a monumental landscape the Grand Canyon had survived; as an ecosystem its future was still seriously in doubt.

Emissions from the growing concentration of coal-fired power plants in the Southwest became especially noticeable during the mid-1970s. In February 1975, for example, Philip Fradkin, an environmental writer for the *Los Angeles Times*, reported reductions in visibility at not only the Grand Canyon but Zion, Bryce, and Cedar Breaks National Monument. "The view from Inspiration Point in Bryce Canyon was hardly inspiring," he wrote. "To the right of Navajo Mountain was the visible plume from the Navajo power plant at Page, Arizona." Two additional stations planned for the region would also soon be covering the parklands with layer upon layer "of gray-blue and yellow-brown smog."[20]

Few revelations demonstrated more pointedly how the situation of the national parks had dramatically changed since the late nineteenth century. Never again could preservationists take comfort in the vision of a boundary separating a park from the impact of civilization. Air pollution alone proved conclusively that whatever boundaries may have existed between the parks and modern America were fast disappearing. Supposedly pollution was a phenomenon of the city. That dirty air now drifted deep into the American wilderness confirmed that the national parks had become as dependent on the lifestyle of their neighbors as on the conscience of their friends.

In the 1970s the problem of educating the American public about the threat of air pollution over the national parks was much like the predicament of trying to defend the Grand Canyon as an ecosystem during the 1960s. The changes to the parks caused by air pollution were basically incremental and therefore difficult to illustrate. Historically, both preservationists and the public responded with far greater intensity to threats against the national parks of a more direct and immediate nature. Monumentalism, however dated, was still far more easily understood than ecology. The announcement in mid-1975 of stepped-up mining operations in Death Valley National Monument, extractions allowed under the monument's enabling legislation of 1933, was another example of a battle cry that aroused Americans because the threat to Death Valley was simultaneously traditional, visible, and immediate. "Thank God these same people weren't guarding Michelangelo's *Pieta* or Rembrandt's *Night Watch*," an irate reader of the *Los Angeles Times* wrote, striking the popular chord. "They would still be engaged in some endless discussion on how to limit the damage. . . . I shudder to think," he concluded, summing up a century of preservationists' fears, "that there may be borax or oil in the Grand Canyon."[21]

Again the strength of the allusion was its simplicity. The pending changes to Death Valley were not incremental and, as a result, could not be as easily discounted in the public mind. Most environmental issues, by way of contrast, invited public apathy. Each had its own complexity and core of special data; just to understand the problem required scientific knowledge beyond the training of the average citizen. Above all, many environmental issues seemed to have no solution in the first place. Pessimism and a sense of helplessness often characterized discussions of overpopulation and pollution. These were not simply threats to a specific place within the United States alone but dilemmas suggesting that both the nation and the world needed to make radical changes in contemporary lifestyles and social values.

The Grand Canyon dams controversy of the 1960s averted public indifference because preservationists appealed directly to the chasm's symbolic importance rather than to its still intangible values as an ecosystem. "If we can't save the Grand Canyon," asked David Brower, executive director of the Sierra Club, "what the hell can we save?"[22] Here was language any

American could well understand. In rebuttal, the Bureau of Reclamation relied on the standard argument that the enjoyment of national parks by a few wilderness enthusiasts at the expense of many people who needed water and power was elitist. The dams would also allow visitors in motorboats, not merely those hardy people who floated the Colorado River in rubber rafts to enjoy the scenic beauty of the inner canyon. The Sierra Club replied in 1966 through the publication of a series of full-page newspaper advertisements, the most famous of which carried the following headline: "SHOULD WE ALSO FLOOD THE SISTINE CHAPEL SO TOURISTS CAN GET NEARER THE CEILING?"[23] Considered in light of the nation's long-standing insistence that its national parks were a source of cultural identity and pride, no analogy could have been used more effectively. Indeed, its impact was borne out on July 31, 1968, when Congress struck down the bureau's proposal.

Like similar decisions in the past, however, Congress's rejection of the Grand Canyon dams did not lead to a lasting precedent for the protection of national parks in the future. Barely within the decade, mining activity in Death Valley National Monument served notice that the national park system as a whole was still not safe in perpetuity. In 1971 Tenneco, the largest producer of borates, talc, and other minerals in Death Valley, stepped up operations on its claims just inside the boundaries of the national monument. "The main impact on the monument," Nathaniel P. Reed, assistant secretary of the interior, reported to Congress in 1975, "is the use of open pit methods." The company's Boraxo pit, Reed noted, "now is some 3,000 feet by 600 feet and is 220 feet deep, while its Sigma pit is 500 by 400 feet, and is more than 75 feet deep." Not only were both mines "being enlarged"; more alarmingly, "the spoil or waste dumps" had become "highly visible from the scenic road to the Dante's View overlook." Fortunately, he concluded, the biggest deposits of borates "in the same general area of the monument" had "not been developed for production as yet."[24]

Growing opposition to the mining during the summer and fall of 1975 led to congressional hearings on legislation to prohibit further entry into the six existing national parks and monuments, including Death Valley, where mining claims could still be filed.[25] On all previous claims, however, such as Tenneco's Boraxo and Sigma pits in Death Valley National Monument, operations would still be allowed. Similarly, Reed recommended to Congress that Glacier Bay National Monument in Alaska, with its important stores of nickel and copper, also remain "open" pending a study of the magnitude of those deposits to be completed in 1978 by the U.S. Bureau of Mines.[26]

Predictably, the compromises proved unsatisfactory to preservation interests. Representative John F. Seiberling of Ohio, for example, sponsor of the legislation to curb the mining, noted the paradox of telling the public that Death Valley "is to be preserved and even collecting rocks is not allowed," while, "at the same time," legally permitting "huge economic interests for their own personal profit to go in and rip it off." Charles Clusen, testifying before Congress on behalf of the Sierra Club, wholeheartedly supported Seiberling's indignation. "[Even] if these were the last borates and talc," Clusen said, "even if there was no substitute for their use, we must still ask if this gives us the right to destroy the one and only Death Valley that we have." Eventually the United States would have to "come to grips with the fact that there are finite supplies of minerals, and that we cannot allow the destruction of everything we treasure in the pursuit of those resources."[27]

Representatives of the affected mining companies, supported by their own champions in Congress, proposed the more traditional solution—eliminating the disputed claims from the monument altogether. Toward that end Representative Joe Skubitz of Kansas, for example, asked rhetorically whether cutting "that area completely out of the monument" would "do irreparable damage." Arguing that the excision would not injure the park, Representative Philip E. Ruppe of Michigan observed that the lands currently affected amounted to only four thousand acres, but .2 percent of the entire monument: "Who cares then if they mine 4,000 acres? . . . If one mined the whole 4,000 acres, does one make an appreciable dent in either the geology or ecology of Death Valley?" Concluding his own testimony, Robert E. Kendall, executive vice president of the United States Borax and Chemical Corporation, answered that the impact of the mining was indeed minimal. He nonetheless recommended that Congress consider the obvious solution to the whole problem, namely, "a realignment of monument boundaries to exclude areas of low scenic value and high mineral value." Similar alignments might also "be the most practical approach to easing the adverse reaction to mining within units of the national park system" elsewhere in the country. At least in Death Valley, Kendall argued, outright removal of the affected claims offered "a better solution" by insuring that "this highly valuable borate area [is] out of the park, so it is not in conflict with national park objectives."[28]

Although Kendall reassured Congress that his company's large mine at Boron, 110 miles southwest of Death Valley, would meet current levels of demand for borates well into the future, his concession did nothing to dilute the seriousness of his attack on the principle of park integrity. "Does it not destroy the integrity of our park system," Congressman Seiberling asked, driving home the point, "that every time somebody comes up with a new mineral deposit within the park, to say that we will solve the problem, we will just change the boundary?" "I don't think that," Kendall replied, finding additional support for his point of view by citing the history of Death Valley National Monument. "In 1933 when the park was created, a portion of the eastern border was shifted so as to exclude an existing mining operation."[29]

For preservationists, the issue still was not that Death Valley had already been mined in the past or that its unmined portions might be spared development until sometime in the future—the point was that the national monument should *never* have been burdened with those compromises in the first place. As a result, there was little for preservationists to applaud in the legislation signed by President Gerald R. Ford on September 28, 1976, which ostensibly had been introduced in Congress to *prohibit* mining in Death Valley. In fact the law did little more than regulate the miners, who might continue excavation on all claims worked prior to February 29, 1976. The stipulation in effect sanctioned the open-pit mining that had aroused the public the previous year. The secretary of the interior was further required to identify those portions of the monument that might be abolished outright "to exclude significant mineral deposits and to decrease possible acquisition costs."[30] Those portions of Death Valley that survived, in short, apparently would contain nothing of lasting economic value.

The threatened realignment of Death Valley National Monument further testified to the unspoken criterion that national parks could not be justified on the basis of ecological principles alone. Indeed, the plea of George Catlin in 1832 for "A *nation's Park*," replete with Indians and wild animals of the plains, was significant not only as the first recorded statement of the national park idea—it was all the more notable as the exception to the rule in the evolution of parks themselves. The national park idea evolved out of the concern for natural wonders as monuments rather than from an appreciation of the value of landscape in its broadest sense, both animate and inanimate. From the standpoint of both geography and plant life, Catlin's proposal was revolutionary. As late as 1985, the United States had yet to establish a national park devoted exclusively to the protection of America's grasslands and their fauna.[31]

Even where the United States had come closest to the ideal of biological conservation, as in the Florida Everglades, the reluctance of Congress to protect enough territory at the outset threatened the longevity of the respective areas. During the late 1960s the Everglades itself was once more threatened, this time by ground breaking for a huge jetport immediately adjacent to the park's northern perimeter. Before the project was halted in 1970, an entire runway had been cleared and graded.[32] The struggle in part led to passage of the Big Cypress National Preserve four years later. With its approval Congress recognized the legitimacy of fears that Everglades National Park could not survive without protecting its flow of fresh

water from the north, particularly from Big Cypress.[33] Yet
again, neither Congress's denial of the jetport nor passage of
the bill to protect the freshwater preserve had committed the
federal government to preserving the integrity of the national
park system as a whole. No sooner had the jetport in the
Everglades been thwarted than developers advanced a similar
scheme in Jackson Hole.[34] Moreover, mining, hunting, grazing, drainage, agriculture, fishing, trapping, and other traditionally unacceptable uses of the national parks were only to
be regulated rather than abolished outright in Big Cypress.[35]

Because Big Cypress was not considered a national park in
its own right, however, but more accurately a measure of
insurance for one, the compromises were overlooked. In either
case, the regulation of noncompatible activities in Big Cypress
was preferable to no regulation at all. Somewhat the same
philosophy lay behind the trend to national recreation areas,
scenic rivers, national lakeshores, parkways, and urban preserves. If few were national parks in the traditional sense, they
were methods of luring purely recreational interests away
from overused areas such as Yosemite and Yellowstone.

The ecological issues raised by the Yellowstone Conference, however, were still far from being resolved. The studies
which had grown out of the centennial observance had been
uncompromising—there was nothing romantic about survival. The failure of the national parks to preserve representative
examples of the earth's life zones conceivably had jeopardized
the future of man himself by limiting his field for scientific
study and experimentation. In Yellowstone, Mt. McKinley,
and Glacier national parks, for example, the pressure of human numbers threatened extinction of the grizzly bear.[36] Be-
lated efforts to expand Redwood National Park by forty-eight
thousand acres further demonstrated how often the national
parks had been denied from the start enough territory to protect an entire ecosystem.[37]

America's historical preoccupation with monumentalism
masked the nation's failure to establish national parks of unquestionable ecological significance. In what was seen as the
final opportunity for the United States to protect a complete

ecological record, throughout the 1970s preservationists proposed national park status for tens of millions of acres of the
public domain in Alaska. Yet even in the forty-ninth state, the
Conservation Foundation warned, resource interests were determined to restrict parklands "to lands covered with ice and
snow," despite the contention of ecologists that the reserves
"should extend to adjacent lowlands as well."[38]

Preservationists still confronted the paradox of their own
achievements. For one hundred years the success of the national parks movement lay in its concentration on protecting
unique scenery. Now that preservationists understood the necessity of designing the reserves along ecological boundaries
as well, they first had to undo the national parks image they
themselves had once helped encourage.[39] Because the nation's
fascination with rugged scenery had made few demands on the
material progress of the United States, however, broadening
the concept of the national park would be difficult. The limitation of preservation to rugged terrain assured developers of
either the absence of commercially valuable resources in the
parks or the impracticality of exploiting them. From the standpoint of natural beauty, of course, spectacular landscapes
hardly struck their admirers as "worthless." But although the
national parks were inspiring, rarely had value judgments
based on emotion overridden the precondition that inspiring
scenery must also be valueless for all but outdoor recreation.
Not until the substitution of environmentalism for romanticism would the American public be reeducated to understand
that the magnificence of the parks physically distracted attention from their ecological shortcomings. Given the sincerity of
fears that mankind might perish without the knowledge
locked up in wilderness, at least this much seemed certain: The
United States could not afford to wait another hundred years
to preserve the land for what it was instead of what it was not.

10

Management in Transition

I can remember Dr. A. Starker Leopold, on a zoology class field trip in Lake County, California, in 1951, telling some of his students that before long fire would be restored to national parks. It seemed a startling and revolutionary idea at the time.

Bruce M. Kilgore, 1974

More visitation, better roads, and improved accommodations—the traditional concerns of national park management—were gradually challenged during the 1960s and early 1970s by the need to address the ecological issues summarized at the Second World Conference on National Parks in 1972. Meanwhile, America's historical preoccupation with monumentalism masked the nation's failure to establish national parks of unquestionable ecological integrity. The result was renewed interest in the biological significance of the larger national parks and monuments already in existence. Again precedent could not be ignored. Granted, the old-line parks and monuments had been established with cultural rather than ecological ends in mind. Only the larger reserves, however, regardless of their imperfections, possessed the diversity of natural features necessary to begin widespread experimentation with the principles of biological management.

Among the Park Service's existing management policies, none seemed more inconsistent with the needs of plants and animals than providing opportunities for mass recreation. As overcrowding worsened, however, a few scientists occasionally spoke out against accommodating people in the parks at the expense of the natural scene. Finally, these random notes of criticism achieved special credibility in 1963, when the distinguished Leopold Committee, chaired by A. Starker Leopold of the University of California at Berkeley, released its sweeping report, *Wildlife Management in the National Parks*. If the document had appeared but a few years earlier, undoubtedly it would have been largely ignored. A new generation of conservation leaders, however, influenced by Rachel Carson's *Silent Spring* and caught up in the emotion of the environmental movement, instead found the Leopold Committee's conclusions too provocative to dismiss.[1]

Central to the committee's report was its recommendation that protection, defined as the strict maintenance of park features, must give way to greater respect for the importance of the natural forces that had brought about those features in the first place. For example, the scientists reported, "It is now an accepted truism that maintenance of suitable habitat is the key to sustaining animal populations, and that protection, though it is important, is not of itself a substitute for habitat." Habitat had less to do with artifacts or physical wonders and more to do with natural processes, such as wind, rain, and fire. It followed that habitat could not be regarded as "a fixed or stable entity that can be set aside and preserved behind a fence, like a cliff dwelling or a petrified tree." Biotic communities evolved by "change through natural stages of succession." Managers who chose to alter the parks biologically must therefore resort to the direct "manipulation of plant and animal populations."[2]

How that manipulation might be directed, and toward what ends, comprised the most significant portion of the Leopold report. "As a primary goal," the committee suggested, "we would recommend that the biotic associations within each park be maintained, or where necessary recreated, as nearly as possible in the condition that prevailed when the area was first visited by the white man." In short, the scientists concluded, "A national park should represent a vignette of primitive America."[3]

The obstacles to achieving "this seemingly simple aspiration are stupendous," the committee wrote, admitting the obvious: "Many of our national parks—in fact most of them—went through periods of indiscriminate logging, burning, livestock grazing, hunting, and predator control." Once those areas became national parks they again "shifted abruptly to a regime of equally unnatural protection from lightning fires, from insect outbreaks, absence of natural controls of ungulates, and in some areas elimination of normal fluctuations in water levels." Meanwhile, exotic species of plants and animals had "inadvertently been introduced." Finally, factors of human visitation, including "roads and trampling and camp grounds and pack stock," had taken their toll of park environments. It was small wonder that restoring "the primitive scene" would not be "done easily nor can it be done completely," the committee concluded. The point was that the National Park Service needed a new perspective from which to begin a more sensitive management program.[4]

At least among scientists familiar with the national parks, the suggestion that they be restored to their appearance at the time of European contact with North America had been discussed as early as the 1910s.[5] With the growing popularity of the environmental movement during the 1960s, more Americans, including eminent scientists such as those of the Leopold Committee, found the ideal of pristine wilderness a comforting vision in a rapidly changing world. Few at the time noted the apparent contradiction in the committee's own conclusions. Having argued that natural forces were dynamic, the committee nonetheless recommended that national park environments be restored to an approximation of their original state four hundred years earlier. Obviously the committee, much like preservationists in general throughout the 1960s, had been influenced by the opinion that human beings were disruptive and therefore were an "unnatural" presence in wilderness areas. Yet another contradiction was the committee's reluctance to extend this bias to Native Americans as well as to their European conquerors. Instead, the committee endorsed manipulation of the environment by the Indians, particularly their use of fire, as a practice in keeping with the need to restore periodic burning to many park landscapes.[6]

By "natural," in other words, the committee meant "original," or at the time of European contact. Put another way, Native Americans were "original" and therefore a "natural" presence in North America. Europeans rather than Indians had been responsible for changing the continent ruthlessly and unsystematically. "The goal of managing the national parks and monuments," the committee restated, "should be to preserve, or where necessary recreate, the ecologic scene as viewed by the first European visitors."[7]

The use of the term "visitors" to describe European pioneers again strongly implied that they and their descendents, not Native Americans, were the unnatural element in the New World. As white Americans moved westward, wildlife was greatly reduced in numbers, some species to the point of extinction. Similarly, Europeans had permanently introduced exotic varieties of plants and animals as well as human diseases alien to North America into practically every environment. "All these limitations we fully realize," the committee wrote by way of confession. "Yet, if [our] goal cannot be fully achieved it can be approached." Since perfection was impossible, the next best alternative was to restore the national parks to at least suggest what North America may have looked like in the precolonial period. "A reasonable illusion of primitive America could be recreated," the scientists maintained, "using the utmost in skill, judgment, and ecologic sensitivity."[8]

With the publication of the Leopold report in 1963, preservation interests eagerly endorsed its substitution of the "illusion of primitive America" for the existing illusions of monumentalism.[9] Much as Americans of the nineteenth century had found comfort in the cultural symbolism of Yosemite, Yellowstone, and the Grand Canyon, so preservationists of the 1960s

The 1970s campaign for national park expansion in Alaska sought to include ecologically sensitive lands, such as wildlife breeding grounds, in all protected areas. Park expansion was least controversial when the territories proposed for wilderness status encompassed only monumental topography, such as the Arrigetch Peaks, Gates of the Arctic National Park and Preserve, above, and the Great Gorge of Ruth Glacier, Denali National Park and Preserve, below.

The gentle beauty of Great Outer Beach, Cape Cod National Seashore, Massachusetts, above, contrasts sharply with the boiling, windswept surf of Point Reyes National Seashore, California, below.

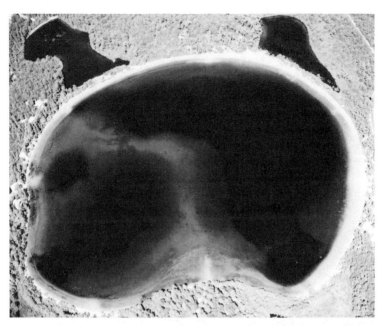

PHOTOGRAPH BY M. WOODBRIDGE WILLIAMS, COURTESY OF THE NATIONAL PARK SERVICE

PHOTOGRAPH BY RICHARD FREAR, COURTESY OF THE NATIONAL PARK SERVICE

National seashores, lakeshores, riverways, and urban recreation areas, although not often monumental, were consistently advocated for their ecological treasures. Above is Great Pond, a freshwater remnant of the Ice Age, in Cape Cod National Seashore, Massachusetts. Scenic riverways, such as the St. Croix National Scenic Riverway in Wisconsin and Minnesota, below, offer a picturesque retreat from urban surroundings.

Rugged topography often explains why open spaces near major American cities have not been extensively developed. Here, the Marin Headlands of the Golden Gate National Recreation Area frame the Golden Gate Bridge and San Francisco, California.

Gateway National Recreation Area, New York and New Jersey, offers recreation for nearby population centers, such as bird watching, above. But urban parks must also cope with urban problems. Below, a high rise and car abandoned at Breezy Point in the same park.

This controversial observation tower, constructed during the early 1970s on private land just outside Gettysburg National Military Park, Pennsylvania, dramatizes the continuing threat to all national parks from commercial encroachments.

A prescribed burn to remove competitive vegetation among the Giant Sequoias in Giant Forest, Sequoia National Park, California, September 1980, contrasts sharply with the principles of total protection generally followed by the National Park Service before the introduction of fire ecology during the late 1960s and 1970s.

As secretary of the interior between 1981 and 1983, James Watt drew fire from environmentalists for his outspoken opposition to national park expansion and inspired literally hundreds of political cartoons. Above, Watt is shown at Yellowstone National Park, September 1981. David Horsey depicts him as the serpent in a national park Garden of Eden, below.

found reason for hope in the suggestion that some of the ecological damage experienced in the United States—at least in
the national parks—might be reversed or undone. Indeed, the
lasting significance of the Leopold report lay not in its own
romantic images of pristine America but in its guiding principle that the biological management of the national parks was
just as important as—if not more so than—the strict protection of their natural features.

Of all the attractions of the national park system none
more dramatically symbolized the slow but steady adoption of
the principles of biological management than the Giant
Sequoias of the High Sierra. Recognition of their cultural
symbolism as America's "living antiquity" had led to the protection of scattered groves of the Big Trees as early as the
Yosemite Grant of 1864. With their protection against logging
and vandalism, however, had not come ecological understanding of their life cycle. The biological sciences were still in their
infancy and still basically obsessed with cataloging data rather than viewing it comprehensively. As a result, few but the
Native Americans who resided in the High Sierra understood
that fires were a common occurrence among the redwood
trees. Government wardens of the Sequoia groves instead tried
to suppress the ground fires that periodically crept toward the
boundaries of the early parks.[10]

Strict protection of the Giant Sequoias against fire
seemed in the best interest of their perpetuation as natural
monuments. Fire burned other forests; as a result, awareness
of the fact that its presence was not universally destructive
grew slowly. For example, as late as 1929 Curtis K. Skinner, a
respected conservationist, upheld the popular view that fire
"without a doubt" was "the greatest threat against the perpetual *scenic* wealth of our largest National Parks" [italics
added]. Throughout the 1880s and 1890s, Skinner wrote, arguing his point, "a fire might rage in the mountain forests for
weeks without exciting any more attention than an occasional
remark between ranchers concerning the dryness of the weath-
er." Not until the early 1900s, following greater publicity
about the needs of the national parks, did the government fully

adopt a policy of "increased vigilance and much careful attention to fire-fighting equipment" that the protection of their forests required.[11]

Given the depth of support for Skinner's point of view among the general public, anyone who questioned the wisdom of excluding fire from every forest inevitably drew strong criticism from professional and amateur foresters alike. Still, although they were a distinct minority, proponents of the so-called light burning theory occasionally managed to get a public hearing.[12] One of the first to defend the use of fire as a management tool in the national parks was Captain G. H. G. Gale, commandant of the Fourth U.S. Cavalry, which was assigned to the patrol of Yosemite in 1894. "Examination of this subject," he reported in June to the secretary of the interior, "leads me to believe that the absolute prevention of fires in these mountains will eventually lead to disastrous results." Fire did not appear to be the enemy of the Sierra forest but a presence crucial to the forest's very survival. Annual fires removed the litter of fallen needles and toppled trees on the forest floor, leaving "the ground ready for the next year's growth." Enough younger trees escaped the flames to replace the forest, "and it is not thought," Gale remarked, appealing to the common wisdom of Sierra natives and pioneers, "that the slight heat of the annual fires will appreciably affect the growth or life of well-grown trees. On the other hand," he concluded with a warning, "if the year's droppings are allowed to accumulate they will increase until the resulting heat, when they do burn, will destroy everything before it."[13]

As a proponent of light burning, Captain Gale was little more persuasive than his counterparts in introducing the sustained, systematic use of fire to the national parks. Nor did the establishment of the National Park Service in 1916 lead to any relaxation in the policy of fire suppression. As a result, over the years the superintendents of the respective parks lost sight of the composition of the parks' original forests as younger, competitive vegetation and debris accumulated among the older growth. Finally, scientists during the 1950s turned increasingly to the problems of fire suppression, later publishing their findings in both respected general and professional journals. Not until 1963 and the publication of the Leopold Committee Report, however, did the National Park Service pay serious attention to this new research. Meanwhile, the Park Service was caught up in its Mission 66 program to open the parks to greater numbers of visitors. Thus it was during the 1960s that the need for periodic burning in most of the larger national parks and monuments was recognized as a management necessity.[14]

The Tuolumne and Mariposa groves of Giant Sequoias in Yosemite National Park served as early examples of the consequences of fire suppression. "Two great changes have taken place as a result of fire protection," wrote H. H. Biswell, a professor of forestry with the University of California, in 1961: "First, the more shade-tolerant white fir and incense cedar have developed in dense thickets in the understory of many Big Trees and pines. They greatly add to the fire hazard." Visitors to the park who considered this accumulation "natural" failed "to recognize that fire, too, was a natural and characteristic feature of the environment in earlier times." "The second change of great importance in the Sierra Nevada forests," Biswell said, continuing his pathbreaking article, "is the large increase in debris on the forest floor." Sierra forests "were relatively clean, open, and park-like in earlier times, and could be easily traveled through." After decades of fire suppression, however, most were "so full of dead material and young trees and brush as to be nearly impassable."[15]

By so increasing the fire hazard, such conditions only invited a major conflagration that would wipe out the forest entirely. Fires in the original, primeval forest had been "friendly," limited to the smaller accumulations of "herbs, needles, and leaves on the ground." The Giant Sequoias themselves, "with their asbestos-like bark," easily resisted the low flames and mild heat. In contrast, a modern fire among the redwoods would be enormously destructive, fed by "the development of a solid fuel layer in many places from the tops of the tallest trees to the young saplings and brush and litter on the ground. Is it any wonder," Professor Biswell asked in conclusion, "that the wildfires in such situations are so devastating and difficult to control?"[16]

The significance of these findings aside, additional research during the 1960s and early 1970s further established the importance of fire not only in clearing the Sequoia groves of competitive vegetation, but in actually providing for their existence in the first place. Once again, the observations of a few perceptive individuals writing in the nineteenth century were confirmed. As early as 1878, for example, John Muir wrote that "fire, the great destroyer of Sequoia, also furnishes bare, virgin ground, one of the conditions essential for its growth from seed."[17] Although Muir greatly exaggerated the destructiveness of natural fires, he was nonetheless among the few people prior to 1900 to recognize their significance in the regeneration of Giant Sequoias.

After 1900, fire suppression throughout the High Sierra undermined the advancement of this hypothesis well into mid-century. Finally, both private and government scientists admitted few Sequoia seedlings were growing in the mountains, even in the protected groves. That startling revelation led to the first major studies of the intricacies of the Sequoia forests, studies that widely confirmed that Sequoia seeds rarely germinated unless simultaneously exposed to bare mineral soils in open sunlight. Not only were young Sequoias found to be intolerant of shade and competitive vegetation, but they required fire to burn away the forest litter that prevented their seeds from reaching bare ground in the first place. Historically many of the seedlings had perished in the ground fires that later swept through the groves every few years. The point was that enough of the younger growth had survived the flames to grow up into a new and complete Sequoia forest. In contrast, the suppression of all fires over a period of several decades had choked the open areas of the Sequoia groves with cedar and white fir. Coupled with their own growth, which shaded out the forest floor among the Big Trees, the competitors contributed increasing amounts of needles and fallen branches to the forest litter, simultaneously strangling any Sequoia seedlings that managed to take root in debris as well as darkness.[18]

With the problem in the Sequoia groves so graphically identified, scientists devoted the remainder of their research to finding a practical solution. Among them was John L. Vankat, assistant professor of botany at Miami University in Oxford, Ohio. "Our great challenge," he wrote, summing up the recent findings in the Big Tree groves, "is to return disturbed ecosystems to the point where natural processes may act as primary management agents." In other words, ideally the appearance of the Sierra forest a century ago might be restored, at least in the national parks. As the basis for his conviction, Professor Vankat extensively quoted the Leopold Committee Report of 1963. "When the forty-niners poured over the Sierra Nevada into California, those that kept diaries spoke almost to a man of the wide-spaced columns of mature trees that grew on the lower western slope in gigantic magnificence. The ground was a grass parkland, in springtime carpeted with wildflowers. Deer and bears were abundant." Ground fires were primarily responsible for this pristine environment; with fire suppression began the changes leading to the "dog-hair thicket of young pines, white fir, incense cedar, and mature brush" common along the western slope of the Sierra in 1963.[19]

At least for a government agency, the National Park Service reacted rather swiftly to the findings of the Leopold Committee Report. In September 1967 the Park Service officially reversed its long-standing policy of suppressing all fires in the great majority of its parks. "Fires in vegetation resulting from natural causes are recognized as natural phenomena," read the agency's new policy statement. Accordingly, wherever fires might "be contained within predetermined fire management units" and where burning would "contribute to the accomplishment of approved vegetation and/or wildlife management objectives," natural fires "may be allowed to run their course."[20]

To reemphasize, by "natural" was meant the original appearance of North America at the time of European contact. Strictly interpreted, such a definition obviously had to make allowances for the extensive use of fire by Native Americans.

Of course the Park Service had neither the intention nor the means of honoring such authenticity in its forests. Human beings, including Indians, could no longer be recognized as agents of "natural" change. What appeared at first glance to contradict man's original contribution as a factor of biological succession, however, in fact provided park biologists with a resolution to their basic dilemma. Before natural processes could be restored to the national parks as self-perpetuating agents, biologists would have to resort to human intervention yet again. But since Native Americans historically had set fire to forests later protected in the parks, it followed that the adoption of Indian aims and techniques would be consistent with the goal of returning specific ecosystems to the point of self-renewal.

Especially in the Giant Sequoia groves of Yosemite, Sequoia, and Kings Canyon national parks, the unnatural accumulation of dead branches, litter, and competitive vegetation over many decades of protection indicated that any fire, however natural in origin, would nonetheless be highly destructive. In this instance, at least, the biological ends justified any artificial means. The artificial suppression of fires had led to the problem in the first place; clearly, the only way "back to nature," so to speak, was by resorting to an artificial remedy in the interest of eventually recreating the natural rhythms that had been lost. First, the competitive vegetation growing among the Big Trees would have to be cut, stacked by hand, and burned under strict supervision. Afterward, the litter and other accumulated debris on the forest floor might also be burned under carefully monitored conditions when fires were not likely to get out of control. Finally, ground fires of natural origin, obviously from lightning strikes, could again be permitted to burn themselves out in the groves under the watchful eye of park biologists.[21]

As in the past, groves cleared of debris and competitive trees would be subjected only to ground fires, each limited by the scarcity of fuel and the work of previous combustion to lower levels of heat and intensity. The thick, asbestoslike bark of the Giant Sequoias would again protect the mature specimens from harm; equally important, enough of the seedlings would survive the occasional flames to perpetuate the Sequoia forest for centuries to come.

The realization of this scenario, coupled with the ability to restrict controlled burning to the parks proper, spurred its emergence in the 1970s as the most profound and successful response to the principles of biological management outlined in the Leopold Committee Report of 1963. Unlike the committee's other controversial recommendations, such as the reintroduction of natural predators to park environments, allowing fire back into park ecosystems did not depend for its success on the cooperation of other government agencies or private landowners surrounding the preserves. Predators wandering outside park boundaries were almost certain to be shot by farmers, ranchers, and hunters. At least with the proper precautions, fire could be restricted to areas solely under the control of the National Park Service.

As any management philosophy, however, controlled burning also had its detractors, including old-line rangers and concessionaires sensitive to the disappointment of park visitors seeking out the traditional as opposed to the biological. Tourists who had driven hundreds or thousands of miles in search of monumental scenery especially found little to inspire them in mountains obscured by the smoke of smoldering fires, however natural or apparently necessary.[22] Other critics saw another contradiction in allowing natural pollution to hang over the parks, while at the same time objecting to the smoke and dust of distant cities and coal-fired power plants.[23] Manipulation of the environment toward human objectives had long been the basis of American society. Were not the pioneers and their descendents, not merely Native Americans, a natural and therefore legitimate presence in the environment? Was it not illogical to expect that the environment could be suspended at a fixed point no one living could even remember? Weighed against these deeply philosophical issues, monumentalism in comparison seemed so simple to understand.

The appreciation of natural objects, unlike an intimate awareness of natural processes, required only childlike wonder and a sense of imagination. To be sure, America's historical preoccupation with monumentalism still masked the nation's failure to establish national parks of unquestionable ecological significance. In the final analysis, obtaining national parks of adequate size, not simply experimenting with new management techniques, was the key to the survival of resources other than scenic wonders. In this regard, the ecological issues raised by the Leopold Committee Report and underscored by the First and Second World Conferences on National Parks were still years away from being addressed politically, let alone even partially resolved biologically.[24]

11

Ideals and Controversies of Expansion

The main flaw in the performance of many existing conservation associations is that most concentrate on a chosen holy grail, and too few organizations have entered the
fight for the total environment.

Stewart L. Udall, 1963

A park, however splendid, has little appeal to a family that
cannot reach it. . . . The new conservation is built on a new
promise—to bring parks closer to the people.

Lyndon B. Johnson, 1968

If you keep standing for perfection, you won't get anything.

Phillip Burton, 1979

Initially hailed as a milestone of environmental insight, the
Leopold Committee Report of 1963 more accurately reawakened and redirected concerns about the biological health
of the national parks evident since the late 1920s. In a similar
vein, the rapid expansion of the national park system during
the 1960s and 1970s merely intensified the long debate over
Congress's responsibility to protect so-called national park
standards. Again the issue pitted traditional perceptions of the
national parks against the growing determination to protect
all kinds of landscapes, not just those blessed with outstanding
geological wonders. Monumentalism was so fixed in the American mind, however, that its persuasiveness in dictating the
establishment of new national parks was not to be easily dis-
lodged. "Our National Parks are much more than recreational
resorts and museums of unaltered nature," wrote Robert Ster-

ling Yard in 1923, defending the national park standards of his own generation; "they are also the Exposition of the Scenic Supremacy of the United States." The nation's reputation as the leader in world conservation would only be threatened by expansion of the national park system for expansion's sake. "No other trade-mark," he concluded, "has cost so much to establish and pays such dividends of business, national prestige, and patriotism." Nevertheless, he warned, his concerns now fully obvious, "it is proposed to destroy it."[1]

Especially in the East, calls for "inferior" national parks threatened to distract attention from the world-class landscapes already included in the national park system. Public recreation, Yard charged, not scenic preservation, was the true motivation behind these newer parks. He did not consider recreation unimportant; similarly, he had earlier admitted that a limited number of areas might qualify for national park status on the basis of their plants, animals, or wilderness alone.[2] In the absence of monumental scenery, however, the need to protect nondescript resources in national parks must be indisputable. The protection of pretty, yet uninspiring landscapes was itself secondary to the promotion of scenic wonders whose uniqueness required no further justification for national park status. "When Zion National Park was created in 1919," he wrote, offering a recent example, "the whole world knew from the simple announcement of the fact that another stupendous scenic wonderland had been discovered. But when pleasant wooded summits, limestone caves, pretty local ravines, local mountains and gaps between mountains become National Parks, the name 'Zion National Park' will mean nothing at home or abroad to those who have not already seen it." Demeaning the scenic standards of the national parks merely invited "local competition not only for national parks but for national appropriations. If one Congressional District secures its own National Park, why not every other Congressional District in the State, or in many States? . . . What are Congressmen for if not to look out for their districts?" The "increasing dozens of little parks" would undermine the financial support of the larger, spectacular, and clearly legitimate reserves. "A National Park Pork Barrel," he bitterly concluded, "would be the final degradation!"[3]

For the next half century, Yard and other purists fought against the use of the term "national park" to describe battlefields, historic sites, parkways, recreation areas, and other federal preserves of limited scenic impressiveness.[4] Dr. John C. Merriam, president of the Carnegie Institution, defended Yard's objections to park expansion in this vein, writing in 1926 of "the power and order behind nature." "National Parks represent opportunities for worship in which one comes to understand more fully certain of the attributes of nature and its Creator," Merriam said, elaborating on his definition. "They are not objects to be worshipped, but they are altars over which we may worship."[5] Reverence for nature, as exemplified by public respect for the sanctity of the existing national parks, would only be eroded by heedless expansion of the system into areas of commonplace topography. At stake, in other words, was the nineteenth century's sense of "pilgrimage," the feeling that only by journeying west did one come face to face with nature in its most majestic, pristine, and symbolic setting.[6]

In contrast to Yard and Merriam, most preservationists of the succeeding generation—grappling with the deterioration of the environment as a whole—simply had far less in common with the image of national parks as evidence of the country's spiritual evolution and cultural superiority. Certainly by the 1960s, that image had been tempered by the belief that nature as a whole was important. National parks, in addition to protecting the "museum pieces" of the American landscape, might also afford protection to land threatened by housing developments, shopping centers, expressways, and similar forms of urban encroachment. Stemming the tide of urban development in the future hinged on educating Americans in the cities and suburbs to appreciate the significance of the natural world being sacrificed in their own backyards. Indeed, the loss of more than a million acres of open space annually throughout the United States of the 1960s and 1970s greatly alarmed preservation interests.[7] Increasingly they understood the irony of protecting Yellowstone's two million acres, for example, all the while losing half as much land every year to housing, highways, parking lots, and other types of urban sprawl.

Equity of access to the national parks was yet another pressing issue for modern preservationists. By virtue of their remoteness, the great western national parks excluded as many Americans as they accommodated. Even in the East, the largest natural areas were too far distant, especially for the urban poor.[8] For Robert Sterling Yard's generation, the quality of park landscapes rather than equity of access to the parks had been preservationists' major concern. Ignoring the fact that states outside the Far West might deserve national parks, few other regions of the country possessed comparable scenic distinctiveness. Whatever course the United States chose to follow in meeting the everyday needs of its citizens for outdoor recreation, the distinction between national parks and purely recreational areas should never be compromised. "None but the noblest" national parks, Yard pleaded again, "painstakingly chosen, must be admitted" to the system.[9]

By the early 1960s, Yard's brand of purism had been questioned by all but the most tradition-bound preservationists. Most still clung to monumentalism emotionally; politically and socially, however, they realized their movement was changing. For example, if preservationists were to acknowledge the legitimacy of civil rights, it seemed advisable to create more national parks closer to where all Americans lived and worked year-round, not merely where only the middle and upper classes could afford to spend their summer vacations.[10] Even more to the point, only the federal government seemed powerful and wealthy enough to forestall the degradation of natural environments across the country. What Yard had labeled "pork barrel politics," in other words, struck preservationists as perhaps their only hope of providing the environment as a whole with at least minimal protection.[11]

Inevitably, Yard's insistence that recreational needs be addressed apart from scenic preservation was tempered by political realities. So, too, did preservationists ignore his warning that bureaucrats and politicians would be tempted to label any area a "national park," thereby diluting the original significance of the term. As opportunities for preservation dwindled with each passing year, these seemed to be the concerns of a previous generation. What mattered most to preservationists of the 1960s and 1970s was not what the parks were called, or even how they might be used, but whether parks—any parks—would be established in the first place.

Across the United States, preservationists championed dozens of new parks under a wide variety of categories, from seashores and lakeshores to urban recreation areas. The impetus for park expansion reached its peak in 1977 with the appointment of Representative Phillip Burton of California to chair the House Subcommittee on National Parks and Insular Affairs. By the end of the following year, Burton, a strong promoter of local, regional, and urban national parks, had pushed through Congress the largest single legislative package in national park history.[12]

Although opponents in Congress, the Park Service, and the media—echoing Robert Sterling Yard—labeled it the "Parks Barrel Bill," its passage was never seriously in doubt. To the contrary, most preservationists endorsed the legislation as an important milestone in making national parks relevant to an urban-based, industrialized society.[13] Granted, the simultaneous campaign for huge wilderness parks in Alaska indicated that traditional values of landscape protection were also very much alive in the United States. Among individuals and organizations equally committed to the establishment of national parks outside the scenic public lands of the West, however, passage of the Omnibus Bill of 1978 heralded a new era of legitimacy—and success—for their cause.

First applied to Yellowstone, the term "national park" inevitably fixed an indelible image of grandeur and mystery in the public mind. It followed that any national park established subsequently would be measured against Yellowstone, not only because it was the first to be called a national park but because the region held such deep significance as a symbol for

American culture. In that vein, in 1961 the historian John Ise addressed the issue of national park standards: "There were in 1902 six national parks of superlative magnificence; but between 1902 and 1906 three new parks were set aside—Wind Cave, Sullys Hill, and Platt—which did not measure up to this high standard." Ise concluded the problem was the absence of a "Congressional policy governing the establishment of national parks," coupled with the lack of a "Park Service to screen park proposals." As a result, these three "inferior" national parks "just happened to be established."[14]

In fact, preservation of the three areas marked a subtle rather than accidental shift in national park policy. By the early twentieth century, the perception of national parks as the embodiment of American romanticism and cultural achievement had been joined by the identification of their value for promoting public health and physical fitness. Invariably, interest groups advocating hiking, horseback riding, and other forms of outdoor recreation asked: Why should only states in the Far West have national parks? Wind Cave, Sullys Hill, and Platt were but the first examples of the political response to this latent desire for all states in the union to share in the national park experiment.

The problem of compensating for the geological limitations of park projects outside the Rocky Mountains, Sierra Nevada, and desert Southwest compounded the dilemma of trying to justify each proposal on traditional grounds. The term "national park," after all, was first applied to the incomparable wonders of Yellowstone. Where equivalent natural features were lacking, other compensatory values had to be found. In this vein, John F. Lacey of Iowa introduced the proposed Wind Cave national park in South Dakota to the House of Representatives as "substantially what the Yellowstone country would be if the geysers should die. It has been excavated by hot water in the same manner that the geyser land is now being excavated in the Yellowstone." Wind Cave's dramatic past, however, was obviously not the geological equal of Yellowstone's exciting present. "The active forces are no longer in operation there," Lacey admitted; "there is no hot water,

and the conditions that formerly prevailed there have ceased."
Still, he argued, finally abandoning his extravagant comparison, "a series of very wonderful caves remain, and the Land
Department has withdrawn this tract from settlement." The
"few claims" of settlers in the area amounted to but "a few
hundred acres" of the nine thousand proposed for park status;
"I think it is a very meritorious proposition," he therefore concluded, "and that this tract of land ought to be reserved to the
American people."[15]

Wind Cave's projected territory of only nine thousand
acres, in comparison to Yellowstone's 2.2 million, also foreshadowed the fate of most parklands to be created outside the
mountain and desert West. With the exception of national
parks equally restricted to either rugged or undesirable terrain, new reserves in the East, Middle West, and South would
likewise be significantly limited in scope. This factor, too,
posed a dilemma for activists seeking to justify the fact that
areas outside the West still qualified for national park status.
Most simply lacked the diversity of natural features one expected to find as a matter of course in Yellowstone, Yosemite,
Glacier, and the Grand Canyon. Anticipating the problem,
proponents of the so-called lesser parks could not help but
inflate their descriptions, arguing in effect that the quantity of
one type of feature was enough compensation for the absence
of several points of interest. Binger Hermann, the commissioner of the General Land Office, thus quoted extensively
from the reports of his surveyor, who found Wind Cave literally filled with "subterranean wonders." Examples included
"great caverns and grotesque-looking rooms," "large grot-
toes," and "tons of specimens." "Those who visited the Yellowstone National Park and the Mammoth Cave of Kentucky," the
description concluded, "will all accord the Wind Cave only a
second place to the Yellowstone Canyon and the geysers of the
former and declare the Wind Cave superior, in point of attrac-
tiveness, to the Mammoth Cave."[16]

In the final analysis, those and similar linkages to Yellowstone National Park proved decisive in winning park status for
Wind Cave. Supporters of the park effectively if excessively

argued that Wind Cave, like Yellowstone, was a monumental "wonder." One simply had to go underground to appreciate the resemblance. The names of Wind Cave's features further betokened its uniqueness and worthiness for national park status—"Pearly Gates," "Fair Grounds," "Garden of Eden," "Castle Garden," and "Blue Grotto," to name but a few.[17] Besides, Congress could hardly find economic reasons to object to the protection of only nine thousand acres, but a minute fraction of one of the larger existing parks. Indeed, opposition in both the House and Senate was negligible. On January 8, 1903, President Theodore Roosevelt signed the Wind Cave National Park Act into law.[18]

In retrospect, if critics of Wind Cave found little to justify its designation as a national park, Congress in 1902 clearly felt otherwise. Right from the outset, Wind Cave was introduced and discussed as a national park project. Sullys Hill National Park, established by presidential proclamation on June 2, 1904, obviously was not intended to be a national park in the traditional sense of the term. In April of 1904, Congress authorized the president to establish a "park" at Sullys Hill in North Dakota; the authorization was actually an addition to a bill adjusting a previous agreement with the Indians of the Devils Lake Reservation. Never one to forego an opportunity to exercise his discretion, President Theodore Roosevelt set aside 960 acres embracing Sullys Hill on the edge of Devils Lake as "Sullys Hill Park."[19]

Neither Congress's authorization nor Roosevelt's proclamation established a *national* park at Sullys Hill; nevertheless, the area was eventually referred to by that term. Lacking any monumental signficance and barely one and a half square miles in area, Sullys Hill later struck its critics as a perfect example of the depreciation of national park standards. Not until 1914 did Congress appropriate $5,000 to manage the reserve; even then, the money was not used to operate Sullys Hill as a national park but as a game preserve under the direct supervision of the U.S. Biological Survey.[20]

The establishment in 1906 of Platt National Park in Oklahoma seemed to invite further abuse of national park standards. In 1902 Congress purchased 640 acres of spring-fed, low rolling hills near the town of Sulphur from the Choctaw and Chickasaw Indians, designating it the Sulphur Springs Reservation. Four years later, its ordinary topography in no way deterred members of the Connecticut delegation in Congress from seeking the preserve as a memorial to the late senator from their state, Orville Hitchcock Platt. A resolution to that effect cleared both the House and Senate in late June of 1906; afterward, the Sulphur Springs Reservation was known officially as "Platt National Park."[21]

Among Platt, Sullys Hill, and Wind Cave only the latter, eventually enlarged to twenty-eight thousand acres, survived as a national park. Yet the precedent of awarding national park status to only the most inspiring western landscapes had clearly been broken. Gradually, proposals for national parks outside the scenic West were introduced into Congress with a frequency their detractors considered alarming. Stephen T. Mather, as first director of the National Park Service, defended the scenic reputation of the existing parks by channeling this enthusiasm for preserves outside the West into the emerging state parks movement. Under Mather's direction, for example, the Park Service was instrumental in the formation of the National Conference on State Parks, which held its first meeting in Des Moines, Iowa, in 1921. Time and again throughout the coming decade, Mather enlisted the support of the organization to disarm proponents of so-called unworthy national park projects. In each instance he suggested that state ownership and control were probably more appropriate for areas whose natural features were renowned only among residents of the neighboring region or locality.[22]

Mather's initial problems with the preservation community were due in large part to his obvious reluctance to apply any such assessment universally. The Hot Springs Reservation, Arkansas, given national park status in 1921, and the Mammoth Cave in Kentucky, authorized five years later, were two early examples of his own concession to the fact that not every national park could possess outstanding national significance on a par with Yellowstone, Yosemite, and the Grand

Canyon.²³ Mammoth Cave, like Wind Cave, was a subterranean wonder at the very least; in contrast, the Hot Springs Reservation was clearly a resort and little more. The National Parks Association further objected to the lack of study prior to determining that Mammoth Cave itself deserved national park status. Instead, Robert Sterling Yard charged the Park Service with playing "national politics." "A graver situation cannot be imagined," he concluded, "at a time when a number of southern states are clamoring for National Parks to bring them the tourist business which the fame of the title is supposed to guarantee."²⁴

As a purist, Yard would have Americans go west to visit the national parks. As a government official, on the other hand, Mather could not be so politically insensitive to the call for landscape protection in the eastern half of the United States, regardless of its topographical shortcomings. Initially, concessions to monumentalism could be made by supporting parks with at least some semblance of dramatic uplift. Acadia National Park, established in 1919 along the rugged seacoast of Mount Desert Island, Maine, was the first example. The park's highest point is Cadillac Mountain, but 1,530 feet above sea level. Yet the standard description of Mount Desert Island as simply "beautiful," the naturalist Freeman Tilden later wrote, "utterly fails to do justice to this rock-built natural fortress which thrusts forward into the Atlantic and challenges its power." Where else, Tilden asked, "can you find anything in our country to match these mountains that come down to the ocean, . . . altogether such a sweep of rugged coastline as has no parallel from Florida to the Canadian provinces?" Even Robert Sterling Yard, as self-appointed protector of national park standards, defined Acadia in 1923 as "our standard bearer for National Park making in the East." It was "only twenty-seven square miles in area," he conceded; "nevertheless," he agreed, "it includes National Park essentials in full measure."²⁵

Of course rugged scenery was the most important "essential." Next in consideration came uniqueness. Acadia was one of a kind, *the* highest and most rugged portion of the Atlantic coast between Maine and Florida. In contrast, the Shenandoah national park project, authorized in 1926, did not win the universal endorsement of preservation interests. Granted, the Blue Ridge Mountains in Shenandoah National Park are far higher than Cadillac Mountain in Acadia; they were not recognized in 1926, however, as the *highest* mountains of their type. Only "the impressive massing of lofty mountains," Yard argued, "still covered with primitive forest, in the Great Smoky Mountains between Tennessee and North Carolina," not "the much lesser Shenandoah location," met every existing national park standard of sublime scenery and "primitive quality." To recognize Shenandoah as a national park, its value for outdoor recreation aside, would be, in effect, to condone "the fatal belief that different standards can be maintained in the same system without the destruction of all standards."[26]

Among preservationists as a whole, growing recognition of the importance of biological conservation steadily undermined support for Yard's rigid point of view. The National Park Service itself had begun to look beyond its traditional role as steward of the great "primeval" parks—where opportunities for further expansion were limited—by actively promoting additions to the system whose significance was distinctly historical or archeological rather than scenic.[27] With the retirement of Stephen Mather as director of the Park Service in January 1929, Horace M. Albright campaigned for recognition of the agency as the appropriate custodian of all federal historic and archeological sites. Among those areas were the great battlefields of the Civil War, established by Congress beginning in 1890 and placed under direction of the War Department.[28] To Albright's good fortune, he met personally in April of 1933 with the new president, Franklin D. Roosevelt, and presented his case for Park Service administration of the historic and archeological properties managed by other federal agencies. Roosevelt's own enthusiasm for the proposal surfaced on June 10, 1933, when he signed an executive order more than doubling the size of the national park system with the transfer of sixty-four national monuments, military parks, battlefield sites, cemeteries, and memorials from the War Department, Forest Service, and District of Columbia to the National Park Service.[29]

Albright hailed the executive order as a personal victory and an agency milestone, noting that the nation's historic as well as scenic heritage was now under the direction of a single government agency.[30] Robert Sterling Yard and his supporters were nonetheless incensed by the transfers, which, in their view, only seemed to demean national park standards even further. "Self-seeking localities," wrote Ovid Butler, editor of *American Forests*, "whose past attempts to obtain national parks in their own interests have been stopped by public opinion, are unquestionably awake to the confused situation and the opportunities it offers for political park making."[31]

As Albright later confessed, political considerations had in fact influenced his position on the transfers. The survival of the Park Service, not the issue of national park standards, had been uppermost on his mind in 1933. "The order of June 10," he wrote, elaborating on this point, "effectively made the Park Service a very strong agency with such a distinctive and independent field of service as to end its possible eligiblity for merger or consolidation with another bureau." That "bureau," he maintained, was none other than the U.S. Forest Service, the Park Service's perennial nemesis since Gifford Pinchot had helped instigate opposition to its formation. "His associates had opposed the creation of the National Park Service in 1915 and 1916," Albright noted, "and there was rumor current in 1933 that Mr. Pinchot sought to use his influence with President Franklin D. Roosevelt to effect such a transfer." The future integrity of the Park Service as an independent agency, in other words, hinged on its gaining *exclusive* control over the nation's historical, archeological, and geological heritage.[32]

Pinchot's successor, Henry S. Graves, had indeed given the Park Service good reason to be alarmed. Publicly he claimed to support the establishment of the National Park Service; in truth, however, he qualified his endorsement repeatedly by insisting not only that the Park Service, like the Forest Service, should be placed in the Department of Agriculture but that the new agency should have no jurisdiction whatsoever over forested lands.[33]

The sacrifice of the Park Service's autonomy under such an arrangement was not lost on Stephen Mather, Horace Albright, and their friends in Congress. Equally distressing, the emerging debate about national park standards inevitably played directly into the hands of Park Service critics, especially administrators and supporters of the Forest Service. In February 1927, for example, Henry Graves, now dean of forestry at Yale University, wrote menacingly about "the problem of the National Parks." The "problem," he remarked, "arose when with the extension of the system the original standards were departed from when areas of mediocre character were incorporated in the Park system." Specifically, he objected to the apparent inclusion within national parks of commercial stands of timber, not simply geological wonders of "special," "unusual," or "exceptional" interest. In other words, he still opposed the protection of other than worthless lands in the national parks. "There is," he wrote, underscoring this bias, "the serious problem of including in their boundaries natural resources of great economic value." Any deviation from protecting only commercially valueless lands in the parks, he elaborated, only invited threats to their integrity. "The presence of extensive natural resources in the Parks will constitute a standing menace to the system," he warned: "Economic pressure will force the restriction of the boundaries, . . . or will jeopardize the very existence of the Parks."[34]

Graves's ominous assessment, bordering on outright intimidation of preservation interests, was in keeping with the strong convictions of resource managers who believed the national parks should be confined strictly to rugged and inaccessible scenery, areas where their permanence did no possible harm to extractive industries. "If I am right in the views set forth in the first part of this paper," Graves wrote, continuing his argument, "it will be the character of the *natural features only* [italics added] that should determine the location of National Parks, and there should not be an effort to develop a chain of National Parks primarily to secure a distribution of them in all sections of the country or in the majority of the states." National Parks, he concluded, invoking the familiar argument of Robert Sterling Yard and other purists within the preservation movement itself, "are designed to preserve certain extraordinary features of national as distinguished from local interest, regardless of where they may be located."[35]

Unlike Robert Sterling Yard, who seemed willing to accept Graves's assessment as support for his own point of view, Horace Albright shrewdly recognized the forester's appeal for park standards as self-serving. Graves was not in fact committed to the scenic integrity of the parks; rather he was more concerned that they not infringe on stands of commercial timber or mineral deposits. Restricting the parks to rugged scenery, however beautiful or inspiring the landscapes might appear to preservationists, was also the best insurance against losing valuable resources to the nation's economy.

In the long run, Albright further realized, by restricting the national parks to world-class, monumental scenery, only the Far West would have federal preserves within convenient access of its resident population. The problem with that limitation was its obvious failure to enhance either public or political support for the national park system. However much Robert Sterling Yard and his associates decried the thought, outdoor recreation was not in fact a by-product of the national park experience. All Americans did not, in John C. Merriam's words, seek out the national parks for an opportunity to "worship" nature. Of course, the forms of recreation appropriate to a national park setting were still open to debate. The American political system, however, with its emphasis on the ideal of distributing government services evenly among the states, spelled inevitable changes for the national park idea once other regions of the country voiced strong objections to their own lack of sites for outdoor recreation.

The population growth of the United States alone made the call for new parklands outside the West inevitable. By 1920 the population of the country had surpassed 100 million, two and a half times the figure when Yellowstone became the first national park in 1872. Moreover, half the population in 1920 lived in cities and towns with 2,500 or more residents, up from only one in four Americans living in urban areas in 1870.[36]

The formation of the National Conference on Outdoor Recreation, which held its first meeting in Washington, D.C., in May 1924, formally recognized the significance of that trend. The composition of the conference was equally revealing. No fewer than 128 separate organizations with interests in outdoor recreation sent delegates. The influence of the National Parks Association and its executive secretary, Robert Sterling Yard, surfaced in the summary of resolutions, which endorsed the platform that national parks, as distinct from local, state, and city parks, "should represent features of national importance as distinguished from sectional or local significance."[37] Nevertheless, additional reports by the conferees suggested that other regions besides the Far West deserved national parks. Among the natural features recommended to the federal government for study were the White Mountains in New Hampshire, the Appalachian highlands, and the headwaters of the Mississippi River.[38]

Although lack of funding contributed in 1929 to the dissolution of the National Conference on Outdoor Recreation, the needs it had addressed continued to provoke discussion and study throughout the 1930s and early 1940s. In 1936, for example, Congress and the president approved the Park, Parkway, and Recreational Area Study Act, charging the Park Service with planning and coordinating all federal activities in outdoor recreation. The Park Service responded in 1941 with the publication of *A Study of the Park and Recreation Problem in the United States*, which, among other contributions, contained an extensive inventory of recreation sites throughout the country.[39]

The intervention of World War II, coupled with the determination of other federal agencies to protect their own prerogatives in providing outdoor recreation, effectively undermined Park Service coordination of the movement. By the middle of the 1950s, however, the surge in visitation to the national parks provided an important catalyst for further expansion of the system itself. No less influential was growing pressure on Congress to address, once and for all, the imbalance between federal parks in the West and other regions of the country. As in the case of Everglades National Park, greater concern about the biological resources of the United States also lay behind calls for tipping the scales of preservation farther eastward. Preservationists, increasingly referred to as "environmentalists," annually viewed with alarm the loss of fields, woodlands, and marshes surrounding the burgeoning cities of the nation. Unfortunately, most state and local governments seemed to lack either the will or the money to protect some of those lands on their own. Only the federal government, many preservationists concluded, had both the tax base and expertise to tackle the problem.

The major stumbling block to the purchase of threatened areas by the federal government was its traditional frugality, specifically, its fundamental policy of carving national parks only from western lands already in the public domain, or from properties donated to the government by certain states and individuals. Spurred by mounting losses of open space on the urban fringe, however, preservationists at last became intolerant of that policy. Certainly by the 1960s, their environmental concerns forced Congress to reevaluate the Park Service's customary role as custodian of the masterpieces of nature and, since the 1930s, the country's public monuments and historical shrines.

Much as Everglades National Park symbolized the emergence of the biological perspective in the national park idea, so Cape Cod National Seashore, authorized in 1961, set many of the important precedents for the establishment of nontraditional parks in the 1960s and 1970s. Cape Cod, Massachusetts, was not the first national seashore; that honor went in 1937 to Cape Hatteras in North Carolina. Yet Cape Hatteras was authorized on the express condition that the state and private donors would actually purchase the land, which only then could be turned over to the National Park Service for administration.[40] At Cape Cod, the federal government recognized, literally for the first time, the importance of not only authorizing parks or providing limited amounts of money for their completion but of actually committing the United States to the purchase of an entire park project from the outset.

In the West, with its broad expanses of public domain, some parks might still be established simply by transferring territory from the U.S. Forest Service or Bureau of Land Management to the Park Service. Cape Cod foretold the problems of carving larger national parks from any area outside the public domain. Of greatest significance, the national seashore had to be fashioned from lands not only previously owned but actually occupied. Homes, businesses, and cottages dotted the Cape; six separate towns were within or adjacent to the park project. Considering the numbers of people involved, outright condemnation of all the land needed for the seashore was not a viable option, either politically or socially.[41] Outside the public domain, the National Park Service would have to learn new ways of accommodating the concerns of its neighbors and inholders.[42]

The other problem raised by Cape Cod and its counterparts was not administrative but philosophical. Simply, precisely for what reasons did they qualify as *national* parks, or, conceding the fact that most were not actually referred to by that term, why should they still be managed by the National Park Service? In the Everglades, where similar questions had arisen among preservationists in the 1930s, its unquestionable uniqueness had saved the park project. Even its detractors had to admit that the Everglades was the nation's *only* subtropical wilderness. Cape Hatteras, Cape Cod, and others to follow clearly were not one-of-a-kind parks; the United States had more than 1,500 miles of coastline along the Atlantic seaboard alone. Besides, Cape Cod National Seashore was not to be carved from pristine lands but from a combination of open spaces and properties already claimed for recreation and development.

As in the case of Everglades National Park, a redefinition of the term "significance" proved to be the key to winning passage of the Cape Cod National Seashore. The rarity of Cape Cod lay not in its false identity as the only seashore in the

United States but in its threatened status as one of the few remaining seacoasts whose features were yet unspoiled by unrestrained and intensive development. In that vein, Senator Alan Bible of Nevada, as chairman of the Senate Subcommittee on the Public Lands, asked his colleagues to consider the bill authorizing the park as a measure "of tremendous importance." During "the last 15 years," he noted, "there has been a great impetus to buy seashore property for commercial and private uses. Extensive and costly developments now line mile after mile of seashore which before World War II was uninhabited." As a result, more and more Americans, especially in the most populated regions of the country, were being denied unrestricted access to coastal beaches.[43]

Indeed the bill was "unique," Bible remarked, "in that it is the first attempt to develop a unit of the national park system in an area which is highly urbanized, by comparison with other areas of the country in which substantial acreage has been set aside for national park purposes." Truly, Cape Cod would be a park for all Americans, one third of whom lived "within a day's drive of the area." "Cape Cod as a national seashore," Senator Leverett Saltonstall of Massachusetts agreed, would be "dedicated to the spiritual replenishment of American families increasingly locked in by urbanization and commercialization who seek the refreshing beauty and natural grandeur of the clean, open spaces." In this respect, Cape Cod became a precedent. "Favorable action by Congress on this proposal," Saltonstall said, concluding with this line of reasoning, "would give encouragement to other efforts to preserve our rapidly vanishing natural shoreline in such areas as Padre Island, Texas, the Oregon Dunes, and Point Reyes, California."[44]

Cape Cod National Seashore, signed into law by President John F. Kennedy on August 7, 1961, was indeed an important step leading to the establishment of eight additional seashores over the next fifteen years. In another major series of parks, the United States further recognized the desirability of protecting the shorelines of the Great Lakes. The first of four national lakeshores—Pictured Rocks, Michigan, along the southeastern edge of Lake Superior—was authorized on October 15, 1966. Close behind came Indiana Dunes, where the movement for the preservation of the Great Lakes had in fact originated a half century before.[45] As early as 1916, Stephen T. Mather had suggested that the "monumental" grandeur of the great dunes between Chicago, Illinois, and Gary, Indiana, warranted their possible inclusion in a dunelands national park. Simultaneously, pioneer ecologists such as John Merle Coulter and Henry Chandler Cowles drew attention to the Indiana Dunes as a heartland of biological uniqueness, one worthy of protection exclusive of its scenic qualities alone. By 1927 a state park of approximately 2,000 acres realized those early ambitions for the region. Finally, following another forty years of intensive industrial development and urban encroachment, on November 5, 1966, the federal government authorized the protection of roughly 6,500 acres of windswept sand, prairie, woodlands, and marsh as the Indiana Dunes National Lakeshore.[46]

Yet another major crusade among preservation groups was the campaign to protect vestiges of America's wild and scenic rivers. Like seacoasts and lakeshores, riverfront parks also might be located close to urban centers. Still another advantage was the self-contained, generally linear nature of river valleys, which required the acquisition of only limited amounts of adjacent lands. For the cost of buying several hundred yards of territory on either side of the streambed, river enthusiasts could enjoy boating, swimming, or walking beside the waterway without being reminded that civilization lay just beyond the park boundary.

Ozark National Scenic Riverways, Missouri, authorized in 1964, disclosed the growing strength of the movement for wild and scenic rivers in the United States.[47] The Wild and Scenic Rivers Act, approved by Congress four years later, formally established an entire system of national riverways through the designation of eight additional streams in that category.[48] Management by the National Park Service, however, was at first limited to the Ozark National Scenic Riverways and the St. Croix National Scenic Riverway in Wisconsin and Minnesota. Both the U.S. Forest Service and Bureau of

Land Management had successfully defended their right to administer major riverways designated from their respective holdings.[49] Future acquisitions consisting largely of private lands, such as the park bordering the St. Croix River, would customarily be deeded to the Park Service for maintenance and protection.

Whatever their lack of monumental significance, national seashores, lakeshores, and riverways could be justified before Congress on the basis of their rarity in a pristine condition. Time and again supporters of those parks noted the loss of coastlines and wild rivers to all forms of commercial, industrial, and residential development. Most of America's great rivers had been dammed; most of its seacoasts and lakeshores forever altered by roads, vacation homesites, diking, and dredging. Unless the federal government intervened to preserve these threatened environments, it seemed reasonable to conclude that few of the nation's free-flowing rivers or unmarred shorelines outside existing parks would survive into the twenty-first century.

The same could be said of the few extensive tracts of open space remaining in the urban centers of the nation, such as New York, Atlanta, San Francisco, and Los Angeles. Here again, the argument that parks must be closer to where people actually lived was crucial to overcoming standard forms of opposition. Opponents nonetheless insisted that urban recreation areas, like other nontraditional parks, would strain Park Service budgets and thus dilute the agency's effectiveness in managing its wilderness preserves.[50] Gateway National Recreation Area, on the outskirts of New York City, and its counterpart across the continent, Golden Gate in San Francisco, proved these objections could be overcome, as their establishment simultaneously on October 27, 1972, demonstrated.[51] National recreation areas previously authorized had been confined almost exclusively to the sites of large reservoirs in the West and South.[52] Accordingly, those parks, too, exacerbated the long-recognized problem of restricting access to the national parks only to more affluent Americans. With the creation of Gateway and Golden Gate national recreation areas, the National Park Service had literally been charged with the responsibility of bringing parks within a bus or subway ride of both the nation's poor and well-to-do.

Inevitably, such rapid expansion of the national park system only begged again the question of national park standards. Already geologically deficient, most of the new parks further suffered from the absence of biological resources of pristine quality. Everglades National Park, a model for biological management since the 1930s, itself was hamstrung with artificial rather than natural boundaries. At least the Everglades appeared to be an integral block of land, a park with a core large enough to provide plants and animals with a semblance of sanctuary. In contrast, most seashores, lakeshores, and riverways were literally pockmarked with residential and industrial developments. And so the question remained. Should parks so remote from the geological uniqueness, territorial integrity, and natural qualities of their predecessors have been authorized by Congress in the first place?

The other major issue was funding. Obviously, the National Park Service alone could not meet the purchasing requirements of so much private land on its own limited budget. Initially, preservationists saw a solution in the Land and Water Conservation Fund Act of 1964. The act provided that entrance and user fees from federal recreation sites, coupled with monies obtained from the sale of surplus federal properties and the federal tax on motor fuel, could be applied to the purchase of parklands by agencies such as the National Park Service and the U.S. Army Corps of Engineers. A later amendment allowed revenues from the sale of oil and gas leases on the continental shelf to be added to the fund.[53]

By the late 1960s, however, even its limitations in dealing with the pace of park expansion were apparent. The hundreds of millions of dollars the Land and Water Conservation Fund eventually generated still could not keep up with the cost of acquiring so many new parks, especially the most fragile and expensive. As purchasing fell farther behind, speculation in many areas already designated for park status but still unacquired steadily mounted. The added emphasis of the fund on recreation, as opposed to the purchase of lands purely biological in character, further compromised the success of the largest and most ambitious park projects.[54]

The problem of funding the expansion of the national park system only seemed to confirm the common charge that the new parks were simply diverting support from the original, clearly legitimate preserves. In either case, preservationists themselves felt bound by precedent to justify their case for expansion by demonstrating that each of the recent parks did, in fact, measure up to the standards of national parks in the past. The result was an unmistakable tendency to inflate both the range and quality of the natural features present in each region. The strategy was not deliberately dishonest; the problem was that preservationists were trying to bring a certain portion of commonplace topography under the umbrella of protection in *national* parks.

The insistence that the national park system should encompass landscapes at large led to special reliance on the biological perspective. Crucial to expansion was the ability to show that each new park contained a multiplicity of biological resources, especially wildlife and plant life, commingling in combinations found nowhere else in the United States. Thus Stewart Udall, as secretary of the interior, testified in 1961 before Congress that the proposed Cape Cod national seashore contained "not only the most extensive natural seashore area in New England but also one of the finest on the North American coast." In acknowledgment of the standards of the western parks, Udall reassured Congress that the Cape Cod region also possessed evidence of "continental glaciation," "erosion," and "deposition," all providing "important opportunities for geologic study." Still, the biota of the park was unquestionably its greatest natural resource. "The plants and wildlife that mingle on Cape Cod in unusual variety give the area outstanding biological significance," he remarked. Indeed, the features of the proposed seashore should be considered in their totality rather than separately or region by region. "From the highland on Griffin Island," he stated, beginning his elaboration on this point, "one can get magnificent views of scenic upland and marsh typical of the cape." Similarly, scientists had noted that each of the "four general types" of "glacial kettle hole ponds" displayed "a distinct association of plant and animal life." And Morris Island contained not only "a rare white cedar bog and a stand of beech forest, but also . . . one of the most important bird resting and feeding grounds, acre for acre, in New England—and one of the two or three most important such habitats on the entire Atlantic seaboard."[55]

Supporters of other nontraditional parks throughout the 1960s found similar ammunition for their causes in statements to the effect that each of their own areas was also a "biological crossroads," as distinct from a region of purely geological significance. In 1963, for example, Leonard Hall, a self-described "farmer, writer, naturalist," and director of the Ozark National Rivers Association, argued before the House Subcommittee on Public Lands that the proposed national riverway in Missouri possessed "one of the richest floras of any area of its size on this continent. We have Kansas plants there. We have Michigan plants. We have plants from the South and others which have developed there." Later in 1963, James Carver, Jr., assistant secretary of the interior, likewise endorsed the proposed Indiana Dunes national lakeshore on the basis of its "outstanding" flora. Carver's objective, like Hall's, was again to demonstrate both the diversity and commingling of the species present in the Indiana Dunes. "Following the slow retreat of the Wisconsin ice," he wrote, briefly tracing the impact of the Ice Age on the region, "the plants which are now characteristic of the northern forests moved through the dunes area northward." Where soil, moisture, and temperatures were favorable, however, "isolated colonies of northern species held on." For example, cool "moderating breezes" off Lake Michigan allowed both "jack pine and white pine . . . to hang on south of their normal range." In low swamps and bogs, more northern plants lay "cloistered within the larger world of central forest and prairie species. Tamarack, buckthorn, leather leaf, checkerberry, orchids, and other unusual plants characterize these special environments," he added. Elsewhere the botanical mosaic included plants of the "central forests and there are occurrences of flora of both the Prairie Peninsula and the Atlantic Coastal Plain species." "The result," he concluded, "is a natural scientific and scenic asset so diverse that it is difficult to equal anywhere in this country."[56]

Of course, only those preservationists seeking the protection of the Indiana Dunes could afford to take Carver's closing remarks at face value. For the rest of the movement there remained the problem of linking other nontraditional parks with the unquestionable uniqueness found in the original preserves of the West. Nor were the national recreation areas immune from the requirement that precedent, at the very least, ought to be acknowledged. In 1972, for instance, Secretary of the Interior Rogers C. B. Morton noted that the proposed Gateway National Recreation Area in New York City "would contain ten miles of ocean beach and natural and historic features of great significance." Granted, portions of the Jamaica Bay Unit, with "14,000 acres of land and water," had been previously developed. "Despite the inroads of civilization," Morton still argued, "Jamaica Bay remains an ecological treasure." Twenty-nine species of waterfowl and seventy of wading, shore, and marsh birds still used the area for nesting, feeding, and refuge. In a similar vein, Representative John F. Seiberling of Ohio defined the proposed Cuyahoga River national recreation area between Cleveland and Akron as "a pastoral wonder, a quiet haven away from the nearby bustling cities." Yet beyond its obvious potential for outdoor recreation, the region had great value as a "unique meeting ground for plant life." A single one-hundred-acre tract in the valley, Seiberling elaborated, had been found to contain "over 400 species of plants, including some usually found only in the far West, some only in the deep South, and some only at higher altitudes or northern latitudes." Surely, he therefore concluded, the Cuyahoga Valley ought to be recognized as a potential park "for the people of the entire country," not just residents of the Cleveland-Akron metropolitan area.[57]

The presence of historic sites and structures, archeological evidence, and other elements of human history comprised the final assemblage of resources offered as justification for awarding seashores, lakeshores, riverways, and open spaces standing as units of the national park system. Like overtures to the parks' biological uniqueness, most of the historic arguments were further listings, each an inventory of the number of pioneer cabins, old farmhouses, and Indian burial sites found in a particular region. Few of the inventories, as a result, did much to dispel the notion that most of the urban-oriented parks, whatever their ecological or historical assets, still were not intended for mass recreation.[58]

The alternative to compromise, preservationists conceded, would be fewer parks. Besides, few supported the viewpoint of Robert Sterling Yard, an opinion more than a half century old, that parks other than primeval wilderness were either pointless or inappropriate. Just as repugnant was the realization that parks in the remote corners of the nation were open only to more affluent Americans. Thus Senator Alan Cranston of California, speaking on behalf of his disadvantaged constituency, noted that "only a relatively small number of Americans have the opportunity to enjoy the wide range of natural wonders [the national park system] protects and preserves. Those fortunate enough to visit distant units of the National Park System," he declared, "are most likely white, educated, relatively well-off economically, young, and suburban. More than 90 percent of the National Park visitors in 1968 were white." "Therefore," he concluded, "I believe that we have a responsibility to 'bring the parks to the people,' especially to the residents of the inner-city who have had virtually no opportunity to enjoy the marvelous and varied recreation benefits of our national parks."[59]

It remained for Phillip Burton, a crusading representative to Congress from San Francisco, California, to orchestrate the grand finale to nearly two decades of park making along the seacoasts, lakeshores, and riverways of urban America. As chairman of the House Subcommittee on National Parks and Insular Affairs, Burton was instrumental in winning passage of the National Parks and Recreation Act of 1978. In essence, the bill combined under one piece of legislation a host of national park projects of special concern to many members of Congress, including increased appropriations and acquisition ceilings for existing parks, boundary changes, wilderness designations, and final authorization for new parks, historic sites, and wild and scenic rivers. Benchmark additions to the national park system included authorization of the Santa Monica Mountains National Recreation Area near Los Angeles and the New River Gorge National River in West Virginia. All told, the bill added fifteen units to the national park system, appropriated $725 million over five years to renovate recreational facilities in urban areas, created eight new wild and scenic rivers, and designated seventeen additional rivers for study and possible inclusion in the wild and scenic rivers system.[60]

The bill further established a system of national historic trails, designating four—the Oregon Trail, Mormon Pioneer Trail, Lewis and Clark Trail, and Iditarod Trail (Alaska)—as initial components. Similarly, Congress authorized another addition to the national system of scenic trails already in existence, the Continental Divide Trail, to span the length of the Rocky Mountains between the Canadian border in Montana and the Mexican border in New Mexico.[61] With few exceptions, in other words, the new parks were basically linear preserves, slices of landscape rather than major blocks of territory whose management might come in conflict with neighboring development.

Seen in terms of the *number* of areas affected, however, the legislation was both impressive and unprecedented. Higher development ceilings were authorized for no fewer than thirty-four existing units of the national park system; similarly, thirty-nine units received boundary adjustments ranging from a few acres to several thousand acres of land.[62] Even supporters of the bill, as a result, occasionally joined its skeptics in labeling it the "parks barrel bill." Critics were in the distinct minority, however, especially in Congress, since the legislation had such a positive financial impact on so many separate states and on more than two hundred congressional districts.[63]

For a different set of reasons, most preservationists them-selves hailed rather than questioned the Omnibus Parks Bill of 1978. Over the past two decades they had spoken out against the loss of millions of acres of land to highways, airports, shopping centers, and similar forms of urban encroachment on open space. Land afforded protection under the National Parks and Recreation Act of 1978, whatever the scenic limita-tions of those properties, was land at least temporarily saved from the threat of urbanization and industrial development. It remained to be seen whether or not Robert Sterling Yard had been correct. Perhaps national parks largely historic or urban in emphasis would in fact dilute both the financial base as well as the international fame of the original park system. In the meantime, however, preservationists were not willing to risk the alternative, the chance of saving the great parks at the expense of compromising the integrity of the American land as a whole.

Nor did preservationists have any intention of abandon-ing the tradition of national parks as broad, monumental ex-panses of pristine territory. The problem in the continental United States was that most opportunities for such parklands had either been lost or already exercised. Only Alaska, with its vast forests, tundra, and mountain ranges, still offered the hope of establishing great national parks with natural as op-posed to political boundaries. Indeed, long before the National Parks and Recreation Act of 1978 itself had been passed by Congress, preservationists had recognized that its provisions would not go far enough. From the environmental as distinct from the recreational perspective, Alaska was the greatest challenge for preservation of them all. How national parks were established in the forty-ninth state might well determine, once and for all, whether or not Americans could truly coexist with their natural surroundings as its custodians rather than as its conquerors.

12

Decision in Alaska

If you think that Alaska is a long way to go for a national park, so was Yellowstone in 1872. Now Yellowstone is irreplaceable. So is Alaska and so are its unspoiled wildlands and magnificent wildlife.

Alaska Coalition brochure, 1977

Our decisions on the designation of Alaska lands for conservation will shape the Nation's future as surely as our decisions on questions of energy, taxes, or the national budget.... In making that determination, we are confronting probably for the last time an opportunity which we have missed so many times before as our Nation's civilization has spread from coast to coast and border to border.

John F. Seiberling, 1977

Alaska is more than an environmental treasure, it is a resource storehouse.

Don Young, 1977

Born of romanticism and cultural nationalism, the first great national parks of the United States were clearly the result of nineteenth-century perceptions of the American landscape. Outside of the continental United States, only Alaska offered preservationists of the twentieth century one final opportunity to have national parks in keeping with the principles of biological management. In preservationists' own words, Alaska was "our last chance to do it right," to design national parks around entire watersheds, animal migration routes, and similar ecological rather than political boundaries.[1] "This will require the largest possible blocks of land to be set aside as national-interest lands," wrote Peggy Wayburn, arguing the case for expansive parks on behalf of the Sierra Club: "This alone can prevent the loss of perhaps the greatest remaining wildlife, wilderness, and scenic resources on earth."[2]

Even the largest national parks in the lower forty-eight states, among them Yellowstone, Yosemite, and the Everglades, were but pieces of far larger biological wholes. Alaska, in contrast, offered the best of both the monumental and the biological in nature. Scenically, its mountains, glaciers, and volcanic areas were unsurpassed on the North American continent. In other words, preservationists need not speak against their own traditions in their quest for Alaskan parks. More importantly, however, Alaska's vastness and near complete ownership by the federal government made the realization of the biological ends in national park management no less attainable. At least, preservationists had good reason to be optimistic at the outset of their campaign for parklands in the forty-ninth state.

In Alaska, as elsewhere in the United States, organized opposition to the expansion of the national park system came from a wide variety of resource interests. For industrialists, Alaska's importance lay beyond its role as the last great refuge for plants and animals. Instead, the nation's last major repository for timber, minerals, oil, natural gas, fresh water, and hydroelectric power seemed to be at stake. "I think we are all acutely aware," noted John H. LaGrange, representing the Kennecott Copper Corporation, "that our Nation and, indeed the world, is passing from an era of surplus to an era of shortage in many mineral and energy commodities." New national parks in Alaska, it followed, again should be restricted to monumental topography, areas rich in scenery but poor from the standpoint of natural resources. "National park and critical habitat withdrawals should not contain more than 15 million acres," LaGrange argued. Otherwise national parks would conflict with the nation's pressing need to find more oil and, in the meantime, to exploit its vast deposits of coal and other minerals. Alaska had all of those resources in abundance. Unfortunately, between 40 and 80 percent of the richest copper deposits alone were located in areas where preservationists wanted to establish national parks.[3]

For preservationists, the opposition of resource interests to the establishment of national parks—as typified by La-

Grange's remarks—was nothing new. As preservationists soon discovered, the problem in Alaska was the tendency of the resource issue to overlap the question of Native American rights. Unlike the continental United States, where Indians had been forced onto reservations outside the national parks long before the parks themselves had been created, Alaska was still largely inhabited by groups of native peoples. In Alaska, the creation of national parks could not be divorced from the issue of civil rights. Drawing the boundaries of each new park demanded simultaneous respect for native traditions, cultures, and means of subsistence—customs deeply intertwined with national park lands. "If we are to err," argued Elvis J. Stahr, president of the National Audubon Society, "let us not err on the side of destroying a truly unique culture."[4]

Indeed, it was almost as if the national park idea had come back full circle to 1832 and George Catlin's plea for "a *nation's Park*, containing man and beast, in all the wild and freshness of their nature's beauty!" On the plains of South Dakota, the artist had called for precisely the kind of sensitivity that planning for the Alaskan parks demanded if the right of Native Americans to reside on their ancestral hunting grounds was also to be protected. Of course, his perspective was as much a product of the period's romanticism as it was evidence of embryonic concern in the United States for the rights of native peoples. For Catlin, preserving the Indians of the plains added charm to the landscape at the same time it advanced the morality of American culture. Alaska was the final opportunity not only to establish national parks with biological boundaries but to create parks that did not—as Catlin himself would have opposed—drive out or exclude native cultures in the process.[5]

With the establishment of Yellowstone National Park in 1872, Catlin's revolutionary point of view was rejected in favor of the strict protection of monumental scenery. By preservation was meant to protect landscapes, not to preserve the historical relationships between landscapes *and* people. Not until the 1960s was the policy of protecting natural features in the national parks exclusive of natural processes widely criticized. Biologists at last fully acknowledged the role of Native Americans in changing park landscapes through the use of fire. The Alaska lands issue also drew attention to the fact that native peoples throughout North America had long exerted great influence on the biological composition of the continent.

Native Americans, it followed, were themselves "part of nature," a key link in the chain of natural processes so many biologists hoped to reintroduce to national park environments. At least in Alaska, preservationists conceded, the chain had not been broken. "Indeed," argued Anthony Wayne Smith, president of the National Parks and Conservation Association, "the practice of subsistence hunting, as understood by the Native cultures, can well be looked upon as part of *a natural ecosystem* which has sustained itself in Alaska for something like 10,000 years and which has proved itself compatible with the stability and diversity of both wildlife and human population" [italics added]. The historical opposition of the National Parks and Conservation Association to hunting, Smith said, elaborating on his point, dealt "only with sports hunting, and if the distinction is kept quite clear along the lines of the pending legislation, no violence can be done to established traditions of national park management."[6]

The naïveté of preservationists like Smith was their assumption that native cultures, like park environments, could be maintained at a fixed approximation of their appearance at some earlier and more ideal period of history. Catlin's romanticism might not be dead but neither were the forces that made changes in the native cultures inevitable. Perhaps the best that could be done in Alaska was to honor the civil rights of the natives and hope that change would not overwhelm their traditions at the expense of the parks. "No conservation group of which I am aware," remarked Louis S. Clapper, a representative of the National Wildlife Federation, "would deny a Native the right to take whatever fish and wildlife he needs for his own family's welfare." That said, so-called subsistence hunting was often "a much abused practice," a "subterfuge" for "the recreational practices" of "employed and 'modernized' natives."[7] Clapper's outspoken comments were compromised by

the National Wildlife Federation's own defense of sport hunting among its members. Yet even the most ardent defenders of
subsistence hunting could not dismiss the impact of modern
technology on native cultures. Ideally, Alaskan natives would
resist the temptations and pressures of modern life. It was just
as likely, however, that the national parks would be eroded
from within as well as from without by what was in fact a vain
attempt to uphold the past against the relentless forces of the
present.

The resource at stake was wilderness—remote, pristine,
and teeming with animals. Before World War II, the natives of
Alaska had hardly made a dent in either its wildness or its
wildlife. But that was before modern firearms and the introduction of airplanes in effect shrank the boundaries of the
Alaskan wilderness.[8] Still, as late as the 1970s, preservationists saw legitimate reason to compare Alaska to Yellowstone a
hundred years earlier. Much as Yellowstone had been America's frontier in the nineteenth century, so Alaska was its frontier in the twentieth. The difference was nonetheless striking—
Americans must make do with Alaska for centuries to come, at
least with respect to wilderness on earth. "What we save now
is all we will ever save," declared another popular slogan of the
period.[9] Especially in the forty-ninth state, no statement
seemed to be a more appropriate—or compelling—call to
action.

The wilderness movement, as distinct from campaigns to
establish new national parks per se, won its most important
victory on September 3, 1964, when President Lyndon B. Johnson signed the Wilderness Act into law. For eight years wilderness enthusiasts had sought its passage, citing the need to
protect not only the remote unspoiled corners of the national
parks but the best of the nation's roadless areas remaining in
the national forests and elsewhere on the public domain. Nine
million acres of land within the national forests were immediately designated as wilderness; meanwhile, the National
Park Service was authorized to study and recommend to Congress which portions of the national parks should also be
protected in a wild and undeveloped state.[10]

For a variety of reasons, the study and establishment of wilderness areas in the national parks, especially the largest preserves, moved slowly. Preservationists themselves were far more concerned about the fate of wilderness areas controlled by the U.S. Forest Service and Bureau of Land Management. In contrast to the Park Service, those were the agencies historically renowned for their determination to open the public domain to multiple use, including logging, grazing, and mining. Granted, the National Park Service itself was often accused of overdeveloping the most popular points of interest within the national parks. Still, the agency had neither the authority—nor the incentive—to open its backcountry areas to resource exploitation.[11]

Of greater concern to the Park Service was the threat wilderness posed to the agency's bureaucratic autonomy. The management of wilderness areas came under the directives of the Wilderness Act of 1964, not the Park Service's own Organic Act of August 25, 1916. Prohibitions in wilderness areas against the use of any motorized means of access or equipment, not to mention roads, clearly restricted the Park Service's discretion in managing its backcountry zones. Formal wilderness designations would also forfeit the potential for using at least some of those areas to accommodate overflows of visitors in the future. That restriction, too, concerned many concessionaires, themselves an influential body in determining national park policy. Like tradition-minded Park Service employees, concessionaires were highly skeptical of anything that might undermine their own options for further expansion of visitor services.[12]

Not until October 23, 1970, six years after the passage of the Wilderness Act, did Congress designate portions of Petrified Forest National Park, Arizona, and Craters of the Moon National Monument, Idaho, as wilderness. In October 1972, parts of Lassen Volcanic National Park and Lava Beds National Monument, both in California, also received wilderness status. Four more years elapsed before Congress approved the first truly major additions to the wilderness system in national parks. On September 22 and October 1, 1976, the House and Senate, respectively, approved legislation creating wilderness

areas in portions of thirteen existing parks and monuments—
Badlands National Monument, Bandelier National Monu-
ment, Black Canyon of the Gunnison National Monument,
Chiricahua National Monument, Great Sand Dunes National
Monument, Haleakala National Park, Isle Royale National
Park, Joshua Tree National Monument, Mesa Verde National
Park, Pinnacles National Monument, Point Reyes National
Seashore, Saguaro National Monument, and Shenandoah Na-
tional Park. President Gerald R. Ford approved the legislation
on October 20, 1976.[13]

The Omnibus Park Bill of 1978, also known as the National
Park and Recreation Act, further designated 1,854,424 acres of
wilderness in eight additional units of the national park system—Buffalo National River, Carlsbad Caverns National
Park, Everglades National Park, Guadalupe Mountains National Park, Gulf Islands National Seashore, Hawaii Volcanoes
National Park, Organ Pipe Cactus National Monument, and
Theodore Roosevelt National Park. In addition, the bill declared another 119,581 acres in the eight preserves as "potential" wilderness, bringing the grand total to nearly two million
acres. Supporters of the legislation in Congress, eager to draw
attention to their achievement, were quick to point out that
this figure exceeded "the total acreage of all lands previously
designated as wilderness in the National Park System."[14]

Most of the largest and most popular national parks, however, among them Yellowstone, Yosemite, Glacier, and the
Grand Canyon, still lacked approval for their wilderness proposals. Designating wilderness in those parks remained controversial. Although the Park Service endorsed the wilderness
idea in public, many high level officials privately expressed
their doubts about the wilderness movement. The larger the
roadless areas within the national parks, the less opportunity
remained for the Park Service to expand its traditional visitor
services and overnight accommodations. The Park Service
would be left with no alternative but to restrict the number of
visitors in the already developed portions of its parks. For an
agency that measured its success by how many people it
served, such restrictions seemed politically unwise. And even

in those parks where management seemed strongly in favor of formal wilderness designations, concessionaires usually were quietly suspicious of, if not overtly hostile to, the concept.[15]

With each frustration of their attempts to establish large wilderness areas in the national parks of the continental United States, preservationists looked upon Alaska as a battleground of even greater importance. If national parks were in fact to be managed as sanctuaries, not merely as scenic wonders divorced of biological considerations, wilderness appeared to be the crucial prerequisite. Wildlife biologists warned repeatedly that the remote roadless corners of America were the only remaining refuges of any real consequence for many species of plants and animals. The management of habitat could accomplish only so much. The alternative to greater and greater reliance on the manipulation of plant and animal populations was providing both with enough territory to survive on their own in the first place.

For a land so rich in natural resources and wilderness, the history of Alaska as an American possession began on a distinct note of irony. Ratification of the treaty in 1867 authorizing purchase of Alaska from the Russians passed the Senate over the objections of opponents who denounced the territory as nothing but a worthless region of snow, rocks, and icebergs. Among most Americans that image of the frozen north held well into the twentieth century. Occasionally, authors, artists, and travelers broke down that perception, yet it was not until World War II, following completion of the Alaska Military Highway through Canada, that Americans finally began to appreciate the true richness and diversity of what was to become the forty-ninth state.[16]

Statehood, which came in 1959, still did not end the bitterness among many Alaskans over their decades of treatment as second-class citizens by the federal government. For a territory of roughly 365 million acres, Alaskans believed federal officials had been far too conservative in allowing the exploitation of its natural resources. In either case, residents were eager to get on with development, not only logging, fishing, and trapping—pursuits comprised in the state's traditional economy—but also opening oil and gas fields and mineral deposits. The legislation granting statehood allowed Alaska to select approximately 104 million acres of federal lands in the state; similarly, the federal government relinquished title to tens of millions of acres of submerged lands along the continental shelf. Only one major obstacle stood between Alaska and the process of completing its selection of federal lands— few politicians had stopped to consider the claims of Native Americans to many of those same properties. Finally, in 1966, as Aleuts, Eskimos, and Indian tribes prepared to take their grievances to court, Secretary of the Interior Stewart Udall froze all land selections pending congressional consideration of the argument that Native Americans as well as the state of Alaska were entitled to share in the allocation of the public domain.[17]

The ensuing stalemate was not resolved until October of 1971 and passage of the Native Claims Settlement Act. The legislation awarded forty million acres of land and one billion dollars in additional compensation to the Alaskan groups. During the five years Congress considered this apparent departure from federal Indian policy, preservationists themselves were no less aware of the unique opportunity the bill presented to voice their own concerns about the future of public lands in the forty-ninth state. Although most preservationists sympathized with the demands of the natives for a secure land base, native selections, in addition to the selections already guaranteed to Alaska, conceivably might undercut the protection of the best wilderness areas even before they had been identified and established. Alaska, to reemphasize, represented the final opportunity to establish national parks, wilderness areas, and wildlife refuges of irrefutable ecological significance and integrity. Without simultaneously addressing the need to preserve the Alaskan wilderness, preservationists argued, all hope of coordinating the development of the state with its protection would be lost.[18]

With the environmental movement, like the civil rights movement, at the peak of its influence, Congress was in little mood to ignore the concerns of preservationists any more than the grievances of Native Americans. Accordingly, Section 17 (d)(2) of the Alaska Native Claims Settlement Act further recognized the desirability of designating up to eighty million acres of the public domain in Alaska as national parks, national forests, wildlife refuges, and wild and scenic rivers. The act gave the secretary of the interior nine months to withdraw lands deemed suitable for consideration as additions to each of the four categories; similarly, the secretary was given until December 19, 1973, to make his final recommendations to Congress concerning which of the lands initially withdrawn from entry should in fact be protected in perpetuity by the federal government.[19]

Yet another opportunity for preservation was provided by Section 17 (d)(1) of the Alaska Native Claims Settlement Act. Under its provisions, the secretary of the interior was allowed ninety days after the enactment of the legislation to select additional "public interest" lands for withdrawal from entry. Apparently the provision did not affect state and native selections around native villages but took precedence over all other state and native selections elsewhere on the public domain. In the confusion over interpretation of the (d)(1) provision, however, the state of Alaska, in January 1972, proclaimed the selection of its entire remaining allotment of seventy-seven million acres under the Statehood Act of 1958.[20]

Such complexity and confusion only foreshadowed the coming battle over Alaskan lands, a struggle that would last for nearly a decade. By September of 1972, Secretary of the Interior Rogers C. B. Morton had withdrawn seventy-nine million acres of the public domain under subsection (d)(2) of the Native Claims Settlement Act, in addition to forty-seven million acres under subsection (d)(1). The state of Alaska immediately protested that the withdrawals conflicted with many of its own selections and, as a result, filed suit in federal court to have Secretary Morton's duplicate choices that were in dispute revoked. In an out-of-court settlement, Alaska won concessions affecting some fourteen million acres of the (d)(1) and (d)(2) withdrawals; for its own part of the compromise, the state agreed to relinquish its claims to thirty-five million of the seventy-seven million acres it had selected in January.[21]

In the end, Secretary Morton's own final recommendations for lands to be protected in Alaskan parks, wilderness areas, and wildlife refuges pleased no one. The state of Alaska again filed suit; meanwhile, preservationists also protested against his proposal to include over eighteen million acres of the (d)(2) lands in national forests rather than in wilderness areas. The objective of the act, preservationists argued, was the protection of those lands rather than the development of their resources, even on a sustained-yield basis. Adding urgency to preservationists' concerns was the deadline established by Congress for the resolution of the entire debate by December 18, 1978. That gave preservationists but seven years to make their case, and already two of those years had slipped by without an acceptable compromise between development and preservation of the state even in sight.[22]

Despite their frustration, preservation groups still used the interval preceding congressional consideration of the Alaska lands issue very wisely. The lull offered them an opportunity for further study and redefinition of their park proposals, for educating their memberships, and, most importantly, for unifying on behalf of a concerted political effort on Capitol Hill. The so-called Alaska Coalition, representing the National Audubon Society, Wilderness Society, Sierra Club, National Parks and Conservation Association, and Defenders of Wildlife, officially organized in 1971 during the debate about native claims in the state. Cooperation among the groups was still relatively informal until January 1977, when Congress itself took up the Alaska lands controversy. Under the circumstances, the five member organizations of the Alaska Coalition agreed to pool both staff and financial resources as they prepared to contest what they collectively considered "the most important conservation issue of the century."[23]

The battle was finally joined on January 4, 1977, when Representative Morris Udall of Arizona introduced his bill, H.R. 39, to the Ninety-fifth Congress. By early April, H.R. 39 was accompanied by a host of similar bills; numerous cosponsors had also attached their names to Udall's original legislation. To sift through the complex array of proposals and to assess public opinion, the House Committee on Interior and Insular Affairs, with Udall as chairman, approved the creation of a special Subcommittee on General Oversight and Alaska Lands. On April 21 and 22, Representative John F. Seiberling of Ohio, chairman of the subcommittee and a cosponsor of H.R. 39, convened the first public hearings on the Alaska lands issue in Washington, D.C.[24]

Five months and sixteen volumes of testimony later, the Subcommittee on General Oversight and Alaska Lands concluded its work. In addition to holding hearings in Washington, D.C., the committee took testimony in Chicago, Atlanta, Denver, and Seattle. Afterward the committee moved to Alaska, where it heard the residents of sixteen separate towns and cities, including Sitka, Juneau, Ketchikan, Anchorage, and Fairbanks.[25] Never before in national park history had any issue sparked so much public interest and discussion. Even the more noted controversies of the recent past, such as the campaign to preserve the redwood groves of the California coast, had not come close to arousing such a nationwide insistence that the general public, as well as renowned figures in the preservation movement and their principal adversaries, should be heard by a major congressional panel.

By itself, however, the sheer number of people who participated in the controversy still had little effect on the arguments used to sway the opposing sides. To be sure, although many people took the opportunity to speak their minds before Congress, their positions were both traditional and predictable. The hearings, in other words, contained no real surprises. Simply, those with a personal stake in the economy of Alaska pushed for smaller parks and greater development of the state's natural resources. Likewise, those who looked to Alaska as the last American wilderness wanted desperately to protect its mountains, forests, rivers, and wildlife in parks that were not only spacious but clearly of ecological as well as scenic significance.

It followed that support for the Alaskan parks was greatest

outside the state. Indeed, much as people living on the Alaskan frontier universally opposed the parks, so citizens in the lower forty-eight states overwhelmingly endorsed H.R. 39.[26] Not surprisingly, supporters and opponents of the legislation lined up similarly in the halls of Congress. Senators Ted Stevens and Mike Gravel of Alaska, in addition to the state's lone member of the House, Don Young, strongly opposed H.R. 39 in its original form. After all, their constituents believed they had the most to lose if the bill were enacted. In contrast, Representatives Udall and Seiberling, among the seventy-two other sponsors of H.R. 39, spoke out for preservation with the obvious assurance that their own political futures would in no way be determined by voters in the state of Alaska.

As if to rationalize their immunity from the Alaskan electorate, the sponsors of H.R. 39 noted repeatedly that their bill was of national rather than local importance. "Obviously, this is a national issue, not just a regional or sectional one," said Representative Seiberling, setting this important theme of the hearings a id congressional debates. "The lands involved are public lands, the property of all the American people." Granted, the residents of Alaska deserved protection of their interests. "But they must also be harmonized with the interests of the other 220 million Americans," he maintained. "As Members of the Congress of the United States, we must act in the interests of all the people."[27]

By definition, Congressman Udall agreed, that meant preservation as well as economic development of the state. "If you go to Europe," he remarked, using comparison to emphasize his point, "you don't participate in making new national parks. In the Lower 48 States, we are rounding out the system." Only Alaska still offered Americans "a chance to display some vision" and "some foresight" in national park planning. Since the establishment of Yellowstone in 1872, he observed, approximately twenty-five million acres of land had been set aside as national parks. For the first time in history, Americans had the opportunity in Alaska to double or perhaps even triple that figure. "So I am looking forward to participating in this endeavor," Udall concluded. "I don't know of any major piece of legislation that will have more far-reaching consequences in the country in the future than this one will."[28]

Predictably, opponents of H.R. 39 took precisely the opposite stance, that of stressing Alaska's significance for the United States as a storehouse of natural resources. "D-2 lands are obviously critical to the State of Alaska," remarked Representative Don Young, admitting the biases of the Alaska delegation, "but, more importantly, they are critical to the Nation as a whole." Congress must consider what the United States stood to lose if preservation of the state got "out of hand." Alaskan oil alone would soon "comprise 20 percent of our domestic oil supply," Young noted. Yet "another natural treasure" of the state was its "critical metals." The national parks and wilderness areas as proposed were simply too large to allow adequate exploitation of these resources. "The key issue is how much needs to be set aside to provide appropriate protection without going overboard," he said, reemphasizing his basic theme. "I trust that the subcommittee will act to set aside those unique areas which everyone agrees need preserving but place other lands in less restrictive management systems where diversified uses will be permitted."[29]

Taking up where Young's testimony left off, Senator Mike Gravel of Alaska proposed the protection of no more than twenty-five million acres of land in national parks, wilderness areas, wildlife refuges, and wild and scenic rivers. "Let me just say," he remarked, justifying his figure, "there is a body of land in Alaska where there is no question, no dispute, that should be preserved in the four conservation Systems." The figure of twenty-five million acres, as opposed to the more than 100 million acres requested by preservationists, was the more "balanced," "moderate," and "reasonable position." Gravel did not need to admit the obvious; the twenty-five million acres he had in mind clearly contained nothing of economic value to the state. Only with that assurance did he freely concede that preservation "is the highest and best use of the land."[30]

Where natural resources might in fact exist in abundance, Gravel further proposed delaying any decisions affecting those lands pending the formation of a joint federal-state commission, "a legislative body, or, as the press has characterized it, in Alaska, a beefed-up zoning commission for the entire State." The object of the commission "would be the development of policy" with respect to all state and federal lands outside the parks. Deposits of oil, gas, and coal, for example, had "not even been scratched." A federal-state commission to protect access to those resources would insure flexibility in future management decisions. "It would be a terrible tragedy in our human existence," he concluded, again revealing his bias for development, "to foreclose the possibility of making an intelligent adjudication when the time came to do it."[31]

Gravel's proposal was endorsed by his Senate colleague, Ted Stevens, as well as Governor Jay Hammond and Representative Don Young. In several meetings with Alaskan residents the previous fall, the four had basically agreed on accepting twenty-five million acres of land for parks, refuges, and wilderness areas. The key objection among preservationists was the unmistakable limitation of those lands to monumental topography at the expense of rounding out the parks to include areas of greater biological significance. In that respect, national park history once more played into the hands of Senator Stevens and the Alaska delegation. "I view the process that we are in now of trying to determine which of our lands have national significance in the true sense that the Grand Canyon and Yosemite and Yellowstone and the other areas that have been made national parks had," he stated, sensing his opportunity to quote precedent. As he implied, the preservation of similar natural wonders, areas both rugged and devoid of natural resources, certainly would arouse little opposition among residents of the forty-ninth state. Instead, they were concerned preservationists would in fact seek a decision by Congress "which may well impede future generations of Alaskans from having the ability to utilize the land bank that Congress wisely gave us as an economic floor for the future of our State."[32]

Its legislative complexity aside, the Alaska lands issue was basically another manifestation of the traditional struggle between preservation and use. Only the object of the debate, not its political intrigue, had changed. Just as resource interests worked to thwart a comprehensive protection bill, so preservationists campaigned diligently to effect a parks and wilderness package of both biological substance and legislative permanence. Advocates of greater development and fewer parks invariably relied on the Alaska delegation to espouse their views in Congress. Similarly, preservation groups, rallying under the banner of the Alaska Coalition, looked to Representatives Udall and Seiberling, among other concerned members of Congress, for their own leadership on Capitol Hill.

Much to their advantage, by 1977 and the introduction of H.R. 39, preservationists knew more about Alaska than their predecessors a century before had ever known about Yosemite or Yellowstone. By the late 1960s, writers for the major conservation magazines were traveling throughout the state, informing the memberships of their respective organizations of the areas considered worthy of protection. The discovery of oil at Prudhoe Bay in 1968, coupled with the completion of the controversial Trans-Alaska Pipeline in 1977, lent further credence to preservationists' claims that Alaska, much as the lower forty-eight states, was in danger of being subdivided into economic spheres of influence. Initially, preservationists feared the search for oil and the construction of the pipeline would destroy the Alaska tundra and decimate the great herds of migrating caribou. Proposals to dam the largest rivers in Alaska, then shunt their water southward through Canada into the thirsty American West, also struck preservationists as the epitome of utilitarian arrogance and callousness toward the natural world.[33]

For preservationists, Alaska was a chance for beginning anew rather than for repeating errors common to the lower forty-eight states. "In Alaska we have the opportunity to learn from our past mistakes," remarked Edgar Wayburn, chairman of the Sierra Club's Alaska Task Force. "We have given away the Redwoods of California, the Big Thicket in Texas, and the Big Cypress Swamp in Florida, just to name a few, and we have had to buy them back at exorbitant prices," he pointed out.

Large parks in Alaska would still be "free as far as the exchange of cash is concerned."[34] David Brower, president of Friends of the Earth, likewise emphasized the unique opportunity offered by federal ownership of so much of the state. "Alaska, as a late maturing child in the society's scheme of things," he said, "is still richly endowed, as youth always is, and we should think carefully before we let qualities that only Alaska still possesses be made as ordinary, or even as repugnant, as too many other places have been driven to become." As examples, he confessed he was "mindful" of California, "my native State, not to mention Texas." The unrestrained development of Alaska would do nothing more than turn an extraordinary environment into another commonplace one, thereby undermining preservationists' own fervent hope of sustaining "Alaska's appeal, productivity, and creativity for centuries."[35]

Such idealism was to prove important for buoying preservationists' spirits in the months and years ahead. The entirety of 1977 passed without any action on H.R. 39, with the exception of the public hearings conducted by the House Subcommittee on General Oversight and Alaska Lands. As preservationists feared, the delay only worked to the advantage of their opponents, especially Representative Don Young, who succeeded in adding no fewer than eighty-five amendments to the original bill once the subcommittee convened early in 1978 to draft the final version. Not until April 7, 1978, was the Interior Committee prepared to report to Congress as a whole; by then only eight months remained until December 18, 1978, the deadline established for the resolution of the Alaska lands issue under the Native Claims Settlement Act. If the controversy had not been resolved by that date, technically all of the lands withdrawn from entry pending congressional review would once again revert to the unreserved public domain and be subject to both state and native selections.[36]

Under the circumstances, preservationists were indeed fortunate to have the support of the new administration. Granted, President Jimmy Carter and his secretary of the interior, Cecil Andrus, proposed a ceiling of only 92 million acres of parks and wilderness as opposed to the 115 million acres of land sought by the Alaska Coalition and specified in the original version of H.R. 39. Still, with Senators Mike Gravel and Ted Stevens threatening delay of the legislation in the Senate, and in light of their call for the protection of a mere 25 million acres of territory, the endorsement of the White House was crucial. On May 17, 1978, the House of Representatives began debate on H.R. 39 and two days later approved the bill by a vote of 277 to 31. Preservationists were jubilant, not only because the House proposed to protect more than 120 million acres as national parks, wildlife refuges, and wild and scenic rivers, but because passage of the bill had been won by such a stunning, lopsided margin.[37]

The celebration, however, proved to be premature. In the Senate, Mike Gravel successfully thwarted serious consideration of the Alaska lands bill throughout the summer and into the fall. Although his delaying tactics grew unpopular, even with Senator Stevens, they nonetheless had the desired effect of preventing final action on H.R. 39 in 1978.[38]

The December 18 deadline, in other words, would not be met. Once again preservationists were extremely fortunate to have the support of the Carter administration. Even as the Ninety-fifth Congress disbanded, President Carter and Secretary of the Interior Andrus had considered their options. As early as October 11, Andrus had informed the public in a signed editorial: "If Congress is unable to act, President Carter and I will."[39] On November 16 Andrus made good his promise by withdrawing 110 million acres of public lands in Alaska from entry under the authority of the Fish and Wildlife Act of 1956 and the Federal Land Management Act of 1976. Each allowed the secretary of the interior broad discretion in the protection of wildlife and wilderness areas on the public domain. Finally, on December 1, further invoking the articles of the Antiquities Act of 1906, President Carter gave added protection to 56 million of the 110 million acres withdrawn by Andrus as national monuments. Andrus's withdrawals were to stand for only three years; Carter's designation of the national monuments would be permanent if Congress itself refused to decide the Alaska lands issue.[40]

Carter's objective was in fact to force Congress to make the final decision. In that respect, his action was like President Franklin D. Roosevelt's veto in 1943 of the bill to abolish Jackson Hole National Monument in Wyoming. Like Roosevelt, Carter believed the protection of Alaska transcended local prejudices and special interests; at least, the decision was too important to allow a few legislators manipulating the political process to forestall the ultimate test of the nation's true will. Nevertheless, 1979 was another year of postponement; indeed, the political season began as another period of frustration and despair for preservation interests, with new amendments threatening the integrity of the original legislation passed by the House of Representatives in 1978. In the second House vote, taken on May 16, 1979, preservationists withstood the new opposition by a tally of 268 to 157, only to lose ground once again in the Senate. Its final version of the bill not only considerably weakened the management safeguards approved by the House but granted protection to twenty-six million fewer acres of Alaska lands in the process.[41]

Ironically, the fate of Alaska was sealed in 1980 not only by compromise but by the intimidation of preservation interests. On August 19, the Senate finally passed a considerably less protective Alaska lands bill. Dismayed but defiant, preservationists would have worked to postpone the legislation yet another year, but for the election on November 4 of Ronald Reagan as the next president of the United States. Unlike Carter's, Reagan's attitude toward environmental legislation was openly hostile. Fearing that he might kill the Alaska lands legislation entirely, preservationists both within and outside the Congress saw no choice but to make their peace with the Senate version of H.R. 39. "Political realities dictate that we act promptly on the Senate-passed bill," Representative Morris Udall said, issuing a personal warning. "We must accept the fact that Reagan is here for four years."[42] On November 12, the House agreed to recognize the wisdom of the Senate, and on December 2, 1980, President Jimmy Carter signed the compromise legislation into law. Granted, the bill was a disappointment for preservationists, although it did, in Udall's words, "accomplish 85–90 percent of the things the House wanted."[43] The penalty of further delay under the Reagan administration might well have been the sacrifice of legislation of any kind.

Considering what they might have lost, preservationists understandably celebrated what they had won in Alaska as a milestone of American conservation. "Never has so much been done on conservation for future generations with one stroke of the pen," wrote Charles Clusen, chairman of the Alaska Coalition. The acreages protected were indeed impressive, a total of more than 100 million acres or 28 percent of the state, including 43.6 million acres of new national parks, 53.8 million acres of new wildlife refuges, and 1.2 million acres for the national wild and scenic rivers system. Of those lands, 56.7 million acres were to receive further protection as wilderness, subject only to accessibility by foot, horseback, raft, or canoe. "Not since the days of Theodore Roosevelt's large public land withdrawals," Clusen concluded, "have we seen such boldness, dynamism, and leadership for the protection of our land heritage. The Alaska 'victory' also shows that the American people believe in a conservation ethic and support environmental protection more than at any previous time in history."[44]

Only after more careful reflection were most preservationists willing to concede that their battle for Alaska may in fact have just begun on December 2, 1980. In park after park, critical wildlife habitat had either been fragmented to accommodate resource extraction or excluded entirely. As a concession to copper mining interests, for example, approximately one million acres in Gates of the Arctic National Park were denied wilderness protection. Similarly, state selections threatened grizzly bear habitat, salmon streams, and caribou breeding grounds bordering Mount McKinley National Park. The Alaska Lands Act renamed the park Denali and expanded it by a whopping 3.7 million acres. The point again was that size by itself was no guarantee that wildlife, especially migrating populations such as caribou, could be sustained without further extending protection to their lowland breeding grounds.[45]

Other preservationists sensed a troublesome precedent in the use of the term "preserve" to describe large expanses of wilderness that historically would have been labeled "national parks" or "national monuments." The management principles of national parks and monuments were clearly defined by precedent, but what was a "national preserve?" One unsettling answer could be gleaned from the legislative histories of the Big Thicket National Preserve in Texas and the Big Cypress National Freshwater Preserve in Florida. In each instance, Congress had granted wide discretion to the secretary of the interior to allow mining, oil drilling, grazing, hunting, trapping, and other extractive uses both within and adjacent to the parks.[46] On the roughly twenty million acres of land designated as "preserves" in Alaska, much the same discretion prevailed. The management of a preserve, in other words, could easily be determined by administrative fiat rather than established by public consensus.

Ideally, preserves would act as buffers for more sensitive park areas. In fact, however, often the preserves themselves were in greater need of protection. The mountainous, inaccessible landscapes forming the core of the new parks and monuments rarely had the same potential for economic development. In keeping with the size and ruggedness of Alaska, its parks could be far larger than those in the lower forty-eight states. In the final analysis, however, national park history had repeated itself. The only unchallenged mandate in Alaska was the endorsement of monumentalism. Beyond its mountainous terrain, especially along the seacoasts of Alaska and in the forests of its southeastern panhandle, entrenched commercial interests, both native and non-native, successfully resisted most long-range efforts to effect preservation over economic use.

In defense of their right to make such a choice, Alaskans argued that pioneer Americans in the past had also enjoyed the freedom to exploit the land as each saw fit. Now that the rest of the country had been developed, residents of the lower forty-eight states had no right to dictate to Alaskans that they and they alone must sacrifice economic opportunity for wilderness preservation. Besides, Alaskans loved the frontier way of life and themselves wished to preserve the land base supporting it.[47]

In rebuttal, preservationists asked again whether or not Alaskans could in fact resist unwanted or undesirable forms of change indefinitely. "Big, outside corporations are looking all over the world for resources," noted Representative John F. Seiberling, for example. He warned Alaskans to support H.R. 39: "And with the kind of machinery and airplanes and the kind of money that people have in the outside, they are going to come in here and each one is going to take a cut of the salami and when he gets through, there will not be much left for the people of Alaska unless we set aside certain areas."[48] Persistent opposition to H.R. 39 on the question of personal freedom led to the allowance of subsistence hunting and the establishment of national preserves to accommodate it. Gradually, however, even preservationists who supported the practice came to recognize the potential for its abuse, especially since the snowmobile, airplane, and high-powered rifle had replaced the dogsled, spear, and hunting knife as tools of the chase.[49]

Alaska, it seemed, eventually would change much as the rest of America had changed. Writing on behalf of the Alaska Coalition, an anonymous preservationist was among those who conceded the point, "For a land which is expected to give so much material wealth to the nation, we only ask in return that the nation seek to protect certain lands and wildlife so that this priceless natural heritage will survive for future generations."[50] Margaret Murie, the noted author and longtime Alaskan adventurer, was even more eloquent, "My prayer is that Alaska will not lose the heart-nourishing friendliness of her youth, . . . that her great wild places will remain great, and wild, and free, where wolf and caribou, wolverine and grizzly bear, and all the Arctic blossoms may live in the delicate balance which supported them long before impetuous man appeared in the north. This is the great gift Alaska can give to the harrassed world."[51] On a scale unique in American history, the passage of the Alaska Lands Act of 1980 realized this fondest of preservationists' dreams. But could the dream be sustained?[52] Indeed, even in the vastness of Alaska, one fundamental accomplishment still eluded the movement—effecting its dreams in perpetuity, in physical reality as well as in transitory laws.

Epilogue

National Parks for the Future: Encirclement and Uncertainty

> The results of this study indicate that no parks of the System are immune to external and internal threats, and that these threats are causing significant and demonstrable damage.
>
> *State of the Parks Report, 1980*

> I will err on the side of public use versus preservation.
>
> *James Watt, 1981*

True to precedent, the jubilation of preservationists following their achievements in Alaska proved to be short lived. On January 20, 1981, Ronald Reagan assumed the presidency on a platform of government austerity and conservative retrenchment. In keeping with his conservative principles, his appointee as secretary of the interior, James Watt, soon made it clear that expansion of the national park system itself had come to an abrupt end. More alarming to preservationists, Watt showed little respect for their conviction that national parks, above all, ought to be managed as sanctuaries for wilderness and wildlife. To Watt, the greatest problem facing the parks was the deterioration of their physical plant, especially roads, parking lots, overnight accommodations, and sewage systems. What funds might be added to the existing park budget obviously would be spent on the access, comfort, and safety of park visitors rather than on the sanctity of park resources. To be sure, that wilderness should be protected for its own sake was the last thing on either the president's or the secretary's agenda.[1]

By itself, Watt's shift in emphasis from the protection of the national parks to recreational development reminiscent of Mission 66 would have been enough to arouse preservationists across the country. Coupled with his outspoken disdain for the environmental movement, however, his obvious indifference to the fate of endangered lands and wildlife assured him a place in history as the most controversial secretary of the interior since Albert B. Fall. In 1922, Fall secretly and improperly leased the nation's petroleum reserve at Teapot Dome, Wyoming, to the Sinclair Oil Company.[2] Among preservationists of the 1980s, it seemed as if James Watt had attempted far worse. Most disconcerting was his steadfast refusal to spend appropriations allocated by Congress for national park acquisitions. No act more openly defied preservationists' assessment that the underlying problem of the national parks since their inception had been the government's failure to provide them with enough land for sustained protection in the first place.[3]

As a critic of national park expansion, Watt epitomized the continuing threat to preservation from within the federal bureaucracy itself. Although Congress and the president alone had the power to establish national parks and wilderness areas, by and large their administration fell to government officials. How those officials interpreted their responsibility in the field often determined whether or not the apparent wishes of Congress would in fact be honored. In the person of James Watt, preservationists relearned bitter lessons from national park history, namely, that what the federal government gave it could always take away. Even with Congress firmly behind the national park idea, Watt's broad discretionary powers as secretary of the interior left him with enough authority to promote the maintenance and development of the nation's "crown jewels," as opposed to acquiring new lands for so-called nontraditional park areas.

Watt, in other words, sensed that he might support the national parks without actually supporting preservation. The key to his subterfuge was in the nature of the parks he endorsed. Protection of the *original* park system required that Watt respect only park tradition; no new lands and few natural resources of great economic value would be affected by his approval of past policies designating the natural "wonders" of the nation as its "crown jewels." By the same token, the policy kept preservationists constantly on the defensive. Once again they were forced to convince the public that the protection of monumental scenery alone no longer met the needs of environmental preservation. As Watt realized, tradition was on the side of monumentalism. Because he did not directly attack the legitimacy of Yosemite, Yellowstone, the Grand Canyon, and their counterparts, the public was not as likely to oppose his conviction that urban parks especially were frivolous and wasteful.[4]

If preservationists had one argument to discredit James Watt, it was that external threats to the national parks, especially mining, air and water pollution, and land development, jeopardized even the most remote and pristine of the nation's "crown jewels." Maintaining the status quo in land acquisitions, among other policies of retrenchment, merely insured that outside threats to the national parks would continue to escalate. Early publicity describing the scope of the problem understandably concentrated on compromises to the parks' scenic integrity. Particularly in the Southwest, meteorologists and other pollution experts noted the deterioration of visibility over the Grand Canyon, Bryce, Zion, Canyonlands, and neighboring national monuments. At stake was the sensation of spaciousness those areas long had evoked. On a clear day, visitors at the most popular scenic overlooks might see mesas and mountain ranges more than one hundred miles distant. Nowhere were the sensations of boundless horizons and personal freedom more pronounced and, accordingly, more in danger of being lost to atmospheric degradation. Indeed, by 1980, due to the spread of coal-fired power plants, smelters, and urbanization throughout the Southwest, scientists had concluded that none of its national parks any longer had "pristine" air quality more than one day out of every three.[5]

The conclusions seemed inescapable. In its own report to the Congress, *State of the Parks—1980,* the National Park Service agreed that external threats to the national parks posed the gravest danger to their resources throughout the 1980s and beyond. "The 63 National Park natural areas greater than 30,000 acres in size reported an average number of threats nearly double that of the Service-wide norm," the document began on an ominous note. The category, of course, included "Yellowstone, Yosemite, Great Smoky Mountains, Everglades, and Glacier. Most of these great parks were at one time pristine areas surrounded and protected by vast wilderness regions," the report continued, underscoring the extent of the changes that had taken place in recent decades. "Today, with their surrounding buffer zones gradually disappearing, many of these parks are experiencing significant and widespread adverse effects associated with external encroachment."[6]

Preservationists themselves were particularly alarmed by a proposal to lease portions of the Targhee National Forest, bordering the southwestern corner of Yellowstone National Park, for a large geothermal power project. In a direct line, the core of the project would be only fifteen miles west of the Upper Geyser Basin and Old Faithful Geyser. Immediately at issue was whether or not the drilling would be harmful to the intricate geothermal systems underlying both the park and its adjacent forest lands. In 1980 an environmental impact statement released by the U.S. Forest Service admitted the possibility of losing Yellowstone's geysers if the project were built. "The exact boundaries of the Yellowstone geothermal reservoir(s) are uncertain," the Forest Service concluded. "Thus, it is difficult to say how much of a connection—if any—there is between the possible geothermal resource . . . and thermal areas inside the park, or if any adverse effects might result."[7]

Individually, the project stood a good chance of being defeated. Collectively, however, both existing and proposed projects of a similar nature bordering other parks, including

Yellowstone, underscored the futility of fighting the national lifestyle indefinitely. In essence, the enemy of preservation was growth. As long as the demands of the economy and a growing population strained the supply of natural resources, the best preservationists could still hope for was not to win environmental battles, but merely to trim their losses.

Toward that end, preservationists and Park Service rangers asked the public to visualize parks in the 1980s in conjunction with their total surroundings. Parks at the center of threatened ecosystems were no more secure than the security of their outlying parts. Yellowstone National Park, for example, depended for its survival on "greater Yellowstone," the territory comprising not only the park proper but the millions of acres of national forest lands, wilderness areas, and private property surrounding it. As a concept, "greater Yellowstone" was especially relevant to wildlife protection. Of all park management goals, wildlife preservation still had the least to do with the placement of national park boundaries. If the grizzly bear in particular were to survive in the continental United States, both Yellowstone and Glacier national parks—either through expansion or strict regulations controlling land use outside their perimeters—would have to accommodate the bears' need to wander freely beyond the national parks themselves.[8]

Symbolically, the administration of James Watt suggested that Americans as a whole still refused to accept the legitimacy of such lines of argument. Respect for grizzly bears and other potentially dangerous animals called for levels of understanding and tolerance usually discernible only among preservationists themselves. To be sure, when Watt himself was forced to resign in 1983, a prejudicial joke reflecting on disabled Americans and minorities, not his disdain for the environment, was the actual basis for his fall from grace. His successor, William Clark, generally followed Watt's direction more quietly and diplomatically. At least with respect to national park policy, little at Interior had changed.[9]

In the final analysis, it seemed as if only a dramatic change in the nation's lifestyle itself could save the national parks from continuing deterioration. During the nineteenth century, the relative isolation of parklands in the West had allowed Americans the luxury of simply stating that their commitment to protection was—as vowed in the Yosemite Park Act of 1864—"inalienable for all time." The promise in 1864 was uncomplicated by immediate threats to the integrity of Yosemite and its successors. Perhaps the nation was sincere, but Americans had not yet been challenged to prove that sincerity by sacrificing any substantive economic goals.

In the absence of national sacrifice, threats to the national parks observable in the 1980s loomed as a potential fact of life well into the twenty-first century. Past the midpoint of the decade, air and water pollution, energy development, and urban encroachment outside the national parks still underscored the significance of economic motives in shaping American values. Writing for an earlier generation, Aldo Leopold, the distinguished wildlife biologist, saw materialism as the basic threat to the integrity of anything wild. Before wilderness could be saved in perpetuity, Americans as a whole would have to reject their destructive perceptions of the natural world as simply a commodity of exchange. "Obligations have no meaning without conscience," he wrote, "and the problem we face is the extension of the social conscience from people to land." More than anything else, the United States needed a responsible, sustainable, and sincere land ethic. "A thing is right when it tends to preserve the integrity, stability, and beauty of the biotic community," he concluded. "It is wrong when it tends otherwise."[10]

It followed that the national parks themselves no longer could accommodate every public whim. If their biological resources were in fact important, then the protection of park environments must take precedence over all forms of consumptive recreation. The Reagan administration's own emphasis on park maintenance aside, such development could only postpone but not suppress further questioning regarding the legitimacy of roads, hotels, campgrounds, and automobiles in the midst of fragile environments. Eventually, the American people would have to choose preservation over development, or accept development and fewer parks. As monuments to American culture, the largest national parks were perhaps nominally secure. But if monumentalism in fact no longer met the nation's environmental needs, then the time for acting decisively was indeed running out.

Notes

Prologue

1. Interpretive writings on the social, cultural, and intellectual significance of the national park idea are almost nonexistent. The standard work to date, for example, John Ise, *Our National Park Policy: A Critical History* (Baltimore: Johns Hopkins University Press, 1961), is better described as a legislative and administrative history. Similarly, Freeman Tilden, *The National Parks*, 2d ed. (New York: Alfred A. Knopf, 1970), is a park-by-park compilation intended for general readers and tourists. Somewhat more interpretive, but now dated, is Harlean James, *Romance of the National Parks* (New York: Macmillan Co., 1939). Two books which have placed the national parks in a limited cultural context are Hans Huth, *Nature and the American: Three Centuries of Changing Attitudes* (Berkeley and Los Angeles: University of California Press, 1957), and Roderick Nash, *Wilderness and the American Mind* (New Haven: Yale University Press, 1967). As their titles imply, however, neither deals specifically with the national parks; similarly, Huth devotes little attention to the reserves beyond the formative years of Yosemite and Yellowstone. An important article-length study on the origins of national parks as a

democratic ideal is Roderick Nash, "The American Invention of National Parks," *American Quarterly* 22 (Fall 1970): 726–35.

2. George B. Tobey, *A History of Landscape Architecture: The Relationship of People to Environment* (New York: American Elsevier, 1973), pp. 25–52. Also relevant are Charles E. Doell and Gerald B. Fitzgerald, *A Brief History of Parks and Recreation in the United States* (Chicago: Athletic Institute, 1954), pp. 12–15; and Norman T. Newton, *Design on the Land: The Development of Landscape Architecture* (Cambridge, Mass.: Harvard University Press, Belknap Press, 1971), pp. 1–20.

3. *Webster's New Collegiate Dictionary* (Springfield, Mass.: G. and C. Merriam Co., 1961), p. 611.

4. More detailed discussions of Romanticism, deism, and primitivism may be found in Nash, *Wilderness and the American Mind*, pp. 44–66, and Huth, *Nature and the American*, pp. 1–53.

5. Doell and Fitzgerald, *Parks and Recreation in the United States*, p. 19; Newton, *Design on the Land*, pp. 221–32; Frederick Law Olmsted, *Walks and Talks of an American Farmer in England* (Ann Arbor: University of Michigan Press, 1967), p. 54.

6. The definitive biography of Olmsted is Laura Wood Roper, *FLO: A Biography of Frederick Law Olmsted* (Baltimore: Johns Hopkins University Press, 1973). Also of value is Albert Fein, *Frederick Law Olmsted and the American Environmental Tradition* (New York: George Braziller, 1972).

7. Huth, *Nature and the American*, pp. 66–67. A more detailed analysis is Thomas Bender, "The 'Rural' Cemetery Movement: Urban Travail and the Appeal of Nature," *New England Quarterly* 47 (June 1974): 196–211.

8. Roper, *FLO*, pp. 126–28; Newton, *Design on the Land*, pp. 267–73; Doell and Fitzgerald, *Parks and Recreation in the United States*, pp. 23–41.

9. See Alfred Runte, "How Niagara Falls Was Saved: The Beginning of Esthetic Conservation in the United States," *The Conservationist* 26 (April–May 1972): 32–35, 43; idem, "Beyond the Spectacular: The Niagara Falls Preservation Campaign," *New-York Historical Society Quarterly* 57 (January 1973): 30–50. These should be supplemented with Roper, *FLO*, pp. 378–82, 395–97; and Charles M. Dow, *The State Reservation at Niagara: A History* (Albany, N.Y.: J. B. Lyon Company, 1914).

10. Charles M. Dow, for example, in his *Anthology and Bibliography of Niagara Falls*, 2 vols. (Albany, N.Y.: J. B. Lyon Company, 1921), 2:1059–93, annotates no less than seventeen published criticisms of this type between 1832 and 1859.

11. As quoted in George Wilson Pierson, *Tocqueville in America* (New York: Doubleday and Co., Anchor Books, 1959), p. 210.

12. As quoted in Dow, *Anthology and Bibliography of Niagara Falls*, 2:1070–71.

13. Ibid., p. 1075. Bonnycastle followed with a call of his own for protection of the cataract. "Niagara is . . . a public property . . . and should be protected from the rapacity of private speculators, and not made a Greenwich fair of; where peddlers and thimble-riggers, niggers and barkers, and lowest trulls of the vilest scum of society, congregate to disgust and annoy the visitors from all parts of the world, plundering and pestering them without control." Ibid., p. 1076.

14. The significance of the West in American culture continues to enjoy considerable treatment. Standard works include Henry Nash Smith, *Virgin Land: The American West as Symbol and Myth* (Cambridge, Mass.: Harvard University Press, 1950); Ray Allen Billington, *America's Frontier Heritage* (New York: Holt, Rinehart and Winston, 1966); and Earl Pomeroy, *In Search of the Golden West: The Tourist in Western America* (New York: Alfred A. Knopf, 1957). Also relevant is Huth, *Nature and the American*, pp. 129–47.

15. Roper, *FLO*, pp. 6, 14, 378.

16. Runte, "Beyond the Spectacular," pp. 30–50. The Olmsted Papers, in the Library of Congress, Washington, D.C., are also rich on the Niagara campaign.

Chapter 1

1. The role of American culture as a factor of environmental perception is a topic of increasing popularity among historians and geographers. Two recent studies are Robert Lemelin, *Pathway to the National Character, 1830–1861* (Port Washington, N.Y.: Kennikat Press, 1974), and David Lowenthal, "The Place of the Past in the American Landscape," chapter 4 in *Geographies of the Mind: Essays in Historical Geosophy*, ed. David Lowenthal and Martyn J. Bowden (New York: Oxford University Press, 1976). Neither study, however, does more than mention the national parks. Closer to my own interpretation of the origins of the national park idea is Paul Shepard, *Man in the Landscape* (New York: Alfred A. Knopf, 1967), pp. 246–58. Shepard, for example, notes the popularity of the image of the ruin among Yellowstone's early explorers. Also selective is Earl S. Pomeroy, *In Search of the Golden West: The Tourist in Western America* (New York: Alfred A. Knopf, 1957), which focuses on the period between 1880 and 1920, after Yosemite and Yellowstone parks were established. A synthesis of both contemporary and historical literature as they pertain to cultural nationalism toward landscape is Roderick Nash, *Wilderness and the American Mind* (New Haven: Yale

University Press, 1967), pp. 67–83, although again, Nash's vehicle is wilderness rather than the national parks per se.

2. The dated but still definitive biography of Samuel Bowles is George S. Merriam, *The Life and Times of Samuel Bowles*, 2 vols. (New York: Century Company, 1885).

3. Dumas Malone, ed., *Dictionary of American Biography*, 11 vols. (New York: Charles Scribner's Sons, 1963), 1:516; ibid., 4:530; Merriam, *Samuel Bowles*, 2:2, 81.

4. Samuel Bowles, *Our New West* (Hartford, Conn.: Hartford Publishing Company, 1869), pp. v–viii.

5. Samuel Bowles, *Across the Continent* (Springfield, Mass.: Samuel Bowles and Company, 1865), p. 231; idem, *Our New West*, p. 385.

6. The definitive biography of Moran is Thurman Wilkins, *Thomas Moran: Artist of the Mountains* (Norman: University of Oklahoma Press, 1966). For Bierstadt there is Gordon Hendricks, *Albert Bierstadt: Painter of the American West* (New York: Henry N. Abrams, 1974). Relevant article-length studies are Gordon Hendricks, "The First Three Western Journeys of Albert Bierstadt," *The Art Bulletin* 46 (September 1964): 333–65; David W. Scott, "American Landscape: A Changing Frontier," *Living Wilderness* 33 (Winter 1969): 3–13; and William S. Talbot, "American Visions of Wilderness," *Living Wilderness* 33 (Winter 1969): 14–25. For an overall interpretation I am indebted to James Thomas Flexner, *That Wilder Image* (New York: Bonanza Books, 1962), pp. 135–36, 293–302.

7. Thomas Jefferson, *Notes on the State of Virginia* (New York: Harper and Row, 1964), p. 17.

8. As quoted in Nash, *Wilderness and the American Mind*, p. 68.

9. Ibid., p. 72.

10. James Fenimore Cooper, "American and European Scenery Compared," Chapter 3 of Washington Irving, et al., *The Home Book of the Picturesque* (New York: G. P. Putnam, 1852), pp. 61, 69.

11. Ibid., pp. 52, 66, 69.

12. Susan Fenimore Cooper, "A Dissolving View," Chapter 5 in ibid., pp. 81–82, 88–94.

13. Regarding the Atlantic coast, for example, James Fenimore Cooper noted: "[it] is, with scarcely an exception, low, monotonous and tame. It wants Alpine rocks, bold promontories, visible heights inland, and all those other glorious accessories of the sort that render the coast of the Mediterranean the wonder of the world." Ibid., p. 54. Similarly, Washington Irving bemoaned that the mountains of the East "might have given our country a name, and a poetical one, had not the all-controlling powers of common-place determined otherwise." Ibid., p. 72. European writers as well picked up on the theme; see, e.g., Alexis de Tocqueville's impressions of the East in George

Wilson Pierson, *Tocqueville in America* (New York: Doubleday and Co., Anchor Books, 1959), pp. 122, 178–79.

14. Irving, et al., *Home Book of the Picturesque*, p. 52.

15. Histories of the acquisition of the public domain include Marion Clawson, *The Land System of the United States* (Lincoln: University of Nebraska Press, 1968), pp. 38, 41–42; Roy M. Robbins, *Our Landed Heritage* (Lincoln: University of Nebraska Press, 1962); and Everett Dick, *The Lure of the Land* (Lincoln: University of Nebraska Press, 1970).

16. A general treatment of the discovery of both wonders may be found in Francis P. Farquhar, *History of the Sierra Nevada* (Berkeley and Los Angeles: University of California Press, 1965), pp. 71–85. Yosemite, which means "great full-grown grizzly bear," was the stronghold of the Ahwahneechee Indians until 1851, when they were finally dispossessed of their home by a battalion of California miners. For a complete history of the valley see Carl P. Russell, *One Hundred Years in Yosemite* (Yosemite National Park: Yosemite Natural History Association, 1968).

17. A. V. Kautz, "Ascent of Mount Rainier," *Overland Monthly* 14 (May 1874): 394; James M. Hutchings, *Scenes of Wonder and Curiosity in California* (London: Chapman and Hall, 1865), p. 134; William H. Brewer, *Up and Down California in 1860–64*, ed. Francis P. Farquhar (New Haven: Yale University Press, 1930), pp. 404–405.

18. Horace Greeley, *An Overland Journey from New York to San Francisco in the Summer of 1859* (New York: C. M. Saxton, Barker and Co., 1860), pp. 306–307; Bowles, *Across the Continent*, pp. 223–24. Bowles' patriotism was further swelled by "The Three Brothers," "Cathedral Rocks," and "The Cathedral Spires." Indeed, he maintained, the formations united "the great impressiveness, the beauty and the fantastic form of the Gothic architecture. From their shape and color alike, it is easy to imagine, in looking upon them, that you are under the ruins of an old Gothic cathedral, to which those of Cologne and Milan are but baby-houses." See pp. 226–27.

19. The Staubach is in the Bernese Alps in southern Switzerland.

20. Thomas Starr King, "A Vacation Among the Sierras," *Boston Evening Transcript*, January 26, 1861, p. 1.

21. Bowles, *Across the Continent*, pp. 228–29; Albert D. Richardson, *Beyond the Mississippi* (Hartford, Conn.: American Publishing Company, 1867), p. 426.

22. The Sierra redwoods, *Sequoia gigantea*, are not to be confused with the California coast redwoods, *Sequoia sempervirens*. For the sake of clarity and consistency I have chosen to call each by their most popular common name as determined by Farquhar, *History of the Sierra Nevada*, pp. 83–89.

23. Clarence King, *Mountaineering in the Sierra Nevada* (Boston:

James R. Osgood and Co., 1872), pp. 41–43; Greeley, *An Overland Journey*, pp. 311–12. Similar observations, again, may be gleaned from the chronicles of the large majority of other early explorers. See, for example, Bowles, *Across the Continent*, p. 237; and Fitz Hugh Ludlow, "Seven Weeks in the Great Yo-Semite," *Atlantic Monthly* 13 (June 1864): 744–45.

24. Richardson, *Beyond the Mississippi*, p. i.

25. Ibid.

26. Again I am indebted to Flexner, *That Wilder Image*, pp. 60–76, 266–84. Also relevant is Nash, *Wilderness and the American Mind*, pp. 78–83.

27. Flexner, *That Wilder Image*, pp. 293–302.

28. Ironically, both were European-born. In 1831, when Albert Bierstadt was one year old, his family moved from its home near Dusseldorf, Germany, to New Bedford, Massachusetts. Between 1853 and 1857 young Albert returned to Germany to study landscape painting. Moran, born in Bolton, England, in 1837, also left Europe at an early age when his father moved the family to Baltimore, Maryland, in 1844.

29. Hendricks, *Albert Bierstadt*, p. 94. Other scholarly accounts of Bierstadt's early career include Harold McCracken, *Portrait of the Old West* (New York: McGraw-Hill, 1952), pp. 137–42; Flexner, *That Wilder Image*, pp. 294–99; and Hendricks, "The First Three Western Journeys of Albert Bierstadt," pp. 333–65.

30. Hendricks, *Albert Bierstadt*, pp. 130–35, 154–65. Both *The Rocky Mountains* and *Domes of the Yosemite* are beautifully reproduced in this volume, on pp. 150–51 and 162–63 respectively.

31. On Watkins see Hans Huth, *Nature and the American: Three Centuries of Changing Attitudes* (Berkeley and Los Angeles: University of California Press, 1957), pp. 145, 149–51; and Brewer, *Up and Down California in 1860–64*, pp. 406, 413.

32. See Hendricks, *Albert Bierstadt*, passim.

33. These paintings in 1977 were owned by Hirschl and Adler Galleries, Inc., New York City, and the National Collection of Fine Arts, Smithsonian Institution, Washington, D.C.

34. George Catlin, *Illustrations of the Manners, Customs, and Conditions of the North American Indians*, 2 vols. (London: H. G. Bohn, 1851), 1: 262.

35. Robert Lemelin, in *Pathway to the National Character*, p. 24, notes that 40,000 visitors annually saw Niagara Falls as early as 1849.

36. The most entertaining account of this exchange is Farquhar, *History of the Sierra Nevada*, p. 87.

37. Ibid., pp. 84–85.

38. As quoted in Joseph H. Engbeck, Jr., *The Enduring Giants* (Berkeley: University Extension, University of California, in cooperation with the California Department of Parks and Recreation, Save-the-

Redwoods League, and the Calaveras Grove Association, 1973), p. 77.

39. The best account of the deliberations leading up to the preservation of Yosemite Valley is Hans Huth, "Yosemite: The Story of An Idea," *Sierra Club Bulletin* 33 (March 1948): 63–76. Also relevant is Holway R. Jones, *John Muir and the Sierra Club: The Battle for Yosemite* (San Francisco: Sierra Club, 1965), pp. 28–29.

40. U.S., Congress, Senate, *Congressional Globe*, 38th Cong., 1st sess., May 17, 1864, pp. 2300–2301.

41. U.S., *Statutes at Large*, 13 (1864): 325.

42. Ibid.

43. Frederick Law Olmsted, "The Yosemite Valley and the Mariposa Big Trees," ed. Laura Wood Roper, *Landscape Architecture* 43 (October 1952): 16–17; idem, "Governmental Preservation of Natural Scenery," March 8, 1890, printed circular, United States Library of Congress, Washington, D.C., Olmsted Papers, Box 32.

44. The standard biography of Muir is Linnie Marsh Wolfe, *Son of the Wilderness: The Life of John Muir* (New York: Alfred A. Knopf, 1945). Roderick Nash adds measurably to her interpretation, however, in *Wilderness and the American Mind*, pp. 122–40. Also of importance is William F. Bade, ed., *The Life and Letters of John Muir*, 2 vols. (Boston: Houghton Mifflin Company, 1924).

45. John Muir, "Flood-Storm in the Sierra," *Overland Monthly* 14 (June 1875): 496.

46. The impact of the quote is discussed in Merle Curti, *The Growth of American Thought*, 3d ed. (New York: Harper and Row, 1964), pp. 237–38.

Chapter 2

1. The latest scholarship on Yellowstone National Park is Richard A. Bartlett, *Nature's Yellowstone* (Albuquerque: University of New Mexico Press, 1974); Aubrey L. Haines, *Yellowstone National Park: Its Exploration and Establishment* (Washington, D.C.: Government Printing Office and National Park Service, 1974); and Aubrey L. Haines, *The Yellowstone Story*, 2 vols. (Yellowstone National Park: Yellowstone Library and Museum Association in cooperation with Colorado Associated University Press, 1977). None of these studies, however, adds to our knowledge about the origins of the national park idea. Bartlett, for example, p. 194, lays the foundation of Yellowstone to "the growth of the American's love for his land for its beauty rather than for its wealth," yet does not define precisely what emotions provoked that "love."

2. As its name implies, Yellowstone was named after the brilliantly-colored rocks found throughout the region, particularly in the walls of the Grand Canyon of the Yellowstone River.

3. For the history of Yellowstone during the fur-trade era, see Bartlett, *Nature's Yellowstone*, pp. 93–116.

4. With the revelation of Yellowstone to the nation at-large, the literature, both contemporary and historical, becomes more voluminous. Included for the ventures of 1869 are Charles W. Cook, David E. Folsom, and William Peterson, *The Valley of the Upper Yellowstone*, ed. Aubrey L. Haines (Norman: University of Oklahoma Press, 1965), pp. 3–7; W. Turrentine Jackson, "The Cook-Folsom Exploration of the Upper Yellowstone, 1869," *Pacific Northwest Quarterly* 32 (July 1941): 307–12; and Bartlett, *Nature's Yellowstone*, 117–21, 147–51.

5. Both Cook and Folsom were born and raised in the East, in Maine and New Hampshire respectively. Peterson, from Denmark, may also be considered among those whose native geographical inheritance was scant preparation for the full impact of Western scenery. For a more detailed suggestion of the cultural legacy that influenced the perceptions of Yellowstone's early explorers, consult the biographical data in Haines, *Yellowstone National Park*, pp. 133–52.

6. Charles W. Cook, "The Valley of the Upper Yellowstone," *Western Monthly* 4 (July 1870): 61.

7. Ibid., p. 64.

8. Their article, just cited above, initially was rejected by the *New York Tribune*, *Scribner's*, and *Harper's*, all of which considered it either fictitious or unreliable. Jackson, "The Cook-Folsom Exploration," pp. 316–17.

9. Louis C. Cramton, *Early History of Yellowstone National Park and Its Relation to National Park Policies* (Washington, D.C.: Government Printing Office and National Park Service, 1932), pp. 12–13; W. Turrentine Jackson, "The Washburn-Doane Expedition into the Upper Yellowstone," *Pacific Historical Review* 10 (June 1941): 189–91; Nathaniel Pitt Langford, *The Discovery of Yellowstone National Park*, (Lincoln: University of Nebraska Press, 1972), pp. vii–xvii.

10. There is no standard title for the expedition; for clarity and consistency only Washburn's name will subsequently be used.

11. Nathaniel P. Langford, "The Wonders of the Yellowstone," I, *Scribner's Monthly* 2 (May 1871): 13.

12. Evert's personal account appeared the following year as "Thirty-Seven Days of Peril," *Scribner's Monthly* 3 (November 1871): 1–17.

13. *The Report of Lieutenant Gustavus C. Doane upon the so-called Yellowstone Expedition of 1870*, S. Ex. Doc. 51, 41st Cong., 3d sess., March 3, 1871, as quoted from Cramton, *Early History of Yellowstone National Park*, p. 142; Nathaniel P. Langford, "The Wonders of the Yellowstone," II (June 1871): 127.

14. A selection is reprinted in Cramton, *Early History of Yellowstone National Park*, pp. 90–110.

15. The explorers named the stream "Tower Creek" and its cataract "Tower Fall." Langford, *The Discovery of Yellowstone Park*, pp. 21–22.

16. "The Yellowstone Expedition," *New York Times*, October 14, 1870, p. 4.

17. Washburn, however, had died in January.

18. W. Turrentine Jackson, "Governmental Exploration of the Upper Yellowstone, 1871," *Pacific Historical Review* 11 (June 1942): 189–90; Bartlett, *Nature's Yellowstone*, pp. 188–89. The progress of the Hayden Survey through Yellowstone is further detailed in Richard A. Bartlett, *Great Surveys of the American West* (Norman: University of Oklahoma Press, 1962), pp. 40–56; and William H. Goetzmann, *Exploration and Empire: The Explorer and the Scientist in the Winning of the American West* (New York: Alfred A. Knopf, 1966), pp. 504–508.

19. Bartlett, *Great Surveys of the American West*, pp. 40–41; idem, *Nature's Yellowstone*, p. 189.

20. W. H. Jackson's autobiography, *Time Exposure* (New York: G. P. Putnam's Sons, 1940), pp. 186–203, is a very entertaining account of his work on the Hayden Survey.

21. A brief history of this painting is in Thurman Wilkins, *Thomas Moran: Artist of the Mountains* (Norman: University of Oklahoma Press, 1966), pp. 3–5, 68–70.

22. The springs were already known to invalids and miners in the region. See W. H. Jackson, *Time Exposure*, p. 198.

23. *Preliminary Report of the United States Geological Survey of Montana and Portions of Adjacent Territories; Being a Fifth Annual Report*, by F. V. Hayden (Washington, D.C.: Government Printing Office, 1872), pp. 83–84. Moran's painting, since restored, now hangs in the National Collection of Fine Arts, Smithsonian Institution, Washington, D.C.

24. Bartlett, *Great Surveys of the American West*, pp. 49–56; Jackson, "Governmental Exploration of the Upper Yellowstone," pp. 194–97.

25. On this debate see Haines, *Yellowstone National Park*, pp. 111–12; Hans Huth, "Yosemite: The Story of An Idea," *Sierra Club Bulletin* 33 (March 1948): 72–76; and Holway R. Jones, *John Muir and the Sierra Club: The Battle for Yosemite* (San Francisco: Sierra Club, 1965), pp. 26–28.

26. Langford, *Discovery of Yellowstone Park*, pp. 117–18.

27. Bartlett, *Nature's Yellowstone*, pp. 202–206; Cramton, *Early History of Yellowstone National Park*, pp. 28–35; Roderick Nash, *Wilderness and the American Mind* (New Haven: Yale University Press, 1967), p. 110; Haines, *Yellowstone National Park*, p. 180, fn. 9.

28. U.S., *Statutes at Large*, 17 (1872): 32–33.

29. Langford, *Discovery of Yellowstone Park*, pp. 96–97.

30. Cornelius Hedges, "The Great Falls of the Yellowstone: A

Graphic Picture of Their Grandeur and Beauty," *Helena Daily Herald*, October 15, 1871, as quoted in Cramton, *Early History of Yellowstone National Park*, p. 100.

31. Langford, "Wonders of the Yellowstone," I, pp. 7, 8, 12; II, p. 124. The host of similar perceptions would also include Ferdinand V. Hayden, "The Wonders of the West—II: More About the Yellowstone," *Scribner's Monthly* 3 (February 1872): passim; idem, "The Hot Springs and Geysers of the Yellowstone and Firehole Rivers," *The American Journal of Science and Arts* 103 (February 1872): 105–15; (March 1872): 161–76; and Walter Trumbull, "The Washburn Yellowstone Expedition," *Overland Monthly* 6 (May 1871): 431–37; (June 1871): 489–96.

32. W. Turrentine Jackson, "The Creation of Yellowstone National Park," *Mississippi Valley Historical Review* 29 (September 1942): 192–93. Similarly, at Mammoth Hot Springs, F. V. Hayden noted that "two men have already pre-empted 320 acres of land covering most of the surface occupied by the active springs, with the expectation that upon the completion of the Northern Pacific Railroad this will become a famous place of resort for invalids and pleasure-seekers." Hayden, "The Wonders of the West—II," pp. 390–91.

33. As quoted in Bartlett, *Nature's Yellowstone*, pp. 206–207.

34. Jackson, "Creation of Yellowstone National Park," p. 202.

35. U.S., Congress, House, Committee on the Public Lands, *The Yellowstone Park*, H. Rept. 26 to accompany H. R. 764, 42d Cong., 2d sess., February 27, 1872, pp. 1–2.

36. The bill's sponsor in the Senate, for example, Samuel Pomeroy of Kansas, introduced it "as the result of the exploration, made by Professor Hayden. . . . With a party he explored the headwaters of the Yellowstone and found it to be a great natural curiosity, great geysers, as they are termed, water spouts, and hot springs, and having platted the ground himself, and having given me the dimensions of it, the bill was drawn up, as it was thought best to consecrate and set apart this great place of national resort, as it may be in the future, for the purposes of public enjoyment." U.S., Congress, Senate, *Congressional Globe*, 42d Cong., 2d sess., January 23, 1872, p. 520.

37. Hiram Martin Chittenden, *The Yellowstone National Park* (Cincinnati: The Robert Clarke Company, 1895), pp. 93–95; Wilkins, *Thomas Moran*, pp. 69–71; Bartlett, *Great Surveys of the American West*, p. 57. The park movement, if not all of its motives, has now been extensively treated; see, e.g., Haines, *Yellowstone National Park*, Part III; and Bartlett, *Nature's Yellowstone*, Chapter 9.

38. Jackson, "Creation of Yellowstone National Park," pp. 195–97; Cramton, *Early History of Yellowstone National Park*, p. 32; Bartlett, *Nature's Yellowstone*, pp. 198–99. Others believed to have worked on the bill include Delegate William Clagett of Montana, Nathaniel P. Langford, and F. V. Hayden.

39. U.S.,*Statutes at Large*, 17 (1872): 32–33. The inclusion of timber on the list, however, should not be taken as evidence that Yellowstone was also intended to be a forest preserve. The absence of high-quality timber in the region was mentioned by Cornelius Cole before the Senate; the assessment could only have come from the explorers themselves, who undoubtedly based their claim on their experiences with the maze of thin, tumbled pines south of Yellowstone Lake. More likely the wording was intended to forestall the cutting of trees by those who wished to fence off the geysers and hot springs.

Chapter 3

1. U.S., Congress, Senate, *Congressional Globe*, 38th Cong., 1st sess., May 17, 1864, pp. 2300–2301.

2. Initial expressions of this thesis include Alfred Runte, "Yellowstone: It's Useless, So Why Not a Park?" *National Parks and Conservation Magazine: The Environmental Journal* 46 (March 1972): 4–7; and idem, " 'Worthless' Lands: Our National Parks," *American West* 10 (May 1973): 4–11.

3. U.S., *Statutes at Large*, 13 (1864): 325.

4. William H. Goetzmann, for example, in *Exploration and Empire: The Explorer and the Scientist in the Winning of the American West* (New York: Alfred A. Knopf, 1966), p. 498, refers to Hayden as "par excellence the businessman's geologist."

5. U.S., Congress, House, Committee on the Public Lands, *The Yellowstone Park*, H. Rept. 26 to accompany H. R. 764, 42d Cong., 2d sess., February 27, 1872, pp. 1–2.

6. U.S., Congress, Senate,*Congressional Globe*, 42d Cong., 2d sess., January 30, 1872, p. 697.

7. Ibid.

8. Ibid.

9. U.S., Congress, House,*Congressional Globe*, 42d Cong., 2d sess., February 27, 1872, p. 1243.

10. U.S., Congress, Senate,*Congressional Globe*, 42d Cong., 2d sess., January 30, 1872, p. 697.

11. U.S., Congress, House,*Congressional Globe*, 42d Cong., 2d sess., February 27, 1872, p. 1243.

12. John Ise, *Our National Park Policy: A Critical History* (Baltimore: Johns Hopkins University Press, 1961), pp. 20–22.

13. U.S., Congress, Senate, *Congressional Record*, 48th Cong., 1st sess., May 27, 1884, pp. 4547–53; Ise, *Our National Park Policy*, pp. 42–43; Richard A. Bartlett, *Nature's Yellowstone* (Albuquerque: University of New Mexico Press, 1974), pp. 141–42.

14. Although several were proposed, none were enacted.

15. U.S.,*Statutes at Large*, 18 (1875): 517–18. Actually the park was

superimposed on a military site. Section 3 of the enabling act, for example, provided that "any part of the park hereby created shall be at all times available for military purposes, either as a parade ground or drill ground, in time of peace, or for complete occupation in time of war. . . ." The reserve might "also be used for the erection of any public buildings or works."

16. Two detailed analyses of the anxiety aroused by the close of the frontier are Earl Pomeroy, *In Search of the Golden West: The Tourist in Western America* (New York: Alfred A. Knopf, 1957), pp. 93–103, 152–58; and Roderick Nash, *Wilderness and the American Mind* (New Haven: Yale University Press, 1967), pp. 143–47.

17. George B. Tobey, Jr., *A History of Landscape Architecture: The Relationship of People to Environment* (New York: American Elsevier, 1973), p. 271.

18. As quoted in Kermit Vanderbilt, *Charles Eliot Norton: Apostle of Culture in a Democracy* (Cambridge, Mass.: Harvard University Press, Belknap Press, 1959), p. 190. Norton, a committed scenic preservationist, participated in the campaigns to save Niagara Falls and the Adirondack forests of northern New York State, the former in cooperation with Frederick Law Olmsted. The Olmsted Papers, housed in the Library of Congress, Washington, D.C., contain a considerable number of letters written between the two men.

19. Alfred Runte, "Beyond the Spectacular: The Niagara Falls Preservation Campaign," *New-York Historical Society Quarterly* 57 (January 1973): 30–50.

20. State of New York, State Land Survey, *Report on the Adirondack State Land Surveys to the Year 1886*, by Verplanck Colvin (Albany: Weed, Parsons and Co., 1886), pp. 5–7.

21. Ibid., pp. 5–7; Runte, "Beyond the Spectacular," pp. 48–50; N. F. Dreisziger, "The Campaign to Save Niagara Falls and the Settlement of United States-Canadian Differences, 1906–1911," *New York History* 55 (October 1974): 437–58.

22. John Muir, "Studies in the Sierra: Mountain Building," *Overland Monthly* 14 (January 1875): 65; William Frederick Bade, ed., *The Life and Letters of John Muir*, 2 vols. (Boston: Houghton Mifflin Co., 1924), 2: 237.

23. State of California, Geological Survey, *The Yosemite Guide-Book*, by J. D. Whitney (Cambridge, Mass.: University Press, 1869), p. 21; Robert Underwood Johnson, "The Case for Yosemite Valley," *Century Magazine* 39 (January 1890): 478.

24. Linnie Marsh Wolfe, *Son of the Wilderness: The Life of John Muir* (New York: Alfred A. Knopf, 1945), pp. 244–46; Nash, *Wilderness and the American Mind*, pp. 130–32.

25. Robert Underwood Johnson, *Remembered Yesterdays* (Boston: Little, Brown, 1923), pp. 279–80; Holway R. Jones, *John Muir and the*

Sierra Club: The Battle for Yosemite (San Francisco: Sierra Club, 1965), p. 43.

26. John Muir, "The Treasures of the Yosemite," *Century Magazine* 40 (August 1890): 487–88.

27. John Muir, "Features of the Proposed Yosemite National Park," *Century Magazine* 40 (September 1890): 666–67; idem, "The Treasures of the Yosemite," p. 483.

28. Ise, *Our National Park Policy*, pp. 100–104; Douglas Hillman Strong, *A History of Sequoia National Park* (Ph.D. diss., Syracuse University, 1964), pp. 61–62.

29. Strong, *A History of Sequoia National Park*, pp. 63–92.

30. Ibid., pp. 112–22; Jones, *John Muir and the Sierra Club*, pp. 46–47.

31. Bade, *Life and Letters of John Muir*, 2: 244–45.

32. Actually Sequoia passed as two separate bills. The first created a small reserve of roughly 75 square miles; the second enlarged it to 250. Who championed the follow-up piece of legislation remains a question of considerable intrigue. Strong, *A History of Sequoia National Park*, pp. 110–12.

33. U.S., *Statutes at Large*, 26 (1890): 478, 650–52; U.S., Congress, House, *Congressional Record*, 51st Cong., 1st sess., August 23, 1890, pp. 9072–73; U.S., Congress, Senate, *Congressional Record*, 51st Cong., 1st sess., September 8, 1890, p. 9829; U.S., Congress, House, *Congressional Record*, 51st Cong., 1st sess., September 30, 1890, pp. 10751–52; U.S., Congress, Senate, *Congressional Record*, 51st Cong., 1st sess., September 30, 1890, p. 10740.

34. U.S., Department of the Interior, *Annual Report of the Secretary of the Interior for the Year 1890* (Washington, D.C.: Government Printing Office, 1890), pp. 123–26. Noble also named the parks, since Congress had merely set forth their boundaries.

35. U.S., Congress, Senate, *Report of the Yosemite Park Commission*, S. Doc. 34, 58th Cong., 3d sess., December 13, 1904, pp. 1–20. The figures are given in Ise, *Our National Park Policy*, p. 70.

36. Muir's petition against the deletion, authored with Joseph N. Le Conte and William E. Colby on behalf of the Sierra Club, is reprinted in U.S., Congress, Senate, *Report of the Yosemite Park Commission*, p. 51.

Chapter 4

1. Carl Snyder, "Our New National Wonderland," *Review of Reviews* 9 (February 1894): 164, 169, 171.

2. John Muir, "The Wild Parks and Forest Reservations of the West," *Atlantic Monthly* 81 (January 1898): 26–28.

3. John Ise, *Our National Park Policy: A Critical History* (Baltimore: Johns Hopkins University Press, 1961), pp. 121–25; U.S., *Statutes at Large*, 30 (1899): 993–95. An administrative history of the reserve is Arthur D. Martinson, "Mount Rainier National Park: First Years," *Forest History* 10 (October 1966): 26–33. Also see idem, *Mountain in the Sky: A History of Mount Rainier National Park* (Ph.D. diss., Washington State University, 1966).

4. Freeman Tilden, *The National Parks* (New York: Alfred A. Knopf, 1970), pp. 115–16; Ise, *Our National Park Policy*, pp. 128–29.

5. W. G. Steel, *The Mountains of Oregon* (Portland, Ore.: David Steel, 1890), pp. 32–33. Steel first visited Crater Lake in 1885.

6. U.S., Congress, House, *Congressional Record*, 57th Cong., 1st sess., April 19, 1902, p. 4450.

7. Ibid., pp. 4450, 4453; U.S., *Statutes at Large*, 32 (1902): 202–3.

8. The standard departure for the origins of utilitarian conservation is Samuel P. Hays, *Conservation and the Gospel of Efficiency: The Progressive Conservation Movement, 1890–1920* (Cambridge, Mass.: Harvard University Press, 1959). Also valuable is Elmo R. Richardson, *The Politics of Conservation: Crusades and Controversies, 1897–1913* (Berkeley and Los Angeles: University of California Press, 1962). Donald C. Swain extends the period of their investigation with *Federal Conservation Policy, 1921–1933* (Berkeley and Los Angeles: University of California Press, 1963).

9. Of the national population in 1910 (91,972,266), but 2,633,517 lived in the Rocky Mountain states, and only 4,192,304 in all of Washington, Oregon, and California. U.S., Bureau of the Census, *Thirteenth Census of the United States, 1910*, 13 vols. (Washington, D.C.: Government Printing Office, 1913), 1:30.

10. John Ise, *The United States Forest Policy* (New Haven: Yale University Press, 1920), pp. 109–18, 120; Hays, *Conservation and the Gospel of Efficiency*, p. 47.

11. Hays, *Conservation and the Gospel of Efficiency*, pp. 14–15, 122–46; Ise, *The United States Forest Policy*, pp. 143–63; Roderick Nash, *Wilderness and the American Mind* (New Haven: Yale University Press, 1967), pp. 149–53.

12. Gifford Pinchot, *The Fight for Conservation* (New York: Doubleday, Page and Co., 1910), p. 45. Pinchot, an 1889 graduate of Yale University, immediately sailed to Europe to study forestry in England, France, and Germany, there being no equivalent training available in the United States at that time. He describes his life and career in *Breaking New Ground* (New York: Harcourt, Brace, Jovanovich, 1947). On his early relationship with President Roosevelt, see pp. 188–97. Two important biographies of Pinchot are M. Nelson McGeary, *Gifford Pinchot* (Princeton: Princeton University Press, 1960), and Harold T. Pinkett, *Gifford Pinchot: Public and Private Forester* (Urbana: University of Illinois Press, 1970). Douglas H. Strong also

provides a detailed synthesis of Pinchot's influence in *The Conservationists* (Menlo Park, Calif.: Addison-Wesley Publishing Company, 1971), pp. 65–89.

13. Hays, *Conservation and the Gospel of Efficiency*, pp. 39–44.

14. Pinchot, *Breaking New Ground*, pp. 263–76.

15. U.S., *Statutes at Large*, 34 (1906): 225.

16. A detailed account of the national monuments and their establishment may be found in Ise, *Our National Park Policy*, pp. 143–62. He ignores, however, the cultural significance behind their creation.

17. U.S., Department of the Interior, National Park Service, *National Parks and Landmarks* (Washington, D.C.: Government Printing Office, 1970), pp. 14, 20; Ise, *Our National Park Policy*, pp. 231, 383–84.

18. U.S., *Statutes at Large*, 34 (1906): 225; Ise, *Our National Park Policy*, pp. 383–84.

19. The establishment of the park is described in Ise, *Our National Park Policy*, pp. 164–70.

20. Grinnell's early career is revealed in John F. Reiger, ed., *The Passing of the Great West: Selected Papers of George Bird Grinnell* (New York: Winchester Press, 1972).

21. See, for example, George Bird Grinnell, "Protection of the National Park," *New York Times*, January 29, 1885, p. 6. John F. Reiger provides a sympathetic account of Grinnell's work on behalf of Yellowstone in *American Sportsmen and the Origins of Conservation* (New York: Winchester Press, 1975), pp. 98–141.

22. U.S., Department of the Interior, National Park Service, *Early History of Glacier National Park, Montana*, by Madison Grant (Washington, D.C.: Government Printing Office, 1919), pp. 5–7; George Bird Grinnell, "The Crown of the Continent," *Century Magazine* 62 (September 1901): 660–72.

23. Rufus Steele, "The Son Who Showed His Father: The Story of How Jim Hill's Boy Put a Ladder to the Roof of his Country," *Sunset Magazine* 34 (March 1915): 473–85; Alfred Runte, "Pragmatic Alliance: Western Railroads and the National Parks," *National Parks and Conservation Magazine: The Environmental Journal* 48 (April 1974): 15.

24. U.S., Congress, Senate, *Congressional Record*, 61st Cong., 2d sess., January 25, 1910, pp. 958–60; ibid., February 9, 1910, pp. 1639–41.

25. Ibid., April 14, 1910, p. 4669; U.S., *Statutes at Large*, 36 (1910): 354–355. Two recent histories of the park are Curt W. Buchholtz, *Man in Glacier* (West Glacier, Mont.: Glacier Natural History Association, 1976), and Warren L. Hanna, *Montana's Many-Splendored Glacierland* (Seattle: Superior Publishing Company, 1976).

26. U.S., Congress, House, Committee on the Public Lands, *Rocky Mountain National Park, Hearings* on S. 6309, 63d Cong., 3d sess., December 23, 1914, pp. 7–22.

27. U.S., Congress, House, *Congressional Record*, 63d Cong., 3d sess., January 18, 1915, pp. 1789–91; U.S., *Statutes at Large*, 38 (1915): 798–800.

28. See, for example, John Muir, "Hetch Hetchy Valley: The Lower Tuolumne Yosemite," *Overland Monthly* 2 (June 1873): 42–50; Nash, *Wilderness and the American Mind*, pp. 161–62.

29. U.S., Department of the Interior, *Report of the Secretary of the Interior for the Fiscal Year Ending June 30, 1903* (Washington, D.C.: Government Printing Office, 1903), p. 156.

30. Holway R. Jones, *John Muir and the Sierra Club: The Battle for Yosemite* (San Francisco: Sierra Club, 1965), pp. 95–100.

31. Prior histories include Jones, *John Muir and the Sierra Club*, pp. 85–169; Nash, *Wilderness and the American Mind*, chapter 10; Elmo R. Richardson, "The Struggle for the Valley: California's Hetch Hetchy Controversy, 1905–1913," *California Historical Society Quarterly* 38 (September 1959): 249–58; and Ise, *Our National Park Policy*, pp. 85–96. None of these accounts may be considered definitive, however, inasmuch as each approaches the controversy within the context of simply events or of other major themes.

32. The House vote was 183 to 43, with 194 absent. U.S., Congress, House, *Congressional Record*, 63d Cong., 1st sess., September 3, 1913, p. 4151. In the Senate the tally was 43 for, 25 against, and 27 either absent or not voting. U.S., Congress, Senate, *Congressional Record*, 63d Cong., 2d sess., December 6, 1913, pp. 385–86.

33. See, for instance, James D. Phelan, "Why Congress Should Pass the Hetch Hetchy Bill," *Outlook* 91 (February 13, 1909): 340–41.

34. John P. Young, "The Hetch Hetchy Problem," *Sunset Magazine* 22 (June 1909): 606.

35. The photograph is reproduced in Jones, *John Muir and the Sierra Club*, opposite p. 112. It originally appeared as part of a series in San Francisco, California, Board of Supervisors, *On the Proposed Use of a Portion of the Hetch Hetchy . . . by John R. Freeman* (San Francisco: Rincon Publishing Co., 1912), pp. 5–56.

36. Letter, J. Horace McFarland to Robert Underwood Johnson, October 31, 1913, University of California, Berkeley, Bancroft Library, Robert Underwood Johnson Papers, Box 3.

37. Ise, *Our National Park Policy*, p. 94.

Chapter 5

1. John Muir, "The Wild Parks and Forest Reservations of the West," *Atlantic Monthly* 81 (January 1898): 15; Allen Chamberlain, "Scenery as a National Asset," *Outlook* 95 (May 28, 1910): 169.

2. An article-length study of the role of the railroads in national park development is Alfred Runte, "Pragmatic Alliance: Western

Railroads and the National Parks," *National Parks and Conservation Magazine: The Environmental Journal* 48 (April 1974): 14–21.

3. A noted confrontation between John Muir and Gifford Pinchot over development of the national forests is recounted in Linnie Marsh Wolfe, *Son of the Wilderness: The Life of John Muir* (New York: Alfred A. Knopf, 1945), pp. 275–76. The emerging split between preservationists and utilitarianists is further documented in Douglas H. Strong, "The Rise of American Esthetic Conservation," *National Parks Magazine* 44 (February 1970): 5–7; and Samuel P. Hays, *Conservation and the Gospel of Efficiency: The Progressive Conservation Movement, 1890–1920* (Cambridge, Mass.: Harvard University Press, 1959): 189–98.

4. U.S., *Statutes at Large*, 26 (1890): 651.

5. Holway R. Jones provides a complete listing in *John Muir and the Sierra Club: The Battle for Yosemite* (San Francisco: Sierra Club, 1965), pp. 4–5, n. 5.

6. The role of nature in suburbia is discussed by Peter J. Schmidt, *Back to Nature: The Arcadian Myth in Urban America* (New York: Oxford University Press, 1969), pp. 1–32.

7. The J. Horace McFarland Papers, housed in the William Penn Memorial Museum, Pennsylvania Historical and Museum Commission, Division of Archives and Manuscripts, Harrisburg, is an invaluable collection for both the Niagara controversy and national park history between 1904 and 1949.

8. J. Horace McFarland, "Shall We Make a Coal-Pile of Niagara?" *Ladies' Home Journal* 23 (October 1906): 39.

9. Ibid.

10. Chamberlain to McFarland, April 22, 1908, McFarland Papers, Box 16; Colby to Chamberlain, April 16, 1908, McFarland Papers, Box 16.

11. Colby to Pinchot, April 20, 1908, McFarland Papers, Box 16.

12. McFarland to Pinchot, November 26, 1909, McFarland Papers, Box 16.

13. See, for example, James D. Phelan, "Why Congress Should Pass the Hetch Hetchy Bill," *Outlook* 91 (February 13, 1909): 340–41.

14. William Frederick Bade, for example, director of the Sierra Club and vice-president of the Western Branch of the Society for the Preservation of National Parks, wrote: "As soon as a good road is built to Hetch-Hetchy and transportation facilities provided, hotels will spring up, and the tide of tourist travel . . . will turn to Hetch-Hetchy in both winter and summer." Bade to Richard A. Ballinger, undated, McFarland Papers, Box 16.

15. J. Horace McFarland, "Shall We Have Ugly Conservation?" *Outlook* 91 (March 13, 1909): 595; Chamberlain to McFarland, March 18, 1909, McFarland Papers, Box 16.

16. Chamberlain, "Scenery as a National Asset," pp. 162–64.

17. Roderick Nash, in *Wilderness and the American Mind* (New Haven: Yale University Press, 1967), p. 170, maintains that preservationists' lack of mention about wilderness was a "tactical error" which cost them "considerable support." In retrospect, however, it must be conceded that the American public as a whole still viewed the national parks as a visual experience rather than an emotional one.

18. Chamberlain, "Scenery as a National Asset," pp. 165, 169.

19. Runte, "Pragmatic Alliance: Western Railroads and the National Parks," pp. 14–21. The topic is further explored in idem, "The Yosemite Valley Railroad: Highway of History, Pathway of Promise," *National Parks and Conservation Magazine: The Environmental Journal* 48 (December 1974): 4–9; and idem, "Blueprint for Comfort: A National Park-to-Park Railway," *National Parks and Conservation Magazine: The Environmental Journal* 50 (November 1976): 8–10.

20. Watrous to McFarland, August 18, 1911, McFarland Papers, Box 17; Watrous to McFarland, September 6, 1911, McFarland Papers, Box 17.

21. U.S., Department of the Interior, *Proceedings of the National Park Conference Held at Yellowstone National Park September 11 and 12, 1911* (Washington, D.C.: Government Printing Office, 1912), p. 4.

22. Ibid., pp. 5–17.

23. U.S., Congress, Senate, *Congressional Record*, 61st Cong., 2d sess., January 25, 1910, p. 961; U.S., Congress, House, *Congressional Record*, 63d Cong., 3d sess., January 18, 1915, p. 1790.

24. U.S., Congress, House, *Congressional Record*, 63d Cong., 3d sess., January 18, 1915, p. 1790.

25. Earl Pomeroy develops this perception of the West and its impact on tourism throughout *In Search of the Golden West: The Tourist in Western America* (New York: Alfred A. Knopf, 1957). See especially chapter 1.

26. Runte, "Pragmatic Alliance: Western Railroads and the National Parks," pp. 14–15; Mary Roberts Rinehart, "Through Glacier National Park with Howard Eaton," Part II, *Collier's* 57 (April 29, 1916): 26.

27. Mary Roberts Rinehart, "Through Glacier National Park with Howard Eaton," Part I, *Collier's* 57 (April 22, 1916): 11.

28. Typed transcript, R. B. Marshall, "Our National Parks," March 6, 1911, McFarland Papers, Box 22.

29. George Otis Smith, "The Nation's Playgrounds," *American Review of Reviews* 40 (July 1909): 44; R. B. Marshall, "Our National Parks."

30. Typed transcript, Mark R. Daniels, "Address Before the Tenth Annual Convention of the American Civic Association," December 3, 1914, McFarland Papers, Box 22.

31. McFarland to C. R. Miller, November 24, 1911, McFarland Papers, Box 19.

32. Ibid.

33. John Ise, *Our National Park Policy: A Critical History* (Baltimore: Johns Hopkins University Press, 1961), p. 384.

34. H. Duane Hampton, *How the United States Cavalry Saved the National Parks* (Bloomington: University of Indiana Press, 1971), passim.

35. Ise, *Our National Park Policy*, pp. 27, 133.

36. Ibid., p. 188.

37. McFarland to C. R. Miller, November 24, 1911, McFarland Papers, Box 19; Frederick Law Olmsted, Jr., to John Olmsted, December 19, 1910, McFarland Papers, Box 20.

38. McFarland to Overton W. Price, October 30, 1911, McFarland Papers, Box 20; McFarland to Olmsted, April 17, 1916, McFarland Papers, Box 20.

39. Pinchot to McFarland, March 4, 1911, McFarland Papers, Box 20; McFarland to Chamberlain, April 2, 1914, McFarland Papers, Box 18. For a summary of the circumstances surrounding Pinchot's removal as chief forester, see Hays, *Conservation and the Gospel of Efficiency*, pp. 165–74.

40. Harold J. Howland to Richard B. Watrous, January 9, 1912, McFarland Papers, Box 21; editorial, "A National Park Service," *Outlook* 100 (February 3, 1912): 246.

41. McFarland to Olmsted, April 17, 1916, McFarland Papers, Box 20; Pinchot to McFarland, March 4, 1911, McFarland Papers, Box 20.

42. See, for example, U.S., Congress, House, Committee on the Public Lands, *National Park Service, Hearings* on H. R. 434 and H. R. 8668, 64th Cong., 1st sess., 1916, pp. 63–69.

43. As quoted in U.S., Congress, House, Committee on the Public Lands, *National Park Service, Hearings* on H. R. 104, 63d Cong., 2d sess., 1914, p. 9.

44. U.S., Congress, House, Committee on the Public Lands, *Establishment of a National Park Service, Hearings* on H. R. 22995, 62d Cong., 2d sess., 1912, p. 7.

45. U.S., Congress, House, Committee on the Public Lands, *National Park Service, Hearings* on H. R. 434 and H. R. 8668, 64th Cong., 1st sess., 1916, pp. 55–56.

46. Congressman John E. Raker, of California, and Congressman William Kent, also of the Golden State, supported the legislation in the House. For a lively interpretation of the bill and the significance of its passage, see Donald C. Swain, "The Passage of the National Park Service Act of 1916," *Wisconsin Magazine of History* 50 (Autumn 1966): 4–17.

47. Both Mather and Albright have been treated in superb biographies; they are Robert Shankland, *Steve Mather of the National Parks*, 3d ed. (New York: Alfred A. Knopf, 1970), and Donald C. Swain, *Wilderness Defender: Horace M. Albright and Conservation* (Chicago:

University of Chicago Press, 1970). A brief synthesis of Mather's career may also be found in Douglas H. Strong, *The Conservationists* (Menlo Park, Calif.: Addison-Wesley Publishing Company, 1971), pp. 117–38. The famous letter from Lane is quoted in both Shankland and Strong, on pp. 7 and 117, respectively.

48. Shankland, *Steve Mather of the National Parks*, p. 66.

49. Stephen T. Mather, "The National Parks on a Business Basis," *American Review of Reviews* 51 (April 1915): 429–30.

50. U.S., *Statutes at Large*, 39 (1916): 535.

51. Ibid. Olmsted's role in guiding the preparation of this paragraph is exhaustively credited in the correspondence of the J. Horace McFarland collection.

52. U.S., Department of the Interior, National Park Service, *Proceedings of the National Parks Conference*, January 2–6, 1917 (Washington, D.C.: Government Printing Office, 1917), p. 20.

Chapter 6

1. Mary Roberts Rinehart, "The Sleeping Giant," *Ladies' Home Journal* 38 (May 1921): 21.

2. Ibid.

3. Joseph Grinnell and Tracy Storer, "Animal Life as an Asset of National Parks," *Science* 44 (September 15, 1916): 377.

4. Rinehart, "The Sleeping Giant," p. 21.

5. Preservationists eventually succeeded in thwarting the projects; interested historians will wish to consult the J. Horace McFarland Papers, Pennsylvania Historical and Museum Commission, Division of Archives and Manuscripts, Harrisburg, for numerous materials relating to the campaign. Relevant contemporary articles include Stephen T. Mather, "Do You Want to Lose Your Parks?" *Independent* 104 (November 13, 1920): 220–21, 238–39; Frank A. Waugh, "The Market Price on Landscape," *Outlook* 127 (March 16, 1921): 428–29; and William C. Gregg, "The Cascade Corner of Yellowstone Park," *Outlook* 129 (November 23, 1921): 469–76.

6. U.S., *Statutes at Large*, 17 (1872): 33.

7. See John F. Reiger, *American Sportsmen and the Origins of Conservation* (New York: Winchester Press, 1975), pp. 97–113, 125–41.

8. The Glacier park debates of 1910 were among the first to deal with wildlife protection as a primary justification for national parks. Senator Thomas H. Carter of Montana, for example, sparked brief discussion with a reminder that the proposed reserve would save the mountain sheep as well as unique scenery. U.S., Congress, Senate, *Congressional Record*, 61st Cong., 2d sess., January 25, 1910, p. 960.

9. Robert Sterling Yard, *National Parks Portfolio* (New York: Charles Scribner's Sons, 1916), pp. 3–6.

10. Robert Sterling Yard, "The People and the National Parks," *The Survey* 48 (August 1, 1922): 547; Rinehart, "The Sleeping Giant," p. 21; Grinnell and Storer, "Animal Life as an Asset of National Parks," p. 377. The emerging role of wildlife conservation in the national parks may also be traced in Charles C. Adams, "The Relation of Wild Life to Recreation in Forests and Parks," *Playground* 18 (July 1924): 208–9; John C. Merriam, "Scientific, Economic, and Recreational Values of Wild Life," *Playground* 18 (July 1924): 203–4; and Horace M. Albright, "Our National Parks as Wildlife Sanctuaries," *American Forests and Forest Life* 35 (August 1929): 505–7, 536.

11. Robert Sterling Yard, "Economic Aspects of Our National Parks Policy," *Scientific Monthly* 16 (April 1923): 384–85.

12. U.S., Department of the Interior, *Annual Report of the Director of the National Park Service, June 30, 1920* (Washington, D.C.: Government Printing Office, 1920), p. 66; C. Edward Graves, "The Yosemite School," *School and Society* 32 (November 1, 1930): 592; Stephen T. Mather, "National Parks are Field Laboratories for the Study of Nature," *School Life* 12 (November 1926): 41. Mather consistently returned to the theme in his annual reports to the secretary of the interior. Other publications of interest on the development of outdoor education in the national parks include: Isabelle F. Story, "National Parks Afford Education by Unconscious Absorption," *School Life* 14 (February 1929): 104–6; Harold C. Bryant, "Nature Lore for Park Visitors," *American Forests and Forest Life* 35 (August 1929): 501–4, 540; and Horace M. Albright, "Says the NPS to the NEA," *School Life* 16 (May 1931): 165–66. A more recent analysis is C. Frank Brockman, "Park Naturalists and the Evolution of National Park Service Interpretation through World War II," *Journal of Forest History* 22 (January 1978): 24–43.

13. John Burroughs, "The Grand Canyon of the Colorado," *Century* 81 (January 1911): 425, 428.

14. The establishment of Zion and Bryce Canyon national parks is described in John Ise, *Our National Park Policy: A Critical History* (Baltimore: Johns Hopkins University Press, 1961), pp. 241–48; and Robert Shankland, *Steve Mather of the National Parks*, 3d ed. (New York: Alfred A. Knopf, 1970), pp. 136–39.

15. Rufus Steele, "The Celestial Circuit," *Sunset Magazine* 56 (May 1926): 24–25; *Nature Magazine* 13 (June 1929): endpiece; *Nature Magazine* 13 (April 1929): 277; and *Nature Magazine* 13 (May 1929): 353. Similar Union Pacific advertisements appeared throughout the 1920s in *National Geographic* and *Sunset Magazine*. Additional examples of monumental perceptions of the Southwest include: Paul C. Phillips, "The Trail of the Painted Parks," *Country Life* 55 (April 1929): 65–66; Charles G. Plummer, "Utah's Zion National Park," *Overland Monthly* 81 (June 1923): 27–28; Stephen T. Mather, "The New Bryce Canyon National Park," *American Forests and Forest Life* 35 (January

1929): 37–38; and Santa Fe Railroad, Passenger Department, *The Grand Canyon of Arizona* (Chicago: Santa Fe Railroad, 1902), passim.

16. U.S., *Statutes at Large*, 39 (1916): 432–34; U.S., *Statutes at Large*, 39 (1917): 938–39. Lassen has its biographer in Douglas H. Strong, *"These Happy Grounds": A History of the Lassen Region* (Red Bluff, Calif.: Walker Lithograph Co., 1973).

17. Ise, *Our National Park Policy*, pp. 238–41, 251; U.S., *Statutes at Large*, 40 (1919): 1178–79.

18. Copy, H. W. Temple et al. to Hubert Work, December 12, 1924, McFarland Papers, Box 18.

19. Isabelle F. Story, "The Park of the Smoking Mountains," *Home Geographic Monthly* 2 (August 1932): 45; Robert Sterling Yard, "Great Smokies: Mountain Throne of the East," *American Forests* 39 (January 1933): 32.

20. William C. Gregg, "Two New National Parks?" *Outlook* 141 (December 30, 1925): 667; U.S., Department of the Interior, *Report of the Director of the National Park Service, June 30, 1925* (Washington, D.C.: Government Printing Office, 1925), p. 3.

21. U.S., *Statutes at Large*, 44 (1926): 616–17. With the establishment of national parks from private instead of public property, it becomes necessary to distinguish between their date of authorization and actual dedication. Usually the interval was at least a decade.

22. Shenandoah National Park awaits a definitive history. Portions of the park campaign, however, are chronicled in Darwin Lambert, *The Earth-Man Story* (New York: Exposition Press, 1972), chapter 5; and Ise, *Our National Park Policy*, pp. 248–58, 262–64. A participant in the Great Smokies crusade, Carlos C. Campbell, has left a detailed account in *Birth of a National Park* (Knoxville: University of Tennessee Press, 1969). A sampling of other appropriate publications would include: Plummer F. Jones, "The Shenandoah National Park in Virginia," *American Review of Reviews* 72 (July 1925): 63–70; Laura Thornborough, "A New National Park in the East: The Great Smokies," *American Forests and Forest Life* 36 (March 1930): 137–40, 190; and Charles Peter Rarich, "Development of the Great Smoky Mountains National Park," *Appalachia* 21 (December 1936): 199–210.

23. Yard, "The People and the National Parks," p. 550.

24. A definitive geological history of the region is J. D. Love and John C. Reed, Jr., *Creation of the Teton Landscape* (Moose, Wyo.: Grand Teton Natural History Association, 1971). Also of value is F. M. Fryxell, *The Tetons: Interpretations of a Mountain Landscape* (Berkeley and Los Angeles: University of California Press, 1938). The Tetons, French for "breasts," were named by voyageurs around 1810. See the recent history by David J. Saylor, *Jackson Hole, Wyoming: In the Shadow of the Grand Tetons* (Norman: University of Oklahoma Press, 1970), p. 54.

25. To the mountain men who first penetrated the region, the term

"hole" defined a valley encircled by peaks. "Jackson Hole" derived from David E. Jackson, a trapper of the 1820s. Saylor, *Jackson Hole, Wyoming*, pp. 60–63.

26. The process is described in ibid., pp. 117–23.

27. Dillon Wallace, "Saddle and Camp Life in the Rockies: The Tragedy of the Elk," *Outing* 58 (March 1911): 187–201; Saylor, *Jackson Hole, Wyoming*, pp. 159–63.

28. U.S., Congress, Senate, *Region South of and Adjoining Yellowstone National Park*, Sen. Doc. 39, 55th Cong., 3d sess., 1898, pp. 4–32.

29. Saylor, *Jackson Hole, Wyoming*, p. 161.

30. As quoted in U.S., Congress, Senate, Subcommittee of the Committee on Public Lands and Surveys, *Enlarging Grand Teton National Park in Wyoming, Hearings* on Sen. Res. 250, 75th Cong., 3d sess., August 8–10, 1938, p. 6. Hereafter cited as Sen. Res. 250, *Hearings*.

31. U.S., Department of the Interior, *Report(s) of the Director of the National Park Service to the Secretary of the Interior, June 30, 1918* (Washington, D.C.: Government Printing Office, 1918), p. 40; and *June 30, 1919* (Washington, D.C.: Government Printing Office, 1919), p. 48.

32. U.S., Congress, Senate, *Congressional Record*, 65th Cong., 3d sess., February 18, 1919, p. 3646. The measure had passed the House the previous day.

33. The Records of the National Park Service, Record Group 79, National Archives, Washington, D.C., File 602, Yellowstone National Park Boundaries, Box 460, detail the care taken by Stephen Mather and Horace Albright to assure the citizens of Jackson Hole that no valuable land would be included in the project. It was with this assurance that the bill was sponsored in Congress by Representative Frank Mondell of Wyoming.

34. Sen. Res. 250, *Hearings*, p. 7.

35. See, for example, Mather to George Bird Grinnell, December 11, 1919, Yellowstone Park Boundaries, R. G. 79, Box 460.

36. S. Res. 250, *Hearings*, p. 7.

37. Albright to Mather, October 16, 1919, Yellowstone Park Boundaries, R. G. 79, Box 460.

38. U.S., Department of the Interior, *Annual Report of the Director of the National Park Service, June 30, 1920* (Washington, D.C.: Government Printing Office, 1920), p. 104.

39. Ibid., p. 112.

40. U.S., Congress, House, *Congressional Record*, 69th Cong., 1st sess., May 26, 1926, p. 10143; U.S., *Statutes at Large*, 44 (1926): 820.

41. S. Res. 250, *Hearings*, pp. 9–10; Struthers Burt, "The Battle of Jackson's Hole," *The Nation* 122 (March 3, 1926): 226.

42. S. Res. 250, *Hearings*, pp. 10–11.

43. Ibid., pp. 13–14. Donald C. Swain provides an additional

perspective on the Jackson Hole controversy in *Wilderness Defender: Horace M. Albright and Conservation* (Chicago: University of Chicago Press, 1970), passim. Swain, however, as does David J. Saylor, *Jackson Hole, Wyoming*, pp. 149–204, concentrates on the events of the campaign itself rather than the relationship of the controversy to the national park idea as a whole. A similar perspective pervades another recent study, Robert W. Righter, "The Brief, Hectic Life of Jackson Hole National Monument," *American West* 13 (November–December 1976): 30–33, 57–62.

44. U.S., Congress, Senate, Subcommittee of the Committee on Public Lands and Surveys, *Investigation of Proposed Enlargement of the Yellowstone and Grand Teton National Parks, Hearings* on S. Res. 226, 73d Cong., 2d sess., August 7–10, 1933, pp. 49–80.

45. S. Res. 250, *Hearings*, p. 15.

46. Fritiof M. Fryxell, "The Grand Tetons: Our National Park of Matterhorns," *American Forests and Forest Life* 35 (August 1929): 455.

47. The characteristics of the reserve are detailed in Ise, *Our National Park Policy*, pp. 338–40.

48. U.S., Congress, Senate, *Congressional Record*, 70th Cong., 2d sess., February 7, 1929, pp. 2982–83; U.S., Congress, House, *Congressional Record*, 70th Cong., 2d sess., February 18, 1929, p. 3699; U.S., Congress, Senate, *Congressional Record*, 70th Cong., 2d sess., February 20, 1929, p. 3810; U.S., *Statutes at Large*, 45 (1929): 1314–16.

49. Struthers Burt, "The Jackson Hole Plan," *Outdoor America* (November–December 1944), reprint, J. Horace McFarland Papers, Box 22.

50. Popular histories of the region include Marjory Stoneman Douglas, *The Everglades: River of Grass* (New York: Rinehart and Co., 1947), and Charlton W. Tebeau, *Man in the Everglades: 2000 Years of Human History in the Everglades National Park* (Miami: University of Miami Press and Everglades Natural History Association, 1968). Patricia Caulfield, *Everglades* (San Francisco: Sierra Club, 1970), is a readable study by an environmental activist, while Luther J. Carter provides a detailed, scholarly treatment of the ecology of the Everglades in *The Florida Experience: Land and Water Policy in a Growth State* (Baltimore: Johns Hopkins University Press and Resources for the Future, 1974), pp. 86–88.

51. U.S., *Statutes at Large*, 46 (1931): 1514; Albert Stoll, Jr., "Isle Royale: An Unspoiled and Little Known Wonderland of the North," *American Forests and Forest Life* 32 (August 1926): 457–59, 512; Arthur Newton Pack, "Isle Royale National Park," *Nature Magazine* 26 (September 1935): 176–77; Ben East, "Park to the North," *American Forests* 47 (June 1941): 274–76, 300–301.

52. William J. Schneider, "Water and the Everglades," *Natural History* 75 (November 1966): 32–40.

53. Ibid., pp. 32–33.

54. Tebeau, *Man in the Everglades*, pp. 169–70; Caulfield, *Everglades*, pp. 43–44.

55. Caulfield, *Everglades*, pp. 48–49; Schneider, "Water and the Everglades," pp. 32–36; Carter, *The Florida Experience*, pp. 83–84.

56. Van Name to Ernest F. Coe, October 6, 1932, Proposed Everglades National Park, History and Legislation, R. G. 79, File 101; Grosvenor to David Fairchild, January 24, 1929, Proposed Everglades National Park, History, R. G. 79, File 101.

57. Fairchild to National Park Service, January 21, 1929, Proposed Everglades National Park, History, R. G. 79, File 101.

58. Hornaday to John K. Small, December 30, 1932, Proposed Everglades National Park, Legislation, R. G. 79, File 120.

59. Albright to Ray Lyman Wilbur, May 10, 1930, Proposed Everglades National Park, Inspections and Investigations, R. G. 79, File 204-020.

60. Ibid.

61. In 1931, for example, Yard wrote to the secretary of the interior: "This is a promoter's proposition. It has scarcely been touched by competent specialists. . . . What's the hurry? Nobody wants the Everglades." Yard to Ray Lyman Wilbur, January 7, 1931, Proposed Everglades National Park, History, R. G. 79, File 101.

62. Yard publicly opposed the inclusion of Jackson Hole in Grand Teton National Park in "Jackson Hole National Monument Borrows Its Grandeur From Surrounding Mountains," *Living Wilderness* 8 (October 1943): 3–13.

63. Frederick Law Olmsted and William P. Wharton, "The Florida Everglades," *American Forests* 38 (March 1932): 143, 147. The investigation was presented to Congress by Senator Duncan U. Fletcher of Florida as: U.S., Congress, Senate, *The Proposed Everglades National Park*, S. Doc. 54, 72d Cong., 1st sess., January 22, 1932.

64. Olmsted and Wharton, "The Florida Everglades," pp. 145–46, 192.

65. National Park Service Memorandum, Arno B. Cammerer, April 2, 1934; and Ickes to Louis B. DeRouen, April 9, 1934, Proposed Everglades National Park, Legislation, R. G. 79, File 120.

66. Ernest F. Coe, "America's Tropical Frontier: A Park," *Landscape Architecture* 27 (October 1936): 6–10. Coe was not above injecting a touch of cultural nationalism into the campaign, however. In 1929, for example, he proclaimed the Everglades "a veritable natural Venice." See Coe, "The Land of the Fountain of Youth," *American Forests and Forest Life* 35 (March 1929): 159.

67. U.S., *Statutes at Large*, 48 (1934): 817; Coe, "America's Tropical Frontier," pp. 6–7; Small to William T. Hornaday, February 28, 1933, Proposed Everglades National Park, Legislation, R. G. 79, File 120.

68. U.S., *Statutes at Large*, 50 (1937): 670. The state of North Carolina, of course, was charged with the acquisition of the property.

Accordingly, the reserve was not formally dedicated until 1953.

69. Other major seashores and their dates of authorization are: Cape Cod, Massachusetts (1961); Padre Island, Texas (1962); Point Reyes, California (1962); Fire Island, New York (1964); Assateague Island, Maryland-Virginia (1965); Cape Lookout, North Carolina (1966); Gulf Islands, Florida and Mississippi (1971); Cumberland Island, Georgia (1972); and Cape Canaveral, Florida (1975). With Cape Cod the federal government broke with its almost universal requirement that the majority of parklands outside the public domain be donated to the United States.

70. Although management of the nation's historic properties by the National Park Service is outside the scope of this volume, their takeover from other federal agencies in 1933 might later be interpreted as further evidence of the emerging ideal of total preservation. See Horace M. Albright, *Origins of the National Park Service Administration of Historic Sites* (Philadelphia: Eastern National Park and Monument Association, 1971), for the events leading to the transfer.

Chapter 7

1. Brief descriptions of their careers may be found in John Ise, *Our National Park Policy: A Critical History* (Baltimore: Johns Hopkins University Press, 1961), pp. 593–96; Carl P. Russell, *One Hundred Years in Yosemite* (Yosemite National Park: Yosemite Natural History Association, 1968), pp. 134–36, 143; and Robert Shankland, *Steve Mather of the National Parks*, 3d ed. (New York: Alfred A. Knopf, 1970), pp. 274–75, 314, 331.

2. U.S., Department of the Interior, National Park Service, *Fauna of the National Parks of the United States: A Preliminary Survey of Faunal Relations in National Parks*, by George M. Wright, Joseph S. Dixon, and Ben H. Thompson (Washington, D.C.: Government Printing Office, 1933), pp. 37–39.

3. Ibid. Further studies appeared as U.S., Department of the Interior, National Park Service, *Fauna of the National Parks of the United States: Wildlife Management in the National Parks*, by George M. Wright and Ben H. Thompson (Washington, D.C.: Government Printing Office, 1935). Partly in anticipation of the findings of both reports, in 1931 the National Park Service reevaluated its long-standing predator-control program. In noting its endurance the scientists concluded: "There is sometimes a tendency in men in the field to hold any predator in the same disreputable position as any human criminal. It seems well to comment that no moral status should be attached to any animal. It is just as natural (just as much a part of nature) for [predators] to prey upon other animal life as it is for trees to grow from

the soil, and nobody questions the morality of the latter." Wright et al., *Fauna of the National Parks: A Preliminary Survey*, p. 48.

4. The components of the park are discussed in Ise, *Our National Park Policy*, pp. 379–82.

5. John B. Yeon, "The Issue of the Olympics," *American Forests* 42 (June 1936): 255. For the opposing point of view see Asahel Curtis, "The Proposed Mount Olympus National Park," *American Forests* 42 (April 1936): 166–69, 195–96.

6. U.S., *Statutes at Large*, 52 (1938): 1241–42. President Franklin D. Roosevelt used his authority to further expand the park in 1940. For a complete legislative history see Ise, *Our National Park Policy*, pp. 382–95. An excellent history of both the region and the park campaign is Ruby El Hult, *Untamed Olympics: The Story of a Peninsula* (Portland, Ore.: Binforde and Mort, 1954). A more recent article-length study by a professional historian is Elmo R. Richardson, "Olympic National Park: Twenty Years of Controversy," *Forest History* 12 (April 1968): 6–15.

7. Numerous contemporary articles document the controversy; among the more relevant are Herb Crisler, "Our Olympic National Park—Let's Keep All of It," *Nature Magazine* 40 (November 1947): 457–60, 496; Fred H. McNeil, "The Olympic Park Problem," *Mazama* 29 (December 1947): 42–46; Herb Crisler, "Our Heritage—Wilderness or Sawdust?" *Appalachia* 27 (December 1948): 171–77; Weldon F. Heald, "Shall We Auction Olympic National Park?" *Natural History* 63 (September 1954): 311–20, 336; E. T. Clark and Irving Clark, Jr., "Is Olympic National Park Too Big?" *American Forests* 60 (September 1954): 30–31, 89, 98; editorial, "Olympic Park Viewpoints," *Nature Magazine* 49 (August–September 1956): 369–70, 374; and Anthony Wayne Smith, "Hands Off Olympic Park!" *National Parks Magazine* 40 (November 1966): 2.

8. John Muir, "A Rival of Yosemite: The Canyon of the South Fork of the Kings River," *Century Magazine* 43 (November 1891): 77–97; Ben H. Thompson, "The Proposed Kings Canyon National Park," *Bird-Lore* 37 (July–August 1935): 239–44; U.S., *Statutes at Large*, 54 (1940): 44.

9. Approximately 47,000 acres of private land, however, soon were added to Olympic National Park through purchase of the Queets River corridor and a strip along the Pacific coast. Ise, *Our National Park Policy*, p. 390.

10. U.S., Congress, House, Committee on the Public Lands, *To Abolish the Jackson Hole National Monument, Wyoming, Hearings* on H. R. 2241, 78th Cong., 1st sess., May–June 1943, p. 81; Donald C. Swain, *Wilderness Defender: Horace M. Albright and Conservation* (Chicago: University of Chicago Press, 1970), pp. 262–64.

11. H. R. 2241, *Hearings*, pp. 17–18, 68.

12. U.S., Congress, House, *Congressional Record*, 78th Cong., 2d sess., December 11, 1944, pp. 9183–96; U.S., Congress, Senate, *Congressional Record*, 78th Cong., 2d sess., December 19, 1944, pp. 9769, 9807–08.

13. Ise, *Our National Park Policy*, pp. 506–8; U.S., *Statutes at Large*, 64 (1950): 849.

14. U.S., *Statutes at Large*, 64 (1950); 849; Ise, *Our National Park Policy*, p. 508. As early as 1933, for example, George M. Wright, Joseph S. Dixon, and Ben H. Thompson opposed recreational hunting as a means of reducing overpopulated wildlife species. "Shooting for sport is unsatisfactory," they noted, "because it is selective of the finest specimens instead of the poor ones which, by rights, should be removed first." Wright et al., *Fauna of the National Parks: A Preliminary Survey*, p. 35.

15. U.S., Congress, House, *Congressional Record*, 73d Cong., 2d sess., May 24, 1934, p. 9497; U.S., *Statutes at Large*, 48 (1934): 817.

16. U.S., *Statutes at Large*, 48 (1934): 816; William J. Schneider, "Water and the Everglades," *Natural History* 75 (November 1966): 35; Patricia Caulfield, *Everglades* (San Francisco: Sierra Club, 1970), p. 53.

17. Luther J. Carter provides a comprehensive listing and interpretation of the multitude of recent studies of the south Florida ecosystem in *The Florida Experience: Land and Water Policy in a Growth State* (Baltimore: Johns Hopkins University Press and Resources for the Future, 1974). Especially see chapters 7 and 8.

18. Peter Farb, "Disaster Threatens the Everglades," *Audubon* 67 (September 1965): 303. Also of relevance are Verne O. Williams, "Man-Made Drought Threatens Everglades National Park," *Audubon* 65 (September 1963): 290–94; and Joan Browder, "Don't Pull the Plug on the Everglades," *American Forests* 73 (September 1967): 12–15, 53–55.

19. Schneider, "Water and the Everglades," p. 39.

20. Wallace Stegner, "Last Chance for the Everglades," *Saturday Review* 50 (May 6, 1967): 23, 73.

21. The coast redwood *(Sequoia sempervirens)* is also generally younger than the Sierra species *(Sequoia gigantea)*. Among the recent scientific analyses of its characteristics are Edward C. Stone and Richard B. Vasey, "Preservation of Coast Redwood on Alluvial Flats," *Science* 159 (January 12, 1968): 157–60; Samuel T. Dana and Kenneth B. Pomeroy, "Redwoods and Parks," *American Forests* 71 (May 1965): 1–32; and Emanuel Fritz, "A Redwood Forester's View," *Journal of Forestry* (May 1967): 312–19.

22. Dana and Pomeroy, "Redwoods and Parks," p. 5. The Sierra redwoods, moreover, had state-park recognition as early as 1864.

23. Charles Mulford Robinson, "Muir Woods—A National Park,"

Survey 20 (May 2, 1908): 181–83. An interesting footnote to the careers of Muir and Kent is Roderick Nash, "John Muir, William Kent and the Conservation Schism," *Pacific Historical Review* 34 (November 1967): 423–33.

24. Dana and Pomeroy, "Redwoods and Parks," pp. 9–10. Including cutover lands and second growth, redwood land in the state parks was almost 103,000 acres.

25. Promotional circular, Save-the-Redwoods League, 1967; Stone and Vasey, "Preservation of Coast Redwood on Alluvial Flats," p. 157.

26. As quoted in Dana and Pomeroy, "Redwoods and Parks," p. 11.

27. Russell D. Butcher, "Redwoods and the Fragile Web of Nature," *Audubon* 66 (May–June 1964): 174.

28. The discrepancy was in large part based on the size of both projects, approximately 43,000 acres for Mill Creek as opposed to 90,000 for Redwood Creek.

29. The particulars of the various proposals are argued exhaustively by their sponsors in House and Senate hearings. See, for example, U.S., Congress, House, Subcommittee on National Parks and Recreation of the Committee on Interior and Insular Affairs, *Redwood National Park* (3 parts), *Hearings* on H. R. 1311 and Related Bills, June–July 1967, May 1968, passim.

30. Promotional circular, Sierra Club, 1967.

31. H. R. 1311, *Hearings*, pp. 439–509, passim.

32. The relationship of these provisions to the failure to establish Redwood National Park as a self-contained ecosystem is detailed in John Graves, "Redwood National Park: Controversy and Compromise," *National Parks and Conservation Magazine: The Environmental Journal* 48 (October 1974): 14–19.

33. Ibid.

34. Promotional circular, Sierra Club, undated.

35. Paul A. Zahl, "Finding the Mt. Everest of All Living Things," *National Geographic* 126 (July 1964): 10–51.

36. "Logging Practices Still Ravaging State's Forests," *Los Angeles Times*, August 24, 1975, pt. 2, p. 1; "Curb on Logging of Redwoods Rejected," *Los Angeles Times*, September 13, 1975, pt. 2, p. 1; "Redwood Grove Periled: State Moves to Save World's Tallest Tree," *Los Angeles Times*, August 29, 1975, pt. 1, p. 3; "State Asks Expansion of U.S. Redwood Park," *Los Angeles Times*, September 19, 1976, pt. 1, p. 3.

37. A. Starker Leopold et al., "Wildlife Management in the National Parks," *National Parks Magazine* 37 (April 1963): iii; F. Fraser Darling and Noel D. Eichhorn, "Man and Nature in the National Parks: Reflections on Policy," *National Parks Magazine* 43 (April 1969): 14, 17. Darling, an ecologist, and Eichhorn, a geographer, were sponsored by the Conservation Foundation of Washington, D.C. The

Leopold Committee report, originally published by the Interior Department, was widely reprinted in most of the major conservation journals.

Chapter 8

1. Edward H. Hamilton, "The New Yosemite Railroad," *Cosmopolitan* 43 (September 1907): 569–70. Another contemporary opinion is Lanier Bartlett, "By Rail to the Yosemite," *Pacific Monthly* 17 (June 1907): 730–38. Two recent studies are Hank Johnston, *Railroads of the Yosemite Valley* (Long Beach, Calif.: Johnston and Howe, 1964), and Alfred Runte, "Yosemite Valley Railroad: Highway of History, Pathway of Promise," *National Parks and Conservation Magazine: The Environmental Journal* 48 (December 1974): 4–9.

2. U.S., National Archives, Natural Resources Division, Record Group 79, Yosemite National Park, "Travel," Pt. 1, Box 727. An entertaining departure on the admission of automobiles into Yosemite Valley is Richard Lillard, "The Siege and Conquest of a National Park," *American West* 5 (January 1968): 28–31, 67, 69–71.

3. Charles J. Belden, "The Motor in Yellowstone," *Scribner's Magazine* 63 (June 1918): 673; Enos A. Mills, "Touring in Our National Parks," *Country Life in America* 23 (January 1913): 36. Mills often is considered the "father of Rocky Mountain National Park," whose establishment he strongly supported for many years.

4. Arthur Newton Pack, "Hunting Nature on Wheels," *Nature Magazine* 13 (June 1929): 388; Robert Sloss, "Camping in an Automobile," *Outing* 56 (May 1910): 236.

5. H. P. Burchell, "The Automobile as a Means of Country Travel," *Outing* 46 (August 1905): 536; Frank E. Brimmer, "Autocamping—the Fastest Growing Sport," *Outlook* 137 (July 16, 1924): 439; Gilbert Irwin, "Nature Ways by Car and Camp," *Nature Magazine* 10 (July 1927): 27.

6. Anonymous, "Neighbors for a Night in Yellowstone Park," *Literary Digest* 82 (August 30, 1924): 45.

7. Ethel and James Dorrance, "Motoring in the Yellowstone," *Munsey's Magazine* 70 (July 1920): 268–70. A sampling of other relevant articles detailing the rise of pleasure motoring in the national parks would include: W. A. Babson, "Motor in the Wilderness," *Country Life in America* 8 (June 1905): 247–48; Hrolf Wisby, "Camping Out with an Automobile," *Outing* 45 (March 1905): 739–45; Samuel M. Evans, "Forty Gallons of Gasoline to Forty Miles of Water: Recipe for a Motor Trip to Crater Lake, Oregon," *Sunset Magazine: The Pacific Monthly* 27 (October 1911): 393–99; Arthur E. Demaray, "Our National Parks and How to Reach Them," *American Forestry* 27 (June 1921): 360–70; Ronne C. Shelse, "The Pageant Highway: A 6,000-Mile Ride

from Park to Park," *Mentor World Traveler* 12 (July 1924): 29–45; Hazel R. Langdale, "To the Yellowstone," *Woman's Home Companion* 56 (May 1929): 120–21; and Anonymous, "Seeing the Western National Parks by Motor," *American Forests and Forest Life* 35 (August 1929): 508–9.

8. The implications of the statistic for rail-passenger service are noted in George W. Long, "Many-Splendored Glacierland," *National Geographic Magazine* 160 (May 1956): 589–90.

9. James Bryce, "National Parks—The Need of the Future," *Outlook* 102 (December 14, 1912): 811–13.

10. Lorimer to McFarland, November 12, 1934, Pennsylvania Historical and Museum Commission, Division of Archives and Manuscripts, McFarland Papers, Box 18.

11. McFarland to Lorimer, November 13, 1934, McFarland Papers, Box 18.

12. U.S., *Statutes at Large*, 39 (1916): 535.

13. Robert Sterling Yard, "Economic Aspects of Our National Parks Policy," *Scientific Monthly* 16 (April 1923): 381.

14. Frederick Law Olmsted, "The Yosemite Valley and the Mariposa Big Trees," ed. Laura Wood Roper, *Landscape Architecture* 43 (October 1952): 17, 22.

15. The advantages and disadvantages of this policy are discussed at length in John Ise, *Our National Park Policy: A Critical History* (Baltimore: Johns Hopkins University Press, 1961). See especially pp. 606–18.

16. Olmsted, "The Yosemite Valley and the Mariposa Big Trees," pp. 22–24.

17. For conditions in the valley see Shirley Sargent, *Galen Clark: Yosemite Guardian* (San Francisco: Sierra Club, 1964), p. 124.

18. Olmsted, "The Yosemite Valley and the Mariposa Big Trees," p. 16.

19. Grace Greenwood, *New Life in New Lands* (New York: J. B. Ford and Co., 1873), pp. 358–60. Grace Greenwood was the pen name of Mrs. Sara Jane Clarke Lippincott (1823–1904), one of the more renowned women correspondents of the period.

20. As quoted in Carl P. Russell, *One Hundred Years in Yosemite* (Yosemite National Park: Yosemite Natural History Association, 1968), pp. 108–109.

21. Ibid., p. 109.

22. Laurence V. Degnan to Douglas H. Hubbard, January 24, 1959, U.S., National Park Service, Yosemite National Park Library Papers, Firefall Collection, Y-22.

23. E. P. Leavitt to Agnes L. Scott, September 20, 1928, Yosemite National Park Library Papers, Firefall Collection, Y-22; G. B. MacKenzie, "The Flaming Wonder of the Sierras," *Travel* 45 (June 1925):

15, 44; Anonymous, "Let the Fire Fall!" *Collier's* 130 (August 16, 1952): 66.

24. Olmsted, "The Yosemite Valley and the Mariposa Big Trees," p. 17.

25. W. G. Marshall, *Through America; or, Nine Months in the United States* (London: H. G. Bohn, 1881), pp. 340–41; Frank Strauser to Ansel F. Hall, July 27, 1925, Yosemite National Park Library Papers, Y-21a.

26. Allen Kelley, "Restoration of Yosemite Waterfalls," *Harper's Weekly* 36 (July 16, 1892): 678. A similar plea is Hiram Martin Chittenden, "Sentiment *versus* Utility in the Treatment of Natural Scenery," *Pacific Monthly* 23 (January 1910): 29–38. Chittenden further included Hetch Hetchy and Niagara Falls as scenic wonders whose beauty could be both preserved and developed. Two additional schemes also afoot were an elaborate cable-car system in the Grand Canyon and an elevator beside the Lower Falls of the Yellowstone River in Yellowstone National Park. Although neither was successful, both were seriously considered. See U.S., Congress, House, Committee on the Public Lands, *Granting Right of Way Over Certain Sections of the Grand Canyon National Monument Reserve in Arizona to the Grand Canyon Scenic Railroad Company, Hearings* on H. R. 2258, 61st Cong., 2d sess., 1910; and U.S., Congress, Senate, *David B. May*, S. Doc. 151, 54th Cong., 2d sess., 1897.

27. Victor H. Cahalane, "Your National Parks—and You," *Nature Magazine* 33 (May 1940): 264–65.

28. Ibid., p. 264.

29. Martelle W. Trager, *National Parks of the Northwest* (New York: Dodd and Mead, 1939), pp. 31–33, 45–48. The bear feedings originally became popular in conjunction with construction of the grand hotels, such as the Old Faithful Inn. Thomas D. Murphy, for example, a British globe-trotter and writer of the period, described the shows and their distracting influence as early as 1909. See his *Three Wonderlands of the American West* (Boston: L. C. Page and Co., 1912), pp. 15–16.

30. Henry Baldwin Ward, "What Is Happening to Our National Parks?" *Nature Magazine* 31 (December 1938): 614; Albert W. Atwood, "Can the National Parks be Kept Unspoiled?" *Saturday Evening Post* 208 (May 16, 1936): 18–19.

31. Robert Sterling Yard, "The People and the National Parks," *Survey* 48 (August 1, 1922): 552; idem, "Economic Aspects of Our National Parks Policy," p. 387; Wallace W. Atwood, "What Are National Parks?" *American Forests* 37 (September 1931): 543.

32. Arno B. Cammerer, "Maintenance of the Primeval in National Parks," *Appalachia* 22 (December 1938): 207.

33. Robert Sterling Yard, "Historical Basis of National Park Standards," *National Parks Bulletin* 10 (November 1929): 4.

34. U.S., Bureau of the Census, *Historical Statistics of the United States: Colonial Times to 1957* (Washington, D.C.: Government Printing Office, 1960), p. 222.

35. "U.S. Is Outgrowing Its Parks," *U.S. News and World Report* 38 (June 10, 1955): 79; Runte, "Yosemite Valley Railroad," p. 7.

36. Joseph Wood Krutch, "Which Men? What Needs?" *American Forests* 63 (April 1957): 23, 46; "U.S. Is Outgrowing Its Parks," p. 78.

37. John Muir, "The Wild Parks and Forest Reservations of the West," *Atlantic Monthly* 81 (January 1898): 16; Bernard DeVoto, "The National Parks," *Fortune* 35 (June 1947): 120–21; Krutch, "Which Men? What Needs?", pp. 22–23. Bernard DeVoto, an indefatigable friend of the national parks, has his biographer in Wallace Stegner, *The Uneasy Chair: A Biography of Bernard DeVoto* (New York: Doubleday, 1974). See pp. 301–22 for DeVoto's efforts on behalf of national park integrity. Another of his outspoken comments is "Let's Close the National Parks," *Harper's Magazine* 207 (October 1953): 49–52.

38. Devereux Butcher, "Resorts or Wilderness?" *Atlantic* 207 (February 1961): 47, 51; F. Fraser Darling and Noel D. Eichhorn, "Man and Nature in the National Parks: Reflections on Policy," *National Parks Magazine* 43 (April 1969): 17.

39. U.S., Bureau of the Census, *Statistical Abstract of the United States: 1974*, 95th ed. (Washington, D.C.: Government Printing Office, 1974), p. 204.

40. Edward Abbey, *Desert Solitaire: A Season in the Wilderness* (New York: Ballantine Books, 1968), pp. 57–61.

41. Garrett Hardin, "The Economics of Wilderness," *Natural History* 78 (June–July 1969): 20–27.

42. Krutch, "Which Men? What Needs?," p. 23.

43. Cammerer, "Maintenance of the Primeval in National Parks," pp. 210–11; Krutch, "Which Men? What Needs?," p. 23.

44. Eric Julber, "Let's Open Up Our Wilderness Areas," *Reader's Digest* 100 (May 1972): 126; idem, "The Wilderness: Just How Wild Should It Be?" reprinted in cooperation with the Western Wood Products Laboratory (undated), p. 1.

45. Butcher, "Resorts or Wilderness?," p. 50.

46. Ibid. Similar contemporary arguments include Paul Brooks, "The Pressure of Numbers," *Atlantic* 207 (February 1961): 54–56; Benton MacKaye, "If This Be Snobbery," *Living Wilderness* 77 (Summer 1961): 3–4; and Jerome B. Wood, "National Parks: Tomorrow's Slums?" *Travel* 101 (April 1954): 14–16.

47. Jack Hope, "Hassles in the Park," *Natural History* 80 (May 1971): 22–23; "Yosemite: Better Way to Run a Park?" *U.S. News and World Report* 72 (January 24, 1972): 56.

48. George B. Hartzog, Jr., "Changing the National Parks to Cope with People—and Cars," *U.S. News and World Report* 72 (January 24, 1972): 52.

49. Jack Anderson, "Yosemite: Another Disneyland?" *Washington Post*, September 15, 1974, reprint; Philip Fradkin, "Sierra Club Sees Damage in Yosemite Filming," *Los Angeles Times*, August 28, 1974, Pt. 1, pp. 1, 22; "Yosemite National Convention Center Proposed by New Concessionaire," *Sierra Club Bulletin* 59 (September 1974): 29.

50. Julber, "The Wilderness: Just How Wild Should It Be?," p. 5.

51. Krutch, "Which Men? What Needs?," p. 23.

52. "America's 'Magnificent Seven,'" *U.S. News and World Report* 78 (April 21, 1975): 56–57. In order, the outstanding natural attractions of the United States included: The Grand Canyon, Yellowstone, Niagara Falls, Mount McKinley, California's "big trees"—the sequoias and redwoods—the Hawaii volcanoes, and the Everglades. Some correlation, quite obviously, exists between both the tourist and resident populations of the states containing each wonder, as well as the greater publicity accorded areas such as Yellowstone.

53. A superb example of the belief that the flow of Niagara Falls can be reduced even further without destroying its scenic integrity, as well as a good overview of the diversion issue, is B. F. Friesen and J. C. Day, "Hydroelectric Power and Scenic Provisions of the 1950 Niagara Treaty," *Water Resources Bulletin* 13 (December 1977): 1175–89.

Chapter 9

1. As quoted in U.S., National Parks Centennial Commission, *Preserving a Heritage* (Washington, D.C.: Government Printing Office, 1973), pp. 79–80.

2. A listing of major publicity efforts covering the centennial may be found in ibid., pp. 52–61.

3. The Conservation Foundation, *National Parks for the Future* (Washington, D.C.: The Conservation Foundation, 1972), p. 31. For a discussion of the national park idea abroad, see Roderick Nash, *Nature in World Development: Patterns in the Preservation of Scenic and Outdoor Recreation Resources* (New York: The Rockefeller Foundation, 1978), and Jeremy Harrison, et al., "The World Coverage of Protected Areas: Development Goals and Environmental Needs," *Ambio*, vol. 11, no. 5 (1982): 238–45. Also pertinent, but now dated, is John Ise, *Our National Park Policy: A Critical History* (Baltimore: Johns Hopkins University Press, 1961), chapter 31.

4. Rachel Carson, *Silent Spring* (New York: Fawcet Crest, [1962] 1964), pp. 24, 169.

5. U.S., Department of the Interior, National Park Service, *First World Conference on National Parks, Proceedings* (Washington, D.C.: Government Printing Office, 1962), pp. 433–47.

6. Ibid., p. xxxi.

7. International Union for Conservation of Nature and Natural

Resources, et al., *Second World Conference on National Parks, Proceedings* (Morges, Switzerland: International Union, U.S. National Parks Centennial Commission, 1974), p. 38; Paul R. Ehrlich, *The Population Bomb*, rev. ed. (New York: Sierra Club/Ballantine Books, 1971), p. xi.

8. Conservation Foundation, *National Parks for the Future*, p. 9.

9. International Union, *Second World Conference, Proceedings*, p. 15.

10. See, for example, Norman Myers, "National Parks in Savannah Africa," *Science* 178 (December 22, 1972): 1255–63; Meyers, "Wildlife Parks in Emergent Africa: The Outlook for Their Survival," *Chicago Field Museum of Natural History Bulletin* 45 (February 1974): 8–14; and David Western, "Amboseli National Park: Enlisting Landowners to Conserve Migratory Wildlife," *Ambio*, vol. 11, no. 5 (1982): 302–8. The theme that even the largest national parks of Africa are threatened also consistently reappears in the proceedings of the world national parks conferences.

11. See, for example, Paul W. Richards, "National Parks in Wet Tropical Areas," International Union, *Second World Conference, Proceedings*, pp. 219–27.

12. Ibid., pp. 443–44. Regarding potential threats to Antarctica from recent reassessments of its economic potential, see P H C Lucas, "International Agreement on Conserving the Antarctic Environment," *Ambio*, vol. 11, no. 5 (1982): 292–95.

13. A detailed overview of the struggles for the Colorado River is Roderick Nash, "Conservation and the Colorado," chapter 9 of T. H. Watkins, et al., *The Grand Colorado: The Story of a River and Its Canyons* (Palo Alto, Calif.: American West Publishing Co., 1969). Also relevant is Roderick Nash, *Wilderness and the American Mind*, 3d ed. (New Haven: Yale University Press, 1982), pp. 209–20.

14. Wallace Stegner, ed., *This is Dinosaur: Echo Park Country and Its Magic Rivers* (New York: Knopf, 1955).

15. See, for example, Eliot Porter, *The Place No One Knew: Glen Canyon on the Colorado* (San Francisco: Sierra Club Press, 1963).

16. Preservationists' arguments for a "greater" Grand Canyon National Park are summarized in Roderick Nash, ed., *Grand Canyon of the Living Colorado* (San Francisco and New York: Sierra Club/Ballantine Books, 1970), pp. 106–7.

17. Robert Dolan, et al., "Man's Impact on the Colorado River in the Grand Canyon," *American Scientist* 62 (July–August 1974): 392–401.

18. Nash, "Conservation and the Colorado," p. 269; Laurence I. Moss, "The Grand Canyon Subsidy Machine," *Sierra Club Bulletin* 52 (April 1967): 89–94.

19. The issue of air pollution is summarized in Jerome Ostrov, "Visibility Protection under the Clean Air Act: Preserving Scenic and Parkland Areas in the Southwest," *Ecology Law Quarterly*, vol. 10, no. 3 (1982): 397–453.

20. Philip Fradkin, "Smog from Power Plants Threatens Utah 'Color Country'," *Los Angeles Times*, February 9, 1975, pt. 2, p. 1.

21. *Los Angeles Times*, December 28, 1975, pt. 7, p. 2.

22. As quoted in Nash, *Wilderness and the American Mind*, p. 230.

23. The advertisement is reprinted in Watkins, *The Grand Colorado*, p. 270.

24. U.S., Congress, House, Subcommittee on National Parks and Recreation of the Committee on Interior and Insular Affairs, *To Prohibit Certain Incompatible Activities within Any Area of the National Park System, Hearing* on H.R. 9799, 94th Cong., 1st sess., October 6, 1975, p. 5.

25. In addition to Death Valley National Monument the parks included: Glacier Bay National Monument and Mount McKinley National Park, Alaska; Crater Lake National Park, Oregon; Organ Pipe Cactus National Monument, Arizona; and Coronado National Memorial, Arizona. Ibid., pp. 4–5.

26. Ibid., p. 38.

27. Ibid., pp. 66–68.

28. Ibid., pp. 45, 52, 101–3.

29. Ibid., pp. 103–4.

30. U.S., *Statutes at Large*, 90 (1976): 1342–44.

31. E. Raymond Hall, "The Prairie National Park," *National Parks Magazine* 36 (February 1962): 5–8; F. Fraser Darling, "The Park Idea and Ecological Reality," ibid. 43 (May 1969): 21–24.

32. "Jetport and the Everglades—Life or Runway?" *Living Wilderness* 33 (Spring 1969): 13–20; "Jets vs. the Call of the Wild," *Business Week* (August 30, 1969): 76–77; "The Newest Trouble on Everglades Waters," *Business Week* (June 5, 1971): 45–46.

33. Melvin A. Finn, "Fahkahatchee: Endangered Gem of the Big Cypress Country," *Living Wilderness* 35 (Autumn 1971): 11–18; George Reiger, "The Choice for Big Cypress: Bulldozers or Butterflies," *National Wildlife* 10 (October–November 1972): 5–10; Luther J. Carter, *The Florida Experience: Land and Water Policy in a Growth State* (Baltimore: Johns Hopkins University Press and Resources for the Future, 1974), chapter 8; Nelson M. Blake, *Land into Water—Water into Land: A History of Water Management in Florida* (Tallahassee: University Presses of Florida, 1980), pp. 231–35.

34. Robert Belous, "Hello, Jet Age; Goodbye, Wilderness," *Living Wilderness* 37 (Spring 1973): 40–49.

35. U.S., *Statutes at Large*, 88 (1974): 1258–61.

36. George H. Harrison and Frank C. Craighead, Jr., "They're Killing Yellowstone's Grizzlies," *National Wildlife* 11 (October–November 1973): 4–8, 17; Christopher Cauble, "The Great Grizzly Grapple," *Natural History* 86 (August–September 1977): 74–81.

37. Efforts leading to the expansion of Redwood National Park in 1978 are admirably interpreted in Susan R. Schrepfer, *The Fight to*

Save the Redwoods: A History of Environmental Reform, 1917–1978 (Madison: University of Wisconsin Press, 1983), pp. 186–244.

38. Conservation Foundation, *National Parks for the Future*, p. 19; Robert Cahn, "Alaska: A Matter of 80,000,000 Acres," *Audubon* 76 (July 1974): 2–13, 66–81.

39. With the approach of the Yellowstone Centennial the National Park Service addressed the shortcomings of the system in U.S., Department of the Interior, National Park Service, *Part Two of the National Park System Plan: Natural History* (Washington, D.C.: Government Printing Office, 1972). Predictably, there was little reason for surprise in its overriding conclusion that only the mountain and desert landscapes of the West were adequately represented in the national park system.

Chapter 10

1. U.S., Department of the Interior, Advisory Board on Wildlife Management, *Wildlife Management in the National Parks*, by A. S. Leopold, et al., Report to the Secretary, March 4, 1963. Hereafter cited as Leopold Committee, *Report*. As testimony to its importance, it was reprinted in its entirety in *Living Wilderness, Audubon, National Parks Magazine*, and *American Forests*.

2. Ibid., pp. 1–2.

3. Ibid., p. 4.

4. Ibid., p. 5.

5. See, for example, Joseph Grinnell and Tracy Storer, "Animal Life as an Asset of National Parks," *Science* 44 (September 15, 1916): 377.

6. Leopold Committee, *Report*, passim.

7. Ibid., p. 21.

8. Ibid., p. 5.

9. "Leopold Report Appraised," *Living Wilderness* 83 (Spring 1963): 20–24; Anthony Wayne Smith, "Editorial Comment on the Leopold Report," *National Parks Magazine* 37 (April 1963): I.

10. An overview of this history is Richard J. Hartesveldt, "Effects of Human Impact upon *Sequoia gigantea* and Its Environment in the Mariposa Grove, Yosemite National Park, California" (Ph.D. diss., University of Michigan, 1962).

11. Curtis K. Skinner, "Fire, the Enemy of Our National Parks," *American Forests and Forest Life* 35 (August 1929): 519–20. Changing American attitudes toward fire are superbly documented in Stephen J. Pyne, *Fire in America: A Cultural History of Wildland and Rural Fire* (Princeton: Princeton University Press, 1982).

12. Pyne, *Fire in America*, pp. 100–22.

13. U.S., Department of the Interior, *Report of the Acting Superinten-*

dent of the Yosemite National Park for the Fiscal Year Ended June 30, 1894, H. Exec. Doc. 1, pt. 5, vol. 3, 53d Cong., 3d sess., 1894, p. 675. Gale further elaborated: "It is a well-known fact that the Indians burned the forests annually." Ibid., p. 676. J. W. Zevely, acting superintendent of Yosemite in 1898, was among those who later endorsed the light burning theory. See U.S., Department of the Interior, *Report of the Acting Superintendent of the Yosemite National Park for the Fiscal Year Ended June 30, 1898*, H. Doc. 5, 55th Cong., 3d sess., 1898, pp. 1056–57. An influential opponent of proposals to reintroduce fire to the Giant Sequoia groves was Colonel S. B. M. Young, acting superintendent of the park in 1896. See U.S., Department of the Interior, *Report of the Acting Superintendent of Yosemite National Park*, August 15, 1896, in H. Doc. 5, vol. 3, 54th Cong., 2d sess., 1896, pp. 736–37.

14. A lengthy bibliography of the scientific literature is contained in U.S., Department of the Interior, National Park Service, *Giant Sequoia Ecology: Fire and Reproduction*, by H. Thomas Harvey, et al., Scientific Monograph Series No. 12 (Washington, D.C.: Government Printing Office, 1980), pp. 163–68.

15. H. H. Biswell, "The Big Trees and Fire," *National Parks Magazine* 35 (April 1961): 13–14.

16. Ibid., p. 14.

17. Quoted in R. J. Hartesveldt and H. T. Harvey, "The Fire Ecology of Sequoia Regeneration," *California Tall Timbers Fire Ecology Conference, November 9–10, 1967, Proceedings* (Tallahassee: Tall Timbers Research Station, 1968): 65.

18. Ibid., pp. 65–76. The scientific literature grew voluminously throughout the late 1960s and 1970s. Also see, for example, H. H. Biswell, "Forest Fire in Perspective," ibid., pp. 43–63; Bruce M. Kilgore, "Impact of Prescribed Burning on a Sequoia–Mixed Conifer Forest," *Annual Tall Timbers Fire Ecology Conference, June 8–9, 1972, Proceedings* (Tallahassee: Tall Timbers Research Station, 1973): 345–75; Peter H. Schuft, "A Prescribed Burning Program for Sequoia and Kings Canyon National Parks," ibid., pp. 377–89; John McLaughlin, "Restoring Fire to the Environment in Sequoia and Kings Canyon National Parks," ibid., pp. 391–95; Bruce M. Kilgore, "Fire Management in the National Parks: An Overview," *Tall Timbers Fire Ecology Conference and Fire and Land Management Symposium, October 8–10, 1974, Proceedings* (Tallahassee: Tall Timbers Research Station, 1976): 45–57; John L. Vankat, "Fire and Man in Sequoia National Park," *Annals of the Association of American Geographers* 67 (March 1977): 17–27; and Bruce M. Kilgore and Dan Taylor, "Fire History of a Sequoia–Mixed Conifer Forest," *Ecology* 60 (February 1979): 129–42.

19. Vankat, "Fire and Man in Sequoia," pp. 17, 25; Leopold Committee, *Report*, p. 6.

20. Vankat, "Fire and Man in Sequoia," p. 26; U.S., Department of the Interior, National Park Service, *Compilation of the Administrative*

Policies . . . of the National Park System (Washington, D.C.: Government Printing Office, 1968), p. 20.

21. The most detailed justification of this perspective is Kilgore, "Impact of Prescribed Burning on a Sequoia–Mixed Conifer Forest," pp. 366–72.

22. In 1974, for instance, a lightning-caused fire burned 3,500 acres in the Tetons, obscuring the mountains periodically from the middle of July until November. In the Park Service's own words, allowing the fire to burn "was quite controversial." U.S., National Park Service, Grand Teton National Park, Wyoming, "Natural Resources Management Plan and Environmental Assessment," bound typescript, March 1985; pp. 72–73. The incident is also mentioned in Pyne, *Fire in America*, p. 304.

23. Pyne, *Fire in America*, p. 122; McLaughlin, "Restoring Fire to the Environment in Sequoia and Kings Canyon National Parks," p. 394.

24. A survey of the literature addressing management issues in addition to fire ecology includes: Robert Dolan, Bruce P. Hayden, and Gary Soucie, "Environmental Dynamics and Resource Management in the U.S. National Parks," *Environmental Management*, vol. 2, no. 3 (1978): 249–58; Thomas M. Bonnicksen and Edward C. Stone, "Managing Vegetation within U.S. National Parks: A Policy Analysis," *Environmental Management* 6 (March 1982): 109–22; Robert Dolan and Bruce Hayden, "Adjusting to Nature in Our National Seashores," *National Parks and Conservation Magazine: The Environmental Journal* 48 (June 1974): 9–14; Robert Dolan, et al., "Man's Impact on the Barrier Islands of North Carolina," *American Scientist* 61 (March–April 1973): 151–62; and James K. Agee, "Issues and Impacts of Redwood National Park Expansion," *Environmental Management* 4 (September 1980): 407–23. The Leopold Committee Report itself should be supplemented with the National Academy of Sciences, National Research Council, Advisory Committee to the National Park Service on Research, "Report to the Secretary of the Interior," by William J. Robbins, et al., bound typescript, August 1, 1963.

Chapter 11

1. Robert Sterling Yard, "Gift-Parks the Coming National Park Danger," *National Parks Bulletin* 4 (October 9, 1923): 4.

2. See, for example, Robert Sterling Yard, *National Parks Portfolio* (New York: Charles Scribner's Sons, 1916), pp. 3–6.

3. Yard, "Gift-Parks," p.4.

4. Robert Sterling Yard, "To Double Our National *Military* Parks System—But Let Us Not Mix Systems," *National Parks Bulletin* 5 (January 21, 1924): 8.

5. John C. Merriam, "Our National Parks," *American Forests and Forest Life* 32 (August 1926): 478. The John C. Merriam Papers, Library of Congress, Washington, D.C., further develop this perspective through correspondence with the principal leaders of American conservation.

6. For a pathbreaking analysis of these emotions with respect to efforts to protect the California coast redwoods, see Susan R. Schrepfer, *The Fight to Save the Redwoods: A History of Environmental Reform, 1917–1978* (Madison: University of Wisconsin Press, 1983), chapters 3–6.

7. A seminal analysis of the period is Samuel P. Hays, "The Environmental Movement," *Journal of Forest History* 25 (October 1981): 219–21.

8. Urban concerns are summarized in Peter Marcuse, "Is the National Parks Movement Anti-Urban?" *Parks and Recreation* 6 (July 1971): 17–21, 48.

9. Yard, "Gift-Parks," p. 5.

10. Marcuse, "National Parks Movement," passim.

11. See, for example, "NPCA Interviews Phillip Burton: Meeting the Needs of Tomorrow Today," *National Parks and Conservation Magazine: The Environmental Journal* 53 (May 1979): 22–26.

12. See U.S., Congress, House, Committee on Interior and Insular Affairs, Subcommittee on National Parks and Insular Affairs, *Legislative History of the National Parks and Recreation Act of 1978*, Committee Print No. 11, 95th Cong., 2d sess., December 1978. Hereafter cited as National Parks and Recreation Act, *Legislative History*.

13. "NPCA Interviews Phillip Burton," p. 22.

14. John Ise, *Our National Park Policy: A Critical History* (Baltimore: Johns Hopkins University Press, 1961), p. 136.

15. U.S., Congress, House, *Congressional Record*, 57th Cong., 2d sess., December 6, 1902, p. 81.

16. U.S., Congress, Senate, *Wind Cave National Park*, S. Rept. 1944 to accompany S. 6138, 57th Cong., 1st sess., June 17, 1902, pp. 2–3.

17. Ibid.

18. U.S., Congress, Senate, *Congressional Record*, 57th Cong., 2d sess., January 12, 1903, p. 666.

19. Ise, *Our National Park Policy*, pp. 139–40.

20. Ibid. Congress approved the official transfer in 1931. See U.S., Congress, House, *Congressional Record*, 71st Cong., 3d sess., January 14, 1931, pp. 2163–65.

21. Ise, *Our National Park Policy*, pp. 140–42; U.S., Congress, House, *Sulphur Springs Reservation to be Known as Platt National Park*, H. Rept. 5016 to accompany H. J. Res. 181, 59th Cong., 1st sess., June 26, 1906.

22. U.S., Department of the Interior, National Park Service, *Report of the Director for the Fiscal Year Ended June 30, 1921* (Washington,

D.C.: Government Printing Office, 1921), pp. 32–33. Mather's role in the state parks movement is further treated in Robert Shankland, *Steve Mather of the National Parks*, 3d ed. (New York: Knopf, 1970), chapter 14.

23. National Park Service, *Report of the Director, 1921*, p. 60. Mather rationalized that Hot Springs National Park did in fact have some national significance, inasmuch as the park drew "heavily from the South and Southwest."

24. Robert Sterling Yard, "Politics in Our National Parks," *American Forests and Forest Life* 32 (August 1926): 485.

25. Freeman Tilden, *The National Parks* (New York: Knopf, 1970), pp. 257–58; Yard, "Gift-Parks," p. 5.

26. Yard, "Politics in Our National Parks," pp. 486, 489.

27. The origins of historic preservation are admirably documented in Charles B. Hosmer, Jr., *Preservation Comes of Age: From Williamsburg to the National Trust, 1926–1949*, 2 vols. (Charlottesville: University of Virginia Press, 1981). A contemporary assessment is Carl P. Russell, "The Conservation of Historic Values," *National Parks Bulletin* 14 (December 1938): 16–19. Also relevant is F. Ross Holland, Jr., "The Park Service as Curator," *National Parks and Conservation Magazine: The Environmental Journal* 53 (August 1979): 10–15.

28. See Ronald F. Lee, *The Origin and Evolution of the National Military Park Idea* (Washington, D.C.: Office of Park Historic Preservation, National Park Service, 1973).

29. Horace M. Albright, *Origins of National Park Service Administration of Historic Sites* (Philadelphia: Eastern National Park and Monument Association, 1971), pp. 17–23.

30. Ibid., p. 24.

31. Ovid Butler, "The New National Park Emergency," *American Forests* 40 (January 1934): 21.

32. Albright, *Park Service Administration of Historic Sites*, p. 23.

33. See, for example, "Remarks by Mr. H. S. Graves," in U.S., Department of the Interior, *Proceedings of the National Park Conference Held at the Yellowstone National Park, September 11 and 12, 1911* (Washington, D.C.: Government Printing Office, 1912), pp. 66–68; and U.S., Department of the Interior, *Proceedings of the National Park Conference Held at Berkeley, California, March 11, 12, and 13, 1915* (Washington, D.C.: Government Printing Office, 1915), pp. 142–46. Graves's outspoken private views are clearly revealed in his lengthy correspondence with J. Horace McFarland, president of the American Civic Association. See the J. Horace McFarland Papers, Pennsylvania Historical and Museum Commission, Division of Archives and Manuscripts, Harrisburg, Box 18, especially Graves to McFarland, March 30, 1916. "My own view has always been that the National Park Service should be in the Department of Agriculture," Graves wrote. "I expressed my views on this subject to [the secretary of the interior] in

1911 in various conferences and also in official correspondence."

34. Henry S. Graves, "National and State Parks," *American Forests and Forest Life* 33 (February 1927): 97–100.

35. Graves, "National and State Parks, Part II," ibid., (March 1927): 150.

36. U.S., Department of Commerce, Bureau of the Census, *1980 Census of Population: Characteristics*, vol. 1, pt. 1, chapter 5, pp. 35–37.

37. "Summary of Resolutions Adopted by President's National Conference on Outdoor Recreation," *Playground* 18 (July 1924): 247.

38. Ibid.

39. U.S., Department of the Interior, National Park Service, *A Study of the Park and Recreation Problem of the United States* (Washington, D.C.: Government Printing Office, 1941), p. 90.

40. U.S., *Statutes at Large*, 50 (1937): 670.

41. U.S., Congress, Senate, Committee on Interior and Insular Affairs, Subcommittee on the Public Lands, *Cape Cod National Seashore Park, Hearing* on S. 857, 87th Cong., 1st sess., March 9, 1961.

42. Secretary of the Interior Stewart Udall described possible methods of long-term acquisition in ibid., p. 10. Section 4 (a)(1) of the bill further provided: "The beneficial owner or owners of improved property which the Secretary acquires by condemnation may elect, as a condition to such acquisition, to retain the right of use and occupancy of the said property for noncommercial residential purposes for a term of twenty-five years, or for such lesser time as the said owner or owners may elect at the time of such acquisition." Ibid., p. 5.

43. U.S., Congress, Senate, *Congressional Record*, 87th Cong., 1st sess., June 27, 1961, p. 11391.

44. Ibid., pp. 11391–92.

45. Significant facts and dates of establishment for all the national parks are provided in U.S., Department of the Interior, National Park Service, *Index of the National Park System and Related Areas as of June 1, 1982* (Washington, D.C.: Government Printing Office, 1982).

46. R. M. Strong, "Indiana's Unspoiled Dunes," *National Parks Magazine* 33 (August 1959): 6–7. A social, cultural, and intellectual history of the region is J. Ronald Engel, *Sacred Sands: The Struggle for Community in the Indiana Dunes* (Middletown, Conn.: Wesleyan University Press, 1983). This should be supplemented with a provocative political history, Kay Franklin and Norma Schaeffer, *Duel for the Dunes: Land Use Conflict on the Shores of Lake Michigan* (Urbana and Chicago: University of Illinois Press, 1983).

47. National Park Service, *Index*, p. 37. Hearings on the park were first held in 1961. See U.S., Congress, Senate, Committee on Interior and Insular Affairs, Subcommittee on Public Lands, *Ozark Rivers National Monument, Hearing* on S. 1381, 87th Cong., 1st sess., July 6, 1961.

48. U.S., Congress, Senate, Committee on Interior and Insular Affairs, *Wild and Scenic Rivers, Hearings* on S. 119 and S. 1092, 90th Cong., 1st sess., April 13–14, 1967; U.S., Congress, House, *Providing for a National Scenic Rivers System*, H. Rept. 1623 to accompany H.R. 18260, 90th Cong., 2d sess., July 3, 1968.

49. To be sure, one of the most consistent themes of all of the federal hearings regarding wild and scenic rivers, national seashores, and national lakeshores is opposition to the parks by competitive resource management agencies and influential commercial interests. For another revealing example of those pressures, specifically, major limitations imposed on Ozark National Scenic Riverways through the elimination of twenty thousand acres along the Eleven Point River, see U.S., Congress, Senate, Committee on Interior and Insular Affairs, Subcommittee on Public Lands, *The Ozark National Rivers, Hearings* on S. 16, 88th Cong., 1st sess., April 8–9 and May 22, 1963.

50. For a recent analysis of this argument and its implications for policy see Ronald A. Foresta, *America's National Parks and Their Keepers* (Washington, D.C.: Resources for the Future, 1984), pp. 46–47, 218–22.

51. National Park Service, *Index*, pp. 19, 43.

52. Lake Mead National Recreation Area, formed by Hoover Dam on the Colorado River, bordering Arizona and Nevada, was the first. Ibid., p. 39.

53. U.S., *Statutes at Large*, 78 (1964): 897–904; ibid., 82 (1968): 354–56.

54. See Foresta, *America's National Parks*, pp. 237–40.

55. S. 857, *Hearing*, pp. 11, 34–35.

56. U.S., Congress, House, Committee on Interior and Insular Affairs, Subcommittee on National Parks, *Ozark National Rivers, Missouri, Hearings* on H.R. 1803, H.R. 2884, and S. 16, 88th Cong., 1st sess., April 9 and May 6, 1963, pp. 22, 27; U.S., Congress, Senate, Committee on Interior and Insular Affairs, Subcommittee on Public Lands, *Indiana Dunes National Lakeshore, Hearings* on S. 2249, 88th Cong., 2d sess., March 5–7, 1964, p. 5. For similar statements, also see U.S., Congress, Senate, Committee on Interior and Insular Affairs, Subcommittee on Public Lands, *Sleeping Bear Dunes National Recreation Area, Hearing* on S. 2153, 87th Cong., 1st sess., November 13, 1961, pp. 11–13; and U.S., Congress, Senate, Committee on Interior and Insular Affairs, Subcommittee on Public Lands, *Pictured Rocks National Lakeshore, Hearing* on S. 1143, 88th Cong., 2d sess., July 20, 1964, pp. 8–11.

57. U.S., Congress, House, Committee on Interior and Insular Affairs, Subcommittee on National Parks and Recreation, *Gateway Area Proposals, Hearings* on H.R. 1370, H.R. 1121, and Related Bills, 92d Cong., 1st sess., June 26, July 19–20, 1971, p. 55; U.S., Congress, House, Committee on Interior and Insular Affairs, Subcommittee on

National Parks and Recreation, *Proposed Cuyahoga Valley National Historical Park and Recreation Area, Part I, Hearing* on H.R. 7167 and Related Bills, 93d Cong., 2d sess., March 1, 1974, p. 9.

58. See, for example, Representative Seiberling's continuing remarks in H.R. 7167, *Hearing*, pp. 9–10.

59. U.S., Congress, Senate, Committee on Interior and Insular Affairs, Subcommittee on Parks and Recreation, *Golden Gate National Recreation Area, Hearings* on S. 2342, S. 3174, and H.R. 16444, 92d Cong., 2d sess., September 22 and 27, 1972, p. 74. Also see U.S., Congress, Senate, Committee on Interior and Insular Affairs, Subcommittee on Parks and Recreation, *Santa Monica Mountain and Seashore National Urban Park, Hearings* on S. 1270, 93d Cong., 2d sess., June 15 and August 1, 1974, passim.

60. National Parks and Recreation Act, *Legislative History*, pp. 978–86.

61. Ibid., p. 985.

62. Ibid., p. 981.

63. "NPCA Interviews Phillip Burton," p. 22.

Chapter 12

1. Robert A. Jones, "Alaska Parks: Battle Lines Form around Last Frontier," *Los Angeles Times*, September 5, 1977, pt. 1, p. 1.

2. Peggy Wayburn, "Great Stakes in the Great Land: Alaska Parks for Public Good," *Sierra Club Bulletin* 59 (September 1974): 17–18.

3. U.S., Congress, House, Committee on Interior and Insular Affairs, Subcommittee on General Oversight and Alaska Lands, *Inclusion of Alaska Lands in National Park, Forest, Wildlife Refuge, and Wild and Scenic Rivers Systems, Hearings* on H.R. 39, H.R. 1974, H.R. 2876, H.R. 5505, et al., 95th Cong., 1st sess., April 21–September 21, 1977, pt. 1, pp. 184, 188. Hereafter cited as H.R. 39, *Hearings*.

4. Ibid., p. 162.

5. George Catlin, *Illustrations of the Manners, Customs, and Conditions of the North American Indians*, 2 vols. (London: H. G. Bohn, 1851), 1:262.

6. H.R. 39, *Hearings*, pt. 1, p. 635.

7. Ibid., pp. 944–45.

8. See Morgan Sherwood, *Big Game in Alaska: A History of Wildlife and People* (New Haven: Yale University Press, 1981).

9. The quote is attributed to Allen H. Morgan, former executive vice president of the Massachusetts Audubon Society. Les Line, ed., *What We Save Now . . . : An Audubon Primer of Defense* (Boston: Houghton Mifflin, in cooperation with the National Audubon Society, 1973), p. vii.

10. I have avoided duplication of the history of the wilderness movement and parklands in Alaska as previously treated in Roderick Nash, *Wilderness and the American Mind*, 3d ed. (New Haven: Yale University Press, 1982); Michael Frome, *Battle for the Wilderness* (New York: Praeger Publishers, 1974); and Craig W. Allin, *The Politics of Wilderness Preservation* (Westport, Conn.: Greenwood Press, 1982).

11. See Allin, *Politics of Wilderness Preservation*, chapter 5; and Ronald A. Foresta, *America's National Parks and Their Keepers* (Washington, D.C.: Resources for the Future, 1984), pp. 69–70.

12. Conrad L. Wirth, as director of the Park Service between 1951 and 1964, literally felt betrayed by preservation interests because of their growing opposition to roads. See Wirth, *Parks, Politics, and the People* (Norman: University of Oklahoma Press, 1980), pp. 358–61.

13. U.S., *Statutes at Large*, 84 (1970–71): 1105–6; U.S., National Park Service, *Index of the National Park System and Related Areas as of June 1, 1982* (Washington, D.C.: Government Printing Office, 1982), p. 20; U.S., Congress, House, *Congressional Record*, 94th Cong., 2d sess., September 26, 1976, pp. 31888–91; U.S., *Statutes at Large*, 90 (1976): 2692–96. The controversial side of national park wilderness is also revealed in U.S., Congress, House, Committee on Interior and Insular Affairs, Subcommittee on National Parks and Recreation, *Designation of Wilderness Areas, Part IV, Hearings* on H.R. 13562 and H.R. 13563, 93d Cong., 2d sess., March 22, 25, and 26, 1974, passim; and U.S., Congress, House, Committee on Interior and Insular Affairs, *Designating Certain Lands within Units of the National Park System as Wilderness . . . and for Other Purposes*, H. Rept. 94–1427 to accompany H.R. 13160, 94th Cong., 2d sess., August 13, 1976.

14. U.S., Congress, House, Committee on Interior and Insular Affairs, Subcommittee on National Parks and Insular Affairs, *Legislative History of the National Parks and Recreation Act of 1978*, Committee Print No. 11, 95th Cong., 2d sess., December 1978, p. 982.

15. See, for example, U.S., Congress, Senate, Committee on Energy and Natural Resources, Subcommittee on Parks, Recreation, and Renewable Resources, *National Park Service Concessions Policy, Hearings* on Oversight—the Concessions Policy Act of 1965, 96th Cong., 1st sess., March 29, April 23 and 27, 1979.

16. A brief summary of this history is Nash, *Wilderness and the American Mind*, pp. 281–88.

17. A concise yet detailed history of Alaska lands legislation is Allin, *Politics of Wilderness Preservation*, chapter 7.

18. A further summary of these arguments is Eugenia Horstman Connally, ed., *Wilderness Parklands in Alaska* (Washington, D.C.: National Parks and Conservation Association, 1978).

19. U.S., *Statutes at Large*, 85 (1971): 708–9.

20. Ibid. Also see Allin, *Politics of Wilderness Preservation*, pp. 216–18.

21. Allin, *Politics of Wilderness Preservation*, pp. 218–19.

22. Ibid., p. 219.

23. As quoted in ibid., p. 221.

24. H.R. 39, *Hearings*, pt. 1, pp. 1–8.

25. Ibid., pts. 2–13.

26. For a breakdown of public support, see Allin, *Politics of Wilderness Preservation*, p. 223.

27. H.R. 39, *Hearings*, pt. 1, p. 2.

28. Ibid., pp. 3–4.

29. Ibid., pp. 4–5.

30. Ibid., pp. 103–6.

31. Ibid., pp. 104, 107.

32. Ibid., pp. 118–19.

33. Sierra Club Alaska Task Force, *Alaska Report* 3 (September 1976): 1–8; Robert A. Jones, "Development or Parks?: Wild Alaska to Change; Only Direction is in Doubt," *Los Angeles Times*, September 6, 1977, pt. 1, pp. 1, 3, 16–17.

34. H.R. 39, *Hearings*, pt. 1, p. 624.

35. Ibid., p. 156.

36. Allin, *Politics of Wilderness Preservation*, p. 226.

37. U.S., Congress, House, *Congressional Record*, 95th Cong., 2d sess., May 17, 1978, pp. 14146–73; ibid., May 18, 1978, pp. 14391–14470; ibid., May 19, 1978, pp. 14660–95.

38. Nash, *Wilderness and the American Mind*, p. 298.

39. Cecil D. Andrus, "Guarding Alaska's Crown Jewels," *Los Angeles Times*, October 11, 1978, pt. 2, p. 7.

40. Nash, *Wilderness and the American Mind*, p. 298; Allin, *Politics of Wilderness Preservation*, p. 236; U.S., *Statutes at Large*, 93 (1978–79): 1446–75.

41. U.S., Congress, House, *Congressional Record*, 96th Cong., 1st sess., May 16, 1979, pp. 11457–59. The first vote, 268 to 157, upheld Representative Udall's more generous version of the bill. The final vote, taken after substitutes to Udall's bill were defeated, was 360 to 65. Further Senate limitations on protection are discussed in Allin, *Politics of Wilderness Preservation*, pp. 244–55.

42. As quoted in Julius Duscha, "How the Alaska Act Was Won," *Living Wilderness* 44 (Spring 1981): 9.

43. As quoted in Nash, *Wilderness and the American Mind*, p. 301.

44. Charles M. Clusen, "Viewpoint," *Living Wilderness* 44 (Spring 1981): 3. Acreages, details, and descriptions of the protected lands are to be found in Charles R. Miller, "The New National Interest Lands," ibid., pp. 10–13.; and Celia Hunter and Ginny Wood, "Alaska National Interest Lands: The D-2 Lands," *Alaska Geographic*, vol. 8, no. 4 (1981): 1–240.

45. On preservationists' concerns and disappointments, see Rebecca Wodder, "The Alaska Challenge Ahead," *Living Wilderness* 44

(Spring 1981): 13–19; Charles M. Clusen, "Viewpoint," ibid., p. 3; Bill Curry, "Alaska Land Battle Far from Settled," *Los Angeles Times*, July 25, 1983, pt. 1, pp. 1, 11; and Jim Doherty, "Alaska: The Real National Lands Battle is Just Getting Under Way," *Audubon* 85 (January 1983).

46. The hearings are especially instructive. See U.S., Congress, House, Committee on Interior and Insular Affairs, Subcommittee on National Parks and Recreation, *Proposed Big Thicket National Reserve, Texas, Hearings* on H.R. 4270, et al., 93d Cong., 1st sess., July 16 and 17, 1973; and idem, *Proposed Big Cypress Reserve, Florida, Hearings* on H.R. 46 and H.R. 4866, 93d Cong., 1st sess., May 10 and 11, 1973.

47. See, for example, H. R. 39, *Hearings*, pts. 8–13, passim.

48. Ibid., pt. 13, p. 215.

49. See, for example, Edgar Wayburn, "Hunters Take Aim at Alaska's National Parks," *Sierra* 68 (May–June 1983): 16–19.

50. Alaska Coalition, "Alaska: Imperiled Heritage," undated leaflet.

51. Margaret Murie, *Two in the Far North*, 2d ed. (Anchorage: Alaska Northwest Publishing Co., 1978), preface.

52. By preservationists' own admission, the issue of resource extraction was still unresolved. Important documents portending the fate of commercially productive lands within or adjacent to national parks, wilderness areas, and wildlife refuges include U.S., Congress, Senate, Committee on Interior and Insular Affairs, *An Assessment of Mineral Resources in Alaska*, prepared by the U.S. Geological Survey, the Bureau of Mines, and the Bureau of Land Management, Committee Print, 93d Cong., 2d sess., July 1974.

Epilogue

1. Peter Steinhart, "Interior Motives: Will Watt Get His Way in the Parks?" *Los Angeles Times*, May 3, 1981, pt. 5, p. 2; Michael Frome, "Park Concessions and Concessioners," *National Parks* 55 (June 1981): 16–18; and Peter Steinhart, "The Park Service Feels an Early Winter Chill from Watt's Interior," *Los Angeles Times*, November 8, 1981, pt. 5, pp. 1–2.

2. Then known as the Mammoth Oil Company. See Burl Noggle, *Teapot Dome: Oil and Politics in the 1920's* (Baton Rouge: Louisiana State University Press, 1962), and Morris Robert Werner and John Starr, *Teapot Dome* (New York: Viking, 1959).

3. For an inventory of preservationists' objections to Watt's policies, see "Watt's Wrongs," *Living Wilderness* 45 (Fall 1981): 40–41.

4. Watt's views, of course, were often in keeping with those of conservatives within the National Park Service itself, who likewise saw urban parks as a distraction from the Park Service's original and legitimate mission. See Ronald A. Foresta, *America's National Parks*

and Their Keepers (Washington, D.C.: Resources for the Future, 1983), pp. 77–82, 175–76. For further analyses of Watt's policies, see T. H. Watkins, "James Gaius Watt: An Idea Whose Time Has Gone," *Living Wilderness* 45 (Winter 1981): 34–38; Chuck Williams, "The Park Rebellion: Charles Cushman, James Watt, and the Attack on the National Parks," *Not Man Apart* 12 (June 1982): 11–26; "Battle over the Wilderness: Special Report," *Newsweek* 102 (July 25, 1983): 22–29; and Bil Gilbert and Robert Sullivan, "Inside Interior: An Abrupt Turn," *Sports Illustrated* 59 (September 26, 1983): 66–80, and (October 3, 1983): 96–112.

5. Gordon Anderson, "Coal: Threat to the Canyonlands," *Living Wilderness* (December 1980): 4–11; John J. Kearney, "Is the Air Visibility of Our National Parks Being Adequately Protected?" *EPA Journal* 7 (May 1981): 2–6; Jeff Radford, "Stripmining Arid Navajo Lands in the U.S.: Threats to Health and Heritage," *Ambio*, vol. 11, no. 1 (1982): 9–14; Jerome Ostrov, "Visibility Protection under the Clean Air Act: Preserving Scenic and Parkland Areas in the Southwest," *Ecology Law Quarterly*, vol. 10, no. 3 (1982): 397–453.

6. U.S., Department of the Interior, National Park Service, *State of the Parks—1980: A Report to the Congress*, prepared by the Office of Science and Technology, May 1980, p. viii.

7. U.S., Department of Agriculture, Forest Service, *Final Environmental Impact Statement of the Island Park Geothermal Area, Idaho-Montana-Wyoming*, January 15, 1980, p. 112.

8. Rick Reese, *Greater Yellowstone: The National Park and Adjacent Wild Lands*, Montana Geographic Series No. 6 (Helena: Montana Magazine, Inc., 1984); Dave Alt, Curt W. Buchholtz, et al., *Glacier Country: Montana's Glacier National Park*, Montana Geographic Series No. 4 (Helena: Montana Magazine, Inc., 1983). Wildlife issues have been exhaustively debated in Warren Hanna, *The Grizzlies of Glacier* (Missoula, Mont.: Mountain Press, 1978); Frank C. Craighead, Jr., *Track of the Grizzly* (San Francisco: Sierra Club Books, 1979); Paul Schullery, *The Bears of Yellowstone* (Yellowstone National Park: Yellowstone Library and Museum Association, 1980); Thomas McNamee, *The Grizzly Bear* (New York: Knopf, 1984); and Alston Chase, "The Last Bears of Yellowstone," *Atlantic Monthly* 251 (February 1983): 63–73.

9. Vic Ostrowidzki, "Clark Will Keep Environmentalists Active," *Seattle Post-Intelligencer*, October 24, 1983, pt. A, p. 9.

10. Aldo Leopold, *A Sand County Almanac* (New York: Oxford University Press, 1949), pp. 209, 224–25. An excellent summary of threats to the national parks in the 1980s is Robert Cahn, "Islands in a Storm: Our National Parks," five parts, *Christian Science Monitor*, June 14–18, 1982, passim. Also see Robert Cahn, "The National Parks: The People, the Parks, the Politics," *Sierra* 68 (May–June 1983): 46–55; and Philip Shabecoff, "National Parks under Threat from Civilization They Serve," *New York Times*, July 30, 1984, pt. 1, pp. 1, 11.

BIBLIOGRAPHICAL NOTE

The notes provide a detailed listing and evaluation of the major works used in this study. The following discusses briefly sources of importance for further research.

Manuscript collections of national park history are numerous. Accordingly, scholars will want to consult a superb new bibliography, Richard C. Davis, *North American Forest History: A Guide to Archives and Manuscripts in the United States and Canada* (Santa Barbara, Calif.: Forest History Society, Inc. and Clio Books, 1977). Its title is misleading; in fact all areas of conservation, not just forests, are well covered. Listed, for example, are the collections consulted for this study, including the William E. Colby, Francis P. Farquhar, Robert Underwood Johnson, John Muir, Robert Bradford Marshall, and Sierra Club records in the Bancroft Library at the University of California, Berkeley. The Library of Congress provided other valuable manuscripts, among them the Frederick Law Olmsted and John C. Merriam papers. The J. Horace McFarland collection, located in the archives building of the Pennsylvania Museum and Historical Commission, Harrisburg, proved especially important for its coverage of the decade preceding formation of the National Park Service. By far the most voluminous repository of primary materials is Record Group 79, the Records of the National Park Service maintained by the National Archives in Washington, D.C. Considering its size, R. G. 79 is well catalogued and relatively easy to use. Regional headquarters of the National Park Service are custodians of most documents produced since 1949; similarly, many of the larger parks, including Yosemite and Yellowstone, have libraries and holdings of their own. Finally, specialty departments, most notably the Conservation Library Center of the Denver Public Library, are acquiring private papers on environmental history subjects.

Printed government documents are another important source for national park history. In addition to the House and Senate debates published in the *Congressional Globe* and *Congressional Record*, there are the standard reports on bills, hearings before congressional committees, and similar documents, usually printed in conjunction with establishment of the parks. Testimony pertaining to the Jackson Hole and Redwood National Park controversies, for example, is exhaustive. Major branches of the federal government, including the Interior Department and National Park Service, until recently published the annual reports of the secretary and director respectively. This work draws heavily on each of these sources, as well as *Statutes at Large* for wording of park legislation as finally approved.

No examination of national park history is complete without extensive use of the primary source materials also to be found in major newspapers, periodicals, and conservation journals. *Poole's Index* and *Reader's Guide* list hundreds of relevant articles; researchers should be aware, however, that many popular magazines and specialty journals, among them *National Parks Magazine* and *American Forests and Forest Life*, were not always indexed during their initial years of publication. Indeed, until early 1978 the *Sierra Club Bulletin* was ignored by *Reader's Guide*. For maximum coverage, therefore, collections of the more important journals should be examined off the shelf. Although exhausting, the procedure often yields unexpected dividends, including period advertisements and letters-to-the-editor columns.

For secondary literature there is another excellent guide, Ronald J. Fahl, *North American Forest and Conservation History: A Bibliography* (Santa Barbara, Calif.: Forest History Society, Inc. and A. B. C.—Clio Press, 1977). As a legislative and administrative history of the national parks to 1960, John Ise, *Our National Park Policy: A Critical History* (Baltimore: Johns Hopkins University Press, 1961), is definitive. The value of the study is diminished, nevertheless, by the haphazard use and occasional inaccuracy of its footnotes. Similarly, Ise chose to discuss the parks individually rather than collectively in most instances. As one result, little attention is paid to the formation of the national park *idea* itself, especially the intellectual and nationalistic trends prior to the establishment of Yosemite (1864) and Yellowstone (1872). Leo Marx, *The Machine in the Garden: Technology and the Pastoral Ideal in America* (New York: Oxford University Press, 1964); Roderick Nash, *Wilderness and the American Mind* (New Haven: Yale University Press, 1967); and Hans Huth, *Nature and the American: Three Centuries of Changing Attitudes* (Berkeley and Los Angeles: University of California Press, 1957), are among the more important studies dealing with early perceptions of the environment in general.

Two biographies, Robert Shankland, *Steve Mather of the National Parks*, 3d ed. (New York: Alfred A. Knopf, 1970), and Donald C. Swain, *Wilderness Defender: Horace M. Albright and Conservation* (Chicago: University of Chicago Press, 1970), are excellent for the formative years of the National Park Service. Individual histories of the national parks are usually less interpretive or complete. Exceptions include Richard A. Bartlett, *Nature's Yellowstone* (Albuquerque: University of New Mexico Press, 1974), and Douglas H. Strong, *A History of Sequoia National Park* (Ph.D. dissertation, Syracuse University, 1964). A model popular treatment of a national park is Ann and Myron Sutton, *Yellowstone: A Century of the Wilderness Idea* (New York: Macmillan Co. and the Yellowstone Library and Museum Association, 1972). Harley E. Jolley, *The Blue Ridge Parkway* (Knoxville: University of Tennessee Press, 1969), gives insights into the origins of the national park system's most famous roadway.

Emerging themes in national park history are suggested by essays such as Peter Marcuse, "Is the National Parks Movement Anti-Urban?" *Parks and Recreation* 6 (July 1971): 17–21, 48; and Darwin Lambert, "We Can Have Wilderness Wherever We Choose," *National Wildlife* 11 (August–September 1973): 20–24. A recent treatment of traditional ruptures in the conservation movement is Elmo R. Richardson's *Dams, Parks, and Politics: Resource Development and Preservation in the Truman-Eisenhower Era* (Lexington: University of Kentucky Press, 1973). For the Progressive period and its aftermath, there is Richardson's *The Politics of Conservation: Crusades and Controversies, 1897–1913* (Berkeley and Los Angeles: University of California Press, 1962); Samuel P. Hays, *Conservation and the Gospel of Efficiency: The Progressive Conservation Movement, 1890–1920* (Cambridge, Mass.: Harvard University Press, 1959); and Donald C. Swain, *Federal Conservation Policy, 1921–1933* (Berkeley and Los Angeles: University of California Press, 1963). John F. Reiger, in *American Sportsmen and the Origins of Conservation* (New York: Winchester Press, 1975), invites further debate with his thesis that responsible hunters and fishermen, not preservationists in the traditional sense, launched conservation on all fronts during the second half of the nineteenth century.

Although major professional journals are beginning to recognize the appropriateness of environmental history, the *Journal of Forest History* promises to remain the standard in the field on the basis of its exhaustive updating of all manuscript collections and scholarly articles. In a more contemporary vein, *National Parks and Conservation Magazine: The Environmental Journal*, *Audubon*, and the *Sierra Club Bulletin*, among others, are vital for maintaining contact with current issues which themselves will someday be history.

Supplementary
Bibliographical Note

The following is intended to introduce important secondary literature written since publication of the first edition of *National Parks*. The notes again provide a more comprehensive listing and description of the sources used in the revision.

A provocative new history of the first national park is *Yellowstone: A Wilderness Besieged,* by Richard A. Bartlett (Tucson: University of Arizona Press, 1985). In contrast to previous studies of the park, Bartlett closely examines the life and times of the Yellowstone visitor, manager, and concessionaire, noting the impact of their presence on park wildlife and habitat. Equally provocative is Susan R. Schrepfer, *The Fight to Save the Redwoods: A History of Environmental Reform, 1917–1978* (Madison: University of Wisconsin Press, 1983). Schrepfer also focuses on the people behind the preservation movement, specifically, on the ideological differences that split the Sierra Club and the Save-the-Redwoods League to the detriment of a national park that

was biologically as well as scenically whole. Based largely on personal papers, oral interviews, and other primary materials,
Schrepfer's work, like Bartlett's, is certain to become a standard in
the field.

Other histories of individual parks include C. W. Buchholtz,
Rocky Mountain National Park: A History (Boulder: Colorado Associated University Press, 1983). Again, Buchholtz goes beyond the history of park establishment to include important information on major resource controversies. Similarly, Douglas H. Strong, *Tahoe: An
Environmental History* (Lincoln: University of Nebraska Press, 1984),
concentrates on water quality, air pollution, urban sprawl, and other
land-use problems affecting the establishment and maintenance of
wilderness parks. To be sure, although Lake Tahoe is not a national
park, it has been seriously considered for one. As a result, Strong's
book provides additional insight into the reasons why otherwise
worthy landscapes are still often denied protection in the national
park system.

Another model study in this regard is Kay Franklin and Norma
Schaeffer, *Duel for the Dunes: Land Use Conflict on the Shores of Lake
Michigan* (Urbana and Chicago: University of Illinois Press, 1983). It
should be supplemented with J. Ronald Engel, *Sacred Sands: The
Struggle for Community in the Indiana Dunes* (Middletown, Conn.:
Wesleyan University Press, 1983), a social, cultural, and intellectual
history of the region before its authorization as a national lakeshore
in 1966. Similarly, Robert W. Righter, *Crucible for Conservation: The
Creation of Grand Teton National Park* (Boulder: Colorado Associated
University Press, 1982), reexamines the fifty-year struggle to include
Jackson Hole, Wyoming, in either Yellowstone or Grand Teton national park. Once more, the strength of Righter's version of the controversy is his continuing discussion of the implications for resources
as opposed to a discussion devoted exclusively to political and bureaucratic intrigue. By way of contrast, the more traditional approach to park history, relying heavily on Indian lore, pioneers' tales,
and travelers' accounts, is reflected in Margaret Sanborn, *Yosemite:
Its Discovery, Its Wonders, and Its People* (New York: Random House,
1981).

Policy issues from historical times to the present have been further addressed in three major studies: Joseph L. Sax, *Mountains
Without Handrails: Reflections on the National Parks* (Ann Arbor: University of Michigan Press, 1980); William C. Everhart, *The National
Park Service*, 2d ed. (Boulder, Colo.: Westview Press, 1983); and
Ronald A. Foresta, *America's National Parks and Their Keepers* (Washington, D.C.: Resources for the Future, 1984). At the risk of being
called an elitist, Sax restates familiar concerns about the need to curb
overdevelopment in the national parks. Foresta, meanwhile, takes a
more tolerant view of the average park visitor, noting that the parks,

after all, were established for human enjoyment as well as resource protection. Similarly, Everhart defends the Park Service by drawing attention to the enormous social and political pressures often imposed on the agency. So, too, Conrad L. Wirth, director of the Park Service between 1951 and 1964, defends Mission 66, road-building, and other internal improvements in *Parks, Politics, and the People* (Norman: University of Oklahoma Press, 1980). Again, Wirth's justification for development is the obligation imposed by Congress on the Park Service to make the parks both safe and accessible. The issue of access is further treated in Alfred Runte, *Trains of Discovery: Western Railroads and the National Parks* (Flagstaff, Ariz.: Northland Press, 1984), which, using historical examples of railroad promotion of the national park idea, argues that public transportation is still the only viable solution to the resource damage attributed in large part to the automobile.

Among books dealing with national parks as a component of other themes in environmental history, *Wilderness and the American Mind*, 3d ed. (New Haven: Yale University Press, 1982), by Roderick Nash, still stands apart. In this most recent revision, Nash develops the social, cultural, and intellectual trends behind the wilderness movement in Alaska. Another important study is Barbara Novak, *Nature and Culture: American Landscape and Painting, 1825–1875* (New York: Oxford University Press, 1980). Novak herself is not concerned with national parks per se but with the intellectual and artistic foundations of nature appreciation. In a similar vein, Stephen J. Pyne uses fire as a departure for environmental analysis in *Fire in America: A Cultural History of Wildland and Rural Fire* (Princeton: Princeton University Press, 1982). Like Nash and Novak, Pyne does not deal exclusively with national parks; still, because *Fire in America* also discusses deep-seated emotions toward the natural world in the United States, its importance as a source for national park history has already been firmly established.

Two biographies of John Muir—Stephen Fox, *John Muir and His Legacy: The American Conservation Movement* (Boston and Toronto: Little, Brown, 1981); and Michael P. Cohen, *The Pathless Way: John Muir and American Wilderness* (Madison: University of Wisconsin Press, 1984), are also notable for their wealth of information about the conservation movement as a whole. Fox, for example, devotes but one third of his study to John Muir himself; the remainder of Fox's book is a biographical approach to the history of conservation and its leadership since Muir's death in 1914. Similarly, the memoirs of Horace M. Albright as told to Robert Cahn, *The Birth of the National Park Service: The Founding Years, 1913–33* (Salt Lake City: Howe Brothers, 1985), is a richly detailed recollection of the hierarchy of American conservation in the opening decades of the twentieth century.

An important new journal is *Environmental Review*, published by the American Society for Environmental History. See, for example, Thomas R. Cox, "From Hot Springs to Gateway: The Evolving Concept of Public Parks, 1832–1976," vol. 5, no. 1 (1980): 14–26. Meanwhile, the *Journal of Forest History* remains an important publication for national park subjects. Examples of recent articles include H. Duane Hampton, "Opposition to National Parks," 25 (January 1981): 36–45; and Rick Hydrick, "The Genesis of National Park Management: John Roberts White and Sequoia National Park, 1920–1947," 28 (April 1984): 68–81. Researchers should also consult the *Encyclopedia of American Forest and Conservation History*, 2 vols. (New York: Macmillan, 1983), edited by Richard C. Davis under the sponsorship of the Forest History Society. Contributors include Alfred Runte, Susan R. Schrepfer, Donald C. Swain, Douglas H. Strong, Richard A. Bartlett, Thomas R. Cox, Stephen J. Pyne, Samuel P. Hays, and numerous other historians noted for their expertise on national park topics. Another major sourcebook is a provocative new report by the Conservation Foundation, *National Parks for a New Generation: Visions, Realities, Prospects* (Washington, D.C.: Conservation Foundation, 1985), which, among numerous philosophical contributions to the ideals of national park management, cites many recent books and articles pertaining to national park research.

Finally, Arthur D. Martinson, *Wilderness Above the Sound: The Story of Mount Rainier National Park* (Flagstaff, Ariz.: Northland Press, 1986), offers another innovative approach to national park scholarship, drawing heavily on the latest techniques of public history.

INDEX

Abbey, Edward, 173–74, 176
Acadia National Park, 114–15, 218–19
Across the Continent, 13
Adirondack Forest Preserve, 57
Adirondack Mountains, 13
Africa, 186
Agora, 2
Air pollution. *See* Pollution
Alaska Coalition, 246, 251, 253
Alaska Military Highway, 243
Alaska National Interest Lands Conservation Act, 255–56
Alaska Native Claims Settlement Act: native compensation, provisions for, 244; and park and wilderness designations, provisions affecting, 245–46, 252
Alaska, parks in, 196, 235; and Antiquities Act, invoked to protect, 253; area of, debated, 248–54; and establishment of, 255; as national preserves, meaning of questioned, 256; and parks in continental U.S., compared with, 236–37; and public opinion regarding, 247–48; as wilderness, 255; and wildlife, limitations affecting, 255–57. *See also* Alaska Native Claims Settlement Act; Mount McKinley National Park
Alaska statehood, 243

Albright, Horace M., 102, 104; contributions of, 102; Everglades national park project, reports favorably on, 132; Jackson Hole, works to protect, 120–25; and national monuments, wins transfer of to Park Service, 219–20; and National Park Service, strengthens autonomy of, 220–22; and park system expansion, actively promotes, 219; and purists, frustrated by, 132
Alps, and mountains of the West, compared, 17, 25, 65–66. *See also* Switzerland
American Association for the Advancement of Science, 61, 114
American Automobile Association, 173
American Civic Association, 86, 101, 114, 133. *See also* McFarland, J. Horace
Andrus, Cecil, 253
Antarctica, 186–87
Antiquities Act, 71–73, 253. *See also* National Monuments
Appalachian Mountain Club, 85, 87, 114. *See also* Chamberlain, Allen
Appalachian Mountains, 17; national parks in, 114–17
Appalachian National Park Association, 114